Sandy Koufax

Edited by Marc Z Aaron, Bill Nowlin, and Glen Sparks

Associate editors Len Levin and Carl Riechers

Society for American Baseball Research, Inc.
Phoenix, AZ

Sandy Koufax
Edited by Marc Z Aaron, Bill Nowlin, and Glen Sparks
Associate editors Len Levin and Carl Riechers

Cover and book design: Gilly Rosenthol

Front cover photograph: Courtesy of the National Baseball Hall of Fame
Back cover images: Courtesy of the National Baseball Hall of Fame; action pitching photograph is from
SABR/The Rucker Archive.

978-1-960819-27-7 (paperback)
978-1-960819-26-0 (ebook)

Library of Congress Control Number: 2024913578

Cronkite School at ASU
555 N. Central Ave. #416
Phoenix, AZ 85004
Phone: (602) 496-1460
Web: www.sabr.org
Facebook: Society for American Baseball Research
Twitter/X: @SABR

Sandy Koufax

Contents

My Boyhood Baseball Dream Comes True

As a young teenager growing up in The Bronx, I was a devout Yankees fan.

Then along came the New York Metropolitans and an opportunity to witness National Leaguers on the main stage.

Sandy Koufax became my idol. He and I have the same heritage. My dad had a color photo of Sandy laminated on wood, which hung in my room until I left home for good after college. Though we had never met, I thought of him as Sandy.

On May 30, 1962, my dad took me to the Polo Grounds to see the Dodgers play a doubleheader against the Mets. It was a warm Memorial Day. The Polo Grounds capacity was listed as 55,000. We did not have tickets. The attendance that day was 55,704. My dad and I were part of the 704 who stood. Sandy Koufax pitched a complete game in the opener. I, however, did not complete the game. At the age of 13, I became dehydrated from standing and headed home with my dad before Koufax finished what was for him a lackluster effort against a hapless Mets team (10 strikeouts and a victory but six earned runs allowed over nine innings, the most runs he surrendered in a game all season).

About 13 years ago I received a notification from SABR that Martin Abramowitz was seeking assistance in having the BioProject compile life stories of all the Jewish players. When I realized that no one had signed up to write about Sandy Koufax, I quickly volunteered.

I contacted the Baseball Hall of Fame Research Library and requested, at my expense, all the clippings in their Sandy Koufax player file. A week or two later the boxes arrived.

One of the clippings was a copy of an uncashed check signed by Koufax for $5 made out to Vic Lapiner, with a note from the pitcher stating that this was a bet he was glad to lose. Lapiner was a minor-league pitcher who later threw batting practice for the Dodgers. It was

in that role that Lapiner became friends with Koufax. They shared the same Jewish heritage. I contacted Vic, who explained that over lunch, Vic bet Sandy that he would go into the Hall of Fame on the first ballot.

A question arose when I wrote my bio of Sandy Koufax. I spoke with Vic about the issue. He gave me Sandy's cellphone number. My reaction was "Are you kidding me?" Vic said Sandy owed him a favor. Well, I nervously called and received a generic voicemail greeting. I left a message stating that I wanted to verify some info in connection with the bio. I did not expect to hear anything back, not even knowing if I had the right number. That evening there was a voice message on my office phone from Sandy. His message said to write whatever I wanted, whether the truth or not, as everyone else does. I thought that this was closure. But the very next day another voice message arrived from Sandy. I immediately called him back. It remains a most memorable personal conversation. One that I treasure, like the picture in my room – wherever it may have gone. Sandy's first message is the only saved message I maintain.

In this book you will read of Koufax's pitching performances, his four no-hitters, strikeout records, World Series games, his early career struggles and successes, his rivalries, retirement decisions, life after baseball, the importance of his Jewish faith, and what his career might have been with modern medical technology and procedures.

So sit back, let the magic begin and read everything that is Koufax!

This book represents the collaborative work of 47 members of the Society for American Baseball Research.

– Marc Z Aaron

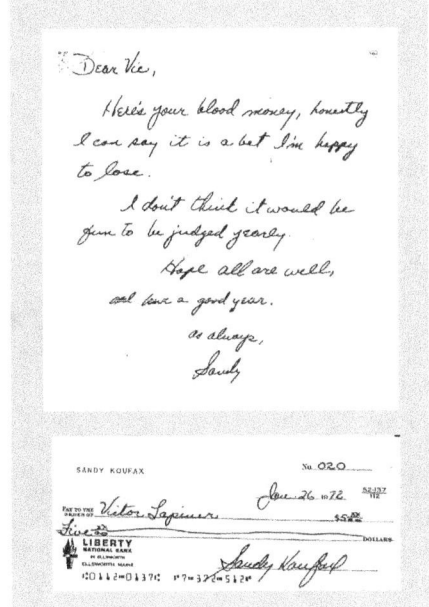

A foolish bet. Courtesy of National Baseball Hall of Fame.

Sandy Koufax

BY MARC Z. AARON

"Mystique" is a word often linked with Sandy Koufax. He was dubbed "The Left Arm of God" for his pitching feats – especially over the five years from 1962 to 1966. A long litany of statistics attests to his brilliance during this period, but perhaps the most salient points are these. Koufax became the first man to win three Cy Young Awards, and was the only pitcher to do so when the prize was given to just one major leaguer. He also won the Triple Crown of pitching in each of those seasons (1963, 1965, and 1966). He pitched four no-hitters, one of them a perfect game.

The great Ernie Banks described what it was like to face Koufax. "It was frightening. He had that tremendous fastball that would rise, and a great curveball that started at the eyes and broke to the ankles. In the end you knew you were going to be embarrassed. You were either going to strike out or foul out."[1] Banks said, "He was the greatest pitcher I ever saw. Most of the time we knew what was coming. He held his hands closer to his head when he threw a curveball, but it didn't matter."[2]

Koufax's build – huge back, long arms, and exceptionally long fingers – enabled him to put extra spin on his pitches. According to Dodgers catcher Norm Sherry, Koufax could "do things with a baseball nobody has been able to do before or since."[3] Pictures show that the baseball was as low as the top of his left ankle when he reached back to throw. He then propelled the ball with a fluid over-the-top delivery that utilized the weight and force of his body.[4]

Koufax believed his natural gifts required him to work hard at his job of winning games. His personal integrity was deep. It took six seasons for him to master his wildness, however, and his career was halted after the 1966 season by an arthritic left elbow. His decision to retire at the age of 30 after such a dominant run left many, both inside and outside of baseball, wondering why he would leave at the top of his game. Yet this too contributed to his aura. When he was elected to the National Baseball Hall of Fame in 1972, he was just 36 years old – the youngest man ever inducted. Decades after his retirement, debate still stirs over Koufax's dazzling peak vs. his career totals.

Two other factors fueled Koufax's legend. As one of the greatest Jewish baseball players ever, he became a hero in that community, especially after refusing to pitch the opening game of the World Series in 1965 because it fell on the High Holy Day of Yom Kippur.[5] The other was his deep sense of privacy. Koufax was, and still is, a greatly admired figure – yet he chose to make few public appearances. Remaining out of the spotlight gave Koufax sightings extra cachet. "Awestruck" is another word frequently attached to this man. Opponents and fans felt that way watching him on the mound, and he retained a unique personal presence.

Sandy Koufax was born as Sanford Braun on December 30, 1935. His parents were Evelyn (née Lichtenstein) and Jack Braun, Sephardic Jews of Hungarian descent.[6] The family lived in the Bensonhurst section of Brooklyn, New York City. Koufax had an older stepsister, Edith, who died in November 1997.

When Sandy was 3, Evelyn (an accountant) divorced Jack Braun.[7] She and the children lived with her parents in Brooklyn. Sandy's grandfather, Max Lichtenstein, was a plumber. The boy's street activities were stoop ball, punch ball, and stickball.[8]

Sandy was 9 when Evelyn married Irving Koufax, the lawyer whom Sandy affectionately came to call his dad.[9] The Koufaxes moved to Rockville Centre, New York. They lived in the first floor of a two-story home owned by his uncle, Sam Lichtenstein, the architect in the family.[10]

Sandy Koufax posted a combined 97-27 won-loss record in his final four seasons. Courtesy of National Baseball Hall of Fame.

After a Long Island Railroad train derailment, the Koufax family moved back to Bensonhurst. They lived alongside the Belt Parkway in a three-story housing development. The young Koufax had just completed ninth grade.

It was then, at the age of 14, that Koufax took up another sport in which he had a lot of talent: basketball. He was a strong rebounder who demonstrated his jumping ability in front of the New York Knicks when the Police Athletic League of Bath Beach arranged for a benefit game to be played at the gym in Lafayette High School, which Sandy began to attend in 10th grade.[11]

During summer vacations from school, Koufax worked as a waiter and counselor at Camp Chi-Wan-Da, near Kingston, New York. He had been going to this camp since the age of 3. His mother was their bookkeeper.[12]

Milton Laurie, a delivery driver for the *New York Journal American*, is believed to be the first man to uncover Koufax's pitching ability. Laurie, a longtime sandlot manager who had years before been signed by the Boston Braves, spotted Koufax pitching for the Tomahawks in the Ice Cream League, a counterpart of the Little League and Babe Ruth League.[13] Even though Koufax walked nine men in two innings, Laurie had his son Walter, who was a classmate, invite Koufax to join his sandlot team. Koufax at first refused, but after much begging by Laurie, he changed his mind. Laurie's team, the Parkviews, were part of the Coney Island Sports League and played their games at Dyker Beach Park on 14th Avenue and 46th Street in Brooklyn.[14] Koufax was busy working in summer camp. As such, he did not play much, but when he did, he would strike out 16-18 batters.

It thrilled Sandy to see Irving Koufax arrive one day at a game. That night, at the dinner table, Irving related how impressed he was and that Evelyn should hand Sandy some money to buy a new pair of spikes. This was a complete surprise to the young Koufax, who had repeatedly heard his father say that "spending on baseball is a waste of money" and "a baseball player you will never be." His parents wanted him to follow in the footsteps of his uncles, who were architects.

Yet it was his interest and skill in basketball that won Koufax a university scholarship. His parents were excited when he accepted the offer from the University of Cincinnati, where the basketball program had a strong reputation. The Bearcat scouts had seen Koufax playing both at high school and at the Jewish Community House.[15]

At the urging of friends, Koufax did go out for baseball in his senior year at Lafayette. He played first base. The team captain was Fred Wilpon, a lefty with a "crackling" curve ball, who became well known decades later as owner of the New York Mets.[16] Their coach was Charlie Sheerin, a utility infielder for the 1936 Phillies.[17]

Koufax stood 6-feet-2 when fully grown (during his major-league career, he weighed as much as 210 pounds). When he went to Cincinnati, he was a starting forward on the freshman team. He was known to be a "savage" rebounder and able to dunk.[18] He was also the third-leading scorer with a 9.7 average. The team won 12 of 14, and according to the coach, Ed Jucker, Koufax could have made it in professional basketball. Jucker led the Bearcats varsity squad to NCAA championships in 1961 and 1962; he later coached the NBA's Cincinnati Royals.[19]

Jucker was also the Bearcats' baseball coach. The team lacked pitchers, so Koufax volunteered to help out. He threw hard but was so wild that catchers wanted no part of him. In his debut game at Keesler Air Force Base in Biloxi, Mississippi, Koufax struggled. He returned to the Cincinnati campus to pitch a four-hitter against Wayne, striking out 16. He next took on Louisville, striking out 18 to set a school record. He finished his first college season with a record of 3-1, 51 strikeouts and 30 walks over 32 innings.[20] He caught the eye of major-league scouts.

Koufax interested each of the three New York City big-league clubs – the Yankees, Giants, and Dodgers – not only because he could throw hard but also because of his religion. Since the days of John McGraw, the New York teams had desired Jewish drawing cards. His faith may have had something to do with it – the bigger factor was his performance – yet it was said in the 1960s that when Koufax pitched, regardless of where, there would be 10,000 more fans in attendance.[21]

The Yankees sent a Jewish scout, which offended the Koufax family. Plus, they offered only $4,000 and a Class-D assignment.[22] Koufax had a tryout with the Giants at the Polo Grounds. He showed up without his glove and had to borrow one from Johnny Antonelli.[23] The team lost interest; tense and frightened, Sandy was wild.[24]

Jimmy Murphy, who covered scholastic sports for the *Brooklyn Eagle*, tipped off Dodgers scout Al Campanis to Koufax. This intro led to a workout at Ebbets Field before both the general manager, Buzzie Bavasi, and the manager, Walt Alston.[25] Campanis offered a $14,000 bonus and a $6,000 salary. Branch Rickey, who by then was general manager of the Pittsburgh Pirates, authorized one of his scouts to top the Dodgers by $5,000. The Milwaukee Braves offered $30,000.[26] But they were too late. Sandy had talked with Irving Koufax frequently, and they decided to sign with Brooklyn. Irving sealed the deal with a handshake. It was on December 14, 1954 that Koufax signed as an amateur free agent (bonus baby).

Sandy then dropped out of Cincinnati and transferred to Columbia University to take some courses at the school of architecture.[27] The demands of playing baseball and the requirement that Koufax fulfill his military service obligation of six months between playing seasons eventually caused him to drop out of Columbia.[28]

Koufax's bonus was rather modest compared to what many "bonus babies" got in that era. Yet the rules then in effect denied clubs the right to send any player to the minors who was given more than $6,000 to sign.[29] Thus, Koufax never spent a day in the minors.[30]

According to his teammate, Carl Erskine, even as a rookie Koufax showed a quiet sense of humor. Erskine related how in the spring of 1955, the Dodgers were on a city bus heading back to the McAllister Hotel after an exhibition game in Miami. The Dodgers had lost and it was a hot night. The bus stopped to let a very slow freight train pass. The passengers grew impatient; coach Billy Herman, sitting across the aisle from Koufax, let out, "Darn, you can give this town back to the Jews." The entire bus went silent. Koufax, not even 20 then, very softly said, "Now Billy, you know we already have it." This defused the situation with no carryover.[31]

It was more than two months into the 1955 season before Koufax made his major-league debut. Early in the season, he injured his ankle and wound up on the disabled list. Tommy Lasorda was the odd man out on June 8, when he was demoted to the minor-league Montreal Royals to make room for Koufax. Lasorda liked to say, "It took the greatest left-handed pitcher in baseball history to get me off that Brooklyn club – and I still think they made a mistake."[32]

Once off the DL, another reason for Koufax's idleness emerged: Alston favored experience over youth. This was true of many big-league managers then, but Alston's tendency was more pronounced because the Dodgers were a World Series contender.

Plus, in those days, big-league pitching staffs were smaller and structured differently. There were four regular starters, and they were expected to pitch deep into the game if not complete it. There were two long-relief men in case a starter got into early trouble. Although the "closer" role was evolving and the concept of saves had not yet come into being, there was also one short man, used sometimes to wrap up the game or often to put out late-inning fires. The eighth and ninth pitchers were the low men on the totem pole. In the normal course of events, they did not get into games. They awaited a blowout by either side or some catastrophe (injury) to occur.[33]

Finally, on June 24, 1955, against the Braves at Milwaukee's County Stadium, Koufax got into a game for Brooklyn. He entered at the start of the fifth inning with the Dodgers trailing, 7-1, and pitched two scoreless innings, striking out two.

After one more relief outing, Koufax got his first start on July 6, 1955. It was the first game of a doubleheader in Pittsburgh. He lasted just 4 2/3 innings. He walked eight batters but allowed only one run on three hits. He was not the pitcher of record. After that, he appeared just three times in a span of 50 days.

Koufax's first win came on August 27, 1955. He started and went the distance, shutting out the Cincinnati Reds on two hits and five walks. He fanned 14, including Gus Bell four times. In his next start, on September 3, Koufax threw another shutout, over Pittsburgh. He allowed just five hits. Those were his only two wins as a rookie.

The Dodgers won their only World Series in 1955, and though Koufax did not appear, he got a full share. He took night classes at Columbia while the Series was in progress, then attended in the day after Johnny Podres finished off the Yankees.[34] Brooklyn won the National League pennant again in 1956; once more Koufax was on the postseason roster, but Alston did not call upon him.

During his first two years as a Dodger, Koufax gained little experience – just 28 total appearances (15 starts) and barely 100 innings pitched. He was frustrated and quick to blame his wildness and unsteadiness on the lack of regular work.[35] It was a vicious cycle. He couldn't pitch until his control improved – but the less he pitched, the worse his control became. While in Brooklyn for three years, Koufax considered himself not a pitcher but an arm. He could not help but feel that some potentially prime years were wasted.[36]

Koufax got a boost in May 1956, however, with the arrival of Sal Maglie. Koufax and Don Drysdale (then a 19-year-old rookie) sat in the bullpen with the savvy veteran and listened to analysis of what was happening on the field.[37]

During the 1956-57 offseason, rather than touring Japan with most of the Dodgers, Koufax got a chance to practice what he was taught in winter ball. The Dodgers arranged for him to pitch in Puerto Rico with the Caguas Criollos. The manager was Ben Geraghty, from the Braves organization, a renowned developer of young talent. Although Koufax posted a won-lost record of just 3-6, he showed more glimpses of brilliance – a one-hit shutout on Halloween night and a two-hit shutout on December 16. The great Roberto Clemente got the only hits off Koufax in the latter game, Sandy's last in Puerto Rico. Caguas had to release him because a league ruling precluded teams from having more than three imported players with big-league experience.[38]

Koufax got more work with Brooklyn in 1957. He pitched in 34 games, starting 13 of them, and logged over 100 innings. That season ended on a distinctive note: Koufax became the last man to throw a pitch in a Brooklyn Dodger uniform. In relief of Roger Craig at Philadelphia, he struck out Willie Jones on three pitches.

During the 1958 season, Koufax revealed to Carl Erskine that he was going to quit baseball and pursue an opportunity to buy into a radio station. But at the end of the season, Koufax felt appreciative of the way the Dodgers had treated him. He had been used more than ever before – 40 games, 26 starts, nearly 160 innings pitched. He said he would give it one more year (1959) before making a final decision.

Erskine believed that because basketball had been Koufax's favorite sport, Koufax did not possess the inner fire for baseball that other rookies and players in general had. Koufax would not approach the other pitchers for advice or ask any questions. He was being self-taught. There was no one trying to show him how to pace himself or how to hold a runner. In addition to the bonus baby rule, which prevented Koufax from getting seasoning, Erskine talked about competition. In the 1950s, players had year-to-year contracts, and thus were not inclined to take a rookie under their wing and show him the ropes. Each man was fighting for his own job. It was not uncommon for players to be released midyear and be replaced by one of the many minor-league aspirants.

Erskine also commented that Koufax may have felt some guilt about leapfrogging over the nine or 10 pitchers that each of the 15 farm teams in the Dodger organization had. Koufax had taken a spot on the roster that another then deserved more. His sensitivity played a role in his image of himself.[39]

Koufax started poorly in 1959. As of May 2, he had started four games – not getting past the fourth inning in any – and relieved once. In just 11 innings, he had allowed 19 hits and 17 walks, and his ERA was a dismal 12.27. Koufax felt that the Dodgers were very close to getting rid of him. Pitching coach Joe Becker said, "He has no coordination and he has lost all his confidence. His arm is sound, but mechanically he is all fouled up…."

Even though Walt Alston said not to give up on Koufax, Sandy believed those were the words of the front office, not the field manager. At this point Koufax was hoping that some other team would claim him on waivers so he could continue in the big leagues.[40] In mid-June, though, it started to come together. Koufax improved his control and pitched three consecutive complete-game victories. He had a similar run in late August. On August 31, against the Giants at the Los Angeles Coliseum, Koufax struck out 18 batters. It was to be his final win of the season. In the bottom of the ninth with the score tied, Koufax was allowed to hit and singled to left field off Giants starter Jack Sanford. After Junior Gilliam singled, Wally Moon launched a three-run walk-off home run. The win streak ended September 6 when, after matching zeroes with Chicago's Art Ceccarelli for nine innings, Koufax gave up a three-run homer to Ernie Banks in the 10th and lost.

Koufax was continuing to mature as a pitcher. In 1959, the Dodgers won another pennant, and so he appeared in a World Series at last. After pitching two innings in Game One, a blow-out victory for the White Sox, Koufax started Game Five. On October 6, in front of 92,706 fans at the Coliseum, he pitched seven innings of five-hit ball, striking out six. He walked only one batter and allowed the game's only run when Sherm Lollar grounded into a double play. The White Sox may have won, but Erskine believed that Koufax realized that he could be truly successful in the major leagues.[41] What also transformed him from an inconsistent pitcher to a Hall of Famer was coming to grips with fear of failure on such a big stage.[42]

The Dodgers realized more fully what they had in 1960, when Yankees GM George Weiss tried to get Koufax in a trade for catcher Elston Howard. Bavasi turned the deal down.[43] The original offer for Howard was Duke Snider and Johnny Podres.[44] Koufax himself may not have agreed. When the 1960 season ended, he was again uncertain about his future. He was disgusted with his performance over 175 innings. Despite 197 strikeouts, both his control (100 walks allowed) and ERA (3.91) had improved just marginally.[45]

It's often observed that the two halves of Koufax's 12-year career stand in stark contrast. From 1955 through 1960, he won 36 and lost 40, with 405 walks in 691 2/3 innings. His ERA over this period was 4.10. But Koufax burst into prominence in 1961, winning 18 games and leading the National League with 269 strikeouts.

During spring training 1961, Norm Sherry, sitting with Koufax on a bus filled with reserves heading out of Vero Beach to an exhibition game, had suggested to Koufax that he ease up a bit – the harder he threw, the wilder he became. Koufax would then tense his massive muscles, and thus his fastball would lose life and his control would erode further. Joe Becker stated, "He needs a loose wrist to get snap in the ball at the position of release, not more muscular tension than he was already creating."[46] Sherry said, "Why not have some fun out there, Sandy? Don't try to throw so hard and use more curve balls and change-ups."[47]

Heeding this suggestion was truly the turning point in Koufax's career. He economized effort, retained velocity, and gained better control of both his pitches and himself. In other words, he went from thrower to pitcher. The mental dimension of his game was prominent.

- At times Koufax put on an act to fool batters into looking for a different pitch. He did not like to shake off signs in a regular manner; he believed it was a tip-off. So he would purposely shake off a series of signs only to come back to where he wanted to be.
- Koufax would not think of the other team's lineup until warming up. He believed that thinking about the hitters that late forced him to concentrate upon them completely.[48]
- He focused on retiring the average hitters, rather than getting out the best opposing batter. His philosophy was that allowing the star(s) to reach base three or four times in a game did not matter if no one else preceded or followed with a hit.
- To be at his best, on the two days before a start Koufax abstained from any activity that might interfere with his performance.[49]

Of interest, however, Koufax believed that luck had a lot to do with success on the mound – particularly line shots hit right at an infielder. Some other noteworthy points include these:

- When Koufax wasn't pitching, he liked to hold a ball with his fastball and curveball grips to strengthen his muscles and tendons.[50]
- He could never throw a slider – it hurt his arm.
- For leverage and push, Koufax pitched from atop the rubber rather than in front of it.
- He believed it necessary to establish the outer half of the plate with a fastball and not get beaten in a close game by throwing a strike on the inner half.[51]
- Koufax never blamed any single play or player for costing him a game, because that same player got him out of trouble in another game.[52]

Koufax's last win in 1961 came in the last big-league game played at the L.A. Coliseum. He earned a complete-game victory after 13 innings and a career-high 205 pitches, to 50 batters. He struck out 15 and walked only three, not allowing a hit over the final five innings.

During his last five seasons, 1962-1966, Koufax ascended to a new level – one of the best peak periods from any pitcher ever (though he did benefit from a notably pitcher-friendly home park in Dodger Stadium). Over that span, he won 111 games and lost only 34, with a 1.95 ERA. He led the National League in ERA in each of those five seasons. *The Sporting News* named him NL Pitcher of the Year from 1963 through 1966. In each of his Cy Young Award/Triple Crown seasons (1963, 1965, and 1966) he won at least 25 games and struck out over 300 batters. In 1963, he was also the NL's Most Valuable Player, and he was the runner-up in the MVP voting of 1965 and 1966.

Koufax enjoyed his fame, but only from afar. Though always elegantly dressed, poised and articulate, he was a basically shy and repressed person. He did not welcome all the commotion that came with his success. He tried very hard to stay out of the news. He would on occasion avoid answering the phone. On urgent matters, a call was often replaced by a wire to Koufax's home.[53] He would often dine in gourmet restaurants at his own expense rather than eat the club's traditional fare, "Dodger steaks."[54] However, he almost never left his hotel room in his final two seasons, preferring to order room service to avoid the attention.[55]

Koufax's 1962 season was off to a good start. On April 24 at Wrigley Field he struck out 18 Cubs as the Dodgers won 10-2. His progress was then interrupted by a career-threatening injury – not to his elbow or shoulder, but to his index finger. It happened in his next start on April 28 in a game against Pittsburgh at Dodger Stadium. By nature a right-handed batter, Koufax decided to protect his throwing arm by swinging lefty instead. In this unfamiliar stance, a pitch from Pirates starter Earl Francis jammed his hand – oddly enough, Koufax got an in-field single on the play. He remained in the game, earning a complete-game 2-1 victory. However, the trauma led to the circulatory condition called Raynaud's phenomenon.[56] It got so bad that if he pressed the finger, it would turn white for hours. His thumb was also affected to a degree.

Despite this numbness, Koufax pitched his first no-hitter, against the Mets, on June 30, 1962. On July 12, he won his 14th game of the season, also against the Mets (he feasted on the expansion club in its weak early years, going 17-2 with a 1.44 ERA). He did not win another game that year. On July

17, Koufax left a game against the Reds after the first inning. He was out of the lineup until September 21. The doctors tried various drugs and intravenous injections designed to dissolve the blood clot in his finger. It alleviated the condition, but at one point the threat of amputation existed.[57]

In the heat of a pennant race with the Giants, Koufax returned, but the layoff cost him endurance. The Dodgers faded down the stretch, and a three-game playoff for the flag ensued. Koufax took the ball for Game One but was knocked out of the box in the second inning.

Going into the 1963 season, there were some lingering doubts about Koufax's condition. He missed three starts in late April and early May with a sore shoulder. His first game back was a victory over the Cardinals, followed by his second career no-hitter on May 11 against the Giants. Koufax was perfect until he walked Ed Bailey with one out in the eighth. Surprisingly, he struck out only four. After the game Koufax stated, "Because of my finger and shoulder injuries and caliber of the Giants, this would have to be my biggest thrill."[58]

The opposing pitcher at Dodger Stadium that night was one of the other premier pitchers in the NL at that time, Juan Marichal. Koufax and the Dominican ace started against each other on four occasions, and this was Koufax's second triumph. Koufax was on the losing side in their next two meetings.

Koufax finished the 1963 season 25-5. He fired 11 shutouts – since then only five other pitchers have had seasons with double-digit shutout totals, and none since 1985.[59]

A teenage Sandy Koufax stands between Dodgers executives Al Campanis, left, and Fresco Thompson. *Courtesy of National Baseball Hall of Fame.*

The Dodgers went on to sweep the World Series against the Yankees. Koufax was named Series MVP, going all the way to win both Game One (5-2) and Game Four (2-1). In Game One, he struck out 15, breaking his old friend Carl Erskine's record, set exactly a decade before. Koufax was aware of it; when he saw Erskine he actually apologized.[60] Koufax set another Series record that day by striking out the first five batters he faced.

By the end of the 1963 season, Koufax had developed traumatic arthritis in his left elbow. Pictures often showed him with his left arm in an ice bath after games. Some experts speculated that the elbow problem came from throwing a few pitches sidearm in his early years. Koufax believed that it happened over a period of 10 to 12 years and may have started in high school when he fell on the basketball court.[61]

The general public had been unaware of the heat treatments that followed.[62] Koufax went to the trainer about an hour before his starts to have Capsolin – basically, chili pepper salve – rubbed on his arm. Capsolin irritates the skin to increase circulation; it burns until the arm goes numb. Excessive application would cause the skin to start peeling.[63] Originally, when his arm blew up, Koufax was given phenylbutazone alka, an anti-inflammatory pill.[64] The nonsteroidal drug was intended for animals and is no longer approved for human use. Today's equivalent is Ibuprofen.

During 1964, Koufax's arthritis became exacerbated. On April 22, he lasted only one inning. He took 12 days off and returned to pitch a complete 10-inning win. One month later in Philadelphia, he pitched his third career no-hitter (and only shutout ever against the Phillies).

In Milwaukee on August 8, Koufax dove back to second base on a pickoff attempt and landed on his elbow. The chronic throbbing after he pitched became more acute; eventually everywhere from his shoulder to wrist swelled up. The team's orthopedic surgeon, Dr. Robert Kerlan, took X-rays that revealed the extent of the arthritis. The treatment was aspirating the fluid build-up with a needle, cortisone injections, and oral medications to relieve the inflammation.[65]

Koufax's final start that season came on August 16. Yet despite taking the mound just 29 times in 1964, he won 19 games. On April 18, 1964 Koufax became the first to pitch three immaculate innings. His first such feat came on June 30, 1962 at Dodger Stadium when he needed just nine pitches in the first inning against the Mets. He finished that game with 13 strikeouts in a 5-0 no-hitter. The second time was April 19, 1963 in the fifth inning with the score 0-0 against Houston at Dodger Stadium. Koufax finished with 14 strikeouts as LA won 2-0. Exactly 365 days later (leap year) in a losing cause against the Reds in Dodger Stadium, with the score tied 0-0 in the third inning, Koufax struck out the side on nine pitches. The Reds scored all three of their runs in the fourth inning on a Deron Johnson home run. Since then this feat of three immaculate innings has been accomplished only twice – Max Scherzer and Chris Sale.

Koufax came up with the idea that if he skipped his customary sideline throwing between starts it would help lessen the pain.[66] The idea seemed to work, as shown by his 1965

record, including a career-high 335 2/3 innings pitched. His 382 strikeouts shattered the modern-era record of 349 that Rube Waddell had set in 1904.

Another memorable matchup against Juan Marichal took place on August 22, 1965 – the game in which Marichal took a bat to Johnny Roseboro's head. Marichal, ejected in the third inning, got no decision. Koufax retired Bob Schroder (who finished Marichal's turn at bat) and Tito Fuentes, but he was still shaken. He walked two and then gave up a three-run homer to Willie Mays that gave the Giants a 4-3 victory.[67]

Koufax, knowing the deadly force of his own deliveries, refrained from beanball wars and never sought to hurt a batter. According to his co-author, Ed Linn, he would not intentionally throw at a hitter and did not try to make batters look bad.[68] Over his career, he hit just 18 batters over 2,324 innings.

By contrast, the National League's other premier pitcher of the day – Bob Gibson – hit 102 batters over 3,884 innings. Gibson (and Don Drysdale) both believed that brushback pitches had a valuable purpose. Yet in his five matchups against Gibson from 1961 through 1966, Koufax was 4-1 with a 0.92 ERA and three shutouts (his 10 against the Cardinals were the most he threw against any team).

With his perfect game at Dodger Stadium on September 9, 1965, Koufax became the first major-league pitcher to throw a fourth no-hitter, surpassing Bob Feller. The Cubs' pitcher, Bob Hendley, allowed just one hit – the teams' combined totals of just one hit and two baserunners are records that have not since been approached.

But the left arm pain remained at times unbearable for Koufax, despite the Capsolin, ice baths, and pain relievers. He found that his left arm was shortening. He had to lean over to reach his face when shaving.

Nonetheless, down the stretch, in yet another heated pennant race with the Giants, he had four complete-game wins in his last five starts. He then pitched two shutouts against Minnesota in the World Series. Though he lost Game Two, he threw a four-hitter in Game Four, striking out 10. In Game Seven, on just two days' rest, he fired a three-hitter. For the second time, he won Series MVP honors.

Koufax's personal decision not to pitch on Yom Kippur, which fell on October 6 in 1965, has been well chronicled. According to media reports, supposedly Koufax was going to consult a rabbi to determine whether he could play. But on October 2, he said simply, "I didn't want to say anything about it before because we were not in a position to clinch the pennant. But at no time did I ever consider it. I will definitely not pitch."[69]

Sports Illustrated named Koufax its Sportsman of the Year for 1965, and writer Jack Olsen asked what drove him. Koufax responded, "I think it's just competition. I want to win, and I want to do things well. And I want to be capable of doing my best. If I were to go out and get beat and then realize after the game that I got beat because of something I did the day before… to me, that's the worst way to lose…I'd be ashamed of myself."[70]

Ahead of the 1966 season, Koufax became embroiled in contract negotiations. He and the Dodgers' other pitching mainstay, Don Drysdale, had grown weary of being played against each other in the process. The two decided to pool their strength and make their salary demands together. The sides were far apart at first; eventually, Buzzie Bavasi made a final offer of $240,000 as a package. This was, at the time, the largest sum ever paid two pitchers on one club for one season – Koufax's portion, $130,000, was then the highest salary in baseball history.[71] However, Koufax and Drysdale had to give up the no-cut clauses in their contracts.[72] Club owner Walter O'Malley was ready to let them both walk if they did not accept that final offer. He mentioned that the Mets were interested in them both.[73]

In 1966, Koufax matched his career highs of the preceding season with 41 starts and 27 complete games. During that season, though, it became necessary for him to receive cortisone injections directly into the elbow joint. The injections became more frequent as the inflammation and fluid in the elbow became more and more difficult to contain. Dr. Kerlan had warned that the traumatic arthritis was incurable. By the end of the 1966 season, Koufax's left arm was bent at a 22.5-degree angle and the bone spurs in the elbow had grown to almost a quarter-inch. Every pitch would bring pain. Combing his hair had become a painful effort. Secretly, he had his suit jackets retailored so that the malformation of his left arm would be hidden.[74]

Yet Koufax never missed a turn – his competitive fire continued to drive him. In midseason, Bob Hunter of the *Los Angeles Times* reported that Koufax had said, "I go out to pitch a no-hitter every game. Of course that can't be, but after I allow one hit, I shoot for a shutout."[75] That dovetailed with his comment the previous year: "And when I give up a run, I want to pitch a one-run game."[76]

In echoes of the 1951 stretch drive, the Giants got hot late in the 1966 race – the threat of a playoff for the Dodgers loomed. But Koufax turned the rivals away in the season's last game. Pitching on just two days' rest in the nightcap of a doubleheader at Philadelphia, he hurled a complete-game 6-3 victory over Jim Bunning to clinch the pennant.[77]

In the 1966 World Series against Baltimore, Koufax started Game Two, going on just three days' rest after his October 2 pennant-clincher. He pitched six innings and allowed four runs; meanwhile, 20-year-old Jim Palmer threw a shutout. The Orioles swept the Series in four games, and so that was the last mound appearance ever by Sandy Koufax.

Before the season was over, the autobiography *Koufax*, written in conjunction with Ed Linn, was published. Among many detailed insights was the following: "I do not think the ballplayer is of an extraordinary importance in our national life. We do not heal the sick or bring peace and comfort to a troubled world. All we do is to provide a few hours of diversion to the people who want to come to the park, and a sort of conflict to those who identify their fortunes with ours through the season…by its nature, it is a brief, self-liquidating life. It is a temporary life, really, a period between the time of our youth and the beginning

of our lifetime career."[78] Whereas Koufax's decision to retire has often been portrayed as "abrupt," this passage supports the idea that he had been contemplating retirement for some time.

It's noteworthy that in 1964, Koufax commented that to be considered a great pitcher, you need to show that you can win games for 10 to 15 years. To be a great ballplayer, your accomplishments need to span not just a couple of years but a whole career.[79]

With this in mind, Carl Erskine's take on Koufax's early retirement becomes even more intriguing. In Erskine's view, once Koufax established his pitching records, he had reached a point where he had nothing more to prove and wanted to leave at the top of the heap. Erskine believed that Koufax never felt totally comfortable as a major-league pitcher. He had never heard or seen any medical report that said Koufax could not go out and pitch.[80]

In his 12 seasons, Sandy Koufax amassed the following notable statistics:

- Winning percentage of .655
- ERA of 2.76
- 40 shutouts, including 10 1-0 victories
- Along with his four no-hitters, two one-hitters, eight two-hitters, and 17 three-hitters
- 9.28 strikeouts per nine innings
- Eight regular-season games with 15 or more strikeouts
- Opponents' batting average of .205
- 6.79 hits allowed per nine innings during his career
- Koufax never won a Gold Glove, but in 1965 he did not commit an error.[81]

As noted, the late Ernie Banks had a hard time facing Koufax. In 143 plate appearances, Banks had only 23 hits (they did include seven home runs) and struck out 31 times. One player who had great success against Koufax was Bill Virdon – .404 in 60 plate appearances despite swinging left-handed, well above his career .267 average.

Even for a pitcher, Koufax was a weak hitter, batting just .097 in his career. He did have two home runs, though. Both came at County Stadium against the Braves and both were off lefthanders. His first, on June 13, 1962, was a solo shot to left center in the fifth inning off Warren Spahn. It proved to be the winning run. The second came a year later off Denny Lemaster. Other batting highlights include a home game against Houston on July 20, 1965. In the ninth with the score tied, Walt Alston allowed Koufax to bat with two out and two on. Koufax delivered a walk-off single to left. Also, in a game against the Mets on June 5, 1966, Koufax had two hits in one inning.

In December 1966, Koufax joined NBC as a broadcaster. His contract (which also called for him to do other work for the network) was for an estimated $1,000,000 over 10 years.[82] Koufax was reassigned to the second broadcasting team in 1969 to gain more experience; Tony Kubek was promoted to join Curt Gowdy, and Pee Wee Reese's contract was not renewed.[83]

After the 1968 season ended, the Dodgers made a formal offer to Koufax to return. He politely turned it down, telling Bob Hunter that he did not want to wind up a cripple and not be able to play a normal game of golf.[84]

According to Carl Erskine, Koufax wanted to have a successful marriage with children. Sandy was regularly seen in the presence of beautiful young women, yet he wondered why he could not meet someone like Erskine's wife. He confessed that his dates had usually been introduced to him at cocktail parties. Erskine told Koufax that was the problem. "You should go to your synagogue or other such similar places to meet a different kind of woman."[85]

Koufax never became a father, but he got married three times. His first wife was Anne Widmark, daughter of actor Richard Widmark. Their wedding was on New Year's Day, 1969.[86] They lived in East Holden, near Ellsworth, Maine. They bought what was known as the Winkumpaugh Farm on October 4, 1971, then proceeded to buy the 300 adjacent acres. Koufax joined the Bucksport Golf Club and got his handicap down to a six. He was able to advance to the championship flights in the 1973 Maine State Amateur Championship. He continued his interest in electronics and dabbled in carpentry and gourmet cooking.[87] Sandy's sister Edith related that when they were growing up, her brother was a pretty good cook and handy around the family home, which he wired for sound. When Edith got married, he even came over to the newlyweds' home and spent three hours persistently fixing a sewing machine.[88]

It was at his Maine home that Koufax received the news that he had been voted into the Hall of Fame.[89] At the time, his 344 votes were the most ever. In his Hall of Fame acceptance speech on August 7, 1972, Koufax referred to his old pitching coach, Joe Becker: "Becker pushed me, shoved me, embarrassed me and made me work and thank God for him. Being a pitcher I feel that it is sometimes very solitary, very lonely…you feel like well everybody on the other team is against you, and they are. The only one that seems to be close, the only friend you have is the catcher, and I'd like to thank every catcher who ever caught in any ball game I was ever in, two in particular, Roy Campanella, who caught the very first one, and John Roseboro, who caught most of the others."

Koufax's contract with NBC was terminated by mutual consent before the start of the 1973 season.[90] From Koufax's side, the decision to leave the broadcast booth stemmed in part from difficulty in talking baseball to people who had not played the game professionally. Other challenges for him were describing pitchers whose repertoires differed from his, and being honest and critical of the men he played with and against. As a result, he was uncomfortable on the air.[91]

In 1974, the Koufaxes sold the Maine property and moved back to California. Koufax played golf, invested in real estate and enjoyed listening to music at home. He rarely attended a baseball game, instead watching on television. He admitted that he missed playing, stating, "It's hard not to miss the one thing in your life you've done very well."[92]

After his retirement, Koufax spent much of his time on a ranch outside Paso Robles. He eventually ran into financial difficulties. Thus, he returned to baseball in 1979 as a special pitching coach for the Dodgers.[93] Over the following 11 years, he worked with prospects during spring training, paying follow-up visits in Double A and Triple A. Keeping a low profile, he had no name on the back of his jacket when on the practice field. During the offseason he retreated to his ranch and eventually to southern Idaho to keep away from the press and baseball.[94]

Anne Widmark and Koufax divorced in 1982. In 1985, Koufax married his second wife, Kimberly Francis, a fitness enthusiast with a passion for the arts. For a time, they lived in Oregon, where she had a gallery. Their marriage ended in the winter of 1998/1999.[95] Koufax married a third time, to Jane Purucker Clarke, a sorority sister of Laura Bush, the former President's wife.[96]

The 1989 season was the last of Koufax's 11 years with the Dodgers as minor-league pitching instructor, although he continued to visit unofficially in spring training. For many years, well into the 21st century, he would also visit the Mets in spring training to catch up with old friend Fred Wilpon and offer sage advice to young pitchers. Sometimes he would disappear, though, before players had a chance to shake his huge hand.

Many books have been written about Sandy Koufax over the years, a testament to enduring public interest in the man. Not a day goes by without his name appearing on the World Wide Web.[97] The year 2002 brought *Sandy Koufax: A Lefty's Legacy*, by Jane Leavy. Koufax authorized the book but declined to be interviewed; thus, Leavy interviewed more than 400 people to gain perspective on the player and person, from the standpoints of both baseball and Judaism. It became a bestseller and was praised for the quality of its writing.

Alas, after the book came out, Koufax's relationship with the Dodgers became severely strained. The *New York Post*, then owned – as were the Dodgers – by News Corp., planted a blind item insinuating that Koufax was gay. The paper quickly withdrew the item and apologized, but Koufax severed his ties with the club for a couple of years. In 2004, however, Frank McCourt bought the Dodgers, and Koufax resumed his unofficial spring-training visits to work with pitchers.[98]

In 2007, 41 years after he retired from baseball, Koufax was the final player chosen in the draft to stock the six teams for the first (and only) season of the Israel Baseball League. Koufax, then 71, was picked by the Modi'in Miracle in the draft conducted by the head of the league's operations, Dan Duquette. Miracle manager Art Shamsky (another noted Jewish big-leaguer) stated, "His selection is a tribute to the esteem with which he is held by everyone associated with this league. It's been 41 years between starts for him. If he's rested and ready to take the mound again, we want him on our team."[99]

Koufax remained a frequent newsmaker. In 2010, President Barack Obama likened himself in jest to Koufax at a White House gathering that honored Jewish Americans. The President stated, "We are both lefties. He can't pitch on Yom Kippur. I can't pitch." Obama started his introduction by saying "This is a pretty fancy…pretty distinguished group and Sandy Koufax."[100] The mention of Koufax's name brought the biggest cheer at this event, which included members of the House and Senate, two Justices of the Supreme Court, Olympic athletes, entrepreneurs, and rabbinical scholars.

Koufax's reputation for privacy endured for decades. Even his own mother saw him as a mystery. When she heard that Sandy was writing his autobiography, she asked if she could get one of the first copies so she could learn about her son. "You never told me anything," she said.[101] One 1999 report noted, "Koufax's tight band of friends…call him The Ghost because of the way he suddenly appears and disappears."[102] Yet this report and others over the years emphasized his loyalty. Fellow Brooklyn native Joe Torre said that once you were in Koufax's inner circle, you were in for good.[103] For example, even though Fred Wilpon got Sandy to become one of the investors in Bernard Madoff's notorious Ponzi scheme, Koufax publicly supported Wilpon. He would have testified on behalf of the Mets' ownership, had a settlement not averted a civil trial.

Koufax himself added balance to the portrait. "I'm trying to figure out who says I'm private," he said with a grin. "I'm at the Final Four. I go to golf tournaments. I go to the movies. I go to dinner. I live my life. Somebody wrote that 50 years ago, and they're still writing that. … I don't care what anybody says. I'm past caring."[104]

In the spring of 2012, Guggenheim Baseball bought the Dodgers, and co-owner Earvin "Magic" Johnson reached out to Koufax. Previously, Sandy had thrown out the first pitch at Dodger Stadium on Opening Day 2008, but in 2013, he forged closer ties with the club again. He continued to impart his wisdom to pitchers and became a special advisor to Chairman Mark Walter. Koufax expressed his delight and said that some of his most cherished memories came at Dodger Stadium. But Ned Colletti, who was then the team's general manager, summed it up perfectly.

"He's as iconic a player as we'll ever have."[105]

NOTES

1   Ira Berkow, "Koufax Is No Garbo," *New York Times*," July 3, 1985.

2   Tom Verducci, "The Left Arm of God," *Sports Illustrated*, July 12, 1999.

3   Maury Allen, "Koufax Labors in Obscurity of Dodger System," *New York Post*, September 15, 1983.

4   Verducci.

5   Ed Gruver, "Two Southpaws – the Best of Their Eras," *Philadelphia Inquirer*, April 9, 2000.

6   Milton Gross, "Call Him Lucky," *New York Post*, October 10, 1965.

7   According to an Associated Press clipping in Koufax's Hall of Fame player file, "Braun Real name of Sandy Koufax," Jack Braun was a six-footer with features that resembled his son's. Braun was part-owner of a business that distributed records. With his second wife, he had a daughter named Marie born in 1946.

8   Sandy Koufax with Ed Linn, *Koufax* (New York: Viking Press, 1966), 16-28.

9   Bob Broeg, "Sandy Started Slowly…But oh What a Finish," *The Sporting News*, August 14, 1971.

10   Koufax with Linn, 16-28.

11   Koufax with Linn, 16-28.

12   Koufax and Linn, 38.

13   Phil Pepe, "Koo: At First He Succeeded," *New York Daily News*, August 6, 1971.

14   http://infinitecardset.blogspot.com/2010/10/52-sandy-koufax-and-coney-island.html

15   Broeg.

16   Pepe.

17   Pepe.

18   Broeg; Richard Sandomir, "Koufax's Change-Up: He Talks with ESPN," *New York Times*, April 2, 1999.

19   Associated Press, "Sandy Was Sometimes Special," *New York Post*, April 2, 1974.

20   Data provided by Connor Boyle, University of Cincinnati, Match 23, 2023.

21   Broeg.

22   Koufax and Linn, 49-50.

23   Koufax and Linn, 47.

24   "Sandy Finally Signed with Persistent Dodgers," *The Sporting News*, August 14, 1971.

25   Broeg.

26   .Broeg

27   Broeg.

28   Broeg.

29   Broeg.

30   Broeg.

31   Carl Erskine, telephone interview with Marc Z. Aaron, October 26, 2012 (hereafter Erskine telephone interview).

32   Joe Resnick, Associated Press, "Lasorda remembers Being Replaced by Koufax," June 7, 2005.

33   Koufax and Linn, 110-111.

34   *The Sporting News*, January 4, 1956: 33; *The Sporting News*, October 26, 1955: 11.

35   Melvin Durslag, "Sandy Koufax the Strikeout King," *Saturday Evening Post*, July 14, 1962.

36   Koufax and Linn, 113-114.

37   Koufax and Linn, 114-118.

38   Thomas E. Van Hyning, *The Santurce Crabbers* (Jefferson, North Carolina: McFarland & Co., 1999), 77.

39   Erskine telephone interview.

40   Koufax and Linn, 134.

41   Erskine telephone interview.

42   Sherman.

43   Durslag, "Sandy Koufax the Strikeout King."

44   Bill Libby, "The Sophistication of Sandy Koufax," *Sport Magazine*, September 1963.

45   Koufax and Linn, 142.

46   Broeg.

47   Broeg.

48   Koufax and Linn, 187.

49   "Koufax on Koufax," *Sports Illustrated*, December 20, 1965.

50   Verducci.

51   Joel Sherman, "Mets Soak in Some Koufax Greatness," *New York Post*, March 17, 1998.

52   Koufax and Linn, 8-9.

53   Melvin Durslag, "Challenging Sandy Was Fascination and Hopeless," *The Sporting News*, February 12, 1972.

54   Richard Lamparski, *"Whatever Became of…"* Seventh Series (New York: Crown Publishers, April 1978).

55   Verducci.

56   *Sports Illustrated*, "Koufax on Koufax," December 20, 1965.

57   Broeg.

58   Broeg.

59   The others: Dean Chance, Juan Marichal, Bob Gibson, Jim Palmer, and John Tudor.

60   Erskine telephone interview.

61   *Sports Illustrated*, "Koufax on Koufax."

62   *Sports Illustrated*, "Koufax on Koufax."

63   Sandy Koufax with Ed Linn, "My Special World Series Memories," *Sport*, October 1966.

64   Koufax and Linn, 237.

65   Broeg.

66   Koufax and Linn, 228.

67   Peter C. Bjarkman, "Dandy Sandy and the Summer of '65'," *Elysian Fields Quarterly*, Winter 1998.

68   Ed Linn, "Koufax Remembered," *Sports Illustrated*, January 20, 1972.

69   Associated Press, "Koufax to Miss Opener, Will Observe Holy Day," October 2, 1965.

70   "Koufax on Koufax," "Sportsman of the Year," *Sports Illustrated*, December 20, 1965.

71   Bob Hunter, "No Hit Game Koufax Goal Every Start," *Los Angeles Times*, June 18, 1966.

72   *New York Post*, April 11, 1966.

73   Koufax and Linn, 288.

74   Linn, "Koufax Remembered."

75   Hunter.

76   Phil Pepe, "Burden on Sandy," *New York World Telegram*, March 18, 1965.

77   Jeff Meyers, United Press International, "Koufax Comes Through and dodgers Clinch Pennant," September 30, 1966.

78   "Koufax 'Right On'," *Binghamton Press*, January 2, 1972.

79   Leonard Koppett, "The Greatest Pitcher of Them All," *New York Times Magazine*, October 4, 1964.

80   Erskine telephone interview.

81   Bob Gibson was the winner even though he committed three errors and had fewer assists than Koufax.

82   Associated Press, "Koufax to Broadcast Baseball," December 30, 1966.

83   Milton Richman, Associated Press, "Pee Wee Reese Gets Word From Network," March 7, 1969.

84   Bob Hunter, "Sandy Says Nix to Comeback Pitch by Dodgers," *Los Angeles Times*, November 9, 1968.

85   Erskine telephone interview

86   Associated Press, "Sandy Koufax, Ann *[sic]* Widmark Are Married," January 2, 1969.

87   Verducci.

88   Broeg.

89   Included among the clippings in Koufax's Hall of Fame library file was a copy of an uncashed check, dated January 26, 1972, made out to Vic Lapiner with a handwritten note that stated, "Dear Vic, Here's your blood money. Honestly I can say it is a bet I'm happy to lose. I don't think it would be fun to be judged yearly. Hope all are well, and have good year. As always, Sandy." Per a telephone interview with Vic Lapiner on May 16, 2012, Vic related that shortly before the HOF voting he and Koufax were sitting in a restaurant when Lapiner bet Koufax he would get into the HOF on the first ballot in January 1972. Lapiner was a pitcher in the Cleveland and Kansas City farm systems and a star athlete at USC. He met Koufax when he continued his baseball career by throwing batting practice for various teams including the Dodgers. They built up a strong friendship, possibly in part because Lapiner is also Jewish.

90   Maury Allen, "Koufax Return Stirs memories," *New York Post*, February 6, 1979.

91   Jack Craig, SporTView column, *Boston Globe*, March 17, 1973 and Ralph Bernstein, "Sandy Koufax Says Transition from Playing Field to Telecasting Was Not an Easy Move," *Utica Daily Press*, February 8, 1968.

92   Maury Allen.

93   Gordon Verrell, "Recluse Koufax Steps Back into the Game," *The Sporting News*, February 17, 1979.

94   Edvins Beitiks, "Koufax Says He's Happy to Be Compared with Gooden," *San Francisco Examiner*, 1986/1987

95   Verducci.

96   Third marriage confirmed with Sandy Koufax by telephone on November 17, 2015. http://old.nationalreview.com/interrogatory/kessler200604032246.asp and Ronald Kessler, *Laura Bush: An Intimate Portrait of the First Lady*, (New York: Broadway Books, 2007.

97   This is the author's observation after a lengthy subscription to Google Alerts.

98   Dylan Hernandez, "Dodgers and Sandy Koufax team up again after years apart," January 22, 2013.

99   http://www.cbsnews.com/2100-500290_162-2735685.html

100   Mark Knoller, "Obama Honors Jewish Americans at White House Reception," www.cbsnews.com, May 27, 2010.

101   Koufax and Linn, 39.

102   Jeff Jacobs, "At 63, Koufax Still Elusive," *Hartford Courant*, October 26, 1999.

103   Jeff Arnold, "Joe Torre Reflects On Sandy Koufax In Advance Of Dodger Legend's Pump Foundation Honor", ThePostGame.com, August 8, 2012 (http://www.thepostgame.com/blog/men-action/201208/sandy-koufax-joe-torre-tony-larussa-pump-brothers-foundation-cancer)

104   Greg Beacham, Associated Press, "Sandy Koufax a commanding presence Dodgers' spring training," February 24, 2013.

105   Hernandez, "Dodgers and Sandy Koufax team up again after years apart."

Wild Thing - From UC Bearcat to Dodgers' Bonus Baby

BY RUSS SPEILLER

When you think of the nickname Wild Thing, which baseball player comes to mind? Perhaps it is Mitch Williams, who earned that moniker while pitching for the Texas Rangers due to his awkward delivery and frequent control issues. More likely, however, the name that pops into your head is Ricky Vaughn, the fictitious Cleveland Indians pitcher, played by actor Charlie Sheen in the classic 1989 movie *Major League*. Most certainly you aren't thinking about Sandy Koufax, who in his 12-year career pitching to 9,497 hitters hit only 18 batters and threw 87 wild pitches.

But if you ask Koufax's teammates at the University of Cincinnati how they would describe the young pitcher, "wild" might be the word most often used. Koufax was most certainly their "wild thing."

It was just before the start of the Bearcats' 1954 season that 18-year-old UC *basketball* player Sandy Koufax arrived between classes to hang out in the office of his coach, Ed Jucker, who also was the head coach of the varsity baseball team. Jucker was busy trying to quickly plan a trip to New Orleans for the baseball team. In Sandy's words, "I heard those two magic words, 'New Orleans,' and I could think of no other place in the world I would rather be." Koufax said, "Coach, I'm a baseball player. I'm a pitcher. I can pitch pretty good."[1]

In 2000, when the university held a ceremony to retire Jucker's jersey, he was asked about the day Koufax informed him of his pitching talents. "I didn't even know he could pitch," Jucker recalled. "At the end of the basketball season, he told me to come over to the gym to take a look at him. I was amazed. It was almost like the wonder man. It struck me in such a fashion.

Sandy Koufax pitched one season for the University of Cincinnati baseball team. He posted a 3-1 record with a 2.81 ERA. Courtesy of University of Cincinnati Athletic Department.

The way he could throw – the speed and the curve – you just didn't find that."[2]

UC captain and right fielder Ike Misali, who was in the office planning the trip with Jucker, later recalled, "All he needed was somebody to teach him control. A kid his age throwing 90 miles an hour – this was 1954. He was strong. He wasn't at all cocky – just a nice guy."[3]

Koufax pitched only one season for the Bearcats, finishing with a 3-1 record and a 2.81 ERA. He led the staff with 51 strikeouts in 32 innings. He also walked 30 batters. His only loss of the season came against the Xavier University Musketeers, in part due to three Cincinnati errors.[4]

To this day it remains a mystery as to what uniform number Sandy wore during that season, as existing individual and team photographs of him don't show the back of his uniform where the number was displayed, nor did team rosters make note of player numbers. When asked by the *Cincinnati Enquirer* what jersey number he wore, Koufax couldn't recall, and neither could his teammates.[5] Perhaps even more a mystery than his uniform number, however, was where the baseball was going to go when he released his unbridled fastball or knee-buckling curve. Koufax later told the *Enquirer* that he didn't have a specific strategy on the mound: "Just throw as hard and as long as you could."[6]

In an exhibition game against a team from Wright-Patterson Air Force Base, Koufax walked the first three batters he faced before striking out the next three on nine pitches.[7] Joe Miller, who was a sophomore catcher for the Bearcats in 1954, recalled, "Koufax was built like a superhuman on the mound, [but] he was damn wild. He couldn't get the ball over the plate ... with consistency."[8] Legend has it that

The Bearcats' hard-throwing lefty, Sandy Koufax, stands in the back row, fifth from the left. Courtesy of University of Cincinnati Athletic Department.

Jucker would have Sandy warm up on the sideline to terrorize opposing teams.[9]

Koufax threw so hard that everyone refused to catch him except for his friend and basketball teammate Dan Gilbert. Thinking back, Gilbert, who was a freshman catcher that spring, said, "We realized early on that Sandy was not a pitcher. He was just a thrower. He was a hard, wild thrower. We practiced inside the old Schmidlapp Hall. There was not much room in there, and it was poorly lighted. I would work with pitchers on the corners. With Sandy, I held my mitt in the center of the plate and prayed that he could get it over or close. I will say this though, when he got the ball over the plate, he was unhittable."[10] Gilbert also recalled using a sponge inside his mitt to help absorb the shock of the baseball, finding it challenging to catch the ball in the webbing.[11] He described the first pitch he witnessed from Koufax in the following way: "You ever take a sledgehammer and hit a knot in a piece of wood? You know how it bounces back? That's how it felt."[12]

There's a story that circulates throughout Oldenburg, Indiana, in which Koufax was invited to come from the University of Cincinnati to Oldenburg and try out for the local semipro baseball team, the Oldenburg Villagers. The gentleman who asked was Ace Moorman Sr., a UC basketball player who had heard about Sandy's pitching talent. "I told Charlie Koester [manager of the Oldenburg Villagers] that there might be a possibility we can get Sandy to come to Oldenburg, but we have two problems," Moorman told the *Indianapolis Star* in 2022. "One, I don't think we have anybody who can catch him, and secondly, that little chicken wire at the back of the backstop, that isn't going to stop him either."[13] In truth, no evidence exists that Koufax ever went to Oldenburg for the tryout, but the myth continues that he was cut from the Villagers because he couldn't throw strikes.

Despite all that wildness, the, 6-foot-1½-inch, 200-pound collegiate pitcher enjoyed some incredible highlights, possibly none greater than on Friday, April 30, 1954, when the hometown Bearcats played against the visiting University of Louisville. Coming off an already incredible 16-strikeout performance against Wayne University (now Wayne State University), the southpaw's sizzling fastball and wicked curve stymied Louisville hitters as Koufax struck out 12 of the first 15 batters he faced, allowing only three hits on his way to an 18-strikeout performance,[14] one he would equal at the major-league level five years later on August 31, 1959, against the San Francisco Giants.

Later in the season, on May 14, in a contest against Lockbourne Air Force Base, Koufax came into the game in relief of starter Bill Norris. He struck out the final two batters he faced in the seventh inning and got three easy taps back to the mound in the eighth before striking out the side in the ninth inning for the victory, his third without a defeat.[15] This was Sandy's final victory as a member of the UC baseball team.

The next day, May 15, 1954, Dodgers scout Bill Zinser noted on his report of the player listed as Sanford Koufax: "A+ arm. Very good prospect. Tall, muscular, quick reflexes, well-coordinated. Going to U. of Cincinnati on Scholarship – not interested in pro ball until he graduates." Moreover, Zinser gave Koufax an A for hitting with a notation that he played first base because of his hitting ability. Sandy himself stated, "I hit better for Cincinnati than I have ever hit in my life."[16] In fact, Koufax's batting average for the 1954 season was a whopping .429, making him the second-best hitter on the team.[17] (Koufax was a famously poor hitter as a major leaguer: just .097 in 776 career at-bats.)

It may seem unbelievable, but Koufax never told his parents of his collegiate baseball endeavors. Sandy explained that "my father got the good word when Gene Bonnibeau, the Eastern scout for the Giants, dropped into his office with a clipping about me from one of the Cincinnati papers."[18]

Koufax recalled Jucker trying very hard to get the Cincinnati Reds interested in him but had heard that their scout, Buzz Boyle, "apparently thought I was too wild."[19] Dodgers scout Al Campanis invited Koufax to try out for the organization at Ebbets Field in front of manager Walter Alston and scouting director Fresco Thompson.[20] In December 1954 Koufax said he would talk to Brooklyn and other interested clubs during his school's Christmas vacation, but "I will not leave school unless I get a bonus to sign."[21] Shortly after, he went from being a UC Bearcat to becoming the Brooklyn Dodgers' $20,000 "bonus baby."[22] For Dodgers fans, "wild thing" Sandy Koufax would eventually make everything "groovy."

NOTES

1   Sandy Koufax with Ed Linn, *Koufax* (New York: Viking Press, 1966), 43.

2   John Bach, "Bearcat Sports, University of Cincinnati." *Magazine – October 2020 | University of Cincinnati*, 2000, https://magazine.uc.edu/issues/0500/sports.html.

3   Mike Dyer, "Sandy Koufax's Season with UC Bearcats Remembered," *Cincinnati Enquirer*, April 30, 2014, https://www.cincinnati.com/story/sports/college/university-of-cincinnati/2014/04/30/sandy-koufax-season-with-uc-bearcats-remembered/8512237/. Accessed March 11, 2023.

4   "XU Wins, 5-2, Over UC 9; Koufax Beaten," *Cincinnati Enquirer*, May 18, 1954: 29.

5   Mike Dyer, "Sandy Koufax's Cincinnati Uniform Number a Mystery." *Cincinnati Enquirer*, April 30, 2014, https://www.cincinnati.com/story/sports/college/university-of-cincinnati/2014/04/30/sandy-koufax-uniform-number-a-mystery/8515119/.

6   Dyer, "Sandy Koufax's Season with UC Bearcats Remembered."

7   Gregg Doyel, "Sandy Koufax Made the Hall of Fame, but Not This Semi-Pro Team in Oldenburg, Indiana," *IndyStar*, June 30, 2022, https://www.indystar.com/story/sports/columnists/gregg-doyel/2022/06/30/sandy-koufax-baseball-indiana-semipro-cut-mlb-hall-fame-pitcher/7703165001/. Accessed March 11, 2023.

8   Dyer, "Sandy Koufax's Season with UC Bearcats Remembered."

9   Gary Cieradkowski, *The League of Outsider Baseball* (New York: Touchstone, 2015), 6.

10 Bach, "Bearcat Sports, University of Cincinnati."

11 "Sandy Koufax's Season with UC Bearcats Remembered."

12 Jane Leavy, *Sandy Koufax: A Lefty's Legacy* (New York: HarperCollins, 2002), 49.

13 Doyel.

14 "Koufax Fans 18," *Cincinnati Enquirer*, May 1, 1954: 16.

15 "Wilson, Koufax Star as 'Cats Nine Wins," *Cincinnati Enquirer*, May 15, 1954: 16.

16 Sandy Koufax with Ed Linn, 45.

17 "Brooks Sign Koufax, Pitching Star at UC," *Cincinnati Enquirer*, December 15, 1954: 28.

18 Sandy Koufax with Ed Linn, 45.

19 Sandy Koufax with Ed Linn, 45.

20 "Sandy Koufax Biography & Los Angeles Dodgers Career," *Dodger Blue*, https://dodgerblue.com/sandy-koufax-biography-los-angeles-dodgers-career-stats/. Accessed March 11, 2023.

21 "Koufax Denies Brooklyn Deal," *Cincinnati Post*, December 14, 1954: 20.

22 Koufax actually had two higher bonus offers, from the Pittsburgh Pirates and Milwaukee Braves; however, as his father, Irving, had been in frequent contact with the Dodgers, it was decided to sign with Brooklyn. See Marc Z. Aaron, "Sandy Koufax," SABR BioProject, at https://sabr.org/bioproj/person/sandy-koufax/.

The Road Not Taken: Sandy Koufax, Basketball Player

BY BILL PRUDEN

In his early teen years Sandy Koufax, like most like-minded kids of his era, played the sport of the season, stopping only for dinner and maybe homework. After the family moved from Brooklyn to Rockville Centre, New York, he took full advantage of the comparatively wide-open spaces of the still-developing Long Island to play whatever sports were available. It was, he later recalled, "baseball in the summer and football in the fall. No leagues. No supervision. Just fun and bruises."[1]

But all that changed after ninth grade, when, tired of commuting into the City on the Long Island Rail Road, Koufax's parents returned to Brooklyn, settling in the Bensonhurt section. Suddenly, the city game, basketball, became the center of the sports-obsessed Koufax's world.

In looking back on how the game dominated the athletic landscape when it barely existed in his Rockville Centre world, the aspiring architect, showing his appreciation of space, observed that "in Brooklyn every square foot of recreational space has to be used – and that's about all the space you need to set up a basket."[2]

Koufax's formal high-school basketball career was, in fact, delayed when his arrival at Lafayette High School coincided with the refusal of New York City schoolteachers to supervise any extracurricular activities – including interscholastic sports – unless they received pay instead of leave time. The stalemate meant no organized sports during Koufax's sophomore year. However, there was still gym class, which at Lafayette meant basketball, and when his classmates recognized his athleticism and saw his clear promise, they urged him to join the Jewish Community House on Bay Parkway and play on their team in the JCH league. Years later Koufax recalled that while "the J" offered a range of activities, its basketball court was the heart of the operation. For Koufax, it "became my second home."[3]

Indeed, Koufax recalled playing virtually every day after school during the basketball season and when spring came around and he was also playing baseball, he would go from school to a baseball game "and then stop off for a three-man game of basketball in some playground."[4] Once that was done, it was time for a league game at the J. During the season, he played a Saturday night league game, only to be back at the J on Sunday morning, waiting for someone to arrive and open the doors so he could continue to work on his game.[5] One teammate said Koufax "could jump like a kangaroo," and he devoted most of his time to working on his rebounding.[6] He worked continuously on his timing off the backboard, further honing his jumping ability and seeking to gain ever more control of his body.[7]

While his basketball career proved short-lived, Koufax's love for the game, the way it appealed to his thoughtful side, as well as the memories he took away from his many days and nights on the Brooklyn playgrounds are lovingly recounted in his 1966 memoir, *Koufax*. He offers a take on the game that reflects both the memories of a teenager in love with the sport, as well as the analytical eye of a professional athlete who knows – and deeply appreciates – the elements of the game that go well beyond the physical side, but which are central to success. Too, however unconsciously, the way Koufax describes getting the right angles for snaring a rebound or the ins and outs of both the give-and-go and the way that you had to operate around the iron pole that supported the basket, reflects the same analytical approach of a man who made, spectacularly, the transformation from a thrower to a pitcher.

It may have been a short-lived career, but basketball was a central part of his late teen years. Indeed, so intensely competitive was the basketball-playing Koufax that he earned the nickname the "Animal of Bensonhurst."[8] Consequently, the fact that his formal introduction to the game came in a program and on a team that would, at year's end, win the inaugural National Jewish Welfare Board-sponsored national tournament made the experience all the more rewarding.[9]

While the early stages of the Koufax basketball odyssey were something short of normal, the latter parts were equally distinctive. He did not play for Lafayette High in his sophomore year but made a smooth transition to high-school ball as a junior. He made a team that was composed for the most part of his JHC teammates. Playing for a new coach, Frank Rabinowitz, hopes were high. However, with the New York schools operating on semester rather than yearlong schedules, it was not uncommon for large numbers of students to graduate in December, something that could ravage a basketball team. And that is exactly what happened with two of his former JHC teammates. While Koufax gained more playing time, the team's championship prospects were dashed.

As a senior, Koufax was both a starter and captain, but that team's prospects were also hurt by midseason graduations. While disappointed, Koufax finished the season as the second highest scorer in the division, averaging 16.5 points per game.[10] He was also named one of the forwards on the sportswriter-selected All-City team.[11] For a guy who had only discovered basketball as a sophomore, he had come a long way and his promise was evident. Koufax's limited performances during his high-school years offered clear evidence of his potential while leaving those who saw him with indelible memories that grew ever more vivid as his baseball career took off.

Nothing illustrated that better than a Police Athletic League benefit that the New York Knicks played against Lafayette in February 1953. As the star-struck high schoolers went through their layup line, the pros put on a bit of a show before the boisterous crowd. However, after Knicks star Harry Gallatin unsuccessfully tried a couple of dunks, a part of the game seldom seen at that time, Knicks guard Al McGuire, apparently prompted by Coach Rabinowitz, brought the 6-2 Koufax over and told Gallatin that he had someone who could show him how it was done – and the prep star did – twice. That proved to be only a preview of the game, for while the pros saw the contest as a way to mix with the community and help popularize the still-developing NBA, Koufax and his teammates went all out. When it was over, the young basketball star had earned a memorable headline, with the *New York Post* declaring, "Lafayette Cager Wowed Gallatin."[12] Gallatin reportedly told Coach Rabinowitz, "We'll be coming back for this kid someday," while Koufax recalled that when it was all over Gallatin wrote down his name, telling him, "I am going to be looking for you in future years."[13]

Indeed, despite the unevenness of his high-school career, Koufax hoped to play in college, an ambition fueled by at least casual feelers from the local schools, as well as one from the legendary Frank McGuire, who, having left St. John's for the University of North Carolina, sought to draw upon the city's talent and lift the program into the upper echelons of college basketball.[14]

In the end, Koufax went to the University of Cincinnati, although why remains a mystery. Indeed, years later even he termed the process and his interest in the school a "puzzlement."[15] That certainly was the case when Koufax arrived for the first day of freshman team tryouts. Assistant varsity/freshmen head coach Ed Jucker (also the head coach of the baseball team) admitted years later that he had no idea who the kid was or what kind of player he was getting.[16] But Koufax's early days on the hardwood impressed Jucker enough that he arranged for a partial scholarship.[17] And providentially, it was the basketball connection that led to Koufax joining Jucker's baseball team on a spring travel trip, a venture that arguably served as the launching pad for the left-hander's Hall of Fame baseball career.

Before that happened, there was the matter of Koufax's final year of organized basketball as a member of Cincinnati's freshman team, the affectionately named Bearkittens. Like his previous stops, Koufax's time with the freshman squad showed his potential. On a team that finished 12-2, he was a starter and one of only three players who saw action in all 14 games. Of note,

Sandy Koufax finished fourth in scoring on the University of Cincinnati's freshman basketball team. Courtesy of University of Cincinnati Athletic Department.

he scored 23 points against Miami of Ohio, with future Dodgers manager Walter Alston in attendance.[18] Koufax finished fourth on the team in scoring, but his work under the boards led to his going to the free-throw line more than all but one teammate.[19] Even so, this was the last organized basketball he would play.

The might-have-beens related to Koufax's basketball career are many. From the flashes of talent he showed playing for the JHC squad, for Lafayette, and against the Knicks, not to mention his efforts for the Bearkittens, it was clear he could play. And given the program he was a part of, that potential might have been developed further. Years later, Koufax mused that the roots of Cincinnati's historic run were being planted while he was there. Indeed, as Koufax struggled to harness his baseball talents, in 1959, with George Smith at the helm, the Bearcats made the first of five consecutive Final Fours, finishing third both that year and in 1960. Jucker was promoted prior to the 1960-1961 season and led the team to national championships in 1961 and 1962, with the team's bid for a historic third straight title coming up short when they lost in the championship game to Loyola in 1963.[20]

But Koufax had no regrets. After all, he fulfilled Harry Gallatin's prophecy. Harry just had to look in a different place.

NOTES

1   Sandy Koufax with Ed Linn, *Koufax* (New York: The Viking Press, 1966), 19.

2   Koufax, 22.

3   Koufax, 23.

4   Koufax, 23.

5   Koufax, 23.

6   Richard Sandomir, "Koufax's Roundball Once Trumped His Fastball," *New York Times*, August 14, 2012 (online).

https://www.proquest.com/usnews/docview/2215731904/C66102B78EFE4C08PQ/1?accountid=69. Accessed February 27, 2023.

7   Koufax, 23-24.

8   Steven L. Pease, *The Golden Age of Jewish Achievement* (Sonoma, California: Deucalion, 2009), 81; Talk Today, USA Today Book Club: 'Sandy Koufax: A Lefty's Legacy,' https://archive.ph/MXmv5.

9   Koufax, 27.

10 Koufax, 27.

11 Jerry Mitchell, *Sandy Koufax* (New York: Grosset & Dunlap, 1971), 24.

12 Jane Leavy, *Sandy Koufax: A Lefty's Legacy* (HarperCollins Publishers, 2002), 40.

13 Leavy, 40; Koufax, 28.

14 Koufax, 30; Koufax identified McGuire as being from the University of South Carolina, a post he did not, in fact, assume until 1964, after almost a decade at North Carolina and then a brief foray into the NBA; Typically, while Koufax himself never made the claim, part of the myth of Koufax the basketball player was that he was heavily recruited, fielding offers from a wealth of big-time programs. See Mitchell, 24.

15 Koufax, 30.

16 Leavy, 48; Among the many myths about Koufax and his basketball career was that he was recruited by Jucker at Cincinnati. Indeed, while his record at UC needed no burnishing, the *New York Times* obituary on the coach asserted that he had "recruited a left-handed pitcher from Lafayette High School in Brooklyn and signed him to a basketball scholarship." Frank Litsky, "Ed Jucker, 85, Who Coached Cincinnati to Basketball Titles," *New York Times*, February 6, 2002: B8.

17 Leavy, 48.

18 "Pair Of Guards Star for Bearkitten Five," *Cincinnati Enquirer*, March 16, 1954; Koufax, 31; Leavy, 48.

19 "Pair Of Guards Star for Bearkitten Five."

20 "History of Cincinnati Basketball," gobearcats.com; https://gobearcats.com/sports/2017/6/15/history-of-cincinnati-basketball.aspx.

A Star Pitcher and His Manager

BY BYRON PETRAROJA

Sandy Koufax and Walt Alston will forever be linked in the minds of baseball fans, especially those who consider themselves to be close observers of the national pastime. One was a ferocious competitor who drove himself beyond reasonable thresholds of endurance and pain. The other, nicknamed "the quiet man," was a fiery competitor in his own right, bubbling beneath the surface. Many questions have risen pertaining to the nature of their relationship; the task here is to shed light on this topic and perhaps to stimulate further inquiry.

While Koufax was attending Lafayette High School in Brooklyn, baseball scouts began to show guarded interest in him as he distinguished himself with the Parkviews, a team in the Coney Island League. Joe Labate, a scout from the Philadelphia Phillies, offered Koufax a contract for $1,500 to play in a college league in northern New York state. Koufax made it clear that he wanted a bonus large enough to allow him to pay for college if he found that he wasn't talented enough to make it as a big-leaguer. At this point, he began to realize that a future in baseball might be a possibility.

By the time Koufax graduated from Lafayette High, he had developed into a skilled basketball player through many hours of practice, league games, and pickup games in both the school gymnasium and the Jewish Community House.[1] His parents had clearly communicated to Koufax and his older stepsister that they were expected to go to college; Koufax agreed. Although he hadn't been able to gather any feelers as far as scholarships were concerned, with the aid of letters of recommendation from both his high school and JCH coaches, he was invited to the University of Cincinnati, where he could work out with the basketball team. This workout, which amounted to a tryout, earned Koufax a scholarship offer.

As fate would have it, the basketball coach at the University of Cincinnati also happened to be the varsity baseball coach, and Koufax found himself as a Bearcats pitcher. He experienced enough success to attract scouts. The New York Giants offered him a tryout at the Polo Grounds, which apparently did not produce rave reviews and he never heard from them again.

The New York Yankees made him an offer that didn't include a bonus and was for a Class-D club. The Pittsburgh Pirates stepped forward but never made a concrete offer. The Brooklyn Dodgers and Milwaukee Braves were also expressing interest, which made for a frenetic schedule of traveling and tryouts.

The Dodgers appeared to express the most interest. Of note, Al Campanis, Brooklyn's director of scouting, had a friendly rivalry with Branch Rickey, the executive vice president and general manager of the Pirates, and the former general manager of the Dodgers. Campanis thought that the Pirates were still very much in the running for the teenage pitcher. Koufax worked out with the Dodgers at Ebbets Field in the early fall of 1954 with Walt Alston, the Dodgers manager, also watching.

Walt Alston paid his dues during his climb to the major leagues. From 1940 through 1953, he worked his way up the minor-league managerial ladder. After observing the divergent paths Koufax and Alston took to the major leagues, it may not be too much of a stretch to think that Alston might want Koufax to prove himself before placing his trust in him as reliable member of his pitching staff. With Koufax having the "bonus baby" designation, the Dodgers were required to keep him on the major-league roster for two seasons, which essentially placed him ahead of several more experienced pitchers who were doing their time in the minors, just as Alston had done. Dick Young of the *New York Daily News*, in a column written June 14, 1956, referred to an overall lack of confidence Alston had in Koufax early in his career, writing, "A pitching pinch has to develop before Walt uses the kid. Then, it seems, Sandy must pitch a shutout or the bullpen is working full force and the kid will be yanked at the first long foul ball."[2]

Based on comments he made in his autobiography as he thought back on his early years with the Dodgers, it appears that Koufax may have been frustrated by having been used sparingly. "I could be wrong. It could be argued, I know, that I was brought along slowly, nurtured carefully, and worked into the rotation when I was ready to put what I had learned to use.

Dodgers manager Walter Alston celebrates with his Hall of Fame left-hander. SABR: The Rucker Archive.

The only thing is that you can never convince me of it."[3] At other times however, he seemed to appreciate the predicament of his manager: "I needed experience, I needed work. Walt needed to win." He went on to describe an incident in which he clearly lost his focus and failed to cover first base while pitching on the next to last day of the 1955 season. He was resigned to not getting a chance to pitch in the World Series that year. He conceded, "Any pitcher who doesn't have the basic reflexes to break for first base on a ground ball hit toward the right side of the diamond can hardly be looked upon as a World Series pitcher."[4]

After his first three seasons, Koufax's record stood at 9 wins and 10 losses; hardly one that inspired his manager to view him as a pitcher he could depend on when games were up for grabs. In 1958, the Dodgers' first season in Los Angeles, he went 11-11 with a 4.48 ERA, and 8-6 in 1959, when the Dodgers won the World Series in a season that provided many opportunities for a young pitcher to prove his worth. Koufax's co-author wrote that Alston remained confident Koufax could indeed develop into a reliable pitcher: "Alston however, refused to quit on Koufax. The skipper's attitude toward his young lefty had changed since '56, and despite Koufax's control problems, Alston gave him three straight starts in mid-June [of 1959]."[5]

Koufax rose to his manager's challenge. On June 22, 1959, he struck out 16 Philadelphia Phillies, pitching a complete game and leading his team to a 6-2 victory. Koufax was given the start in a key August 31 game against the San Francisco Giants. He responded in magnificent fashion, fanning 18 and breaking Dizzy Dean's National League record of 17 strikeouts and tying Bob Feller's major-league record of 18 by striking out the side in the ninth inning. He started Game Five of the World Series, a potential Series clincher for the Dodgers. Although he couldn't seal the deal, he held Chicago's "Go-Go" White Sox to just one run over seven innings.

When Koufax finished the 1960 season with an 8-13 record, his frustration had reached the level that he was strongly considering quitting baseball to focus on other pursuits. In another book he related an incident in which he threw some of his equipment into the trash and told Dodgers clubhouse manager Nobe Kawano not to bother storing any of his possessions when the season had concluded. "It wasn't that I had any regrets over the choice I had made. It was just that, having given myself six years, a full apprenticeship, I was convinced that the time had come to admit to myself that I wasn't going to make it."[6]

Koufax may have been more frustrated with himself and his own lack of progress than with Alston. He had been given multiple opportunities to learn the craft of pitching: "It wasn't that I hadn't gotten my chance to pitch in 1960, either, I had been given more chance than ever."[7] He was questioning his ability to master the all-important ability to control where his pitches were headed. Koufax was fully aware of this issue, having seen many pitchers who seemed very hittable but could make hitters look silly by exhibiting impeccable control.

Koufax ultimately decided to give baseball one last try as he entered the 1961 season with the attitude that if he was going to make it, he needed to fully commit himself to baseball. It didn't hurt that he came into camp in the best shape of his life, having lost some unneeded weight which he attributed to having his tonsils out and not being able to eat or drink comfortably for two weeks. At least two other factors turned the tide in Koufax's favor that year: He paid particularly close attention to the information the team statistician, Allan Roth, gave him about the importance of getting ahead of the hitter. And he heeded the advice of his roommate, catcher Norm Sherry, who encouraged him before a B-squad spring-training game to be a pitcher instead of a thrower. "You haven't a thing to lose because none of the brass is going to be there," Sherry told him. "If you get behind the hitters, don't try to throw hard, because when you force your fast ball you're always high with it."[8] Even though he had heard this type of advice many times before, Koufax finally absorbed it. Something clicked in that game and success followed. The 1961 season saw Koufax sprint out to a 10-3 record by the halfway point of the season and earn a spot on the National League All-Star team. By the end of the season he had won a career-high 18 games against 13 defeats and had broken the National League strikeout record, fanning 269 batters.

Koufax experienced his first significant injury during the 1962 season. He was cruising along with a 14-5 record in late July when he was forced to leave the rotation with a serious circulation issue in his left index finger. He came back in late September as his team was battling the San Francisco Giants for the pennant. However, he was largely ineffective in his return and the Giants edged out the Dodgers by taking a three-game tiebreaker series two games to one. Alston's patience with Koufax had paid off, however, as Koufax had developed into a dominant pitcher, one of the stalwarts of the Dodgers staff.

Some might say that Alston's trust and respect for his star pitcher had increased to a fault while Koufax developed into the player he had shown the potential to become. There are numerous examples of Alston leaving Koufax in a game when the situation seemed to dictate taking him out, as well as times in which he pitched him on short rest even though the health of his precious left arm was in question. For example, Alston gave Koufax the start on May 30, 1962; it was the Dodgers' first return to New York since their move to Los Angeles. In the ninth inning, with the Dodgers holding a 13-6 lead over the New York Mets, Koufax had given up four hits in the inning and Alston let him stay in the game.

In late May of 1964, Alston brought in Koufax to pitch in relief on two days' rest when just a month earlier he was out of the lineup with an ailing elbow. For Game Seven of the 1965 World Series against the Minnesota Twins, Alston was faced with the choice of pitching Koufax on two days' rest or starting his other ace, Don Drysdale, who had an additional day of rest. He went with Koufax. Sandy was laboring in the fifth inning after giving up a solid double and a walk and appeared to have only his fastball at his disposal. Alston left him in the game even though Drysdale was warmed up. Koufax rewarded his manager's trust by retiring the Twins and pitching a Series-winning shutout.

Despite the general belief by many observers that Alston had at times misused Koufax, it doesn't appear that Koufax felt that way. Referring to his desire to pitch during the 1962 season with an injured index finger, he seemed to appreciate these opportunities. "I had spent too much of my life *not* pitching to think about missing any turns," his autobiography said.[9]

There were indications that the relationship between pitcher and manager may not have always been smooth. Michael Leahy in his book *The Last Innocents* related an incident in which Maury Wills overheard a confrontation between Koufax and Alston concerning a change in the pitching rotation, Wills described the situation: "[Koufax] was raising hell. There was a lot of shouting between the two of them. Alston basically said, 'Goddammit, I'm the manager.' And Sandy yelled, 'I'm the starting pitcher.'"[10] The confrontation ended at that point as the room fell silent with Koufax emerging from the office.

Another incident involved a brief conversation between Dick Tracewski, a Dodgers infielder, and Koufax in which Tracewski commented on how Alston had relayed his decision to use Koufax over Drysdale to start Game Seven of the 1965 Series. Alston had apparently told the players that he would "start the left hander" and Tracewski felt that Alston's choice to not use Koufax's name was significant. "That rubbed Sandy the wrong way," said Tracewski. Leahy wrote that Tracewski "believed that Koufax regarded Alston's announcement as yet another slight in a relationship that wasn't going to be warm and fuzzy ever."[11]

Koufax gained his manager's trust over time and Alston appeared to develop faith in Koufax. Alston and Koufax may not have had the closest of relationships. There were times when Koufax was frustrated with not being given enough opportunities to pitch early in his career and from time to time disagreed with Alston's decisions. Perhaps, though, the ways in which they related to each other were more a product of their personalities. Some of these traits may have been ones they shared. Alston enjoyed some of the simpler pleasures of life; in his autobiography, *A Year at a Time,* he expounded on the value he placed on being back home in Darrtown, Ohio. "Back behind the barn there were woods of thirty or forty acres. … I loved to ride those woods, and Dad often went with me. The owners didn't object and I've spent many an hour enjoying the quiet and solitude there."[12]

Author Gruver cited former Dodgers general manager Buzzie Bavasi, who spoke of how Koufax's interests were different than those of the typical ballplayer and, respecting Koufax's privacy, said, "I think few ball players had the same interests as Sandy. I don't think too many players had an interest in music, in lectures, or doing some work around the house. Sandy was a loner in that respect. And you never wanted to pry with Sandy, so I never got too close with him."[13]

Gruver used the adjective "phlegmatic" to describe Alston when the Dodgers hired him as their manager in 1954; in addition, he received the nickname "The Quiet Man" somewhere along the way. Alston, however, wrote, "[E]veryone who knows me well realizes that I'm slow to anger but, once I boil – watch out, It's pretty hard to calm me down."[14]

Koufax had his moments as well; Gruver described one of Koufax's challenges as being one of overall self-control, "Even in his great years, he grimaced in disgust following an ill-timed hit or a walk. At times, he kicked the sheet metal on the bottom of the dugout water cooler in anger over a poor pitch."[15] Some of Koufax's teammates, Wills for example, talked about how serious and nontalkative he became when it was time to prepare for a game even during spring training. "Other guys would be looking to have a little fun sometimes. … Not Sandy. All business." Jeff Torborg talked about wanting to communicate with Koufax to make a good impression as his catcher; however, the exchanges between them were typically short and to the point.[16] Between Alston's stoic, calm persona with the potential to erupt and Koufax's desire for privacy, his serious approach to the game, and also with that potential to unleash his fury at times, one can see how a close relationship between the two might never have had a chance to develop.

There were times, though, when Koufax and his teammates were involved in rather comedic situations with their manager. One such incident occurred when Sandy and fellow pitcher Larry Sherry wanted to celebrate a little after each had pitched extremely well during spring training in 1961. They went out and when they returned, they had broken curfew and were loud enough to alert their manager to their transgression. Both Koufax and Sherry slipped into their rooms just before Alston came charging down the hall. When he arrived at Sherry's room, he found it locked and began hammering on it with his fists. In doing so, he managed to break his diamond-studded World Series ring. Both players were fined $100, and the rest of their teammates found the whole thing hilarious.[17]

There are some indications that Walt Alston wasn't one to play favorites and for the most part had the same expectations for all the players he managed. "I've always believed that baseball is still a game," his book said. "You ought to enjoy, get some fun out of playing, yet give it everything you have. As long as I could get that out of a player I was pretty easy to get along with."[18] If you didn't meet those expectations, however, you would potentially be introduced to Alston's wrath. Leahy described an incident in which Lou Johnson, a Dodgers outfielder, was late for batting practice before the seventh game of the 1965 World Series and how angry that made Alston. "Johnson had never seen Alston so upset," Leahy wrote. "That the two men got past the moment had less to do with anything Johnson said than it did with Alston's utter lack of choices."[19] The Dodgers had a dearth of power that season, and Alston needed Johnson's bat in the lineup.

Alston talked about the challenge he faced with being close with his players. He referred to one of his former players and coaches, Tommy Lasorda, who felt that Alston was becoming less close to his players. Alston explained the reason as being basic geography, "no doubt part of that comes from being older and more experienced as a manager. And the mere fact that in Los Angeles we're spread out over half of Southern California rather than living within a few blocks of Dodger Stadium makes it hard to be close." However, he described how his Montreal Royals ballclub from years earlier was "a tight little clique," in part because most players did not speak French and tended to socialize with one another.[20] It seems that Alston genuinely enjoyed down time with family members, other members of his staff, and players, as he talked fondly of playing cards with them during road trips: "During the years when Don Drysdale, Jim Gilliam and Wes Parker were playing for us we played a lot of bridge on the road. But in recent years we just haven't had four bridge nuts on the club."[21]

Both pitcher and manager shared a high level of competitiveness that fueled their drive to succeed. Over the course of their careers, each had a strong impact on the overall success the other experienced. After all, both Koufax and Alston were inducted into the Baseball Hall of Fame – Alston in 1983 and Koufax in 1972. Perhaps this comment by Alston encapsulates how he truly felt about his star pitcher:

"You'd need a book or two to recite all of Sandy's accomplishments. His greatest was himself. He worked tirelessly to achieve success. Once he did he was no different from the Sandy who came to Ebbets Field in 1955 [sic] to try out. He was team-oriented, took coaching well and worked hard."[22]

NOTES

1   The Jewish Community House is on Bay Parkway in the Bensonhurst section of Brooklyn. It was founded in 1927 and as of 2024 still existed. It has always served as a place for the Jewish community and their neighbors to gather and support each other during times of need. (JCHB.org).

2   Edward Gruver, *Koufax* (Latham, New York: Oxford, Taylor Trade, 2000), 119.

3   Sandy Koufax with Ed Linn, *Koufax* (New York: Viking Press, 1966), 114.

4   Koufax with Linn, 105.

5   Gruver, 121.

6   Koufax with Linn, 143.

7   Koufax with Linn, 143.

8   Koufax with Linn, 154.

9   Koufax with Linn, 165.

10 Michael Leahy, *The Last Innocents* (New York: HarperCollins, 2016), 226.

11 Leahy, 320.

12 Walter Alston, *A Year at a Time* (Waco, Texas: World Books, 1976), 76.

13 Gruver, 172.

14 Gruver, 173.

15 Gruver, 4.

16 Leahy, 197.

17 Koufax, 155.

18 Alston, 87.

19 Leahy, 322.

20 Alston, 88.

21 Alston, 100.

22 Alston, 164.

Sandy Koufax and His Home Ballparks

BY PAUL SINCLAIR

Sandy Koufax's baseball career is a tale of two cities, Brooklyn and Los Angeles. It is a tale about a career that contained two disparate time periods, the worst of times and the best of times. For the first seven seasons he was a marginal player and, quite frankly, unremarkable. For the final five seasons he was phenomenal.

How did Koufax have such two distinctly different periods within his career? One possible answer points to the home ballparks where he plied his trade. It is not happenstance that each period of his career aligns with different home ballparks. He pitched at Brooklyn's Ebbets Field and Los Angeles' Coliseum from 1955 to 1961, his unremarkable years. At Los Angeles' Dodger Stadium, his home ballpark from 1962 to 1966, Koufax built the legend that made him a Hall of Famer.

The story of Sandy Koufax and his home ballparks begins in December 1954 when Koufax signed his first professional baseball contract with the Brooklyn Dodgers for an annual salary of $6,000 and a $14,000 bonus. According to the rules in effect in 1954, the bonus guaranteed Koufax, soon to be 19 years old, a spot on the Dodgers roster until the end of 1956, two full seasons. There would be no skill development in minor-league home ballparks during his career.

Ebbets Field, in his hometown of Brooklyn, would be his home ballpark. Located in an area known as Pigtown in the Flatbush district of Brooklyn, Ebbets Field covered a full city block and was a prominent edifice in the community. The ballpark's exterior featured grand arches and windows. Fans made their way to their seats through an Italian marble rotunda. With minimal foul territory, the double-tiered grandstand was close to the playing field, making for an intimate fan experience. In fact, portions of the grandstand and press box hung over the field.

An irregularly configured ballpark, Ebbets Field was considered a hitter's haven. From home plate to the foul poles, the right-field fence was 297 feet, while the left-field fence measured 348 feet. The fences in right-center field and left-center field were roughly equivalent at 352 feet. Dead center field was a deep 393 feet.

Koufax's rookie season was the 43rd season of baseball at Ebbets Field. Originally built in 1913 and renovated several times over the years, Ebbets Field had by 1955 a seating capacity of 31,902, small relative to other National League parks.

With Ebbets Field nearing the end of its useful life and needing a larger ballpark, Dodgers owner Walter O'Malley was negotiating with local government for the development of a new baseball stadium in Brooklyn. Covering a full city block meant the Ebbets site could not accommodate an expanded stadium.

Koufax attended Lafayette High School in a section of Brooklyn just five minutes southwest of Ebbets Field. His first memories of the ballpark were from high-school trips to see the Dodgers play. Annually, the students would go to a game starting at 11 A.M. Those school trips forged fond memories of Dodgers great Jackie Robinson and of other players like Gil Hodges, Duke Snider, Pee Wee Reese, and Don Newcombe who would later become his teammates.

It was in September 1954 that Koufax pitched on the Ebbets Field mound for the first time. Present for this tryout were scouting director Al Campanis, manager Walter Alston, scout Fresco Thompson, and broadcaster Vin Scully. Koufax threw to catcher Rube Walker. His fastball and curve were both rated A+ in Campanis's scouting report.[1]

Koufax was considered a natural for Ebbets Field. A southpaw with highly rated pitching skills and a local Jewish talent, he merited a roster spot and the bonus money. He was added to the Dodgers roster in December 1954. Scout Thompson envisioned the 19-year-old Koufax's development and early career use and decided, "We feel he'll be ready in about four years."[2] It was hoped that Koufax, the lone Jewish player on the Dodgers' major-league roster, would become a star and boost attendance at his home ballpark.

As Koufax's professional career commenced, he saw pitching as an art form to be learned, honed, and perfected. To him, control was the essence of pitching.[3] Control meant throwing strikes. Losing was precipitated by too many walks. Typical baseball pitching statistics show his progress in learning the pitching art form. Three specific pitching statistics measure his progress in the mastery of control: walks and hits per innings pitched (WHIP), strikeouts per nine innings (K/9), and strikeout/walk ratio (K/BB).

Koufax was on the Dodgers roster for the 1955 season, but his debut at Ebbets Field was delayed. Late in spring training, an ankle injury forced him onto the disabled list. Activated on June 8, Koufax made his first Ebbets Field game appearance on June 29. In the ninth inning of a 6-1 loss to the New York Giants, he faced six batters, surrendered two hits, walked one, and did not give up a run.

Entering games late when the Dodgers were trailing was manager Walter Alston's plan for using and developing Koufax. It was 24 days before he next appeared in a home game. He was roughed up for two earned runs in the last two innings of an 11-6 loss to the Milwaukee Braves. The next day Koufax was back on the Ebbets Field mound in the second game of a doubleheader against the Braves. He pitched a perfect ninth inning in a 9-2 loss.

Thirty-two days passed before Koufax next appeared in a home game. He pitched well, pleasing the hometown fans with a perfect ninth inning against Cincinnati. Koufax had two strikeouts, his first at Ebbets Field.

In late August Brooklyn was cruising to the National League pennant with a significant lead over the second-place Milwaukee Braves. But the Dodgers had lost three straight to the fifth-place Reds and with starters Carl Erskine, Billy Loes, and Don Newcombe ailing, manager Alston gave Koufax his first Ebbets Field start on August 27.

It was an amazing debut for Koufax as a starter in his home ballpark. He got his first win, a 7-0 shutout. Surrendering hits only in the first and ninth innings, Koufax had 14 strikeouts, a National League single-game high for the 1955 season. The only negative in this stellar outing for Koufax was his lack of control; he walked five batters.

Koufax pitched twice more during a late August and early September homestand. A disastrous sixth inning against Milwaukee (five hits and four earned runs) on the last day of August did not dissuade Alston from naming him as the starter against Pittsburgh on the Saturday of the Labor Day weekend. That second start at Ebbets Field was another remarkable outing. Koufax picked up his second win of the season, another shutout, with six strikeouts, five hits, and two walks, as the Dodgers defeated the Pirates 4-0.

Highlighted by two shutouts, Koufax's inaugural season at Ebbets Field was impressive. In the seven games he pitched in his hometown ballpark, he shut out opponents for 22 of his 24 innings pitched. Limiting opponents to nine hits (seven singles and two doubles), Koufax had two wins and attractive ERA of 2.25 at Ebbets Field, and contributed to Brooklyn's capture of the National League pennant for the eighth time. Brooklyn defeated the New York Yankees in seven games to win the World Series, though Koufax did not see any action. In the dugout, he had the best seat in Ebbets Field as he watched the Dodgers win their only championship in Brooklyn.

Sandy Koufax posted a career 57-15 won-loss record at Dodger Stadium and a 1.37 ERA. SABR: The Rucker Archive.

Pleased with Koufax's strong rookie performance in 1955, Dodgers leadership hoped that he would be immune from the sophomore jinx, the belief that a player performing well in his first season rarely does well in his second season.

During the 1956 season, Koufax was again infrequently used in home games. His first four appearances (one in April and three in May) were in a relief role. Thereafter, Koufax was limited to four home appearances, all as a starter. He did not play at Ebbets Field after August 5. For the second consecutive season, Koufax did not appear in the World Series, which the Dodgers lost in seven games to their crosstown rival Yankees.

Looking back at season's end, Koufax did experience the feared sophomore slump. He pitched only 18 innings at Ebbets Field and was ineffective. Opponents batted .354 against him. His record of no wins, two losses, an ERA of 7.50, WHIP of 2.167, K/9 of 4.0, and K/W of 0.73 statistically evidence his dismal second season at his home ballpark.

Koufax's away-game statistics starkly contrasted with his Ebbets Field performance (opponents batting average .250, ERA 3.76, WHIP of 1.38, K/9 of 4.9, and a K/W of 1.22). Overall, he was good enough to remain on the Dodgers roster. However, starting in May 1957 there were no restrictions on the Dodgers' ability to assign him to the minor leagues.

As Koufax and the Dodgers finished spring training in 1957 in Vero Beach, the outlook for a new ballpark in Brooklyn was bleak. Surrounded by uncertainty about their future in Brooklyn, the Dodgers fell out of contention early in the season. For his third season, the Dodgers failing to contend for the pennant meant Koufax had increased opportunity and more appearances.

Overall, Koufax's 1957 season at Ebbets Field was much better than the downbeat 1956 season but was again unremarkable. Appearing in 17 games, seven as a starter and 10 in relief, Koufax had a 3-1 record and an ERA of 3.70. His superior season was attributed to improved control. In 56 innings, he had 67 strikeouts and walked only 23. Improvement to his WHIP (1.250), K/9 (10.8), and K/BB (2.91) offer evidence of his improved command. The game on September 20, 1957, against the Philadelphia Phillies turned out to be Koufax's last appearance on the Ebbets Field mound. Entering with two outs in the top of the ninth inning, Koufax retired the only batter he faced.

In October 1957 it was officially announced that the Dodgers were moving to Los Angeles. After three years of infrequent use and long periods of inactivity, Koufax bade farewell to Ebbets Field. He would now have a new home ballpark, 3,000 miles from his hometown.

To lure the franchise to Los Angeles, the Dodgers were deeded 300 acres of land to build a modern stadium in the Chavez Ravine section of Los Angeles. The plan was to develop the site with a baseball-only super-stadium to be known as Dodger Stadium.

However, the completion of Dodger Stadium was still four baseball seasons away. In the interim, the Dodgers needed a temporary home ballpark. After considering the Rose Bowl in suburban Pasadena and the Los Angeles-based, minor-league Wrigley Field, the club selected the Los Angeles Memorial Coliseum.

The Coliseum, a bowl-shaped stadium with a seating capacity of over 90,000 for baseball, was used as a multisport facility, predominantly for college and NFL football. Fitting an appropriate ballpark into a stadium of the Coliseum's shape and size was challenging. Far from ideal for baseball, the ballpark had to be situated in the west end of the stadium to keep the sun from blinding fielders' eyes. In the end, the large seating capacity and its revenue potential outweighed the concerns that the Coliseum was ill-suited for baseball.

Expectedly, the configuration of the Dodgers home field within the Coliseum was highly irregular. Down the left-field line, the six-foot-high chain-link outfield fence was only 251 feet from home plate. Angling sharply toward center field, the fence was only 320 feet in left-center field and a cavernous 420 feet in dead center field. The fence angled back to the first-base foul pole, 380 feet in right-center field and only 300 feet down the first-base line. To allay concerns about the potential for an inordinate number of home runs to right field, a 42-foot-high screen was installed. The screen extended from the left-field foul pole to dead center field. For the first 140 feet, the screen was 42 feet high. Over the next 30 feet it cantilevered down to a height of 8 feet and then to 6 feet in center field.

Foul territory was negligible down the first-base line and massive down the third-base line. The fan experience lacked the intimacy of Ebbets Field. The Coliseum's bowl seating meant poor sight lines. At its worst, seats were almost another ballpark away, 710 feet from home plate.

The Coliseum was clearly not a pitcher-friendly park – particularly for left-handers like Koufax with such a favorable configuration for right-handed pull hitters.

During his first year pitching in the Coliseum, Koufax appeared in 17 home games, 12 as a starter and five as a reliever. His inaugural appearance was pitching the ninth inning of a 15-2 blowout loss to the Cubs. In his one inning, he allowed a hit and no runs for a successful debut. Thereafter, the 1958 season at the Coliseum did not go well for Koufax. He won just two games and lost another six. An inability to consistently throw strikes resulted in 49 walks in 62⅔ innings and contributed

to an ERA of 5.60. He gave up 12 home runs. As a starter, he struggled, completing five innings or less in eight of his 12 starts. Relative to the previous season at Ebbets Field, Koufax's control had declined (WHIP 1.66; K/9 7.6; K/BB 1.08).

The 1958 season did end with a positive outing, although Koufax still ended up on the losing end. In the second game of a doubleheader, he pitched a complete game, with the Cubs winning 2-1. Allowing five hits and one earned run, he had nine strikeouts, but lacked control, walking a season-high seven batters.

The conclusion of the 1958 season meant that Koufax had completed the four-year development horizon originally projected for him. Playing in the strangely configured Coliseum was, as expected, challenging for pitchers, especially left-handers like him. Adapting to his interim home ballpark and harnessing his control were mandatory prerequisites for a successful 1959 season.

The Dodgers used Koufax in home games during the 1959 season in a similar manner to the previous four years. He appeared in 15 games, 10 as a starter and five as a reliever. His control nicely improved as walks per nine innings decreased to 4.4 from 7. His K/9 increased significantly to 11.1 from 7.6. He was also better at keeping the ball in the ballpark, reducing home runs per nine innings to 1.5 from 1.7.

Noteworthy was Koufax's start on August 31, 1959. Pitching before a Coliseum crowd of 82,794 (60,194 paid), he displayed his full potential. He went the distance in a 5-2 win against the San Francisco Giants and tied the modern National League single-game strikeout record by whiffing 18 Giants.[4] Of the final 17 outs, 15 were by strikeout, including a near-immaculate inning in the ninth as Koufax struck out the Giants on just 10 pitches.

The Dodgers ended the 1959 154-game schedule tied with the Milwaukee Braves. Sweeping a best-of-three-game tiebreaker series, the Dodgers won the pennant and would face the Chicago White Sox in the World Series. The pennant-clinching game was a dramatic 6-5 12-inning win for the Dodgers. Koufax faced five batters in the ninth inning and did not give up any hits or runs despite walking three batters.

In Game Five of the Dodgers-White Sox World Series at the Coliseum, Koufax made his first postseason start. He pitched well, going seven innings and giving up five hits and one run, while striking out six and walking one. Despite nine hits, including a triple by Gil Hodges, the Dodgers were shut out 1-0 by White Sox starter Bob Shaw and a strong Chicago bullpen. The Dodgers beat the White Sox in six games for their second World Series championship in the first five years of Koufax's career.

The Dodgers were looking for consistency from Koufax in the 1960 season as they sought to win back-to-back World Series. Koufax had shown signs that he was adapting to the Coliseum. However, his 1960 performance was eerily like 1958, his first season in the Coliseum. A home record of 1-7 and an ERA of 5.27 was very disappointing for him and the Dodgers. Control problems returned as Koufax walked 49 in 70 innings (6.3 per nine innings). His WHIP increased to 1.60, K/9 declined to 9.1, and K/BB decreased to 1.45. Despite this, he set a career high for home appearances with 19. He started 11 times and relieved in eight games. Success was elusive as a starter. In seven of his 11 starts in the Coliseum, he lasted fewer than 5⅔ innings.

The 1961 season was the last of four seasons that the Dodgers played in the Coliseum. Entering his seventh season in the major leagues, having just celebrated his 25th birthday, Koufax was used more frequently, predominantly as a starter. Starting in 18 of his 21 appearances, Koufax pitched a personal-high 132⅓ innings at home. He had a 9-8 record for a Dodgers team that was 89-65. Improving his control (WHIP 1.29; K/9 9.9; K/BB 2.84) and keeping the ball in the park were keys to a better final season in the less than ideally configured Coliseum.

Koufax's last appearance at the Coliseum was on September 20, 1961. It was also the last game the Dodgers played in this temporary home. They won 3-2 over the Chicago Cubs. Koufax pitched an amazing 13-inning complete game, striking out 15 batters while walking only three and allowing seven hits.

Signs of Koufax's potential were displayed best when he was not pitching at the Coliseum. For example, on the road in National League ballparks in 1961, he appeared in the same number of away games as home games but had a 9-5 record and an ERA of 2.77, better by 1.5 runs. Koufax's ascension to star status began in 1961 as he was named to the All-Star team and led the National League in strikeouts.

The Coliseum, as Koufax's home ballpark, was a nemesis to his development as a major-league pitcher. Over his four seasons there, he compiled a record of 17 wins and 23 losses and an ERA of 4.33. Control continued to be a struggle. Even an increase in appearances at the Coliseum did not result in improved control (WHIP 1.41; K/9 9.6; K/BB 1.95). But he did have some great games. The Dodgers were patient with his development as Koufax was now three years past the original four-year development plan. Continuing to be on the Dodgers roster reflected the potential he displayed over the past two seasons as a visitor in National League ballparks.

1960 and 1961	W	L	PCT	ERA	G	GS	IP	H	ER	WHIP	K/9	K/BB
Coliseum	10	15	.400	4.58	40	29	202.1	182	103	1.394	9.61	2.16
Away Games	16	11	.593	2.88	39	32	228.1	163	73	1.134	9.85	2.60

For the 1962 season, finally the Dodgers would fully settle into their brand-new home; Dodger Stadium, opened for a new era of Dodger baseball.

Nestled in the hillside of Chavez Ravine, the setting of Dodger Stadium is beautiful. To the south, it overlooks downtown Los Angeles. To the north, the San Gabriel mountains and palm trees provide a picturesque background.

Built over three years at a cost of $23 million, Dodger Stadium's five seating levels provided for a capacity of 56,000. The first four levels extended from the right-field foul pole to the left-field foul pole. The uppermost level reached from the first-base side to the third-base side.

Quite unlike the Coliseum, the configuration of this ballpark was symmetrical. The right-field and the left-field lines were 330 feet from home plate, right-center and left-center were 375 feet, and dead center measured 395 feet. Consistent with other ballparks of that era, the playing surface was grass.

Dodger Stadium was considered a pitcher's ballpark, significantly different from Ebbets Field and, of course, the Coliseum. The environment in Chavez Ravine was pitcher-friendly, as the heavy evening air restricted fly balls that would have been home runs in the earlier home ballparks. Dodger Stadium's more expansive outfield and regular-sized foul territory were positive features for pitchers.

In his first game at Dodger Stadium, the second game played there, Koufax commenced what became his remarkable career turnaround. He defeated the Reds with a complete-game 6-2 victory. The Reds managed only four hits (two singles and two doubles). Koufax had seven strikeouts and three walks.

On June 30 he made his 11th start at Dodger Stadium, against the New York Mets. Striking out 13 but walking five, Koufax managed through control issues to pitch the first no-hitter of his career. But after the no-hitter, he would make only two more starts at Dodger Stadium that season.

In mid-July, Koufax experienced physical ailments. A circulatory problem in his index finger and shoulder pain sidelined him for much of the second half of the season. He made one final start at home on September 27. In a no-decision outing, he pitched five innings (three hits, two runs) in a Dodgers' loss to Houston.

Koufax was brilliant at Dodger Stadium during the 1962 season. He started in all his 13 appearances and achieved seven complete games. His record of 7-4 included two losses by one run and another loss by two runs. Koufax pitched 102⅔ innings and had an ERA of 1.75. With 118 strikeouts and only 25 walks, his turnaround vis-à-vis his final season at the Coliseum was remarkable. Control had been harnessed (WHIP 0.91; K/9 10.3; K/BB 4.72).

Though curtailed by injury, Koufax's performance in Dodger Stadium during the 1962 season was a precursor to the dominance that he would have in the National League in the seasons ahead.

The 1963 season was the first in a magnificent four-year run. Recovered from his injury setbacks and enjoying his new home ballpark, Koufax elevated his performance and completely dominated National League opponents in Dodger Stadium.

In front of 49,807 fans on May 11, 1963, Koufax pitched a no-hitter as the Dodgers won 8-0 over the Giants. He struck out four and walked two. It was his second career no-hitter, both at Dodger Stadium.

Koufax's no-hitter made him a headliner at Dodger Stadium for each game he started. Not surprisingly, it was generally acknowledged that an extra 5,000 to 10,000 fans would buy tickets to watch a Koufax start at Dodger Stadium.

In 1963 Koufax showed that he was a clutch pitcher in a tight pennant race. In late August the Dodgers led the Giants and the Cardinals by 5½ and 6½ games respectively. The Cardinals embarked on a hot streak, winning 19 of 20 games. From August 21, Koufax made six starts at home, all Dodgers wins including victories over the Cardinals and Giants. Opponents were limited to nine runs in those six starts totaling 51⅓ innings.

The Dodgers won the pennant in 1963. Koufax started Game Four of the World Series at Dodger Stadium against the Yankees with the Dodgers leading three victories to none. He led the Dodgers to a complete-game win and a World Series sweep. He gave up one run on six hits, no walks, and eight strikeouts.

As a starter in all 17 of his appearances, Koufax pitched 143⅔ innings, a personal high for innings pitched in his home ballpark. He won 11 games and lost one. Ten complete-game appearances including six shutouts were evidence of his dominance on the mound.

A home ERA of 1.38 contributed to his winning a well-earned National League ERA title (1.88). His control continued to improve (WHIP 0.74; K/9 9.0; K/BB 6.26). A Koufax start at Dodger Stadium put fear into National League hitters, who hit a dismal .164 against him.

The 1964 season started with much promise as Koufax pitched the home opener, a 4-0 shutout over St. Louis. His start on August 16 was his last home appearance that year. After his final start, a 3-0 shutout win over St. Louis, he was diagnosed with traumatic arthritis, a chronic ailment that put his career on a limited timeline.

Remarkably, Koufax was even more outstanding at Dodger Stadium during the 1964 season. He finished with a home record of 12-2. Since his no-hitter against the Mets in June 1962, Koufax's home record was an incredible 25 wins and 3 losses.

Appearing in 15 games, all but one as a starter, Koufax took his dominance to an unprecedented level. His home ERA, a minuscule 0.85, meant another National League ERA title (1.74). Facing Koufax, opponents' bats went silent at Dodger Stadium, hitting only .179, and his control remained at elite levels (WHIP 0.783; K/9 8.7; K/BB 6.89).

The 1965 season saw Koufax pick up right where he left off after his injury-shortened 1964 season. At home, he continued to trounce opponents. Used solely as a starter with appearances in a personal high of 20 home games, amazingly Koufax pitched 14 complete games and had a home record of 14-3.

The 1965 National League season ended with a memorable pennant race between the Dodgers and the Giants. Consistent with previous Septembers, Koufax was unbeatable at Dodger Stadium in that pennant race.

The game on September 9 against the Chicago Cubs stands alone in the annals of baseball history. Dodgers outfielder Lou Johnson had the only hit in the game, a 1-0 Dodgers victory. Koufax retired all 27 Cubs in order. This game has been marvelously chronicled in Jane Leavy's book, *Koufax: A Lefty's Legacy*.[5] It was Koufax's first perfect game and third no-hitter at Dodger Stadium.

Following that perfect game were three complete games including two shutouts and a 3-1 victory over Milwaukee. Koufax's

stats for those four September starts are unbelievable – wins 4; losses 0; IP 36; hits 11; runs 1; K 52; BB 8. The Dodgers won 15 of their final 16 games to claim the pennant.

The Dodgers faced the Minnesota Twins in the World Series. With the teams tied at two victories each, Koufax started and won Game Five at Dodger Stadium. His mastery of opponents in late-season and postseason home games continued; he blanked the Twins 7-0. The Dodgers went on to win the World Series in seven games.

Koufax bravely faced the 1966 season through much physical suffering. With chronic injuries afflicting him, a decline in performance would have been expected. His performance did decline relative to his otherworldly seasons of 1963 to 1965 but he remained the most elite pitcher in major-league baseball.

Koufax appeared in 21 home games, a career high. His statistics were awesome and remarkably consistent to those of his previous season. Opponents' batting average increased to only .202. His ERA at Dodger Stadium was 1.52 with three shutouts and six one-run games.

The final month of the 1966 season featured another tight pennant race with the Giants. As in September 1963 and September 1965, Koufax was at his best when it mattered most. This time four Koufax starts at home in September resulted in three Dodgers wins. In 34 innings, he allowed only four runs.

The Dodgers won the pennant for the second consecutive year and were at home for Game Two of the 1966 World Series against the Baltimore Orioles. His final game at Dodger Stadium was not the dominant Koufax that fans had seen in recent pennant races and World Series. Betrayed by weak Dodgers hitting and poor fielding, Koufax exited his home ballpark stage after six innings as he took the loss in a 6-0 defeat. The Dodgers were swept by the Orioles.

Koufax's final home game at Dodger Stadium closed the latter portion of his career.

Statistically, there was a consequential difference between the seven Ebbets Field/Coliseum seasons and the five Dodger Stadium seasons.

	W	L	PCT	ERA	G	GS	IP	H	ER	WHIP	K/9	K/BB
Ebbets Field/ Coliseum	22	26	.458	4.27	104	64	442.2	390	210	1.405	9.43	2.00
Dodger Stadium	57	15	.792	1.37	86	85	715.1	446	109	0.822	9.49	5.31

For decades after Koufax's retirement, analysts and commentators have tried to assign meaning to the marked contrast in Koufax and his home ballparks and the trajectory of his success. One interpretation espouses the idea that Koufax owed a lot of his success to the configuration of and location of Dodger Stadium.[6] The dimensions of the ballpark and climatic conditions were most favorable to him and his skills. In other words, what really happened to Koufax was that he moved from a park that was conspiring to stifle his abilities to a park that was a great fit for him. Following this view, some have concluded that he is the most overrated left-handed starter of all time.[7] This view is argued by giving greater weight to the Ebbets Field/Coliseum mediocre years of his career.

Despite the controversy, most find the Sandy Koufax story inspiring. As a late bloomer, he is held up as an inspiration for the importance of focus, perseverance, patience, and encouragement. Metaphorically, Dodger Stadium in Los Angeles was truly Koufax's promised land – a home ballpark that was the setting for his liberation and emergence as the most dominant pitcher in major-league baseball history.

NOTES

1   Sandy Koufax with Ed Linn, *Koufax* (New York: Viking Press, 1966), 64-65.

2   Dave Anderson, "Jewish Southpaw From Boro a Natural for Ebbets Field," *Brooklyn Daily Eagle*, December 17, 1954: 27.

3   *Koufax*, 100-101.

4   Warren Spahn of the Boston Braves had struck out 18 Chicago Cubs on June 14, 1952.

5   Jane Leavy, *Sandy Koufax: A Lefty's Legacy* (New York: Perennial, 2003).

6   Cody Swartz, "Why Sandy Koufax Owes a LOT of His Success to Dodger Stadium," *Bleacher Report*, July 2, 2009. https://bleacherreport.com/articles/211023-why-sandy-koufax-owes-a-lot-of-his-success-to-dodger-stadium.

7   Jayson Stark, "Left-Handed Starting Pitchers," in *The Stark Truth* (Chicago: Triumph Books, 2007), 15-19.

Short-Term Pitching Brilliance – Comparing Sandy Koufax to Other Short-Term-Peak Pitchers

BY SCOTT MARTIRE

Who can truly be compared to the great Sandy Koufax? This article offers a historical comparison between Koufax and other "short-term-peak" pitchers. Ron Guidry and Johan Santana will be the comparisons, with concluding thoughts on a current pitcher, Jacob deGrom. These pitchers had distinct phases in their careers and mirrored each other in some fashion. Each had a period of learning and rising, high-level performance, and ultimately a decline.

Sandy Koufax's contributions to our game are nothing less than spectacular. While his detailed statistics are reviewed elsewhere, we note that his climb to prestige began in 1961, when he gained All-Star status and placed in National League MVP voting. He had continued success through 1966, earning three Cy Young Awards and helping to win a second World Series championship during those years. He was a two-time World Series MVP and had a career ERA of 2.76. With over 2,396 career strikeouts, the seven-time All-Star and Hall of Famer's accolades are the stuff of legend, especially when one keeps in mind how these honors were earned in just six seasons.

The Ramp Up

When Koufax made his debut in 1955, he walked nearly as many batters as he struck out. His first two games were out of the bullpen until he earned his first start in July of 1955. In 1955 he started five of his 12 games, two of them shutouts. During this time, he pitched sporadically, suffering from lack of control and not getting much opportunity to improve. His middling performances continued throughout the late 1950s and into 1960. Over his first six seasons, his won-lost record was 36-40, with an ERA of 4.10. As 1961 began, so did a new dawn in Koufax's career.

Ron Guidry was another dominating southpaw, who rose to prominence in the 1970s with the Yankees, and who had a career trajectory comparable to Koufax's. Guidry played 14 years to Koufax's 12, and started life out of the bullpen in the same way that Koufax did. In his early years in the minors, he struck out plenty of batters, but he also gave up a lot of walks. Guidry earned his major-league debut in 1975. He spent time during his first two years rotating between the minors and majors, not seeing much action. A key start against Seattle in 1977 in which he pitched 8⅓ shutout innings helped to cement him into the regular rotation. That year he made 25 starts and 6 relief appearances, going 16-7 with a sub-3.00 ERA.

Our third lefty, Johan Santana, is from more recent times, the 1990s and 2000s. This comparison often stirs up the most conversation and opinions. Although he and Koufax came from very different eras, they are often considered as two of the greatest left-handed pitchers in baseball history. Santana enjoyed a great run of about eight years in the 2000s of his 12 total years playing. He showed consistency earlier in his career when compared to Koufax and Guidry. A two-time Cy Young Award winner and four time All-Star, Santana shared a similar rise to stardom. He had fantastic years of peak performance and finally an injury-plagued ending, save for a few late-career gems. His minor-league starts were nothing short of atrocious, as he meandered around rookie ball and low A, with an ERA of 7.36 at one stop and 9.45 at another. Ultimately landing with the Minnesota Twins after

Sandy Koufax made the NL All-Star team from 1961-66. SABR: The Rucker Archive.

a trade, Santana made his major-league debut in 2000. He struggled, to say the least, with an ERA of 6.49 in 86 innings, and an elbow injury in 2001. However, something happened in the 2002 season, a weapon was developed and elevated Santana to stardom. The changeup.

Lights Out!

As the 1961 season got underway, so did Sandy Koufax. That year he racked up 18 wins and led the National League with 269 strikeouts. His magical 1963 season is one for the ages. Riding a sub-2.00 ERA, 306 strikeouts, and his second no-hitter (He threw his first in 1962), he was voted the NL MVP. With a record of 25-5, 11 shutouts, and a sweep in the World Series, in which he was voted the Series MVP, Koufax had arrived. He became best known for an overwhelming fastball and a destructive curveball, and he knew how to change up his mix to keep batters off balance. His curveball was one of the most unhittable pitches in all of baseball. Not free from injury, he developed traumatic arthritis in his left elbow by the end of the 1963 season, which would slowly impact his effectiveness and health. At that time there was no Tommy John surgery or other advanced method to alleviate the injury or pain, so Koufax would submerge his throwing elbow in an ice bath after games. Other remedies included heat treatments with a type of chili powder and an anti-inflammatory pill that is no longer approved for humans. His options were limited, and he lived with excruciating pain. He still pitched some gems, including 15 complete games. He threw seven shutouts in 1964, including another no-hitter.

The pain and success continued side by side into 1965, where Koufax pitched a perfect game late in the season, his fourth no-hitter. That campaign culminated with another World Series win and another World Series MVP. The magic ended in 1966 as the injections became more frequent. Koufax also developed bone spurs in his arm. The Dodgers won another pennant but were swept by the Baltimore Orioles. Koufax retired weeks later at the age of 30.

Guidry enjoyed great peak years as well. His contribution to the game was marked by precision and control. His slider was his bread-and-butter pitch, along with a menacing breaking ball, hitting the corners with remarkable accuracy. In 1977 Guidry pitched a complete game in the AL Championship Series against Kansas City and successfully faced the Dodgers for his first World Series win. Guidry performed well, even earning accolades from his cantankerous manager, Billy Martin. The 1978 season was a fantastic one for Guidry, exemplified by dominating the Angels with an incredible 18 strikeouts during a June 1978 game. The hurler earned team records during that year for lowest ERA for a lefty (1.74), most strikeouts (248), highest win percentage (.893), and most shutouts (9). He won the Cy Young Award, along with another World Series ring, as the Yankees again dispatched the Dodgers. His success continued into 1979, although the Yankees were not back to the big game until 1981.

Santana honed his weapons during the 2002 season in Triple A, posting an ERA of 3.14 in 11 appearances, including 9 starts. As he moved back up to the majors, his stats got better, and his changeup more lethal. By 2003 Santana was in the starting rotation; he had a 2.51 ERA in his last 11 starts and struck out 70 batters in 68 innings. His true rise to prominence came in 2004, when he posted a sub-2.00 ERA with 75 strikeouts over 55 innings in his last seven starts before the All-Star break. With the confidence of his finely tuned changeup, Santana won his first Cy Young Award and led the American League in ERA (2.61), ERA+ (182), WHIP (0.921), and strikeouts per nine innings (10.5). He repeated this stellar performance in 2005 and 2006, leading again in many of those categories. Add to that another exceptional performance as 2007 unfolded, and Santana seemed unstoppable. But the unwanted attention of a potential trade with the Twins out of pennant contention brought drama to the Twin Cities. Santana was the talk of the offseason. By January of 2008 he had a new home with the New York Mets. He managed a good first season with the Mets, picking up a heavy workload. As the 2009 season unfolded, his uncharacteristically low strikeout totals and high number of hits suggested something was wrong. By the end of August, Santana underwent surgery to remove bone chips in his throwing elbow.

Sunset, Impact, and Legacy

Koufax retired after the 1966 season. His retirement was abrupt, although it has been reported that he was considering it for some time.[1] Koufax is regarded as one of the top pitchers in baseball. His accolades were tremendous, earning himself election to the National Baseball Hall of Fame in 1972. He remains a fan favorite to this day.

Guidry was getting older along with the rest of the Yankees as the 1980s rolled on. As his fastball slowed, he shifted his focus to inducing weak contact from hitters. Guidry made his first appearance on the disabled list in 1984 but managed a short resurgence during the 1985 season. He led the AL with a win percentage of .786 and 22 wins, but as time went on so did the reduction in his workload. By 1989 he had retired. He continued to work on and off in baseball until 2015. Guidry's impact was shown in his leadership, consistency, and admirable work ethic, which served as an example to his teammates. He often outthought and outmaneuvered hitters, especially in later years when his velocity fell off. He espoused the mental side of the game and earned five Gold Glove Awards for his fielding excellence.

Santana came back for the 2010 season with high hopes, but it was clear that he was not quite the same. The low strikeouts and lower velocity on his fastball were beginning to show. He struggled through the season until he left a start in September after a five-inning outing, followed by the bad news that he needed season-ending shoulder surgery. The injury lingered and he missed the entire 2011 season as well. The Mets and Santana looked forward to 2012, which he started well, with an ERA of just over 2.00 by the end of April. Then he shocked everyone, and with a little help from the third-base umpire's call, Santana threw the first no-hitter in Mets history. The exuberance did not last as he was clobbered in his next start, ran up a high ERA, and ultimately landed on the disabled list by August. Another shoulder injury in 2013 caused him to miss that season. He did not pitch in 2014 after suffering a torn Achilles tendon. Still trying to make a comeback in 2015, another injury caused Santana to end that season, and thus his career. Santana's impact on baseball is not as profound as Koufax's, but he was dependable and remains a fan favorite for the Mets and Twins. He has become an inspiration to young players, especially to those coming from Latin America, particularly his native Venezuela.

A Modern Comparison or "The Asterisk"

One of the questions that is often asked in baseball is: What if? What if Sandy Koufax had the benefit of modern remedies to lengthen his playing career? As noted, some of the treatments used in his day were crude and primitive. In a time before Tommy John surgery, the stalwart Koufax endured agonizing pain and disfigurement in his throwing arm. As we make one final comparison, we leave this essay with an asterisk as we do not know the final chapter of our last comparison.

Jacob deGrom's trajectory is much like those of Koufax, Guidry, and Santana, with clear ramp-up, high performance, and apparent decline at a young age. Although in 2024 we were not sure if deGrom's sunset was final, his injuries in the '20s suggest we may have seen the best and last of deGrom. His rise included switching from the field to the mound in college, where he became a top prospect. After being signed to the Mets, he had Tommy John surgery while still in the minors. He won back-to-back Cy Young Awards in 2018 and 2019 with the Mets, and a had low ERA that rivaled Koufax, Guidry, and Santana in their primes. The four-time All-Star made a World Series appearance, although the Mets were not victorious. With his pitch mix including a lightning four-seamer and slider, deGrom served up a buffet of unhittable fare. As age and time have marched on, he has had a litany of injuries. Many questioned the high price he fetched in his move in 2023 to the Texas Rangers, who paid so much for an aging and injury-prone former All-Star. Early in the 2023 season these arguments gained traction. deGrom was shut down in early June, when it was reported that he would have surgery to repair his UCL for the second time in his career. In 2024 the verdict was still out as to whether deGrom would make a full recovery and return to pitching.

SOURCES

The author consulted Baseball-Reference.com as well as the BioProject biographies of Sandy Koufax and Ron Guidry, and the following:

Rymer, Zachary D. "Retelling Johan Santana's MLB Journey from Untouchable to Unfixable," BleacherReport.com, March 29, 2013. https://bleacherreport.com/articles/1585844-retelling-johan-santa-nas-mlb-journey-from-untouchable-to-unfixable.

Stetson University, gohatters.com: https://gohatters.com/sports/baseball/roster/jacob-degrom/3594.

Jacob DeGrom injuries, FoxSports.com, https://www.foxsports.com/mlb/jacob-degrom-player-injuries.

NOTES

1　　Marc Z. Aaron, "Sandy Koufax," SABRBioProject, https://sabr.org/bioproj/person/sandy-koufax/.

Koufax vs. Other Hall of Fame Pitchers

BY CARTER CROMWELL

From time to time during his career, Sandy Koufax went head-to-head against other eventual Hall of Fame pitchers. Perhaps none was as significant as the last such regular-season confrontation.

Afterward, Koufax called it "the biggest ballgame of my life."[1]

It was the final game of the 1966 regular season, and his Los Angeles Dodgers had to win to capture the last of their three National League titles in the decade. It was also the last regular-season game of Koufax's career and his final victory, as only he and a very select few knew that he had decided to retire after that season because of his injured left elbow.

"It did cross my mind that it might be my last game if we lost," Koufax said. "But it wasn't about me, really."[2]

It came on October 2 in the second game of a doubleheader against the Phillies in Philadelphia's Connie Mack Stadium.[3] Los Angeles had lost the first game and the San Francisco Giants had defeated Pittsburgh to pull to within a game of the Dodgers. A Dodgers loss in the nightcap would leave them just a half-game ahead. If that happened, San Francisco would make up a rained-out game against Cincinnati, and a Giants victory then would tie them with Los Angeles and force a tiebreaker.

So it was up to Koufax, working on only two days' rest, to get the Dodgers across the finish line.

His mound opponent was future Cooperstown inductee Jim Bunning, trying for his 20th victory of the season. The two had started against each other twice before, each getting a no-decision in a Phillies victory on August 18, 1965, and in a Dodgers win July 27, 1966 – the latter a classic duel in which both went 11 innings before exiting. The only other time they pitched in the same game was May 24, 1964, when Bunning went seven innings in a loss and Koufax pitched the last three innings to earn a save.

At first Koufax wasn't sure if he'd be needed on this day, but the Giants-Pirates outcome wasn't decided until past the start time of the Dodgers-Phillies contest, so he pitched.

Bunning, who said, "I just didn't have it that day,"[4] was done after five innings, having allowed four runs, all earned, on five hits and two walks.

Koufax injured his back while pitching in the fifth inning. Trainers labored between innings to work out the kink, and, though it continued to bother him, he pitched through it. "You could see him wince," Philadelphia shortstop Bobby Wine said, "but nothing more than that."[5]

Los Angeles led 6-0 going into the Phillies' half of the ninth. At that point, Koufax said, "I guess I sort of ran out of gas,"[6] as the Phillies rallied to trail 6-3 with no one out. But according to Dodgers first baseman Wes Parker, "I swear I saw that inner fire in his eyes. He was not going to let this game get away from him."[7]

Indeed, Koufax retired the next three hitters to end the game and clinch the NL title.

After the team returned to Los Angeles, Koufax told a reporter that the victory "was bigger than my pennant clincher last year, or winning the seventh game of the World Series against the [Minnesota] Twins [in 1965]."[8]

In a reflective moment 50 years later, he said, "I always wanted to finish a win, and I wanted to finish my career with a win. So, yes, I'm tremendously proud of that game. But the reason I said that then was because of the team. I just wanted to make sure all of us got World Series shares. That money wouldn't seem like much now, but it was important to us then."[9]

The Dodgers were swept by Baltimore in the World Series, each Dodger receiving a loser's share of $8,189.36.

Bunning, of course, wasn't the only Hall of Fame pitcher Koufax battled in direct matchups. For the purposes of this article, we're examining only the period of 1961-1966, during which he morphed from an inconsistent flamethrower with a 36-40 record and bases-on-balls averages as high as six walks per nine innings into one of the greatest pitchers in major-league baseball history. As Willie Mays once said, "For him to do all those things in five years, what guys take 20 years to do, *that's* remarkable."[10]

Aside from Bunning, Koufax also pitched against all-time greats Bob Gibson, Juan Marichal, Gaylord Perry, Warren Spahn, Jim Kaat, Whitey Ford, and Jim Palmer – the last three only in the World Series – from 1961 to 1966. In terms of head-to-head matchups, the pitchers were in different stages of their own careers.

vs. BOB GIBSON

Koufax was 4-1 in five such matchups against Bob Gibson with three shutouts and a 0.92 earned-run average. There was also a game in May 1962 in which Koufax started and got a no-decision. Gibson earned a win with five innings of relief after Koufax left.

Koufax pitched complete games in each of his four victories vs. Gibson, the first on May 25, 1961, when he "announced himself in May with a 1-0 victory ... in St. Louis, a taut three-hitter decided by Tommy Davis's seventh-inning home run."[11]

The others came on June 18, 1962, July 3, 1963, and April 26, 1966. Gibson was almost the equal, pitching complete games in two defeats and going eight innings in the third matchup. Two of the games ended 1-0, and the third was 4-2. Both pitchers were fated to pitch much of their careers for teams not known for offensive prowess.

In the 1962 matchup, "Koufax teamed up with Tommy Davis to beat [Gibson] again. Another 1-0 loss for Gibson, another game-winning home run for Davis. For the first time in his career, Koufax pitched a complete game and walked no one."[12]

Gibson beat Koufax on September 24, 1961, going 6⅓ innings in an 8-7 victory while Koufax lasted just three innings.

Of note, the two were scheduled to battle each other on September 21, 1962, but fate intervened. During batting practice, Gibson fractured a bone above his right ankle. Koufax was making his first start in nearly two months because of an injured pitching hand – said to be a crushed artery in the palm. He was pulled with two out in the first inning, already trailing 4-0 after walking the bases loaded and giving up a grand slam to Charlie James.[13]

vs. JUAN MARICHAL

Koufax and Marichal started against each other four times, and there was another game in May 1965 in which Marichal got the win in relief but came into the game after Koufax had exited. The two most significant of the head-to-head matchups came on May 11, 1963, when Koufax pitched the second of his four no-hitters, and on August 22, 1965 – the infamous game in which Marichal attacked Dodger catcher John Roseboro with a bat.[14]

In the 1963 no-hitter, Koufax struck out an uncharacteristically few four batters and walked two in front of a crowd of 49,807 at Dodger Stadium. He had a perfect game until he walked Giants' catcher Ed Bailey on a full count with one out in the eighth inning. The Dodgers had actually led by just 1-0 before striking for three runs in the sixth inning off Marichal.

"The fellows on the bench didn't say anything about [the] no-hitter," Koufax said afterward, "but I knew it all the time and also knew I was close to a perfect game. That must be the ultimate thing for a pitcher."[15] Koufax, of course, achieved the "ultimate" with a perfect game two years later against the Chicago Cubs.

"It's hard to describe, but the game (against the Giants) gave me more satisfaction [than his first no-hitter the season before against the expansion New York Mets] because I felt I'd overcome my wildness problem."[16] Against the Mets, he had walked five batters.

There were a few hard-hit balls – by Harvey Kuenn, Felipe Alou, Willie Mays, and Orlando Cepeda – but none dropped for hits.

Interestingly, Tommy Lasorda – later the Dodgers manager but then a scout – had been asked the day before to catch a bullpen session to test Koufax's shoulder, which had been stiff

and kept him out of action for a couple of weeks. Lasorda said later that he told Koufax, "With stuff like that, tomorrow you've got to throw a no-hitter." Lasorda didn't see his prediction come true, however, because of a dinner meeting that night. He learned that Koufax was close to making history only when he turned on his transistor radio while at the dinner table.[17]

The second key matchup also made history, but not in a joyful sense. The longtime heated rivals were in a tight pennant race and this was the finale of a tense four-game series at San Francisco's Candlestick Park. Marichal and Koufax had already traded high-and-tight pitches to opposing hitters when Roseboro deliberately threw a ball back to Koufax that Marichal claimed had clipped his ear. He and Roseboro confronted each other, and then Marichal clubbed Roseboro with his bat. Marichal was ejected, suspended for eight game days and fined a then-record $1,750.

When the game resumed, Koufax walked two batters and then gave up a three-run homer to Mays that gave the Giants a 4-2 lead. San Francisco eventually won, 4-3. Koufax, who began the game with a 21-4 mark, also lost his next two starts before rebounding to finish 26-8, win the second of his three Cy Young Awards, and clinch the World Series with a Game Seven victory over Kaat and the Minnesota Twins.[18]

After missing two starts because of his suspension, Marichal went 3-4 over his final nine appearances to finish at 22-13. His ERA was 1.78 before the altercation and 3.55 after it.[19]

The other two occasions in which Koufax and Marichal competed directly against each other came on June 3, 1961, and May 24, 1963. In the 1961 contest, both pitched complete games, and Koufax came out on top in a 4-3 Dodgers victory. Neither was at the top of his game, Koufax giving up seven hits and walking five, while Marichal gave up nine hits and struck out just four. In the 1963 game, Marichal was superior in a 7-1 Giants win. He gave up just four hits and a walk, while striking out 10. Koufax, meanwhile, lasted just one-third of an inning, allowing five runs on five hits and two walks.

vs. WARREN SPAHN

Koufax and Spahn, the winningest left-handed pitcher in major-league history, went against each other four times during the former's glory years, with Koufax winning three times and Spahn once.

Spahn pitched a complete game in a 4-2 Milwaukee Braves win on September 2, 1961. Koufax went seven innings and gave up four runs, just two earned. In a rematch 13 days later, it was Koufax who pitched a complete game while Spahn lasted just one inning in an 11-2 Dodgers victory. On June 13, 1962, Los Angeles defeated Milwaukee 2-1 on a three-hitter by Koufax. Spahn went eight innings in that game.[20]

On June 20, 1965, when Spahn was briefly with the New York Mets, the two matched up with the Dodgers winning, 2-1. Koufax pitched a complete-game one-hitter – the only hit a solo home run by Jim Hickman in the fifth inning – while Spahn went seven strong innings, allowing just four hits and one walk.

vs. GAYLORD PERRY

Koufax and the Giants' Gaylord Perry pitched against each other three times, but only one was a straight matchup. That came on May 9, 1965. The Giants won 6-3, with Koufax taking the loss and Perry getting a no-decision. Koufax went seven innings and Perry 7⅓, but interestingly it was Marichal who got the win with 1⅓ innings of relief after San Francisco scored four runs in the bottom of the eighth.

On July 26, 1964, Koufax pitched a complete game in a 5-2 loss, with the Giants scoring four times in the ninth inning. The big hits were a run-scoring double by Mays and a two-run home run by Jim Ray Hart, but all the runs were officially unearned because of an error by shortstop Maury Wills on Harvey Kuenn's groundball. Perry pitched the last inning for San Francisco and got the save.

Koufax and Perry also pitched on June 25, 1964, but against each other for only one inning. Koufax started and went nine innings of an eventual 13-inning game that San Francisco won 2-1. Perry entered the game in the ninth inning, pitched the last five, and got credit for the victory.

vs. JIM KAAT

Koufax and Kaat faced each other in Games Two, Five, and Seven of the 1965 World Series, with Kaat winning the first and Koufax the last two. Koufax famously did not pitch the Series opener because it took place on the Jewish holy day of Yom Kippur.

In the first matchup – played in a drizzling rain – the Twins won 5-1 behind Kaat's seven-hit, one-run, one-walk effort. Koufax was removed after six innings despite having allowed just two runs – only one earned – on six hits and having struck out nine batters. The game was scoreless after five innings before Minnesota scored twice against Koufax in the sixth.

"The cold weather didn't bother me," Koufax said afterward. "I've pitched and had good stuff on colder days. I knew what I wanted to do out there but I just couldn't do it. If I had had a little better control, or better stuff, I might have gotten away with it. ... Kaat and Minnesota just did a better job."[21]

Four days later, with the Series tied at two games apiece, the two matched up in Game Five at Dodger Stadium and the Dodgers won 7-0. This time, Koufax pitched a complete-game, four-hit shutout with 10 strikeouts while Kaat lasted just 2⅓ innings.[22]

That set up the finale, in which both pitchers started on just two days of rest. Koufax again went the distance, giving up just three hits and striking out 10 in a 2-0 Dodgers victory. Kaat was chased in the fourth inning after giving up both runs.

What made Koufax's performance even more amazing was that his arm was hurting so much, he couldn't control his curveball. So he threw nothing but fastballs from the third inning on.

"I didn't have a curve ball at all," Koufax said. "When I threw it I couldn't get it over. And those first few innings I really didn't know how long I was going to last. Then I seemed

to get my second wind. In the last three, the fastball seemed to move better, and I got stronger."[23]

vs. WHITEY FORD

The two Hall of Fame left-handers competed directly just twice – in Games One and Four of the Dodgers' surprising World Series sweep of the Yankees in 1963.[24]

In the opener at Yankee Stadium, Koufax set a Series record of 15 strikeouts – later surpassed by Bob Gibson with 17 in the first game of the 1968 Series – and held the Yankees to just six hits in a 5-2 victory. Ford, who had led the American League with 24 victories that season, gave up five runs in the first three innings and lasted just five innings.

Game Seven at Dodger Stadium hung in the balance much longer before the Dodgers won 2-1.

Ford gave up just two hits but one was a fifth-inning solo home run by Frank Howard. Mickey Mantle tied the game in the seventh with a homer off Koufax, but the Dodgers got the deciding run in the bottom of the seventh when Willie Davis hit a sacrifice fly to score Jim Gilliam.

One thing not revealed at the time was that Koufax had an open sore between the last two toes of his left foot, the one he used to push off the mound. A corn had torn off two days before and had not healed. He got a shot of Novocain in the affected area, and that apparently did the trick as he gave up just six hits, walked no one, and struck out eight.[25]

vs. JIM PALMER

The final game of Koufax's career came on just three days of rest after the pennant-clinching victory over Bunning and the Phillies, and it was against another eventual Hall of Fame inductee[26] – the not-quite-21-year-old Jim Palmer, who had won 15 games in his second season.

The result was the opposite of that in Philadelphia.

The Orioles broke a scoreless tie with three unearned runs in the fifth inning, thanks in large part to three errors by Los Angeles center fielder Willie Davis. Koufax was lifted after the sixth inning, having allowed six hits, walked two batters, and struck out two. Palmer, meanwhile, went on to throw a four-hit shutout.

A *Sports Illustrated* retrospective said that "Sandy, pitching his third big game in eight days, gave up only one earned run in six innings ... but it was a weak performance for Koufax, who failed to impress the Baltimore hitters. He looked tired, he was forcing his pitches. ..."[27]

In short, it was not a fitting end to one of the most dominant six-season stretches in major-league baseball history.

SOURCES

In addition to the sources in the Notes, the author utilized baseball-reference.com for information contained in this article.

For more detailed information on how about how Koufax's career statistics compare with those of Hall of Famers Gibson and Marichal, refer to Larry DeFillipo's article in this volume titled "First Among Equals."

NOTES

1 Steve Wulf, "Sandy Koufax' Final Victory Might Have Been His Best," ESPN.com, September 30, 2016: https://www.espn.com/mlb/story/_/id/17671148/los-angeles-dodgers-pitcher-sandy-koufax-relives-finest-game.

2 Wulf.

3 See the Games Project account of this game by Jake Bell, which is presented elsewhere in this publication.

4 Wulf.

5 Wulf.

6 Wulf.

7 Wulf.

8 Wulf.

9 Wulf.

10 Jane Leavy, *Sandy Koufax: A Lefty's Legacy* (New York: HarperCollins Publishers, 2002), 120.

11 Leavy, 114. See Tim Odzer's Games Project writeup of the game, presented elsewhere in this publication.

12 Leavy, 116. An account of the June 18, 1962, game by Thomas J. Brown Jr. is also presented in this publication.

13 "Bob Gibson vs. Sandy Koufax: Grand game for Charlie James," retrosimba, August 31, 2012 (updated October 7, 2020): https://retrosimba.com/2012/08/31/gibson-vs-koufax-a-grand-game-for-charlie-james/.

14 Marc Z Aaron has written the May 11, 1963, game account, presented elsewhere in this publication.

15 Kevin Stone, "Koufax's Nearly Perfect in No-Hitter vs. Giants," National Baseball Hall of Fame website, no date provided: https://baseballhall.org/discover/inside-pitch/koufax-pitches-second-career-no-hitter-vs-giants. Article accessed on May 12, 2023.

16 Kevin Stone.

17 Mark Langill, "OTD: Sandy's Second No-No," *Dodger Insider,* May 11, 2020: https://dodgers.mlblogs.com/otd-sandys-second-no-no-782a3c27d304.

18 The Games Project account of Koufax's Game Seven victory has been written by Norm King and appears elsewhere in this publication.

19 Stone.

20 See Tim Otto's account of the June 13 game.

21 Jon Weisman, "Remembering '65: World Series Game 2," *Dodger Insider*, October 7, 2015: https://dodgers.mlblogs.com/remembering-65-world-series-game-2-be26ca5211e4.

22 Norm King has written both Game Five and Game Seven, which are presented elsewhere in this publication.

23 Houston Mitchell, "Greatest Moments in Dodger History, No. 14: Sandy Koufax's Shutout in Game 7 of 1965 World Series," *Los Angeles Times*, March 24, 2021: https://www.latimes.com/sports/newsletter/2021-03-24/world-series-sandy-koufax-dodgers-dugout.

24 Andy McCue has written Games One and Four, and those accounts appear elsewhere in this publication.

25 Andy McCue, "October 6, 1963: Koufax Stifles Yankee Bats Again as Dodgers Sweep World Series," Society for American Baseball Research: https://sabr.org/gamesproj/game/october-6-1963-koufax-stifles-yankee-bats-again/.

26 Mark Kanter's account of Game Two of the 1966 World Series is presented elsewhere in this publication.

27 Jack Mann, "Those Happy Birds!" *Sports Illustrated*, October 17, 1966: https://vault.si.com/vault/1966/10/17/those-happy-birds.

Sandy Koufax versus Hall of Fame Members with at least 100 Plate Appearances

BY KEN CARRANO

Sandy Koufax faced 512 different batters during his Hall of Fame career, from Dick Groat (145 plate appearances, or PA), to Vinegar Bend Mizell (one PA, along with 63 other batters). Along the way, he faced a number of players who have been elected to the National Baseball Hall of Fame, including Ron Santo (87 PA against Koufax), Lou Brock (70), Pete Rose (60), and Stan Musial (44). Seven Hall of Famers whose careers paralleled Koufax's so closely that they had 100 or more plate appearances against the Brooklyn/Los Angeles Dodgers ace:

- Ernie Banks – 143
- Henry "Hank" Aaron – 130
- Willie Mays – 122
- Roberto Clemente – 122
- Frank Robinson – 121
- Bill Mazeroski – 109
- Eddie Mathews – 102

This essay will review Koufax's performance against these legends of the game and highlight some key games in which they competed. Also compared are the performances of these Hall of Famers against the two Sandys – the "bonus baby" Koufax of 1955-1960 who compiled a 36-40 record with 6.7 Wins Above Replacement (WAR), and "The Left Arm of God" years of 1961-1966 (129-47, three Cy Young Awards, 46.4 WAR).

The Dominated

Ernie Banks – faced Koufax 143 times between 1955 and 1966:

Seasons	Player	B	PA	AB	H	HR	RBI	BB	SO	BA	OBP	SLG	OPS
55-60	Ernie Banks	R	73	64	16	5	17	9	14	0.250	0.342	0.531	0.874
61-66	Ernie Banks	R	70	69	7	2	2	1	17	0.101	0.114	0.217	0.332
	Total		143	133	23	7	19	10	31	0.173	0.231	0.368	0.599

Ernie Banks was perhaps the best player in the National League during the bonus-baby Koufax years of 1955-1960. He won two MVP Awards (1958-59) and had three additional top-10 MVP finishes, plus a .294 batting average with 248 home runs and 693 RBIs. Banks' performance against Koufax during these

years was more modest. "What was it like facing Koufax?" Banks said, "It was frightenin.'"[1]

Banks' batting average of .250 was better than the .225 average that all batters had against Koufax during 1955-60. Banks' best day was April 12, 1959, when he went 2-for-2 with a triple in a 5-3 Dodgers victory. The wind blowing in at Wrigley Field helped keep Banks' third-inning drive from leaving the park, and again later in the game when he faced Johnny Klippstein in the fourth with two on.

Banks hit a game-winning home run against Koufax on September 6, 1959, in the first game of a doubleheader sweep that was notable for Koufax's setting a major-league record in defeat with 41 strikeouts in a three-game stretch.[2]

The Banks of 1961-1966 was a very good player, but not quite the same as the Banks of 1955-60. During these six years, Banks' batting average dropped to .264 and his home-run totals dropped to 150. Banks made four All-Star Games and received some MVP votes in 1962. His performance against Koufax was anything but All-Star worthy. Banks hit a triple in his first at-bat vs. Koufax in 1961, one of his three hits against three Dodgers pitchers that day. (Koufax came into the game in relief in the fourth inning.) Banks had only one other hit against Koufax in 1961, a single on June 20, 1961, and faced him twice in 1962, going 1-for-7 with a single in his final 1962 AB against him.

Banks faced Koufax in only two games in 1963 and the second, on June 9, was his best ever, with two home runs in an 11-8 loss. Banks hit a third homer against Larry Sherry in that losing cause. It was almost two years and another 26 appearances before he had another hit against Koufax. Included in that dismal streak were three swinging strikeouts in Koufax's perfect game on September 9, 1965. "He tried to throw the ball right past us," eulogized Banks. "And he did."[3] Banks was able to rebound with two singles in 1966, his final hits against the LA ace. Banks finished his time against Koufax with seven hits in six years, including going hitless in 1964 and 1965.

Bill Mazeroski – faced Koufax 109 times between 1957 and 1966:

Seasons	Player	B	PA	AB	H	HR	RBI	BB	SO	BA	OBP	SLG	OPS
57-60	Bill Mazeroski	R	39	32	4	0	4	6	7	0.125	0.256	0.125	0.381
61-66	Bill Mazeroski	R	70	68	15	0	1	2	12	0.221	0.243	0.265	0.508
	Total		109	100	19	0	5	8	19	0.190	0.248	0.220	0.468

Bill Mazeroski was elected to the Hall of Fame in 2001, based primarily on his superior defense for the Pittsburgh Pirates (eight Gold Glove Awards between 1958 and 1967) and perhaps the most famous home run of all time that ended the 1960 World Series. "Some critics scoffed at his election, saying his offense (career batting average .260) did not live up to that of others already residing at Cooperstown. Others replied that the caliber of pitchers he faced had to be considered, among them Hall of Fame pitchers like Warren Spahn, Don Drysdale, Sandy Koufax, Bob Gibson, Juan Marichal, Gaylord Perry, Tom Seaver, Steve Carlton, and Ferguson Jenkins."[4] There is some validity to this argument – in the years that both Mazeroski and Koufax were both active, 1956 to 1966, only Nellie Fox (20.6) and Johnny Temple (18.1) had an offensive WAR (oWAR) for second basemen higher than Mazeroski's of 17.5, Mazeroski faced a total of 14 Hall of Fame pitchers during his career and, as one would expect, he performed better against the non-Hall hurlers:

Against	PA	AB	H	HR	RBI	BB	SO	BA	OBP	SLG	OPS
HOF	1113	1050	243	15	91	45	118	0.231	0.263	0.314	0.577
Non-HOF	7095	6548	1734	123	750	393	585	0.265	0.306	0.378	0.684
Total	8208	7598	1977	138	841	438	703	0.260	0.301	0.369	0.670
Against	PA	AB	H	HR	RBI	BB	SO	BA	OBP	SLG	OPS
Don Drysdale	144	139	37	3	16	4	16	0.266	0.287	0.367	0.654
Warren Spahn	128	122	36	3	14	4	7	0.295	0.315	0.443	0.758
Sandy Koufax	109	100	19	0	5	8	19	0.190	0.248	0.220	0.468

Mazeroski debuted with the Pirates in 1956 but did not face Koufax until 1957, when he got two hits in eight at-bats, with both hits resulting in RBIs. The highlight of his 11 plate appearances against Koufax in 1958 were three walks, including two in a row on June 13. Mazeroski continued to struggle against the lefty through 1963, scratching only six hits in 48 appearances. Unlike Banks, however, Mazeroski seemed to figure out Koufax the more he faced him. From 1964 on, Mazeroski had 11 hits in 42 at-bats against Koufax, a .262 average, better than his lifetime average of .260 and considerably better than his .154 batting average against Koufax in his three prior years.

While Mazeroski may have had better success against Koufax the longer he faced him, one thing he could not do was drive in any runs. On July 29, 1961, Mazeroski started a remarkable string of appearances against Koufax with little to no effect on the game. He singled in consecutive at-bats, the second giving the Pirates a 2-1 lead. Mazeroski came up again in the fifth inning with the bases loaded and two out but struck out swinging. This at-bat was the first of 57 consecutive plate appearances in which Mazeroski did not record an RBI against Koufax. There was a runner in scoring position in only eight of these appearances, and in one opportunity Mazeroski was intentionally walked.

Frank Robinson – faced Koufax 121 times between 1956 and 1965:

Seasons	Player	B	PA	AB	H	HR	RBI	BB	SO	BA	OBP	SLG	OPS
56-60	Frank Robinson	R	36	30	9	4	9	6	8	0.300	0.417	0.700	1.117
61-65	Frank Robinson	R	85	73	15	3	14	10	12	0.205	0.318	0.425	0.742
	Total		121	103	24	7	23	16	20	0.233	0.336	0.505	0.841

Frank Robinson was one of the most feared hitters in the National League in his years with the Cincinnati Reds. Debuting in 1956, Robinson won the Rookie of the Year Award; he won his first Most Valuable Player Award in 1961, and played in eight All-Star Games during the Koufax era. For his first years competing against Koufax, Robinson had the better of the matchup. From 1956 through 1961, Robinson hit .367 against Koufax while slugging a robust .776. Robinson homered in his second time facing Koufax, a first-inning shot in a 6-4 Reds victory. His second homer off Koufax was more meaningful. Leading off the eighth inning with the Reds trailing by a run, Robinson homered to tie the score. The Reds won a walk-off victory in the ninth inning, moving to one game behind the

Asked what it was like to face Sandy Koufax, Cubs Hall of Famer Ernie Banks said, "It was frightenin'." SABR: The Rucker Archive.

Milwaukee Braves for the NL lead. The Reds stayed in contention all season but finished two games behind the Dodgers for the crown.

Robinson continued to have success against Koufax, especially in the Reds' World Series campaign of 1961. Robinson's three-run homer tied the April 21 game against the Dodgers that the Reds eventually lost. He doubled twice off Koufax on June 24, the second a bases-loaded shot that gave the Reds the lead in another game they lost. Another double on August 15 tied that game. Robinson eventually had 9 hits in 19 at-bats against Koufax in 1961, with 9 RBIs and an OPS of 1.460, easily the best of any hitter against Koufax that year with more than 10 plate appearances.

And then it was gone. Much like Banks, it was as if a switch was flipped in 1962. In the final years of this matchup, Robinson's batting average plummeted to .111 and his slugging percentage shrank to .259. Included in these totals was an 0-for-17 stretch in 1964-65. After a home run in July 1965, Robinson finished his time against Koufax going hitless in his last nine at-bats. Robinson, though, had the last laugh, getting a triple in the sixth inning of Game Two of the 1966 World Series, which the Baltimore Orioles swept. Robinson, who was traded to Baltimore after the 1965 campaign, gave his Orioles teammates some advice: "If it starts at the belt, take it because it's going to choke you."[5]

The Enigmas

Eddie Mathews – faced Koufax 102 times between 1955 and 1966:

Seasons	Player	B	PA	AB	H	HR	RBI	BB	SO	BA	OBP	SLG	OPS
55-60	Eddie Mathews	L	45	37	6	2	3	8	9	0.162	0.311	0.351	0.662
61-66	Eddie Mathews	L	57	52	19	1	4	5	13	0.365	0.421	0.462	0.883
	Total		102	89	25	3	7	13	22	0.281	0.373	0.416	0.788

One of the most feared power hitters in the National League, Mathews struggled against the younger Koufax during the Milwaukee Braves' glory years of the 1950s, then hit Koufax better than anyone else in this essay during the 1960s. Mathews had a hit in one of this three at-bats against the young Koufax, but then went more than two seasons without another one, albeit in limited appearances (eight total). Seeing Koufax more in 1958 than he did in the three prior seasons combined, he had some success, managing 4 hits in 13 at-bats. Two of those hits came on July 30, when Mathews' home run on the first pitch leading off the bottom of the eighth inning gave the Braves a 4-3 victory, moving them into first place in the NL, a lead they did not relinquish for the remainder of the campaign. Warren Spahn broke a streak of his own on this night, defeating the Dodgers for the first time since September 25, 1951. Mathews' next hit off Koufax was more than a year later, and also a home

run, on August 17. It was his only hit off Koufax in 1959, the year he led the NL with 46 homers.

After facing Koufax only four times in 1960 (walking three times), Mathews began a stretch of hitting against Koufax that was unlike anyone else in the NL, except for his teammate Henry Aaron (more on him later). Mathews' .378 batting average against Koufax in 1961-63 compares favorably to the average that hitters against Koufax achieved in these years of .202. Unfortunately for Mathews, 15 of those 17 hits were singles, and he drove in only three runs in this period.

As Mathews' career wound down, so too did his appearances against Koufax. In 1964 the Braves faced the Dodgers in 18 games and Mathews played in 16 of these affairs but managed to avoid Koufax completely. In fact, Mathews went more than two years between appearances against the lefty. Matthews singled in the second inning against Koufax in what was the Braves' final home game in Milwaukee, on September 22, 1965, a 7-6 defeat. Mathews managed just one more hit against Koufax, a home run in his final at-bat against him on August 9, 1966, that gave the Braves a walk-off 2-1 victory. The game was new Braves manager Billy Hitchcock's first after Bobby Bragan was fired. Before the game, Hitchcock said, "I believe (Mathews) still has a lot of sting in his bat,"[6] He was right – Mathews hit eight home runs in the final month and a half of the season to bring his total for the Braves to 493 before being traded to the Houston Astros after the 1966 season.

Roberto Clemente – faced Koufax 122 times between 1955 and 1966:

Seasons	Player	B	PA	AB	H	HR	RBI	BB	SO	BA	OBP	SLG	OPS
55-60	Roberto Clemente	R	44	38	11	1	4	6	7	0.289	0.386	0.447	0.834
61-66	Roberto Clemente	R	78	73	22	5	12	4	13	0.301	0.338	0.603	0.940
	Total		122	111	33	6	16	10	20	0.297	0.355	0.550	0.905

In his 18-year career with the Pirates, Roberto Clemente was one of the most consistent hitters in history. From 1960 until his final season of 1972, Clemente hit under .300 only once (1968), and over .340 five times. He finished in the top 10 of MVP voting eight times (winning in 1966) and missed only one All-Star Game in this period (1968). This consistency was evident against Koufax as well, perhaps not year over year, but over the course of the 12 years of competition between the two.

Koufax and Clemente were both rookies in 1955, and Roberto singled off Sandy in their first meeting, on July 6. They did not face each other very often through 1959, but when they did, Clemente had Koufax's number, reaching base 13 times in their 29 battles. Clemente's single in the fifth inning on August 17, 1957, put the Pirates in the lead to stay and gave Koufax his third loss of the season.

Remarkably, in the Pirates' magical championship year of 1960, Clemente had one of his worst seasons against Koufax, reaching base only four times in 15 appearances, with his only home run providing his lone RBI. That changed in 1961, as Clemente hit .389 against Koufax in 18 at-bats, including a double on June 29 that tied the game in the eighth inning and knocked Koufax out of the game. Koufax held Clement hitless in 1962, but the seasons of 1963 and 1964 were Clemente's best against the left-hander: .500 over the two seasons combined. Clemente missed a cycle by only the home run on May 17 in the first game of a doubleheader, his fly ball to right field coming up short. Clemente got that homer two weeks later, tying the game on May 31 in the third inning before an eventual Pirates loss.

The final two seasons of competition swung toward Koufax, as Clemente struggled with five total hits in 30 at-bats. In a tight pennant race late in 1966, Koufax beat the Pirates 5–1 to increase the Dodgers' lead over the Pirates to 3½ games. Noting his unusually low number of strikeouts (five), Bob Bailey said, "Compared with the way he usually throws, he had nothing."[7] Clemente thought otherwise. "When my back hurts, they call me a goldbrick. Koufax says his elbow hurts and they make him a national hero. He threw as hard tonight as he ever has. He can't have a sore elbow and throw like that."[8] Even with these two offyears, Clemente hit .301 off Koufax in his prime, when the NL as a whole hit only .197 against him.

The Dominators

Willie Mays – faced Koufax 122 times between 1955 and 1966:

Seasons	Player	B	PA	AB	H	HR	RBI	BB	SO	BA	OBP	SLG	OPS
55-60	Willie Mays	R	33	23	9	1	2	10	5	0.391	0.576	0.652	1.228
61-66	Willie Mays	R	89	74	18	4	12	15	15	0.243	0.371	0.500	0.871
	Total		122	97	27	5	14	25	20	0.278	0.426	0.536	0.962

Few rankings of all-time greats don't include Willie Mays as either the best or second-best outfielder to ever play the game. Mays' .278 lifetime average against Koufax was understandably less than the .313 that he averaged over the time he and Koufax competed against each other. What Mays did better than anyone else was, as Billy Beane said in the movie *Moneyball*, "He gets on base a lot."[9]

Mays faced Koufax only 33 times during first six years of the lefty's career, less than anyone else in this essay. That his on-base percentage was .576 likely means that Koufax was happy they did not face each other more often. His first plate appearances against Koufax went like this: walk, home run, walk, double, strikeout swinging, single, single, single. He walked four consecutive times in 1958, including a bases-loaded walk that gave the Giants some insurance in a victory on August 10.

As Mays faced Koufax more often in the 1960s, his batting average declined, but he kept getting on base. On August 20, 1961, Mays doubled and homered (and walked) to drive in the first three runs of an 11–8 Giants victory. The loss was the Dodgers' seventh in a row, their longest streak since they lost eight straight in 1948.[10] Mays also homered twice, the first against Koufax in the first inning, in the first game of the three-game

tiebreaker series to decide the 1962 NL pennant. The season may have taken its toll on Koufax. "I've seen Sandy throw a lot harder. The long layoff hurt him," Mays said after the game.[11]

Mays was also there for Koufax's second ho-hitter, on May 11, 1963. Mays almost broke up the no-hitter with a screaming line drive that was snared by Jim Gilliam at third base. Koufax had not allowed a baserunner to that point. Mays got revenge later in the year, getting a double and home run on September 6, his only hits against Koufax that season in 15 plate appearances. Mays would find his form against Koufax over 1964 and 1965, averaging .385 with an on-base percentage of .484, phenomenal considering that Koufax had overall totals of .184 average against, with an OBP against of .233. Even in their final year together, Mays achieved a .400 OBP thanks to six walks in 20 plate appearances.

Hank Aaron – faced Koufax 130 times between 1955 and 1966:

Seasons	Player	B	PA	AB	H	HR	RBI	BB	SO	BA	OBP	SLG	OPS
55-60	Henry Aaron	R	48	40	19	5	10	8	4	0.475	0.563	0.975	1.538
61-66	Henry Aaron	R	82	76	23	2	6	6	8	0.303	0.354	0.474	0.827
	Total		130	116	42	7	16	14	12	0.362	0.431	0.647	1.077

There are 126 players who faced Sandy Koufax 25 times or more in their careers. (We've discussed six of them.) Of those 126 players, three had an OPS of 1.000 or greater against Koufax. Gene Oliver faced Koufax 54 times in his career with the Cardinals and Braves and hit .392 with 4 home runs and an OPS of 1.073. He also struck out 11 times. Hal Smith (the Cardinal, not the Pirate) faced Koufax 36 times, hitting .364 and accumulating an OPS of 1.053. (For the record, the other Hal Smith faced Koufax 37 times, striking out in 11 of them.) Aaron's 1.077 OPS against Koufax was the best of the seven Hall of Famers with 100 plate appearances against Koufax, and it isn't even close, with Mays the closest at .962. Aaron's strikeout-to-plate-appearance rate of 9.2% is also easiest the best of his contemporaries – 7.2% better than Mays, 12.4% better than his teammate Mathews. He was the one hitter for whom Koufax confessed he never had a plan.[12]

Aaron was there at the beginning for Koufax. Sandy debuted in Milwaukee on June 24, 1955, in the bottom of the fifth inning, replacing Jim Hughes. After a bloop single by Johnny Logan, Mathews grounded to Koufax, who threw the ball into center field. Aaron came up next and walked on four pitches. Koufax managed to get out of that situation, striking out Bobby Thomson and getting Joe Adcock to hit into a double play. "A park-packing crowd of 43,068 witnessed the historic occasion, and doubtless was oblivious to it," Dick Young wrote in the *New York Daily News*. "To them it was just another guy named Koufax. To the Brook brass, however, it marked the start of what they expect to be a fine career. They sank a $20,000 bonus ($6,000 salary included) into the kid, who won't be 20 until December."[13] Aaron didn't get his first hit against Koufax until 1957, but he quickly made up for lost time. Aaron homered and tripled on August 23, 1957, in a game in which the Braves gave up three runs in the bottom of the ninth inning and lost 3-2. The Hammer lived up to his nickname over the next three years – facing Koufax 39 times between 1958 and 1960, Aaron hit .500 with 4 home runs, 8 RBIs, and an OPS of 1.558. In a remarkable stretch from June 24, 1960, through May 16, 1961, Aaron reached base 10 times (five singles, two doubles, a triple, a home run, and one reached on error) in 11 plate appearances.

Koufax would eventually catch up with Aaron – there was likely no way he could have kept up that kind of performance, especially against the post-1960 version of Koufax right after Aaron's 9-for-11 streak. Koufax went on one of his own, retiring Aaron eight times in nine plate appearances, surrounding just an intentional walk. That was the last great year that Aaron had against Koufax. The years 1963-1965 saw Koufax take over, with Aaron dropping to a .156 batting average and a pedestrian OPS of .438 – both figures even lower than Koufax's totals for everyone in those years of .186 and an OPS of .507. Between August 25, 1963, and the end of the 1965 season, Aaron had an especially tough time – one hit and one walk in 20 plate appearances. The move from Milwaukee to Atlanta did give Aaron a chance for redemption as he hit .400 against Koufax in 1966, with an OPS back to an impressive 1.100. Aaron's final hit against Koufax was the 424th home run of his career, on July 9, 1966.

SOURCES

In addition to the sources cited in the Notes, the author consulted SABR's Biography Project (BioProject) and Games Project.

All data from baseball-reference.com.

NOTES

1 Ira Berkow, "Koufax Is No Garbo," *New York Times,* July 3, 1985: B7.

2 Richard Dozier, "Cubs Defeat Dodgers Twice on Homers," *Chicago Tribune,* September 7, 1959: 77.

3 Bob Hunter, "Now Sandy Stands Alone on Summit," *The Sporting News,* September 25, 1965: 3.

4 Bob Hurte, SABR BioProject, https://sabr.org/bioproj/person/bill-mazeroski/.

5 Jane Leavy, *Sandy Koufax: A Lefty's Legacy* (New York: Harper-Collins, 2002), 221.

6 Wayne Minshew, "Cap'n Ed 2, Sandy 1," *Atlanta Constitution,* August 10, 1966: 35.

6 Minshew.

7 Leavy, 224.

8 Leavy, 224.

9 https://www.imdb.com/title/tt1210166/characters/nm0000093

10 Frank Finch, "Dodgers Roll 7, but Just Keep Fading," *Los Angeles Times,* August 21, 1961: 78.

11 Paul Zimmerman, "Mays, Giants Rout Futile Dodgers, 8-0," *Los Angeles Times,* October 2, 1962: 40.

12 Leavy, 86.

13 Dick Young, "Braves win 7th in Row, Diverting Brooks 8-2," *New York Daily News,* June 25, 1955: 242.

1965-66 Pennant Races: LA's Most Artful Dodger

BY ED GRUVER

On the afternoon of Sunday, June 20, 1965, New York Mets announcer Ralph Kiner described for listeners on WHN Radio in New York one of the more awesome sights in major-league baseball in the mid-1960s:

"Sandy Koufax, one of the top left-handers in the history of baseball …"[1]

Baseball Hall of Fame writer Roger Angell said in a 1999 interview that he'd never seen major-league hitters more overmatched than when Koufax was throwing his "terrific fastball and deadly curveball." Angell recalled hitters looking out at Koufax on the mound as if they were wondering what they were facing. Batters sat in their dugout, said Angell, completely riveted by Koufax.[2]

In this Father's Day doubleheader Koufax dueled the man who at the time was statistically the greatest lefty in the game's history, Warren Spahn. The twin bill was critical to the pennant hopes of the Dodgers, who at 41-24 led the Milwaukee Braves by 3½ games and the Cincinnati Reds by 4 games.

Koufax versus Spahn was a classic mound matchup, and the game, historical as it was in that it marked the first time that Koufax and Don Drysdale started in the same doubleheader, lived up to expectations.

Amid near-perfect 68-degree weather, the two legendary lefties matched one another pitch for pitch – Koufax's flame belching fastballs and 12-to-6 curves mystifying the Mets while Spahn's sinking fastballs, screwballs, sliders, and knuckleballs were dazzling the Dodgers.

Claude Osteen, the number-three starter on the 1965-66 Dodgers, said in a 1998 interview that to call Koufax's curveball "outstanding" was not a good enough word for it. Koufax's curve dropped straight down, Osteen remembered, and his fiery fastball flared upward. Osteen said Koufax didn't have a great changeup, but he didn't need one, since his curve and fastball were otherworldly.[3]

Sandy Koufax won two games in the 1965 World Series and boasted a 0.38 ERA. *SABR: The Rucker Archive.*

Osteen recalled Koufax having huge hands and long fingers, the latter allowing him to exert extra spin on the ball. By adjusting his grip on the ball, he could deliver flaring fastballs estimated at between 95 and 100 mph and 85 mph power curves that broke in on right-handed hitters and away from lefties.

Ed Roebuck, a former Dodger teammate of Koufax, said in an interview that the pitcher's long fingers allowed him to put extra spin on the ball and thus aided in his ability to throw his exceptional fastball and curve.[4]

Angell noted that with Koufax, one could see where all the heat was coming from on his pitches. It was generated by the bowed back, powerful arm, and powerful legs. It was very exciting, said Angell.[5]

Koufax's duel with Spahn moved along briskly. At 1 hour and 52 minutes it was the third quickest contest the Dodgers played in 1965. Koufax's 2-1 victory was reminiscent of a mound meeting he and Spahn engaged in nearly three years to the day earlier, June 13, 1962, in Milwaukee, Koufax allowing just three hits in another 2-1 victory.[6]

Decades later, Koufax would joke at a gathering of baseball greats for the All-Century Team that Spahn was the best southpaw pitcher in the room that day. Not because Spahn was so good, Koufax said tongue-in-cheek, but because he pitched "the whole damn century."[7]

In LA, Koufax ignored an arthritic left elbow that caused him constant pain and went the distance, surrendering one hit and two walks while striking out 12. He faced just three batters over the minimum for a nine-inning game and improved his record to 11-3. The victory was his fifth straight in as many outings, a streak he eventually pushed to 11 as the Dodgers fought for their pennant lives.

The blazing National League race in the summer of '65 emerged as one of the most suspenseful ever. The see-saw summer in '65 saw six teams – Cincinnati, Los Angeles, Milwaukee,

Philadelphia, Pittsburgh, and San Francisco – spend time atop the standings.

That the Dodgers were in contention might have surprised some. The 1963 World Series champions plummeted to sixth place in '64, the result of inconsistent play and injuries. The offseason saw the Dodgers bolster their mound rotation but weaken their offense when they acquired Osteen for slugger Frank Howard in a seven-player deal.

The Dodgers' offense grew even more anemic one month into the 1965 campaign, their top hitter Tommy Davis breaking his ankle sliding into second base to break up a double-play attempt in a May 1 game against the Giants in Los Angeles. Davis didn't return to the lineup until the final game of the regular season, and that in a pinch-hit role.

The injury might have doomed the Dodgers if not for the clutch play and pleasing personality of his replacement, Lou Johnson. Called Sweet Lou by teammates for his infectious good humor, Johnson was a journeyman outfielder who had played for the Chicago Cubs, Los Angeles Angels, and Milwaukee Braves.

The injury to Tommy Davis was one of many endured by the Dodgers in '65. Willie Davis, Ron Fairly, John Roseboro, and Maury Wills all missed playing time because of injuries. That the '65 Dodgers did not produce a player with more than 12 home runs or 70 RBIs shows how important pitching was for this team.

Osteen, Drysdale, Johnny Podres, and a deep bullpen headed by relief ace Ron Perranoski picked up the slack, but it was Koufax who proved to be LA's most artful Dodger. It hadn't always been that way. Sportswriter Dave Anderson covered Koufax's signing with the Dodgers for the *Brooklyn Eagle* newspaper in 1955 and recalled in a 1999 interview that Koufax was "a nice kid" but also just the 25th guy on the roster. Even as a rookie, Koufax could throw the ball through a brick, Anderson said, but he often couldn't find the brick because of his lack of control.[8]

By 1965 Koufax was the best pitcher in baseball, but his success came at a costly price from a physical standpoint. The day on which he was scheduled to pitch saw Koufax apply the heating ointment Capsolin to his left arm to loosen the muscles. Capsolin was so hot it would nearly cause the skin to blister, but its effect was to stimulate the circulation beneath the skin.

Minnesota Twins ace southpaw Jim Kaat, who faced Koufax three times in the 1965 World Series, remembered in a 1998 interview standing next to Koufax for pregame publicity photos and having his eyes water from the strong smell of the Capsolin. The ointment heated up the arm, said Kaat, and killed the pain. After the game, Dodgers trainers filled a small plastic tub with crushed ice, dropping the water temperature to 35 degrees, and Koufax would submerge his pitching arm in the freezing water for 35 to 45 minutes.[9]

Eight days before defeating Spahn and the Mets on June 20, Koufax had taken the mound on a sunlit Saturday in Shea Stadium seeking his 11th victory in 12 career starts against New York. By the game's end, his 5-0 shutout had raised his career mark against the Mets to 11-0 and lowered his career ERA

against them to 1.00. He told reporters that he didn't have a good curveball that afternoon; instead, he challenged the Mets with his fastball.[10]

When the Mets mounted even a modest rally, Koufax, according to Joseph Sheehan of the *New York Times*, "put an end to that nonsense."[11]

Five days after his victory over Spahn, Koufax returned to the Dodger Stadium mound and again allowed just one run and struck out 12 in beating Bob Friend and Pittsburgh. Four days later Koufax climbed the hill in San Francisco's Candlestick Park, struck out 10, including future Hall of Fame sluggers Willie Mays and Willie McCovey, and won 9-3.

On Saturday night, July 3, Koufax fanned 10 to beat the Astros beneath the plastic sky of the new Houston Astrodome. It was his fourth straight game of 10 or more strikeouts and his seventh consecutive complete-game victory.

The All-Star break found the Dodgers trailing the first-place Reds by three percentage points. The hotly contested race saw San Francisco 3 games back of Cincinnati, Philadelphia 3½, and Milwaukee 5½ games out.

Koufax's remarkable streaks of consecutive complete games and strikeouts ended abruptly in his next outing, a 7-6 defeat on July 7, which saw Cincinnati score five runs in the first two innings at Crosley Field and drive Koufax off the mound in the fifth. Because the Dodgers rallied to tie the game at 6-6 in the eighth inning, Koufax was not the pitcher of record at game's end.

The defeat dropped the Dodgers into a first-place tie with the Reds. Four days later, in the first game of a Sunday doubleheader in Pittsburgh, Koufax survived a two-run first inning and then slammed the door on the Pirates. Koufax got a run back in the third with an RBI single and the Dodgers added two more runs in the fourth and one in the eighth to claim a 4-2 win.

The complete-game victory, in which Koufax struck out 10, raised his record to 15-3 and allowed the Dodgers to remain tied for first place. Returning to Dodger Stadium, Koufax kept LA tied with Cincinnati with a four-hit shutout of Chicago on July 16, and his 3-2 victory over Houston four days later allowed the Dodgers to increase their cushion atop the standings to 3½ games. Once again Koufax helped his own cause. With the Dodgers tied with the Astros at 2-2 in the ninth inning, LA manager Walter Alston allowed Koufax to bat rather than be pinch-hit for, and Koufax singled to left, scoring Jim Lefebvre with the winning run.

The superlative pitching of Koufax and the rest of the Dodgers' staff was crucial, since LA ranked ninth in the league in runs scored, due in part to the mounting injuries the club continued to suffer. The Dodgers' bench grew so short that Alston had his pitchers hit for themselves in clutch situations and used Drysdale as a pinch-hitter. That Drysdale often came through is evident by his batting average of .300 and slugging average of .508 that season.

The Dodgers dropped decisions in each of Koufax's next two outings, though he took the loss in only one. With LA's lead melting in the summer months, Koufax went the route in a 3-2 win in St. Louis as the calendar flipped to August. The Dodgers led the Reds by 1½ games and were 3½ ahead of the Braves and 4 games in front of the Giants.

On August 8 the Dodgers made national headlines with an 18-0 loss in Cincinnati. Koufax returned his team to normalcy in his next outing, a complete-game 4-3 win in which he fanned 14 Mets and won his 20th game for the second time in his career.

Koufax improved to 21-4 in his next mound appearance, a 1-0 victory over the Pirates on August 14 in which he struck out 12, did not walk a batter, and scattered five hits. Four days later, Koufax matched up against Jim Bunning but neither great pitcher figured in the decision in a 6-3 Phillies win.

On Sunday, August 22, Koufax and Giants ace Juan Marichal opposed one another in a much-anticipated matchup that would result in one of the more infamous games in major-league history. What should have been a memorable mound duel between two all-time greats engaged in a pressure-packed pennant race was marred by one of the sport's all-time ugliest incidents – Marichal attacking Roseboro with his bat after the catcher buzzed the Giants hitter's head as he returned the ball to Koufax. Claiming the ball nicked his ear, Marichal bloodied Roseboro before Mays, Koufax, and others restored peace.

The loss started a streak of four straight games in which the Dodgers dropped a game started by Koufax, who may have been still shaken by the Marichal-Roseboro brawl. Four days later, on August 26, Koufax absorbed his second straight defeat, 5-2 in Shea Stadium in a game that future ace reliever Tug McGraw started for the Mets and earned the win. After working seven innings in New York, Koufax was back on the mound two nights later in Philadelphia, pitching the ninth inning to earn a save in an 8-4 win over the fading Phillies in Connie Mack Stadium. The save was his first of the season and the eighth in his career.

The first day of September saw Koufax drop his third straight start, losing to the Pirates 3-2 when Jim Pagliaroni reached him for a two-out double to left field to score Willie Stargell. Stargell's strikeout in the fourth inning was number 307 on the season for Koufax, the most by a National League pitcher in 73 years.[12]

The game featured an intriguing pitcher-hitter duel between Koufax and Roberto Clemente in the bottom of the sixth. According to the *Pittsburgh Press*, Clemente fouled off "at least 15 pitches" from Koufax before going down on a swinging strikeout.[13]

Koufax struck out 10 in 11 innings in a game rescheduled from the day before due to rain, but the afternoon loss left LA tied for first with the Reds. In the post-mortem, Koufax told reporters that he threw a bad pitch and Pagliaroni hit it good.

Another one-run defeat in that night's game dropped the Dodgers into second place, one percentage point behind Cincinnati.

The NL race listed five teams within 2½ games of first place. Opposing fellow future Hall of Fame pitcher Robin Roberts in the Astrodome on Sunday, September 5, Koufax worked seven innings but did not get a decision in a 4-2 win. The pressure of a pennant race now in its stretch run was such that even the usually unflappable Koufax was affected. After the game Koufax reportedly stormed into the Dodgers locker room, overturned a training table, and threw it against the wall.

When Koufax strode to the Dodger Stadium mound for a Thursday night game against the Cubs on September 9, LA was on a two-game losing streak and had fallen a half-game out of first place. Once again, he was called upon to be the Dodgers' stopper. Leading off for Chicago and making his major-league debut was center fielder Don Young. Koufax got Young on a pop fly to second baseman Jim Lefebvre, and then fanned both Glenn Beckert and Billy Williams looking.

Though the mound matchup looked like a mismatch – the 21-7 Koufax versus the 2-2 Bob Hendley – the Cubs southpaw matched the legendary lefty pitch for pitch, inning by inning. Koufax had five strikeouts through the first four frames; Hendley, on the other hand, retired the Dodgers on a series of groundouts and fly outs. Each had a no-hitter heading into the fifth inning, and the Dodgers broke up the scoreless tie without benefit of a base hit. Johnson led off with a walk, was sacrificed to second, stole third, and scored on catcher Chris Krug's throwing error.

Johnson's walk ended Hendley's perfect-game bid, and his two-out double past first baseman Ernie Banks in the seventh broke up the no-hitter. Koufax, meanwhile, kept the Cubs in check and he said afterward that the seventh inning was when he felt he had a shot at a perfect game.[14]

Koufax whiffed Ron Santo, Banks, and Byron Browne in the eighth. On the verge of baseball history, he finished with a flourish, striking out the side – Krug, Joey Amalfitano, Harvey Kuenn – in the ninth.

"The last three innings I had the best stuff I threw all night, and perhaps all year," Koufax told reporters.[15]

He said he used high heat to set up his breaking pitches. "I had a real good fastball, and that sort of helps your curve," Koufax remarked to reporters.

Frank Finch wrote in the next day's *Los Angeles Times* that Koufax was "[a] Michelangelo among pitchers."[16]

Koufax and Hendley produced more drama five days later in Wrigley Field, though it was the Cubs hurler outpitching the Dodgers' ace with a complete-game 2-1 win. Koufax's no-hit streak lasted one-third of an inning before Beckert doubled to right field.

The loss left the Dodgers 3½ games out of first place, and another loss the next day, the team's third straight, dropped them 4½ games back in mid-September. The season was expiring, and so were the Dodgers' dreams of the pennant. Koufax helped halt the slide the following day, claiming his second save of the season by working the ninth inning in a 2-0 victory over the Cubs. The victory sparked a win streak that eventually reached 13.

Two days later, on September 18, Koufax blanked the defending World Series champion Cardinals 1-0 in Busch Stadium. His complete-game four-hitter kept the Dodgers at 3½ games back with 13 to play.

On September 22 Koufax toed the rubber in Milwaukee's County Stadium and was knocked out in the third inning against the Braves, giving up five runs on six hits. It was one of his shortest starts of the season, but the Dodgers rallied to win 7-6 in 11 innings. The dramatic victory allowed LA to cut its deficit to two games, and three days later Koufax overcame pain and fatigue to fan 12 in a 2-0 win over the Cardinals.

In a day game in Dodger Stadium on September 29, Koufax contributed to Cincinnati's slide with a 5-0 victory that gave him his second straight shutout. Fanning 13, he fired a complete-game two-hitter that lifted LA to a two-game lead over San Francisco with four games to go in the torrid race.

The Dodgers' next to last game of the regular season had them hosting the Braves before a Saturday afternoon crowd of 41,574. Pitching through pain once again, Koufax overcame his chronic sore elbow and a Milwaukee lineup featuring Hank Aaron, Felipe Alou, and Joe Torre. The dangerous trio went a combined 0-for-10 with five strikeouts as Koufax threw his third straight complete-game victory. Striking out 13 for the second straight time, Koufax with his four-hit, 3-1 win clinched the Dodgers' second pennant in three seasons.

After Johnson caught Denis Menke's fly ball to left field for the game's final out, Finch wrote in the *LA Times* that the "magnificent Sandy Koufax" had made the anemic offense provided by the Dodgers – two hits, both by Lefebvre – stand up.

The Dodgers' stretch drive had seen them win 14 of their final 15 games and turn a 4½-game deficit into a two-game margin of victory. Koufax contributed four complete-game victories and a save to the streak, and he finished the regular season by leading the league in wins (26), winning percentage (.765), ERA (2.04), complete games (27), innings pitched (335⅔), and strikeouts (382).

It was enough to earn him his second Cy Young Award in three seasons. In an era when the award was given to only one pitcher across the major leagues, Koufax claimed all 20 first-place votes. He finished second to Mays in the MVP balloting, totaling 177 vote points to Mays' 224.

Koufax continued his dominance in the World Series. After losing Game Two, 5-1, to fellow future Hall of Famer Kaat in Minnesota, he returned to the Dodger Stadium mound and blanked the Twins 7-0 in Game Five to give LA a 3-2 Series lead. Three days later, amid partly sunny and cool conditions on October 14, Koufax pitched what is arguably the signature game of his great career in Game Seven.

Facing Kaat again in Metropolitan Stadium in the rubber match between the two, Koufax overcame an arthritic elbow aching from extreme fatigue and an ineffective curveball and challenged the Twins' top hitters – Harmon Killebrew, Tony Oliva, Don Mincher, et al. – with his blazing fastball. With the World Series on the line, a weary, injured Koufax struck out 10, walked three, and allowed only three hits in a 2-0 victory.

Oliva faced many great pitchers in his career but recalled in a 1999 interview that Koufax was something special. Oliva said Koufax's pitches did something different from other pitchers.

Everyone knew Koufax threw hard, said Oliva, but the fact that he threw every pitch from the same over-the-top motion made it difficult to pick up his pitches. Oliva said the Twins realized what their National League counterparts already knew, and that was that Koufax's curve went straight down, and his high-90s fastball seemed to sail upward. Every delivery was the same, said Oliva, and every pitch was off the same motion.[17]

Oliva was a professional hitter, owning quick wrists and excellent bat control. But he remembered struggling to catch up to Koufax's fastball, which Oliva believed approached 100 mph with great movement. Koufax threw hard, Oliva remembered, and he said there weren't too many hitters who could hit a fastball that had as much movement as the ones fired by Koufax.

Killebrew recalled being impressed by Koufax's outstanding fastball and great control. He said Koufax's curveball looked like his fastball before dropping straight down, and what he and some of the other hitters on the American League championship squad sought to do against the Dodgers ace was the opposite of what teams like the Giants and Pirates did in the National League.[18]

Hall of Fame second baseman Bill Mazeroski remembered in a 1998 interview that the Pittsburgh Pirates would look for the fastball because even if they looked to hit Koufax's curve they still struggled to connect.[19]

Killebrew said the Twins took the opposite approach and laid off Koufax's high fastball since they didn't believe they could catch up to it.

Kaat, a decent hitting pitcher who batted .247 in 1965, couldn't recall being able to put the ball in play or even hitting a foul ball against Koufax in the World Series. His fastballs, Kaat said, were a blur. Kaat said the feeling in the Twins' dugout as Koufax mowed down one batter after another was almost a feeling of sorrow for the next man up.

The Twins were experiencing what the New York Yankees had dealt with two years earlier, when Koufax won Games One and Four to highlight a stunning sweep of the two-time defending World Series champions. Second baseman Bobby Richardson, a clutch World Series player for the Yankees, remembered in a 1998 interview that Koufax's fastball took off so quickly that he was able to throw it past the Yankees hitters. Richardson recalled Koufax's curve dropping as though it was rolling off a cliff. The Yankees won Series in 1961 and '62, but in '63, Richardson said, Koufax took the wind out of their sails.[20]

The 1965 World Series champions followed a similar path to the pennant in '66. Koufax and Drysdale staged a celebrated joint holdout in spring training over contract disputes, but both signed just before the start of the regular season. While Drysdale followed with a sub-.500 season, Koufax won his first three decisions, including a 4-2 victory over Bob Gibson on April 26 under the lights in Dodger Stadium.

From May 10 to June 10, Koufax won eight straight starts, all of them complete games, to raise his record to 11-1. A 3-0 loss to Houston on June 14 snapped the win streak, but Koufax resumed his winning ways in his next outing, a 3-2 complete-game decision over the Giants.

The Dodgers ace amped up his intensity in the summer. Complete-game victories in his next two outings improved Koufax's record to 14-2. He was 15-4 at the time of the All-Star Game on July 12, and was hugely responsible for the Dodgers not trailing the league-leading Giants by more than five games.

In the 1967 documentary *Portrait of Willie Mays*, aired on ABC-TV and narrated by sportscaster Chris Schenkel, the Giants' superstar said that when Koufax was a young hurler in Brooklyn, he threw hard but couldn't control his pitches. Mays said Koufax now made batters hit his pitch. Willie looked for the breaking ball but said Koufax more often than not challenged him with his fastball.

Norm Sherry, a catcher with the Dodgers from 1959 to '62, said in a 1999 interview that Koufax's transition from being a pitcher who struggled with control to one who could pinpoint them with power and accuracy was startling. Sherry recalled Koufax in his peak years, 1963-66, being able to place his pitches wherever he wanted.[21]

Mays told Schenkel that he loved to face Koufax because he felt he hit well against the Dodgers' ace. He believed that even though Koufax threw hard, his overhand delivery made it easier for Mays to see the pitch and decipher if it was a fastball or breaking ball. Mays said his plan against Koufax was to get on base any way he could and use his speed to try to disrupt Sandy's pitching rhythm and the Dodgers' infield defense.

Koufax's 4-2 win in Shea Stadium in the Dodgers' first game after the All-Star break trimmed their deficit to four games, and by the end of July they were tied for first place in the blistering race. Koufax went 4-3 in August and the Dodgers were three games back entering the regular season's final month. On September 11, Koufax's 4-0 win over Houston in the first game of a Sunday doubleheader in LA lifted the Dodgers into sole control of first place for the first time since June 11.

As he had in 1965, Koufax ratcheted up his game in the season's stretch run. Severe muscle spasms caused his back to seize up in pain on the mound, but Koufax soldiered on as the summer gave way to a golden fall. A 5-1 win over Pittsburgh on September 16 increased the Dodgers' lead to 3½ games. An 11-1 final against the Phillies on September 20 gave Koufax his 25th victory of the summer. A 2-1 loss to Ken Holtzman and the Cubs followed before Koufax equaled his personal best with win number 26, a 2-1 decision over the Cardinals in Busch Stadium.

In the final games of the regular season, the Dodgers were in Connie Mack Stadium for a doubleheader against the Phillies. Koufax was warming up on the mound for the second game amid darkening, overcast skies when he heard the crowd roar behind him. He stopped and turned to look at the cause of the commotion and saw that the stadium scoreboard showed the Giants had won in Pittsburgh. San Francisco's victory meant Koufax had to beat Bunning to nail down the pennant. Pushing himself to the limits of his pain and endurance, Koufax threw so hard that he fell off the mound.

For eight innings Koufax shut out the Phillies on four hits as the Dodgers gave him a six-run lead. But he was exhausted by the ninth inning and the Phillies plated three runs with no outs. Manager Alston visited the mound and told the tired Koufax to stick it out. Cameras captured Koufax going through his mannerisms as he prepared to meet the challenge – touching the back of his blue cap with his left hand and tugging on the bill before rubbing the ball with both hands, staring in for the sign, and then rocking and delivering the pitch.

Firing fastballs in dramatic fashion through the deepening shadows, Koufax retired the side and then raced off the mound in celebration when he fanned Jackie Brandt for his 10th strikeout to end the game.

Koufax's 6-3 win gave him career bests in victories (27) and ERA (1.73). His 41 starts and 27 complete games matched his personal bests from the season before. Koufax led the league for the second straight season in wins, ERA, games started, complete games, innings pitched (323), and strikeouts (317), and paced the NL in shutouts (5) for the third time in four years.

Koufax claimed his second consecutive Cy Young Award and was runner-up in the MVP voting for the second straight year, this time to Clemente.

The excellence Koufax achieved on the mound did not surprise former teammate and fellow pitcher Carl Erskine. In a 1999 interview, Erskine recalled that even in Koufax's early years he had shown spurts of greatness. On any given day, Sandy could be awesome, said Erskine, who added that the potential for consistent dominance on the mound was always there.[22]

As he had the year before, Koufax started Game Two of the World Series, this time facing the Baltimore Orioles, surprise champion of the American League. Just as they had against the Twins in the '65 fall classic, the Dodgers trailed in the World Series 1-0 and looked for Koufax to be their stopper. For the second year in a row, Koufax lost Game Two. The "Kiddie Corps" Orioles scored four runs in six innings, though only one run was earned as the Dodgers committed six errors on the sun-soaked afternoon.

Making his third pressure start in just eight days, the workhorse Koufax was undoubtedly fatigued. Writing in *Sports Illustrated*, Jack Mann thought Koufax "looked tired, he was forcing his pitches." Mann added that the tiring Koufax "failed to impress the Baltimore hitters."[23]

Yet Jim Palmer, a 20-year-old future Hall of Fame pitcher making his World Series debut that day, recalled Koufax's flashing fastballs.

"Radio fastballs," Palmer called them in a 1999 interview. He could hear them, Palmer remembered, but he couldn't see them. Everybody says the ball doesn't jump, that you can't get it to rise, said Palmer. "Well, his ball jumped six to eight inches."[24]

Koufax's rising fastballs were a rising tide that helped lift the Dodgers to league titles in the bruising NL pennant races in 1965 and '66. His arthritic elbow forced his retirement after the '66 World Series, ending an era of dominance.

Boston sportswriter George Sullivan was in Michigan to cover college football's latest "Game of the Century" in November 1966 when Koufax announced his stunning retirement. Sullivan recalled it decades later as the sports equivalent to Pearl Harbor in December 1941, one of those days where people would remember exactly where they were and what they were doing when they heard the news.[25]

NOTES

1 Roger Angell phone interview with the author, 1999.

2 Angell interview.

3 Claude Osteen phone interview with the author, 1998.

4 Ed Roebuck phone interview with the author, 1999.

5 Angell.

6 Associated Press, "Spahn Is Beaten in Pitching Duel: Koufax Limits Braves to 3 Hits and Strikes Out 6 in Gaining 9th Victory," *New York Times*, June 14, 1962.

7 Associated Press, "Koufax Considers Spahn Best Lefty," *South Florida Sun Sentinel* (Fort Lauderdale), October 25, 1999.

8 Dave Anderson phone interview with the author, 1999.

9 Jim Kaat interview with the author, 1998.

10 Joe Trimble, "LA's Koufax Blanks Mets, 5-0, to String 11-0 Mark," *New York Daily News*, June 13, 1965: 144.

11 Joseph Sheehan, "Dodgers Triumph Over Mets by 5-0," *New York Times*, June 13, 1965: S1.

12 Lester J. Biederman, "Stargell Fans as Koufax Sets Record," *Pittsburgh Press*, September 2, 1965: 45.

13 Biederman.

14 "Koufax Eyed 'Perfection' All the Way," *Chicago Tribune*, September 10, 1965: 53.

15 Charles Maher, "Even Koufax Admits Game 'Nearly Perfect,'" *Los Angeles Times*, September 10, 1965: 53.

16 Frank Finch, "Hendley Loses, 1-0, on 1-Hitter," *Los Angeles Times*, September 10, 1965: 45.

17 Tony Oliva phone interview with the author, 1999.

18 Harmon Killebrew phone interview with the author, 1999.

19 Bill Mazeroski phone interview with the author, 1999.

20 Bobby Richardson phone interview with the author, 1999.

21 Norm Sherry phone interview with the author, 1999.

22 Carl Erskine phone interview with the author, 1999.

23 Jack Mann, "A Practical Demonstration of Palmer's Law," *Sports Illustrated*, October 17. 1966: 34.

24 Jim Palmer in-person interview with the author, 1999.

25 George Sullivan phone interview with the author, 1999.

Who Had the Best Final Season?

BY PAUL WHITE

The fact that Sandy Koufax had arthritis in his left elbow was well known for the final two years of his career. He woke up after a spring-training game in 1965 unable to straighten his pitching arm and was flown back to Los Angeles for testing. Koufax made no secret of the fact that he'd been diagnosed with "traumatic arthritis." It was reported in the *Los Angeles Times* as early as April 4 of that year[1] and was mentioned later that year in the broadly syndicated columns of Jim Murray[2] and Dick Young.[3]

In short, everyone knew about it for two years before Koufax announced his retirement. So why, in November of the following year, was the news of his retirement reported as a "bombshell"[4] that left people "stunned?"[5]

The answer likely lies in the fact that he was still pitching better than anybody in baseball. As Jane Leavy said in her wonderful biography of Koufax, "No, what was disconcerting, revolutionary even, was the idea. Athletes don't quit, certainly not after their best season. They don't walk away. They limp away."[6]

Leavy may have overstated her case a bit, because 1966 likely wasn't Koufax's best year. According to Fangraphs WAR, it was his third best, behind 1965 and 1963. According to WAR on Baseball-Reference.com, it was his second best, behind 1963. According to traditional statistics, Koufax did, by the barest of margins, win the most games and have the lowest ERA of his career in 1966, but he also had his worst winning percentage and fewest shutouts since 1962, and his lowest strikeout rate since the Dodgers' first season in Los Angeles, 1958.

Yet Leavy's main point is valid. Koufax was still pitching brilliantly, easily the best pitcher in baseball yet again. He won his third Cy Young Award, and, like the first two, the vote was unanimous. He did not just have a great final season but went out with five successive seasons as the ERA leader, something no other retiree can claim. In addition, he led the league in innings pitched his final two seasons.

Since 1966 proved to be his final season, the question has long been asked if it's the finest final season anyone has ever had.

As with most things in life, the answer is: "It depends."

What it depends upon lies in how we choose to define our terms. For instance, are we only talking about baseball players? Because, if we're not, then Koufax may not even have had the best final season among athletes whose final game was played in 1966. Jim Brown's final season with the Cleveland Browns was 1965 (his final game was played on January 2, 1966), and all he did was lead the NFL in rushing, total yards, and touchdowns while winning his fourth league MVP award.

Because it's virtually impossible to compare a baseball season to a football season, it makes sense to limit the discussion to just the one sport that Koufax played.

That still leaves us with a few terms to define. Do we mean a player's final full season, excluding any part-time years that may have finished his career? If so, it might be hard to surpass someone like Dick McBride of the 1875 Philadelphia Athletics, who won 44 games that season, his final full year in baseball. He pitched in just four games the next year before calling it quits.

That situation seems to be outside the spirit of the exercise though, doesn't it? Koufax walked away after 1966. He didn't come back, pitch four ineffective games in 1967, and then retire. So let's stick with the same standard when comparing him to others.

Speaking of Dick McBride, and other players from baseball's earliest days, what about timeframe? When we say best final season "ever," do we mean in the full statistically recorded history of baseball, all the way back to the nineteenth century, when pitchers were routinely posting preposterous innings-pitched totals, it took six balls to walk a batter, the fielders had no gloves, and batters were out if a foul ball was caught on a bounce?

If we choose to go back that far, it seems impossible for Koufax's final season to be considered superior to Jim Devlin's. As the only pitcher on the roster of the Louisville Grays of the National League in 1877, Devlin threw 559 innings, started and completed all 61 games the team played, won 35 of them, led the league in ERA+, and had a WAR total of 13.2, a mark that has been surpassed in a single season only by Babe Ruth, Walter Johnson, and a few other nineteenth-century pitchers.

That was Devlin's final year as a player because, after the season ended, he confessed to purposely losing games and was banned for life. Still, a final season is a final season, and Devlin's numbers would put him well beyond Koufax in 1966. It's hard for any modern pitcher, even a workhorse like Koufax, to compete with the numbers that can be compiled by the only pitcher on a decent team's roster.

In keeping with the spirit of our other definitions, and the attempt to compare apples to apples (or baseballs to baseballs) on as level a playing field as possible, it seems that nineteenth-century pitchers played under such different circumstances than Koufax that they shouldn't be included in the discussion.

There's another tricky situation to address. Many Negro League players continued their playing careers in leagues that still aren't considered major league. That means some of them had their final official "major league" season when they were in the prime middle years of their careers. Should we be considering those as "final" seasons?

For instance, Charlie "Chino" Smith had a remarkable year in 1929 for the New York Lincoln Giants of the American Negro League. The 28-year-old Smith was in his prime, entering that season with a career major-league batting average of .379. Playing in 66 of the Giants' 68 league games, he led the league with 86 runs scored, 29 doubles, 22 homers, and a batting line of .451/.551/.870. His 1.421 OPS is nearly identical to Barry Bonds' mark in 2004. His WAR total of 5.9 extrapolated to a 162-game season would stand at 14.1, the exact mark Babe Ruth posted in 1923, his only MVP season. It's one of the most spectacular seasons in major-league history, and it's the final major-league season Smith played.

So does that count as one of the great final seasons? We could count it, but the problem is that Smith did nothing to stop playing major-league baseball. In fact, at the time, he wasn't even aware that he was playing "major league" baseball, because the American and National Leagues were the only ones considered "major" at that time by both "organized baseball" and the public in general. Only in 2020 was the American Negro League finally categorized as "major."

Smith kept right on playing when the ANL dissolved after that season, and still for the New York Lincoln Giants. He batted .417 in 1930 and led the Giants to a 37-13 record and a place in a postseason series against the Homestead Grays. In the finale of that series, Smith was injured in a collision with Walter "Rev" Cannady, effectively ending his career.[7] He died in January 1932 at the age of just 30, and for years it was believed that Smith's injury and a case of yellow fever contracted while playing in Cuba led to his death, but more recent research points to cancer of the stomach and pancreas as the cause.[8]

It would be very hard to claim that Koufax's final season in 1966 was better than Smith's season of 1929, but Smith's year was "final" only by technicality. He wasn't retired or injured or banned or even demoted. His team continued as before, just outside the league structure that allows it to be viewed as a major-league team. He continued to play top-caliber baseball past 1929, so this, too, is a type of season that seems to fall outside the point of the discussion.

That leaves us with a field of prospects consisting of baseball players from 1900 forward who were playing in their final season on the field at any level. We still must decide one more term, and that is "finest." When we say a player's final season was the "finest," are we speaking of the finest quantitative performance, i.e., he posted the best statistics, or the most recognized performance, i.e., he received the most accolades?

Looking at just one likely doesn't provide a full picture of the season. There have been wonderful statistical seasons that went virtually unrecognized at the time, (John Valentin in 1995, for example[9]), just as there have been seasons rewarded with various honors that likely didn't deserve them (such as Pete Vuckovich in 1982).[10] To get the clearest possible picture of the quality of the season in historical context, and in the context of how it was viewed at the time, we need to look at both.

First, the statistics.

Since 1900, only five pitchers have won at least 20 games in their final season: Koufax, 27 in 1966; Lefty Williams, 22 in 1920; Henry Schmidt, 22 in 1903; Eddie Cicotte, 21 in 1920; and Mike Mussina, 20 in 2008. Clearly, Koufax has a big advantage here, even before noting that two of his competitors, Williams and Cicotte, should lose a few accolade points since they were banned by baseball for throwing the 1919 World Series. Of these five, Koufax also had the lowest ERA, started the most games, completed the most games, and had the most strikeouts, best ERA+, and highest WAR.

Pitcher wins are somewhat out of vogue now and are certainly harder to come by given modern pitcher usage, so let's shift to ERA, and more particularly ERA+ since that accounts for the differences between ballparks and run-scoring eras. Searching for pitchers in their final major-league season who threw at least 100 innings, had an ERA of 2.50 or better, and an ERA+ of 150 or better, we find just 10 men besides Koufax. Six of them – Max Manning, Bill Byrd, Leon Day, Amos Watson, Roy Welmaker, and Dick Matthews – pitched in the Negro Leagues and all but Matthews pitched after their "final" major-league season, either in Black leagues not currently considered major, Mexican baseball, or the minor leagues. There is no known record of Matthews pitching again, but his 2.17 ERA and 161 ERA+ don't approach Koufax's marks of 1.73 and 190, respectively, and didn't lead his league as Koufax did.

Of the four remaining pitchers – Larry French, J.R. Richard, Ned Garvin, and John Tudor – French's 180 ERA+ in 1942 came the closest to Koufax, but he did it in almost 200 fewer innings. Ned Garvin's 1.72 ERA in 1904 was a point better than Koufax's mark, but in 130 fewer innings and in a much lower run-scoring environment as indicated by his much lower ERA+ of 159. None of the 10 men led their respective leagues in either ERA or ERA+ as Koufax did.

Let's move on to strikeouts. Koufax fanned 317 hitters in 1966, leading the National League. The next closest pitcher was José Fernández, who had 253 strikeouts in 2016 before tragically dying in a boating accident at the end of that season. No other pitcher surpassed even 200 strikeouts in his final season, and the only pitchers to lead their league in strikeouts in their final season, as Koufax did, were Leon Day in 1946, and Jim LaMarque in 1948, and both continued their careers elsewhere after those seasons.

Shifting to WAR from baseball-reference.com, we find no pitcher anywhere near Koufax's mark of 10.3 in his final season. The closest was José Leblanc in 1921, when he had 6.2 WAR to lead the Negro National League, but he pitched after that season in Cuba. Other pitchers also led their respective leagues in WAR, but they were all Negro Leagues pitchers, too, and all played somewhere after their final "major league" season, except for the aforementioned Dick Matthews, whose 3.8 WAR in the Negro Southern League, for a team that played just 48 league games, would extrapolate to 12.8 WAR over a 162-game season, so we shouldn't simply ignore it. On the other hand, it's a record posted by a pitcher who was never heard from again, playing in a league that existed for just one season, and we must project performance to put him in the same class as Koufax. It seems safe to go ahead and pass him over as a candidate.

Moving along to accolades, this is a pretty short discussion when it comes to pitchers. There have been 124 Cy Young Awards handed out through the 2022 season. Just one of those was given to a pitcher who was playing his final season – Koufax in 1966. 'Nuff said.

It's clear that no pitcher in the modern era had a final season as good as Koufax had. If we're going to find a player to challenge him, it will have to be a position player. We'll examine the Triple Crown statistics first.

Just eight players have hit as many home runs in their final season as Koufax had wins, 27. The most was 38 by David Ortiz in 2016, but he fell considerably short of leading the league, as Koufax did in wins. Ortiz finished tied for eighth, nine homers behind Mark Trumbo. If we were considering Charlie Smith, we'd have to account for the fact that he led the American Negro League with 22 homers, which projects to 52 for a 162-game season, but we've already noted that 1929 wasn't really Smith's final season. Bill Pierce, Willard Brown, Tom Finley, and Lester Lockett, who led their respective leagues in homers in their final major-league seasons, are all eliminated for the same reason.

But a different Negro Leagues legend is in the running. Josh Gibson led the Negro National League with 13 homers in 1946, his final season before tragically dying that winter of a stroke. He played in just 48 of the Homestead Grays' 77 league games, so his homer total projects to 27 over a 162-game season. Impressive enough to lead that league, but not a particularly notable figure by itself. Gibson's ongoing health issues were already taking a toll on his performance. Other than homers and slugging, he didn't lead the league in any offensive categories, and his 2.4 WAR projects to just 5.0 for 162 games, less than half of Koufax's mark in 1966.

Shifting to RBIs, the case for David Ortiz in 2016 becomes stronger. He led the American League with 127 RBIs, the most ever compiled in a final big-league season. Some Negro Leagues players who weren't actually playing their final seasons also managed to lead their league, but the only player besides Ortiz to lead his league in RBIs in his final year was Turkey Stearnes in 1940, when he drove home 33 runs to lead the Negro American League. That projects to just 107 in a 162-game year, well short of Ortiz's mark, and the rest of his numbers that year weren't particularly noteworthy.

So how strong a candidate is Ortiz for the title of having the finest final season ever? His homerun and RBI totals are impressive, and he also led the American League with 48 doubles, a .620 slugging percentage, and an OPS of 1.021. But he totaled just 5.2 WAR due to his complete lack of defense as a designated hitter, and even his offensive WAR only wasn't in the top 10 in the league. He finished sixth in the MVP voting that season, compared to Koufax winning the Cy Young and finishing second in MVP voting. Overall, we'd have to conclude that Ortiz's final year, though impressive, falls short of Koufax.

There have been some remarkable batting averages posted in players' final seasons, like Charlie Smith's .451 mark in 1929 and Tetelo Vargas's .471 average in 1943, but most of them were achieved by Negro Leagues players who continued their careers in non-major-league venues, including all three of the players who won batting titles in their final big-league seasons. But there is one noteworthy player who hit .382 in his final season that we need to examine more closely.

Joe Jackson, of Black Sox infamy, was third in the AL with that .382 average in 1920. He also led the league with 20 triples, and had an OPS+ of 172, short of Koufax's ERA+ of 190 in his final year, but still impressive and good for third in the league. He finished the season with 7.5 WAR (or 7.9 in a 162-game year), well behind several other players in 1920, but still the highest WAR total for any hitter in his final season. Others, like the seemingly omnipresent Charlie Smith, posted marks that project to a higher total, but remain ineligible for the title due to their continued careers.

Sandy Koufax posted a career-low 1.73 ERA in his final season with the Dodgers and struck out 317 batters. SABR: The Rucker Archive.

So Jackson may have the best claim so far, but he has the obvious drawbacks of falling short of Koufax in accolades (there was no MVP award that year) and in league-leading performances, plus whatever negative points we care to assign for being banned for life after the season due to his involvement in the Black Sox scandal. Ultimately, we'd have to say that Shoeless Joe isn't a contender for the title either.

Speaking of the MVP award, no one has ever won the award in their final season. The closest anyone has come was … Koufax, who finished second in 1966.

All things considered, given the parameters we established at the beginning, the answer to the question of who had the finest final season in major-league history seems obvious. Everyone is free to determine their own standards, though, so if you feel nineteenth-century players deserve consideration, then crown Jim Devlin or Dick McBride or some other candidate. Or include Negro Leaguers even if they continued playing elsewhere when their "major league" careers ended. Granting Charlie Smith, for instance, this small dose of attention and fame certainly wouldn't be inappropriate given the lack of attention he received in life.

But until those rules are redefined, baseball's finest final season belongs to Sandy Koufax.

SOURCES

In addition to the sources cited in the Notes, the author consulted Baseball-Reference.com and Fangraphs.com for any pertinent information, including career statistics.

NOTES

1   Sid Ziff, "Say It Isn't So," *Los Angeles Times*, April 4, 1965: D-3.

2   Jim Murray, "Arm & Hammer," *Los Angeles Times*, May 14, 1965: 43.

3   Dick Young, "Young Ideas," *New York Daily News*, August 12, 1965: 283.

4   Alex Kahn, "Dodgers Need a New Star," *Los Angeles Evening Citizen News*, November 19, 1966: 10.

5   "Arthritis Finally K's Koo's Career," *New York Daily News*, November 19, 1966: 251.

6   Jan Leavy, *Sandy Koufax: A Lefty's Legacy* (New York: Harper Perennial, 2003), 238.

7   John Holway, "Charlie 'Chino' Smith," *The Baseball Research Journal*, 1978. Retrieved from https://sabr.org/journal/article/charlie-chino-smith/.

8   Gary Ashwill, "The Death (And Life) of Charles 'Chino' Smith," www.agatetype.typepad.com, April 7, 2011. Retrieved from https://agatetype.typepad.com/agate_type/2011/04/the-death-and-life-of-charles-chino-smith.html.

9   In 1995 Valentin had one of the most unrecognized great seasons in recent memory, displaying both power (27 homers) and speed (20 steals in 25 attempts) while playing excellent defense at shortstop. He led the AL in both overall WAR (8.3) and defensive WAR (3.0), yet wasn't selected as an All-Star, didn't win a Gold Glove, and finished just 9th in MVP voting while his teammate, Mo Vaughn, was given the award. See Mark Feinsand, "This Was a Divisive MVP Choice, So We Re-Voted…" MLB.com, April 2, 2020. Retrieved from https://www.mlb.com/news/re-vote-for-1995-al-mvp-award.

10 Andrew Stoeten, "How Dave Stieb Was Robbed of the 1982 AL Cy Young Award, and What It's Still Costing Him Today," *The Athletic*, November 7, 1982. Retrieved from https://theathletic.com/1317127/2019/11/07/how-dave-stieb-was-robbed-of-the-1982-al-cy-young-award-and-what-its-still-costing-him-today/. v

First Among Equals

BY LARRY DEFILLIPO

In the run-up to the 1970 season, Commissioner Bowie Kuhn shared plans to continue minor-league trials with what became the designated hitter, begin another trial with livelier baseballs, and explore "bending" foul lines outward by 3 degrees(!). All those prospective changes were designed to tip the balance back to offense, after what Kuhn called "a decade for the pitchers."[1]

Three pitchers stood above all others in making the '60s so; Sandy Koufax, Bob Gibson, and Juan Marichal. And, like Michelangelo, da Vinci, and Raphael, Florentine rivals of the sixteenth century, each excelled with an artistry all his own.

No pitcher in the major leagues won more games (191), threw more shutouts (45), completed more games (197), or compiled a higher WAR (55.3) in the 1960s than Marichal did with his trademark high leg kick. Gibson's unblinking ferocity paved the way for his decade-high 2,071 strikeouts. The highest winning percentage (.695), lowest ERA (2.36), and lowest WHIP (1.005) of any pitcher who hurled 1,200 innings or more in the 1960s (as 66 did) belonged to Koufax, an over-the-top flamethrowing southpaw.

Marichal, Gibson, and Koufax finished one-two-three in cumulative pitcher WAR across the majors in the 1960s. The pecking order changed to Koufax, Marichal, and Gibson for that decade's lowest ERA. The trio also took three of the top four spots in complete games and shutouts.[2]

So dominant were Koufax, Gibson, and Marichal during the seven years in which their careers overlapped (1960-1966), it's surprising the trio appeared together just once on a Topps league-leaders trading card – the 1967 NL Pitching (Wins) Leaders, card #236.

Sandy Koufax pitched 14 complete games in which he gave up two hits or fewer. *Courtesy of National Baseball Hall of Fame.*

Past Assessments

In his eponymous *NEW Historical Baseball Abstract*, sabermetrician Bill James in 2001 used Win Shares, a measure he devised, to compare player contributions across eras, taking into account total, peak (top three and five-year subtotals) and season-average values. Using those values, and subjective adjustments for performance relative to peers of the same era, James ranked Gibson as the number 8 pitcher all-time, Koufax as number 10, and Marichal as number 21.[3]

In 2010 Michael W of *Bleacher Report* ranked the top pitchers of the 1960s by comparing raw career totals, adjusted career totals (eliminating partial or poor seasons), and peak career totals for a slate of traditional (G, GS, innings, ERA, W, H/9, WHIP, SHO, K, etc.) and advanced (ERA+ and one of his own creation, W%+) pitching metrics. Michael W rated Marichal first, followed by Gibson and Koufax. Marichal trumps Koufax in his analysis due to the longer timespan over which Marichal performed at a high level and tops Gibson by outperforming him in six of nine key metrics during his peak years.[4]

A 2014 analysis by Mark Stoler published in the *Things Have Changed* blog compared Koufax's performance in 1963 through 1966 to peak four-year spans for Gibson and Marichal, defined as 1966 to 1969 for each of them. This comparison showed that at their peaks, Koufax stood above Marichal and Gibson in winning percentage when supported by three runs or fewer (.689 vs .578 vs .490 respectively). Stoler reported that Koufax and Marichal each won 75 percent of the 1-0 and 2-1 games that they started in their peak years, but the author's analysis found Koufax earned one fewer victory in those contests than Stoler tallied (17 vs. 18), dropping his winning percentage to a still-impressive 74 percent.[5]

This Assessment

In this article, Koufax, Gibson, and Marichal are compared in categories that include repertoire, debuts and farewells, career pitching totals, top seasons, key splits, head-to-head, high-profile games, and recognition. A review of individual games in which Koufax, Gibson, and Marichal opposed one another, authored by Carter Cromwell, can be found elsewhere in this publication.

REPERTOIRE

Koufax, 6-feet-2 and 210 pounds at his peak, dominated batters with a high-riding (often described as rising) four-seam fastball and a devastating overhand curve. Long fingers and big hands enabled the left-hander to deliver curveballs that broke straight down.[6]

Gibson relied on a four-seam fastball that he liked to throw high, a slider he could sweep or drop nearly vertical and a curveball he took years to perfect.[7] Standing 6-feet-1 and 185 pounds, Gibson was a fast worker, so much so that legendary Dodgers broadcaster Vin Scully once said, "Gibson pitches like he's double parked."[8]

Marichal boasted a five-pitch arsenal that included a slider, fastball, changeup, curve, and screwball, all delivered in either a three-quarters or over-the top-motion by the 6-foot, 185-pound Dominican. "Gibson and Koufax blew hitters away," according to SABR author Jan Finkel. "Marichal toyed with them, embarrassed them."[9]

DEBUTS AND FAREWELLS

Koufax was a 19-year-old bonus baby when he debuted for Brooklyn in relief against the Milwaukee Braves in 1955, having never played a game in the minors. He pitched two scoreless innings with a pair of strikeouts, the first coming against Brooklyn nemesis Bobby Thomson. Koufax was not yet 31 when he pitched his last game, a six-inning losing start against the Baltimore Orioles in Game Two of the 1966 World Series.

Marichal was signed as an amateur free agent in 1957 and spent 2½ seasons in the minors before making his major-league debut at the age of 22: a one-hit shutout over the Philadelphia Phillies.[10] Marichal's last appearance was as a Dodger, when at the age of 37 he made an abbreviated start in April 1975 against the Big Red Machine, the Cincinnati Reds.

An accomplished baseball and basketball player at Creighton University, Gibson split his time between the Harlem Globetrotters and Triple-A Omaha in 1957, his first year as a professional. He was 23 years old when he debuted in relief against the Dodgers during that team's first week in Los Angeles, allowing two earned runs in two innings. Gibson was two months shy of turning 40 when he appeared in his final game, taking the loss after an ineffective inning of relief against the Chicago Cubs in September 1975.

CAREER PITCHING TOTALS

Cumulative

	Yrs	WAR	G	GS	CG	SHO	SV	W	L	SO	BB
Koufax	12	53.1	397	314	137	40	9	165	87	2396	817
Gibson	17	81.7	528	482	255	56	6	251	174	3117	1336
Marichal	16	61.8	471	457	244	52	2	243	142	2303	709

Blessed with good health through most of their careers, Gibson and Marichal pitched significantly longer than Koufax did. Circulatory problems in his throwing arm that first appeared in 1962 cut Koufax's career short after 12 seasons. Each pitcher spent time as a reliever or occasional starter early in his career; Koufax for his three seasons in Brooklyn (1955-1957), Gibson for his first two years (1959 and 1960), and Marichal in his rookie season (1960).

While Marichal topped the trio in 1960s WAR, Gibson came out ahead in career WAR. He also started and completed the most games of the trio, finishing 53 percent of his starts, as did Marichal. Gibson compiled the most shutouts, though Koufax turned a higher percentage of his starts into shutouts than either Gibson or Marichal did (13 percent vs. 12 percent and 11 percent respectively).

Gibson collected more victories than Marichal or Koufax, but was a distant third to Koufax and then Marichal in winning percentage (.591 vs. .655 and .631 respectively).

Gibson was the only member of the group to top 3,000 strikeouts, ranking second all-time when he retired, behind only Walter Johnson. Gibson had 74 double-digit strikeout games, dwarfing Marichal's 25 but exceeded by the 97 that Koufax authored.

Ratios

	ERA	WHIP	SO/BB	SO per 9	BAA	FIP
Koufax	2.76	1.106	2.93	9.3	.205	2.69
Gibson	2.91	1.188	2.33	7.2	.228	2.89
Marichal	2.89	1.101	3.25	5.9	.237	3.04

Koufax topped both Gibson and Marichal in career ERA, despite an ERA after his first six seasons that was over three-quarters of a run higher than at the same point of their careers (4.10 vs. 3.32 and 2.75 respectively). Koufax's ERA from 1961 to 1966 was a sterling 2.19. Koufax allowed five or more earned runs in only 9 percent of his starts (27 times), and never allowed more than six, versus 17 percent for Gibson and 13 percent for Marichal.

Marichal eked out Koufax for lowest career WHIP of the trio (1.101 to 1.106), equivalent to allowing five fewer baserunners per 1,000 innings than the Dodgers ace. A control specialist, Marichal also maintained a higher strikeout-to-walk ratio than either Koufax or Gibson.

Koufax was the only one of the three to fan more than a batter per inning, a career rate unmatched by any pitcher who threw 700 innings or more until Nolan Ryan reached that threshold. Koufax also maintained the lowest FIP and held hitters to the lowest batting average, the latter nearly 50 points below league average over his career.

TOP SEASONS

Best Season (by WAR)

	Year	WAR	W	L	SHO	IP	SO	BB	ERA	WHIP	BAA
Koufax	1963	10.7	25	5	11	311	306	58	1.88	0.875	.189
Gibson	1968	11.2	22	9	13	304.2	268	62	1.12	0.853	.184
Marichal	1965	10.3	22	13	10	295.1	240	46	2.13	0.914	.205

Gibson's historic 1968 season stands apart from the best season posted by either Koufax or Marichal. The first National League pitcher to compile 13 shutouts (or a WAR higher than 11) since Grover Cleveland Alexander, Gibson posted an ERA in 1968 more than a half-run lower than Koufax's in 1963 and a full run lower than Marichal's 1965 campaign. Gibson's WHIP and BAA in 1968 were also superior to Koufax and Marichal's figures for their best seasons.

Koufax's second-best season as measured by WAR was in many ways superior to this best. In 1966, his final season, he posted a 10.3 WAR with a career-high 27 wins, a career-low ERA, and strikeout and WHIP numbers superior to those in his 1963 campaign. All with a painful, arthritic left arm that would end his career soon after.

Gibson and Koufax each earned both MVP and Cy Young Awards during their best WAR season. Marichal led the NL in WAR during his best WAR year but came in ninth in MVP voting behind teammate Willie Mays and saw Koufax become a unanimous Cy Young Award winner.

Number of Years Leading the Pack

Major Lgs	WAR	CG	W	SHO	SO	SO/9	SO/BB	BB/9	ERA	WHIP
Koufax	2	2	3 (1T)	2 (1T)	4	3	2	0	3	3
Gibson	2	1	0	3 (2T)	0	0	0	0	1	0
Marichal	1	2	1T	1	0	0	2	2	1	1

NL	WAR	IP	W	SHO	SO	SO/9	SO/BB	BB/9	ERA	WHIP
Koufax	2	2	3 (1T)	3 (1T)	4	6	3	0	5	4
Gibson	3	0	1T	3 (2T)	1	0	0	0	1	1
Marichal	1	2	2 (1T)	2	0	0	3	4	1	2

T = tied for lead

Koufax sat atop NL and major-league pitching leaderboards more often than either Gibson or Marichal did across their careers. The trio took turns leading the NL in WAR, complete games, wins, and shutouts, but it was Koufax who most often topped the senior circuit in strikeouts, strikeouts per walk, lowest WHIP, and lowest ERA. His six NL crowns for strikeouts per

nine innings were the most since Brooklyn Dodger Dazzy Vance, and his four consecutive WHIP titles were last equaled by Carl Hubbell. Koufax was the first NL pitcher to win five ERA titles since Christy Mathewson, a feat next matched by Clayton Kershaw in 2017.

Gibson and Marichal also demonstrated leaderboard mastery that took decades to equal. Gibson's three consecutive NL WAR titles were next replicated by Randy Johnson in 2001, and Marichal's four times leading the NL in fewest walks per nine innings stood unmatched until Greg Maddux came along.

KEY SPLITS

Strength of Opponent

	Over .500 Team Winning Percentage	Over .500 Team ERA	Over .500 Team WHIP	Under .500 Team Winning Percentage	Under .500 Team ERA	Under .500 Team WHIP
Koufax	.651	2.75	1.094	.659	2.77	1.120
Gibson	.524	3.18	1.224	.672	2.60	1.146
Marichal	.602	3.05	1.114	.669	2.69	1.086

Koufax's level of regular-season success against good (over .500) teams was essentially identical to how he did against lesser (under .500) teams. His winning percentage was only .008 lower, his ERA was 0.02 *lower*, and his WHIP was 0.026 *lower* when facing winning teams as opposed to have-nots.

Gibson outperformed Koufax against weaker teams but was decidedly less successful against stronger teams, with a winning percentage .148 lower and an ERA over a half-run higher than he registered against sub-.500 teams. Marichal also edged Koufax in his success against sub-.500 teams, with a fall-off against better teams that was less severe than Gibson's.

Home Field Advantage

	Peak Yrs Home Ballpark(s)	Home ERA	Home WHIP	Road ERA	Road WHIP	Average ERA+
Koufax	Dodger Stadium	1.37	0.822	2.57	1.038	168*
Gibson	Busch Stadiums I & II	3.08	1.218	2.76	1.159	127
Marichal	Candlestick Park	2.74	1.075	3.03	1.127	123

*Average of Koufax's season ERA+ values from 1962-1966

Analysts credit Dodger Stadium's high mound and spacious outfield with enabling Koufax to disproportionately dominate at home versus on the road. Home/road splits during the five years that Koufax pitched at Dodger Stadium (1962-1966) confirm that assessment as he compiled an eye-popping 1.37 ERA and 0.822 WHIP at home. His ERA was more than a run higher on the road, where he allowed an average of two more hits plus walks per nine innings.

Gibson, who played his home games at the original Busch Stadium through 1965 and Busch Stadium II beginning in 1966, had reverse splits, with a higher ERA and WHIP at home than on the road. Like Koufax, Marichal was more dominant at home, allowing a quarter of an earned run less at San Francisco's Candlestick Park than he did elsewhere.

Another way to adjust for ballpark influence in evaluating the trio is the adjusted ERA metric, ERA+, which normalizes ERA with three-year park factors and league-average ERAs. Koufax's average ERA+ during the years he pitched at Dodger Stadium is well above career values Gibson and Marichal posted in their home ballparks. Koufax twice posted ERA+ values over 185 while Marichal and Gibson never topped 170. Each led the NL in ERA+ twice, Koufax in 1964 and 1966, Gibson in 1962 and 1968, and Marichal in 1965 and 1969.

Low-Scoring and Close Games

	Winning Percentage when Their Team Scored Two Runs or Fewer	Record in Games Where Final Score was 1-0	Winning Percentage in One-Run Complete Games
Koufax	.378	11-3	.837
Gibson	.250	9-10	.643
Marichal	.237	7-8	.653

Koufax won more than a third of his starts in which he received two runs of support or fewer. Neither Gibson nor Marichal won more than a quarter of theirs. Koufax was significantly more successful in games he started where the final score was 1-0, winning over 75 percent of them. Both Gibson and Marichal lost more often than they won in 1-0 games.

In complete games decided by a single run, Koufax shined, going 36-7. Gibson went 54-30 in one-run complete games, while Marichal was 47-25.

HEAD-TO-HEAD

Against Hall of Famers, Plus One

	HoF + One Position Players Faced (Reg. Season)	PA	HR	SO	BB	BAA	SLG
Koufax	24	1584	54	313	170	.241	.412
Gibson	26	2195	70	388	220	.242	.394
Marichal	30	1865	69	292	129	.271	.440

Against the cream of the crop, Hall of Fame position players plus all-time hits leader Pete Rose (HoFs+1), Koufax edged Gibson for the lowest batting average against. The pair traded places for the lowest slugging percentage allowed. Marichal was a distant third in both categories. Marichal's strikeout-to-walk ratio topped Koufax and Gibson by a wide margin (2.26 versus 1.84 and 1.76, respectively).

Koufax had the most trouble with Hank Aaron, who hit .362 against him with seven home runs. Among HoFs+1 that he faced 20 times or more, Koufax was most dominant against Willie Stargell (2-for-23 with 10 strikeouts) and Willie McCovey (6-for-42 with 15 strikeouts).

Gibson's toughest out among HoFs+1 he faced 20 times or more was Eddie Mathews, who hit .326 off him. Billy Williams touched up Gibson for 45 hits, including 10 home runs, and 31 RBIs, each tops among HoFs+1 he faced. Richie Ashburn and Tony Perez struggled the most against Gibson, batting .118 and .121, respectively, with Perez fanning 28 times in 58 at-bats.

Former teammate Orlando Cepeda proved to be Marichal's Achilles heel among HoFs+1 that he faced 20 times or more, hitting .375 against him. Joe Torre slugged .620 off Marichal and nobody topped Torre's 8 home runs and 26 RBIs against the Dominican Dandy. Ted Simmons (4-for-23) and Stargell (19-for-106 with 27 strikeouts) fared the worst of the group against Marichal.

Confrontations

	HBP (Rate)	Career Ejections	Ejections for Throwing at a Batter	Ejections for Using Bat as a Weapon
Koufax	18 (1 per 129 innings)	1	0	0
Gibson	102 (1 per 38 innings)	5	0	1
Marichal	40 (1 per 88 innings)	2	1	1

Koufax was known to dislike hitting batters. So much so that Hank Aaron was able to crowd the plate without concern for getting plunked. Only once did Koufax admit to purposely throwing at a batter – Lou Brock on May 26, 1965, after he'd stolen second and third two innings earlier.[11] Koufax hit batters an average of only once every 129 innings. Frank Robinson, who scored the last run Koufax ever allowed, in the 1966 World Series, was the only batter Koufax hit more than once.

Gibson claimed he rarely threw at batters but didn't hesitate to stand up for his teammates. "I know when I hit a guy, 99 percent of the time it was because the other team was throwing at guys on my team."[12] Aaron reportedly schooled young Dusty Baker about facing Gibson with these words of wisdom. "Don't dig in against Bob Gibson, he'll knock you down. He'd knock down his own grandmother if she dared to challenge him." Gibson hit batters almost 3½ times more frequently than Koufax did.

From the mound, Marichal had a reputation for brushing back batters from time to time but hit batters only once every 88 innings. As a batter, Marichal carried out the most notorious on-field attack in the modern era. Facing Koufax in the third inning of an August 22, 1965, contest at Candlestick Park, Marichal became incensed when a throw from catcher John Roseboro to Koufax came close to his ear. Marichal clubbed

Roseboro on the head with his bat, giving the Dodger backstop a gash that took 14 stitches to close and triggering a brawl that lasted 14 minutes.

Ironically, the only career ejection for the normally quiet Koufax came from arguing balls and strikes (in 1960), and brushback-prone Gibson was *never* ejected for throwing at a batter. Gibson suffered five ejections, two for bench jockeying, two for arguing calls on the bases, and one for throwing his bat at Phillies pitcher Jack Baldschun right after Baldschun had plunked him. Marichal was ejected twice, once for his attack on Roseboro, and the second time for intentionally hitting Dodgers outfielder Bill Buckner.[13]

HIGH-PROFILE GAMES

Low-Hit Games

	# of No-Hitters	# of One-Hitters	# of Two-Hitters
Koufax	4 (1 perfect game)	2	8
Gibson	1	2	8
Marichal	1	3	6

Koufax stands alone in the number of low-hit games he pitched, with 14 versus 11 for Gibson and 10 for Marichal. Koufax threw four no-hitters, with his second, on May 11, 1963, coming opposite Marichal and the Giants. Koufax's last no-hitter, a perfect game against the Chicago Cubs on September 9, 1965, remains the only one in Dodgers history.

Gibson and Marichal each had one no-hitter in their careers. Gibson threw the first no-hitter at Pittsburgh's Three Rivers Stadium, against the Pirates on August 14, 1971. Marichal's no-hitter on June 15, 1963, against the Houston Colt .45s, was the first one thrown at Candlestick Park.

All-Star Games

	Selections	Appearances/ Starts	IP	H	ER	SO	BB	W	L
Koufax	7	4 (1 start)	6	4	1	3	2	1	0
Gibson	9	6 (1 start)	11	11	4	10	5	0	0
Marichal	10	8 (2 starts)	18	7	1	12	2	2	0

Koufax pitched in four All-Star Games, starting once, in 1966. He allowed one earned run in that start, on a wild pitch after Brooks Robinson tripled on a ball Hank Aaron lost in the background of white shirts.

Gibson pitched in six All-Star Games, and also started only once, in his final appearance, in 1972.

Marichal was on the mound in eight All-Star Games, starting twice, in 1965 and 1967. He earned wins in relief in 1962 and 1964, the latter courtesy of a ninth-inning walk-off home run by Johnny Callison. He was also 1-for-2 at the plate, singling off Mudcat Grant in 1965.

World Series

	# of WS	G	GS	CG	SHO	W	L	SO	BB	ERA	WHIP
Koufax	6	8	7	4	2	4	3	61	11	0.95	0.825
Gibson	3	9	9	8	2	7	2	92	17	1.89	0.889
Marichal	1	1	1	0	0	0	0	4	2	0.00	1.000

Koufax was on the roster but never appeared in two World Series with the Brooklyn Dodgers before pitching in four after the club moved to Los Angeles. He lost his only start in the 1959 World Series, to the Chicago White Sox, then won both starts against the New York Yankees in the 1963 World Series, setting a new Series strikeout record with 15 in Game One. Facing the Minnesota Twins in the 1965 World Series, Koufax won two of three starts, both shutouts, the last a grueling effort at Minnesota's Metropolitan Stadium on two days' rest. Koufax lost what would be the last game of his career to 20-year-old Jim Palmer and the Baltimore Orioles in Game Two of the 1966 World Series. Koufax collected one World Series hit; an RBI single in Game Five of the 1965 Series. He earned World Series MVP honors in 1963 and 1965.

Gibson lost his first and last World Series starts, but earned complete-game victories in all seven of the starts he made in between. He won Game Seven of the 1964 World Series over the Yankees, and three starts over the Boston Red Sox in the 1967 World Series, including another Game Seven victory. In the 1968 World Series, Gibson had a record-setting 17 strikeouts in a Game One shutout of the Detroit Tigers but lost Game Seven. He collected four hits in his World Series appearances, including home runs in both Game Seven of the 1967 Series and Game Four of the 1968 Series. Gibson earned MVP awards for the 1964 and 1967 World Series.

Marichal pitched in one Fall Classic and one NLCS. He started Game Four of the 1962 World Series, holding the Yankees scoreless through four innings, but was forced to leave the game after he injured the thumb on his pitching hand while attempting to bunt. Marichal suffered a complete-game loss to the Pittsburgh Pirates in Game Three of the 1971 NLCS. He was hitless in five postseason at-bats.

HITTING and FIELDING

Career Hitting

	Batting Average	OPS	HR	RBI	Stolen Bases
Koufax	.097	.261	2	28	0
Gibson	.206	.545	24	144	13
Marichal	.165	.393	4	75	2

Gibson towered above Marichal and Koufax at the plate and on the bases. A career .206 hitter, he had a .545 OPS, hit 24 home runs (against 24 different pitchers), drove in 144 runs and stole

13 bases. Marichal slashed an anemic .165/.191/.202 with 4 home runs, while Koufax registered a microscopic .097/.145/.116 with 2 career home runs. His first, in 1962, was off Warren Spahn.

Career Fielding

	# of Golden Gloves	Fielding Percentage	Range Factor per 9 Innings	Stolen Bases Allowed per H+BB+HBP	Pickoffs
Koufax	0	.954	1.13	0.28	5
Gibson	9	.949	1.80	0.42	1
Marichal	0	.949	2.23	0.45	43

Gibson earned nine consecutive Gold Glove awards as the NL's top fielding pitcher from 1965 through 1973. Neither Koufax nor Marichal ever earned one, despite lifetime fielding percentages equivalent to Gibson's.

Marichal's range factor (assists plus putouts) per nine innings was double that of Koufax, enabled in part by the higher number of balls batters put in play against Marichal. (He fanned 3.4 fewer batters per nine innings than Koufax did [5.9 vs. 9.3].) Gibson's range factor falls between those of Koufax and Marichal, in line with his 7.2 strikeouts per nine innings.

To no surprise, Marichal, the high-kicking right-hander, allowed the most stolen bases per hits plus walks plus HBP, a proxy for total baserunners (0.045, or 1 for every 22 baserunners). The southpaw Koufax allowed the fewest (0.028, or 1 per 35), with Gibson between the two (0.416 or 1 per 24). All three suffered caught-stealing percentages in their careers that were below league average.

Marichal picked off 43 runners, roughly one every 11 starts. Koufax picked off five runners in his career, one every 63 starts. Gibson had only *one* pickoff in his career, nabbing Johnny Callison, in 1967. Since 1910, when pickoffs were first tracked, through the 2023 season, no other pitcher with 400 or more starts (a group 119 strong) has fewer than two.

RECOGNITION

Records and Rarities

Koufax set a new NL record for the most strikeouts in a nine-inning game when he fanned 18 Giants on August 31, 1959, and tied that record on April 24, 1962, against the Cubs. His record fell in September of 1969 when Steve Carlton struck out 19 New York Mets.

Koufax's perfect game in September 1965 made him the first major-league pitcher with four no-hitters. Only Nolan Ryan has matched Koufax since, with seven career no-hitters.

Koufax broke Rube Waddell's modern-era major-league record for most strikeouts in a season with 382 in 1965. Eight years later, Nolan Ryan topped Koufax's mark.[14]

In 1966 Koufax became the first three-time pitching Triple Crown winner in either league since earned runs became an official statistic in 1913. No pitcher has matched his feat since then.

Koufax's career ERA at Dodger Stadium, 1.37, is the lowest of any pitcher in any ballpark where he's thrown at least 500 innings since the end of the Deadball Era. The next closest through the end of the 2023 season, Jacob deGrom at New York's Citi Field, has an ERA three-quarters of a run higher.[15]

Gibson's 1.12 ERA in 1968 was the lowest in the NL since the Deadball Era, topped in the twentieth century only by Mordecai "Three-Finger" Brown's 1.04 ERA for the 1906 Chicago Cubs.[16]

Marichal's 243 wins and 2,303 strikeouts were records for Latin American pitchers when he retired in 1975. Cuban-born Luis Tiant passed his strikeout totals in 1980 and Nicaraguan Dennis Martinez topped his win total in 1998. Marichal's 6.167 strikeouts per walk in 1966 tied Christy Mathewson's NL record, set in 1908, and his streak of seven consecutive years with an ERA below 2.80, from 1963 to 1969, had last been matched in the majors by Walter Johnson, who strung together 12 such seasons.[17]

MVP & Cy Young Awards

	MVP Awards	Cy Young Awards
Koufax	1 (1963)	3 (1963, 1965, 1966)
Gibson	1 (1968)	2 (1968, 1970)
Marichal	None	None

Koufax earned three Cy Young Awards, in years when only one award was given across the NL and AL. Gibson collected two NL Cy Young Awards. Koufax and Gibson were each voted NL Most Valuable Player one time, with Koufax also finishing second twice (in 1965 and 1966).

Marichal never received a single first-place vote for a Cy Young Award. His best MVP finish was a distant fifth to Gibson in 1968.

Hall of Fame Balloting

	Year Elected	Pct of Ballots (No.)	Year of Eligibility
Koufax	1972	86.9% (396)	First
Gibson	1981	84% (337)	First
Marichal	1983	83.7% (313)	Third

Koufax became the youngest ballplayer inducted into the Hall of Fame after he was elected in 1972, in his first year of eligibility. Other 1972 inductees included Yogi Berra (named on 85.6 percent of ballots) and Early Wynn (named on 76.0 percent).

In 1981 Gibson became the 11th player elected to the Hall of Fame in his first year of eligibility. No other nominees reached the 75 percent threshold for induction that year.

One of those nominees who fell short in 1981 was Marichal, who was also in his first year of eligibility. He received 233 votes that year (58.1 percent) and 305 (73.5 percent) the next. Finally elected to the Hall of Fame in 1983, he became the first Latin American ballplayer inducted in a general election. Speculation at the time was that some electors refused to vote for Marichal until he made amends to Johnny Roseboro for his 1965 attack, which he did in 1982.[18]

The Final Word

Frank Robinson said that if he won a battle with Gibson, he knew he'd beaten the absolute best.[19] Gibson thought otherwise. Long after he'd retired, he told author Roger Angell that Marichal was the best hurler of his time, because of his absolute control. "I had a better fastball and a better slider, but he was a better pitcher than me or Koufax."[20]

When asked to name the greatest pitcher he'd ever faced, Pete Rose said there were three "Hardest thrower – Koufax. Toughest competitor – Bob Gibson. Most complete pitcher – Juan Marichal[. I]n a jam Marichal could throw any one of five pitches for a strike.[21]

Contrary to the Cooperstown outsider's stance, most Hall of Famers who faced the trio with a bat in their hands considered Koufax king of the hill.[22] Richie Ashburn said of Koufax, "Either he throws the fastest ball I've ever seen, or I'm going blind."[23] According to Willie Stargell, "Hitting against Koufax is like trying to drink coffee with a fork."[24] Stan Musial called Koufax the most overpowering pitcher he ever faced.[25] Bill Mazeroski picked Koufax as the best pitcher of his era. "Gibson approached it," Mazeroski said, "but there was no one better than Sandy Koufax… He was the best I ever saw."[26]

Despite hitting for much lower averages off Gibson (.215) and Marichal (.288) than he did against Koufax (.362), Hank Aaron rated Koufax number one. "You talk about the Gibsons and the Drysdales and the Spahns," he said. "And as good as those guys were, Koufax was a step ahead of them. No matter who he pitched against, he could always be a little bit better. If somebody pitched a one-hitter, he could pitch a no-hitter."[27] Warren Spahn, when asked who was the best pitcher he ever saw, answered "Koufax. What do you think I am, crazy?"[28]

Acknowledgments

The author wishes to thank Bill Nowlin for his feedback during initial editing and Carter Cromwell for providing quotes from Bob Gibson and Pete Rose.

NOTES

1   United Press International, "Baseball Planners Tinker with Training Gimmicks," *York* (Pennsylvania) *Dispatch*, February 11, 1970: C48.

2   The trio also earned the three highest scores in the majors for Context Neutral Wins, reported as WPA/LI, a metric devised in the 2000s to compare players' relative offensive contributions via win expectancy, normalized to the average leverage that player experienced. Koufax finished first, with Marichal and Gibson second and third, respectively. Piper Slowinski, "WPA/LI," Fangraphs website, February 17, 2010, https://library.fangraphs.com/misc/wpa-li/.

3   Bill James, *The NEW Bill James Historical Baseball Abstract* (New York: Free Press, 2001), 846.

4   Michael W defined peak years for Koufax as 1961 through 1966, for Gibson as 1961, 1962, 1966, 1968, 1969, and 1972, and for Marichal

as 1960, 1963, 1964, 1965, 1966, 1968, and 1969. Michael W, "MLB's 10 Best Starting Pitchers of the 1960s: Gibson, Koufax, Marichal?" January 1, 2010, Bleacher Report website, https://bleacherreport. com/articles/317776-mlbs-10-best-starting-pitchers-of-the-1960s- gibson-koufax-marichal.

5   Mark Stoler, "Gibson Koufax Marichal Mashup," Things Have Changed website, April 24, 2014, https://havechanged.blogspot. com/2014/04/gibson-koufax-marichal-mashup.html.

6   Edward Gruver, *Koufax* (Dallas: Taylor Publishing, 2000), 38.

7   Bob Gibson with Phil Pepe, *Ghetto to Glory* (New York: Prentice-Hall, 1968), 56.

8   George Smith, "This 'n That," *Anniston* (Alabama) *Star*, June 22, 1972: 17.

9   Jan Finkel, Juan Marichal SABR biography, https://sabr.org/bioproj/ person/juan-marichal/.

10   In his debut, Marichal retired the first 19 batters he faced and had a no-hitter going until two out in the eighth inning.

11   Jane Leavy, *Sandy Koufax: A Lefty's Legacy* (New York: Harper Collins, 2002), 179.

12   Harold Friend, "MLB: Bob Gibson Blamed the Batter for Getting Hit by One of His Inside Pitches," BleacherReport, September 9, 2011, https://bleacherreport.com/articles/842616-mlb-bob-gibson- blamed-the-batter-for-getting-hit-by-one-of-his-inside-pitches.

13   Marichal hit Buckner after he'd thrown two pitches earlier that inning at the head of Dodgers pitcher Bill Singer, in retaliation for Singer hitting Marichal's teammates Willie Mays and Bill Speier earlier in the game.

14   Koufax continues to hold, as of the end of the 2023 season, Dodgers franchise records for the most strikeouts in a game (his mark of 18 was tied by Ramon Martinez in 1990), season records for the most strikeouts, most shutouts (11), and fewest hits per nine-innings (5.79), and career record for the fewest hits per nine innings among Dodger pitchers who hurled 1,000 innings or more (6.79).

15   Andrew Simon, "11 Stats That Show Why Koufax Is a Legend," MLB.com, December 29, 2022. https://www.mlb.com/news/san- dy-koufax-s-best-stats-and-accomplishments. Koufax's lead over deGrom remains unchanged one year after Simon's analysis.

16   As of the end of the 2023 season, Gibson remains the Cardinals career record holder for wins, losses, strikeouts, starts, complete games, shutouts, innings pitched, FIP for pitchers with 1,000 innings or more, home runs allowed, walks, hit batters, and number of batters faced. He also has the top five Cardinals single-season strikeout totals since 1901; 274 in 1970, 270 in 1965, 269 in 1969, 268 in 1968, and 245 in 1964. Gibson set six Cardinals franchise single-season marks in 1968 that still stand: lowest season ERA, most shutouts, highest ERA+ (258), lowest FIP (1.77), lowest WHIP (0.853), and fewest hits per nine-innings (5.8).

17   Marichal is the San Francisco Giants career record holder through 2023 in wins, losses, strikeouts, starts, complete games, shutouts, innings pitched, hits, runs, home runs allowed, and batters faced. Among San Francisco pitchers with at least 1,000 innings pitched, he has the lowest ERA and lowest WHIP.

18   Gruver, *Koufax*, 185; Stan Hochman, "Marichal Finally Where He Belongs," *Philadelphia Daily News*, January 13, 1983: 84. Jack Lang of the *New York Daily News* speculated soon after Marichal failed to get elected in 1981 that he came up short due to voter reluctance over his attack on Roseboro. Jack Lang, "Hall of Fame: Always a Rift," *New York Daily News*, January 8, 1982: 34.

19 Tim Kurkjian, "In His Day, St. Louis Cardinals Great Bob Gibson Was Feared Like No Other Pitcher," ESPN website, October 3, 2020, https://www.espn.com/mlb/story/_/id/20694447/in-day-st-louis-cardinals-great-bob-gibson-was-feared-no-other-pitcher.

20 "Roger Angell, "Distance: The Game Belongs to Bob Gibson," *The New Yorker*, September 22, 1980: https://www.newyorker.com/magazine/1980/09/22/distance.

21 Roger Kahn, "Opinions and 'Fax,'" *Los Angeles Times*, July 15, 1999: D5.

22 "Marichal Finally Where He Belongs."

23 Jim Murray, "Sandy Is Dandy," *Oakland Tribune*, July 4, 1962: 34.

24 Associated Press, "Hitting Against Koufax Like Drinking Coffee with a Fork," *Appleton* (Wisconsin) *Post-Crescent*, June 26, 1965: B3.

25 Gruver, *Koufax*, 229.

26 Gruver, *Koufax*, 226.

27 Jane Leavy, *Sandy Koufax: A Lefty's Legacy* (New York: Harper Collins, 2002), 2.

28 Gruver, *Koufax*, 8.

Sandy Koufax: Symbol of Jewish Pride

BY WILLIAM M. VINES

On May 27, 2010, President Barack Obama welcomed a group to the East Room of the White House to celebrate the inaugural Jewish American Heritage Month. In his opening remarks, the president observed, "This is a pretty distinguished group. We've got senators and representatives, Supreme Court justices, successful entrepreneurs, rabbinical scholars, Olympic athletes – and Sandy Koufax!" As the crowd laughed, the president quipped, "Sandy and I actually have something in common. He can't pitch on Yom Kippur – and I can't pitch!"[1]

Of all the prominent Jewish Americans in the East Room on that occasion, President Obama singled out just one – Sandy Koufax. This speaks volumes about the iconic, almost mythical status Koufax possesses among Jewish Americans. To non-Jewish baseball fans, Koufax is heralded as one of the greatest left-handed pitchers of all time. But to Jewish baseball fans, Koufax is nothing less than a folk hero, a "public emblem for his people."[2] Koufax's success on the mound resonated deeply with Jewish baseball fans and served as a source of immense pride. As one of the few prominent Jewish players during his era, Koufax became a symbol of Jewish achievement.

During his heyday in the mid-1960s, Koufax was without peer among Jewish American athletes. One familiar line was, "Abraham, Moses and Sandy."[3] Former Commissioner Bud Selig recalled that "every Jewish mother was trying to figure out how her daughter could meet Sandy Koufax."[4] Koufax himself never sought the limelight. Unlike many professional athletes, he was reserved and tended to shy away from publicity. But his lack of self-promotion did nothing to diminish his immense standing among baseball fans, particularly Jewish baseball fans. According to Jack Mendelson, who grew up in the same Brooklyn neighborhood as Koufax, "We were so proud [of Koufax] as Jewish kids. We all felt something, some sort of crazy pride. Back then the

U.S. President Barack Obama shakes hands with Baseball Hall of Fame pitcher Sandy Koufax at the Jewish American Heritage Month reception at the White House. Next to Koufax are his wife Jane Clarke Koufax and entertainer Theodore Bikel. May 27, 2010. Photograph by White House photographer Alex Wong.

Holocaust was still fresh, and so when a kid like that makes it, man, it was tremendous for us."[5]

Koufax, of course, was not the first great Jewish major leaguer. In 1935 Hank Greenberg won the American League Most Valuable Player Award and helped the Detroit Tigers win the World Series.[6] It was a watershed year for Greenberg. He led the American League in RBIs, total bases, and extra-base hits, and tied Jimmie Foxx for the most home runs. Greenberg would eventually be named to five All-Star teams, win another MVP award in 1940, and be inducted into the National Baseball Hall of Fame in 1956. But despite his prowess on the field, Greenberg was forced to endure harsh anti-Semitism throughout his career. Greenberg recalled, "Every ballpark I went to, there'd be somebody in the stands who spent the whole afternoon just calling me names. ... If you're having a good day, you don't give a damn. But if you're having a bad day, why, pretty soon it gets you hot under the collar."[7] Birdie Tebbetts, a teammate of Greenberg's in Detroit for seven seasons, lamented, "There was nobody in the history of the game who took more abuse than Greenberg, unless it was Jackie Robinson."[8]

On December 30, 1935, two months after Greenberg won his first MVP Award, Sandy was born in Brooklyn to Evelyn and Jack Braun. The Brauns divorced when Sandy was 3 years old. Six years later, Evelyn married Irving Koufax, and Sandy took his stepfather's last name. Sandy played baseball at Lafayette High School in Brooklyn and went to the University of Cincinnati, where he also played basketball. Dodgers scout Al Campanis, who had seen Koufax pitch while he was still in high school, recalled, "There are two times in my life the hair on my arms stood up – the first time I saw the ceiling of the Sistine Chapel, and the second time I saw Sandy Koufax throw a fastball."[9] Koufax signed with the Dodgers in 1954 when he was just 18 years old. He received a $14,000 signing bonus along with a starting salary of $6,000. As a "bonus baby," he went straight to the Dodgers and never pitched in the minor leagues.

During Koufax's first six years in the majors, he was an average pitcher at best. He had control problems and his ERA hovered around 4.00. The only season he won more than 10 games was 1958, when he went 11-11 with a 4.48 ERA. The turning point in his career came during spring training in 1961 when Dodgers catcher Norm Sherry urged Koufax to ease up a bit on his fastball.[10] Sherry had noticed that the harder Koufax threw the wilder he got. So he told Koufax, "Why not have some fun out there, Sandy? Don't try to throw so hard and use more curveballs and changeups."[11] Koufax wisely followed Sherry's advice, and for the next six seasons, no major-league pitcher was more dominant.

He was a National League All-Star in each of his last six seasons (1961-66) and a World Series MVP twice (1963, 1965). He was a three-time Cy Young Award winner (1963, 1965, 1966) and a National League MVP (1963). He led the majors in wins three times (1963, 1965, 1966) and in strikeouts four times (1961, 1963, 1965, 1966), and he topped the National League in ERA five times (1962-66). He threw four no-hitters, including a perfect game against the Chicago Cubs on September 9, 1965.

But aside from his tremendous accomplishments *on* the field, Koufax is revered by many Jewish baseball fans more for what he did *off* the field. Perhaps the most defining moment of his career was his decision not to pitch Game One of the 1965 World Series against the Minnesota Twins. That game fell on October 6, which was Yom Kippur, the holiest day on the Jewish calendar. Koufax was not known to be a particularly devout or observant Jew; nevertheless, before the start of the 1965 series, Koufax announced he would not pitch Game One because it coincided with the holy day. Koufax always maintained that his decision not to pitch was easy. He said, "There was no hard decision for me. ... It was just a thing of respect."[12] Dodgers owner Walter O'Malley, along with Koufax's teammates and coaches, supported his decision. According to fellow hurler Claude Osteen, "Sandy was such a star on our club, we said, 'If this is Sandy's decision, then it's okay.'"[13]

Dodgers manager Walter Alston named Don Drysdale the starting pitcher for Game One. Drysdale had won 23 games in 1965, so the Dodgers were not particularly concerned about Koufax's absence. But Drysdale got shellacked in the game. In 2⅔ innings, Drysdale gave up seven runs on seven hits, including home runs to Don Mincher and Zoilo Versalles. As Drysdale walked off the mound in the third inning after getting pulled, he looked back at Alston and supposedly said, "I bet right now you wish I was Jewish too!"[14] The Twins won the game, 8-2.

For years, there has been much speculation about where Koufax spent October 6, 1965. Koufax never disclosed where. Rabbis throughout the Minneapolis-St. Paul area claimed to have seen Koufax at their synagogues that day. The late Rabbi Bernard Raskas of the Temple of Aaron Synagogue in St. Paul maintained until his death in 2010 that he brought Koufax

into his synagogue through a side door and sat him in front where almost no one saw him.[15] Koufax biographer Jane Leavy is skeptical. She believes Koufax never left his hotel room on October 6. She writes, "Raskas could not have seen [Koufax] unless he was the room service waiter at midnight [when Koufax would have broken his fast]."[16]

Koufax's decision to sit out the first game of the World Series became a major national news story, sparking intense media attention and igniting debates throughout the country. Some praised Koufax's decision to place religion over sport, while others criticized him for potentially letting down his team. Koufax's decision resonated most deeply with Jewish baseball fans, who saw it as an affirmation of his Jewish identity. As Rabbi Elliot Cosgrove observed, Koufax's decision was a "pivot forever changing Jewish-American identity... [showing] that you could stand in two cultures – you could make it big in America and remain a nice Jewish boy."[17]

Koufax returned to the mound for Game Two. But he did not fare much better than Drysdale had in Game One. Koufax pitched six innings in a 5-1 loss. After the game, Koufax refused to blame his performance on his longer-than-normal layoff. He said, "I knew what I wanted to do out there, but I just couldn't do it. If I had a little better control, or better stuff, I might have gotten away with it."[18]

Koufax got his groove back for games Five and Seven. Both were masterful pitching performances. In Game Five at Dodger Stadium, with the series tied at two games apiece,[19] Koufax pitched a four-hit shutout, striking out 10 and walking only one. The series returned to Minnesota, where the Twins won Game Six. For the decisive seventh game, Alston again went with Koufax even though he had only two days' rest to Drysdale's three. Koufax threw a three-hit shutout, again striking out 10, on his way to his second World Series MVP in three years. Jim Murray of the *Los Angeles Times* wrote, "Drysdale with three days' rest is not as good as Koufax with two days' rest. ... If Alston had started anybody but Koufax, management probably would have demanded a psychiatric examination."[20]

In the years since 1965, several Jewish major leaguers have followed in Koufax's footsteps and refused to play on Jewish holy days. In 1966, 20-year-old Cubs rookie pitcher Ken Holtzman refused to pitch on Yom Kippur. Years later, Holtzman recalled that Koufax's decision not to pitch Game One of the 1965 World Series made it much easier for him not to pitch on the holy day.[21] In 2001 Shawn Green refused to suit up for the Dodgers for a crucial game against the Giants that fell on Yom Kippur. When asked about his decision, Green said, "There is nothing I would rather do than play against the Giants in a pennant race, but some things take precedence over that."[22]

But unlike Koufax, Holtzman, and Green, some Jewish major leaguers have opted to play on holy days. In 1996, Brewers backup catcher Jesse Levis played on Yom Kippur and said, "It's not like I'm Sandy Koufax. I don't have that kind of leverage. I hope God forgives me."[23] In 2019 three Jewish players, Alex Bregman (Astros), Max Fried (Braves), and Joc Pederson (Dodgers), decided to play in playoff games on Yom Kippur. All three of their teams lost. Armin Rosen questioned whether the three losses were caused by a "Koufax Curse."[24] Rosen humorously asked:

> "Why would Yom Kippur observance be the determinative factor in a baseball game? Surely [God] isn't that petty. But consider this: Any one of these outcomes would have been an unlikely event. Two of them? Preposterous. Three of them? On Yom Kippur? What do you wanna bet that it's not the hand of any angry God?[25]"

Sandy Koufax's influence in the American Jewish community has been profound and far-reaching. Through his commitment to his faith, he provided cultural representation and served as a role model for many aspiring Jewish athletes. Indeed, it is almost impossible to overestimate just how important Koufax's decision not to pitch on Yom Kippur 1965 was, and still is, to the American Jewish community. According to David King, "[I]n an America that often vilified the Jewish people, Koufax's act gave Jews a renewed sense of pride in both their religion and their cultural contributions."[26] For this reason, it is unlikely Koufax's decision in 1965 is going to be forgotten by the Jewish community any time soon. In fact, some rabbis are making a concerted effort not to let the story die. As Rabbi Gordon Tucker said, "I've said to the congregation, to the over-60 crowd, 'You have to keep that story alive and tell your grandchildren – you have an obligation to do that.'"[27]

NOTES

1   https://obamawhitehouse.archives.gov/realitycheck/the-press-office/remarks-president-reception-honor-jewish-american-heritage-month.

2   David A. King, "Nostra Aetate and Sandy Koufax," *Georgia Bulletin*, October 29, 2015. https://georgiabulletin.org/commentary/2015/10/nostra-aetate-sandy-koufax/.

3   King.

4   Bud Selig interview, "The Central Theme of Jews in Baseball," https://www.youtube.com/watch?v=zJXKylOeaiY.

5   David Lengel, "Fifty Years Later, Sandy Koufax Still Stirs Up Emotions of Jewish Baseball Fans," *Guardian*, US edition, October 7, 2015. https://www.theguardian.com/sport/blog/2015/oct/07/sandy-koufax-world-series-50-years. Accessed September 2, 2023.

6   Greenberg sprained his wrist in Game Two of the World Series and was unable to play the remainder of the Series.

7   Michael Beschloss, "Hank Greenberg's Triumph over Hate Speech," *New York Times*, July 25, 2014.

8   Beschloss.

9   Jane Leavy, *Sandy Koufax: A Lefty's Legacy* (New York: Harper Perennial, 2002), 55.

10   Marc Z. Aaron, "SABR Baseball Biography Project: Sandy Koufax," Society for American Baseball Research, https://sabr.org/bioproj/person/Sandy-Koufax, citing Bob Broeg, "Sandy Started Slowly … But Oh What a Finish," *The Sporting News*, August 14, 1971.

11   Aaron.

12   Hillel Kuttler, "Why Sandy Koufax Sitting Out a World Series Game Still Matters 50 Years Later," Jewish Federation of Greater Orange County, https://www.jewishorangeny.org/jewish-life/wao-weekly-e-blast-news-articles/why-sandy-koufax-sitting-out-a-world-series-game-still.

13   Lengel.

14   Tess Cutler, "1965: When Dodger Sandy Koufax Didn't Pitch Game One of the World Series," *Jewish Journal*, October 24, 2017, https://jewishjournal.com/los_angeles/226360/dodger-sandy-koufax-yom-kippur/

15   John Rosengren, "Myth and Fact Part of Legacy from Sandy Koufax's Yom Kippur Choice," *Sports Illustrated*, September 23, 2015.

16   Rosengren.

17   Elliot J. Cosgrove, "The Hyphen Within," Park Avenue Synagogue, September 22, 2015, https://pasyn.org/node/320.

18   Paul Zimmerman, "Sandy Loses, but There's a Catch to It," *Los Angeles Times*, October 8, 1965: III-1.

19   The Dodgers won Game Three (4-0) and Game Four (7-2).

20   Jim Murray, "Worker of Art," *Los Angeles Times*, October 15, 1965: III-4.

21   Frederic J. Frommer, "Sandy Koufax Wouldn't Play on Yom Kippur. Neither Would Another Ace Jewish Pitcher," *Forward*, September 29, 2022, https://forward.com/news/sports/519660/sandy-koufax-wouldn't-play-on-yom-kippur.

22   Jeff Merron, "Green, Koufax and Greenberg – Same Dilemma, Different Decisions," ESPN, September 26, 2001, https://www.espn.com./classic/s/merron_on_green.html.

23   Merron.

24   Armin Rosen, "The Koufax Curse," *Tablet*, October 10, 2019, https://www.tabletmag.com/sections/sports/articles/the-koufax-curse.

25   Rosen.

26   King, "Nostra Aetate and Sandy Koufax."

27   Lengel, "Fifty Years Later, Sandy Koufax Still Stirs Up Emotions of Jewish Baseball Fans."

Sandy Koufax As a Jewish American Sports Icon

BY SARAH WEXLER

Ask the average American to name a Jewish athlete. For many, the first to come to mind will be Dodgers great Sandy Koufax, even though it's been nearly six decades since his retirement from major-league baseball.

Like many of his sport's all-timers, Koufax maintains an almost mythic status – especially among Jewish baseball fans, as well as the broader Jewish American community. Early to mid-1960s baseball was in large part defined by Koufax baffling hitters with a high-octane fastball and a devastating curveball en route to becoming a first-ballot Hall of Famer. It remains one of the most dominant peaks for any pitcher.

For the purposes of this article, just as important was his fateful decision to sit out Game One of the 1965 World Series against the Minnesota Twins in recognition of Yom Kippur, the holiest day on the Jewish religious calendar.

Koufax was not the first great Jewish athlete, nor the first Jewish baseball star. Yet the legendary left-hander seems to occupy a special place in the Jewish American imagination, while non-Jewish sports fans also recognize his place as a revered representative of his people.

To understand why Koufax retains this image as a specifically Jewish superstar, the author talked with a Jewish historian, a rabbi, a fan who grew up watching Koufax pitch, and several contemporary Jewish major-league players and personnel. Their views offer insight into why Koufax's legacy as a Jewish American sports icon has endured for so long and with such strength.

What a historian says

Signed by the Dodgers ahead of the 1955 season, Koufax played his first three seasons in his native Brooklyn before the team relocated to Los Angeles in '58, where he truly made a name for himself. From 1961 to 1966, Koufax won three Cy Young Awards and a National League MVP Award while earning seven All-Star selections.[1] He threw four no-hitters – one a year from 1962 to 1965 – culminating in his perfect game against the Cubs. He was a four-time World Series champion.

Location somewhat explains Koufax's national prominence, as he played not just in the country's two biggest Jewish communities, but in the two largest media markets. But even more so, it was the era in which Koufax played that enabled him to build his legend – and not just because the advent of televised games afforded greater exposure than previous generations of players had.

"Koufax would have been part of this assimilating impulse of his parents' generation, seeking to balance full allegiance and loyalty to United States and holding onto some measure of Jewish identity – particularly, Jewish religious and ethnic identity – and that piece of the puzzle was becoming smaller than the American piece," said David Myers, distinguished professor and Sady and Ludwig Kahn Chair in Jewish History at UCLA. "It was a period in which those two dimensions of identity were being balanced and rebalanced and recalibrated."[2]

Assimilation is something of a double-edged sword. It's hard to argue against certain privileges like greater safety and opportunity, but a loss of cultural identity is difficult to reckon with. The mid-twentieth century featured a rediscovering of Jewish pride in America, in no small part due to events following Israel's establishment.[3]

Compare Koufax to Hank Greenberg, the only other Jewish player enshrined in the National Baseball Hall of Fame. The son of Romanian Jewish immigrants,[4] Greenberg broke into the big leagues with the Detroit Tigers for good in 1933, and he played until 1947, missing the 1942-44 seasons due to service in the US Army.[5] Like Koufax, Greenberg also once sat out on Yom Kippur – but that came during a pennant chase in 1934, rather than the World Series.[6]

Because antisemitism in the United States was worse pre-World War II, Greenberg routinely faced anti-Jewish abuse from opposing players and fans[7] in ways that Koufax didn't (although Koufax did endure some, including from his own teammates and in the form of hate mail, as well as stereotypes in the press related to his purported intellectualism).[8] But there's no doubt it was a society more accepting of Jews overall.

"A significant tide of sympathy moves toward Jews and the Jewish experience after the Holocaust," said Myers. "[Before World War II] there was fear, on the part of some, that Jews would assert their own collective interest and drag the United States against its will into a major global conflagration. So, there was that aura of suspicion. Whereas after the war, after the full excesses of the Holocaust became known, that sense of suspicion gave way to a greater sympathy for Jews."

Essentially, because Jews of Greenberg's day had even greater outsider status than Jews of Koufax's day, his affirmations of Jewish identity didn't register in the way Koufax's did. In a time when Jews were more integrated into the mainstream, it was hugely impactful for Koufax to assert that Jewish religion and culture mattered and deserved respect, even when they stood in contrast with societal norms.

"It's precisely Koufax's act in the midst of this assimilatory era that I think lent it a particular power," said Myers. "It may, at least for Jews, grant him a measure of immortality."

What a rabbi says

Like Koufax, Reb Jason Van Leeuwen grew up in New York before moving to California for work. A Syracuse native, Van Leeuwen was a big baseball fan, too young to have seen Koufax pitch but certainly aware of the southpaw's achievements – and he was excited to learn that this accomplished athlete happened to be Jewish.

The head rabbi at Temple B'nai Hayim, a Conservative synagogue in Sherman Oaks, California, Van Leeuwen has come to view Koufax as someone who holds a unique place in Jewish American history.

"Koufax, more than any other Jewish ballplayer, symbolizes the American Jew who makes it, succeeds, is at the top of his field, but does not deny and even affirms his Jewish identity – even to the point where he will observe a religious holiday in the middle of a World Series," said Van Leeuwen. "He's a statement that you can have it all as a Jewish American. You can stay Jewish, and you can be fully American."[9]

Jewish identity, especially in the diaspora, is a multifaceted and deeply personal thing. It comprises religious, ethnic, and cultural components, each bearing significance that varies vastly among members of the community. And it is generally accepted that, while he valued his Jewish heritage, Koufax was not religiously observant. There's even a dispute over whether he attended Yom Kippur services in October 1965, or if he simply stayed in his Twin Cities hotel room.[10]

Asked whether it mattered where Koufax was that day, Van Leeuwen said the act of Koufax prioritizing culture over sport is bigger than any of the smaller details when it comes to his place in Jewish American lore.

"If you ask people what do they know about Koufax: a great pitcher, four no-hitters, didn't pitch on Yom Kippur in the World Series," said Van Leeuwen. "Beyond that, the average Jewish American can't say much else about him."

What a fan says

The Dodgers weren't the only ones who moved to Los Angeles in 1958. That's also when Jim Gilson, then 6 years old, relocated there from Cleveland along with his family. Several times a season, he made the trip from LA's west side to go to games. For their first four years in town, that was at the Los Angeles Memorial Coliseum, where Gilson enjoyed seeing Wally Moon hit his famed "Moon Shots" over the short left-field porch. Then, in 1962, Dodger Stadium opened its gates.

Gilson recalls the thrills of Maury Wills' daring efforts on the basepaths, and the intimidating persona of Koufax's co-ace, Don Drysdale. But to a young Jewish child, it was Koufax himself

who stood out most, with Gilson estimating he attended as many as 10 of the southpaw's starts.

"He had a commanding presence that went beyond his baseball prowess," said Gilson, a retired lawyer and museum executive. "Even to a kid, he appeared to carry himself with supreme confidence. … I have a memory of feeling like he's a master, he knows he's a master, [but] he's not outwardly puffing out his chest about that."[11]

There was a time in the United States when baseball was regarded as a tool for outsiders to gain acceptance,[12] which was true to Gilson's experience. He made friends playing Little League, and a shared passion for the new hometown major-league team was a natural way to fit in with his adopted community. In a more personal sense, Koufax's Jewishness, paired with his unquestioned greatness, made him not just an icon to Gilson and others, but a trailblazer as well.

"You could point to Sandy Koufax as a reason to be accepted," said Gilson. "… Sandy Koufax being accepted and extolled, I think, was part of what made me feel like I can be accepted and maybe even extolled."

Also contributing to Koufax's mystique: his reputation for keeping a low profile and valuing privacy, making his occasional public appearances at Dodgers spring training, Hall of Fame ceremonies, and big games all the more exciting.

The Dodgers retired Sandy Koufax's No. 32 jersey number in 1972. Jersey numbers for Roy Campanella (39) and Jackie Robinson (42) also were retired. SABR: The Rucker Archive.

"He retains both that reserve and impeccable public performance," said Gilson. "And man, he looks like he could pick up the ball and still strike out 18 guys. ... And he still looks like a star. He has movie-star looks, and I don't think that hurts, either."

What players say

Sports fandom usually runs through families, with an oral history component of parents telling children about stars of their youth. That was the case for Astros second baseman Alex Bregman, whose family admired the Dodgers pitcher so much they even named their dog Koufax.

When Bregman learned about Koufax from his father and his grandfather, Jewishness was regularly part of the discussion.

"Sandy Koufax is always the guy," said Bregman. "I think it's just passed on from generation to generation. I'll teach my son about Sandy Koufax as well."[13]

The complex nature of Jewish identity makes it hard to pinpoint just how many Jewish players there have been throughout major-league baseball history. But it is pretty widely agreed that, at least on the athletic side, Jews have been underrepresented in both baseball and sports as a whole.[14]

That's a big reason why so many Jewish major-league players have long looked up to Koufax – there haven't been many others to look up to, certainly not those who could be argued as the best at their position. Take Braves left-hander Max Fried, an LA native who modeled his own curveball on Koufax's[15] – despite the fact that even Fried's father was too young to have watched Koufax.

As much as broader midcentury American society shaped Koufax's story, some baseball-specific aspects factor in as well. For one thing, 1960s sports medicine was not advanced enough to keep Koufax healthy, and he spent his last few seasons dealing with extreme arm pain and swelling. Doctors suggested that he risked losing the use of a limb or finger amputation if he continued, leading Koufax to retire at just 30 years old.[16] As much as Koufax's statistics explain why he is admired, those years he didn't get to play also contribute to the baseball world's fascination.

"There's a little bit of like, 'what could have been,'" said Fried. "... He was so good for a really good amount of time, and he had to pretty much retire in the middle of his prime. ... That leaves a lasting impact. Most people, you see [them have] a little bit of decline, but for him, it still feels like he was on an ascent."

The baseball calendar has also changed substantially. The postseason has expanded from just the World Series to several rounds. It now takes a few weeks of playoff games to reach the fall classic, which comes in late October. Although the High Holy Days move each year on the Gregorian calendar, they almost always occur in late September or early October, with October 14 being the latest date that Yom Kippur can fall.[17] So unless the major-league schedule or the postseason format shifts drastically again, no player will get to make an impact statement like Koufax in 1965.[18]

But that decision still speaks volumes to Jewish players, even those who don't make the same choice for themselves.

"The biggest [act] that made him a legend was the ability to put his faith before baseball and sit out on Yom Kippur," said Fried. "[The World Series was] something that is obviously a big deal and a lot of people really care about, but ... for him to be able to take that and sacrifice maybe what would be a [championship] to respect his religion, it just shows the kind of person and the man he is."

Beyond his sporting skill, Koufax has proven to be a role model for subsequent generations of major leaguers, Jewish and not, when it comes to how to conduct oneself.

"[Koufax] just [rises] in stature and impressiveness when you meet him, because he's such a thoughtful, gentle, normal dude," said Gabe Kapler, then manager of the Giants. "That's what really stands out, is just what a good person he is, and a guy who just doesn't [care] about the spotlight. I don't really think he cares if he is recognized as the best pitcher or any of that."[19]

"Someone that embraces who they are as a person and does something that they think is important to them and not changing based on others' point of view, I think, is the most important thing that you can draw from [Koufax]," said A's second baseman Zack Gelof, who played for Team Israel in the World Baseball Classic in 2023.[20]

Conclusion

Many factors played a part in Koufax becoming the long-lasting paragon of Jewish athletic excellence. A combination of era, talent, personality, and circumstance helped transform him from a mere great ballplayer into something much bigger and more meaningful. The fact that it's not something he actively sought for himself only adds to his mythos – who doesn't love a humble, reluctant star?

This raises the question, then: Will Koufax forever reign as the face of Jewish American sports, or could another Jewish athlete one day rise up and take the mantle?

It might just be a matter of time. As we move further away from Koufax's career and fewer people have firsthand memories of it, that could set the stage for someone else to step into that role. But the circumstances would have to be exactly right.

"The perfect storm is a strong, charismatic Jewish athlete that was as good as Sandy was," said Kapler. "... I think it's possible that that comes up again, but it's got to kind of take a little bit of the stars aligning."

Then again, there's a chance that with the passing decades, Koufax's legend will only grow, firmly cementing his place in history along with a host of other Jewish folk heroes.

"Maybe there'll be some apocryphal text about [Koufax] a thousand years hence," said Rabbi Van Leeuwen.

SOURCES

All stats courtesy of Baseball-Reference.com.

NOTES

1   From 1956-1966, just one Cy Young Award was given for both leagues. From 1959 to 1962, the major-league season featured two All-Star Games; Koufax was selected to both in '61.

2   Interview with David Myers on February 26, 2024.

3   The Six Day War in 1967 was a major inflection point for Jewish American ethnic pride.

4   Scott Ferkovich, "Hank Greenberg," Society for American Baseball Research. Accessed February 26, 2024. https://sabr.org/bioproj/person/hank-greenberg/.

5   "Profile: Hank Greenberg," National Museum of American Jewish Military History. Accessed February 23, 2024. https://nmajmh.org/education/individual-profiles/hank-greenberg/.

6   Greenberg had chosen to play on Rosh Hashanah that year, though he did attend morning services. "Hank Greenberg," Jewish Historical Society of Michigan. Accessed February 23, 2024. https://www.jhsmichigan.org/gallery/2017/05/michigans-first-cemetery-site.html.

7   Michael Beschloss, "Hank Greenberg's Triumph Over Hate Speech," New York Times, July 25, 2014. Accessed February 23, 2024. https://www.nytimes.com/2014/07/26/upshot/hank-greenbergs-triumph-over-hate-speech.html.

8   Michael Leahy, The Last Innocents: The Collision of the Turbulent Sixties and the Los Angeles Dodgers (New York: HarperCollins, 2016), 2, 111, 223-224.

9   Interview with Reb Jason Van Leeuwen on February 14, 2024.

10 Jane Leavy, Sandy Koufax; A Lefty's Legacy (New York: HarperCollins, 2002), 184.

11 Interview with Jim Gilson on February 16, 2024.

12 Peter Dreier, "Chasing Dreams: Baseball and Becoming American," The American Prospect, August 12, 2016. Accessed February 27, 2024. https://prospect.org/culture/chasing-dreams-baseball-becoming-american/.

13 Interview with Alex Bregman, on June 25, 2023.

14 Recall the joke from the film Airplane! about a "Famous Jewish Sports Legends" leaflet as a "light reading" option.

15 According to Max Fried, this was at the suggestion of mentor Reggie Smith, who offered his own insight while also relaying information on pitching technique from conversations with Koufax. Interview with Max Fried on September 2, 2023.

16 Harold Friend, "Sandy Koufax: The Doctors Were Worried They Might Have to Amputate the Finger," Bleacher Report, November 28, 2011. Accessed February 25, 2024. https://bleacherreport.com/articles/959588-sandy-koufax-the-doctors-were-worried-they-might-have-to-amputate-the-finger.

17 Abigail Klein Leichman, "10 Things You Need to Know About Yom Kippur," Texas Jewish Post, October 2, 2022. Accessed February 25, 2024. https://tjpnews.com/10-things-you-need-to-know-about-yom-kippur/.

18 In fact, Koufax had long refused to pitch on Yom Kippur, but it never drew much attention outside of the team before, largely because it had never been in conflict with the World Series. (See Leahy, 113.)

19 Interview with Gabe Kapler on September 22, 2023.

20 Interview with Zack Gelof on August 3, 2023.

"Bigger Than Sinatra": Sandy Koufax in Hollywood

BY VINCE GUERRIERI

In the post-World War II era, New York City was effectively the baseball capital of the nation.

Not only was it the home of the commissioner's office (baseball's initial commissioner, Kenesaw Mountain Landis, kept an office in Chicago; his successor Happy Chandler, a Kentucky native, had his office in Cincinnati), but it was home to three major-league teams, all of which were successful. In fact, from 1947 through 1958, every World Series featured at least one of New York City's teams, with the Yankees and Giants meeting in 1951 and the Yankees and Dodgers meeting six times.

In the 1950s New York City was also the hub for the nascent medium of television. Displayed at the World's Fair in New York in 1939, television was also seen as a potential sports broadcasting medium as well. In fact, the first American sports broadcast was a Princeton baseball game at Columbia University in 1939.[1] Broadcast networks occupied Midtown skyscrapers with business offices and studios.[2]

But by the end of the 1950s, there were seismic shifts for both baseball and television, and both involved a move west. After the 1957 season, the Dodgers decamped for Los Angeles, bringing the Giants with them to San Francisco. (Before too long, there would be an American League team in Los Angeles as well, as baseball expanded to head off a potential third league.) The beloved Bums of Brooklyn had given way to a new team, more oriented toward speed and pitching, with Maury Wills setting a record for stolen bases in 1962 and dominant pitching by Don Drysdale and Sandy Koufax.[3]

Koufax and the Dodgers became a dynasty in the 1960s, winning two World Series and losing a third. Their success and proximity to the new center of the television industry made them darlings of Hollywood, none more so than Koufax himself, who threw four no-hitters and won three Cy Young Awards. His roommate Dick Tracewski said Koufax was "bigger even than Sinatra."[4]

When the film industry moved west in the early twentieth century, there were technical considerations.[5] Los Angeles offered more temperate weather and an abundance of natural sunlight, both aids to filmmaking. Television production also moved west because of new technology.

Initially, television was live, for the simple reason that there wasn't a lot of technology available to record and rebroadcast shows. Film was used for some shows, most notably *I Love Lucy*,[6] ensuring that it would be around for generations.[7] Some programs were recorded on kinescope, which is essentially filming a television screen, at least initially for rebroadcast on the West Coast.[8]

Magnetic tape had been around for audio purposes since the 1920s, and by the 1950s a workable solution was found to use tape recording for video as well as audio, leading to television shows being recorded and played at any time.[9] In 1953 some 80 percent of network television was broadcast live. By 1960 that number had shrunk to 35 percent, and very little of that was scripted television.[10]

Perhaps most importantly, the movie studios were moving into television production themselves. Columbia Pictures recycled the name of its prewar cartoon production company, Screen Gems, into its TV production company, starting first with advertisements and then with original series like *Father Knows Best, I Dream of Jeannie, and The Partridge Family*. When Walt Disney opened his eponymous theme park in California in 1955, it was televised live, and Disney became a Sunday evening television staple for generations. In fact, by 1959 Warner Bros. supplied one-third of ABC's prime-time schedule.[11]

There has always been a connection between athletes and Hollywood. The Hollywood Stars of the Pacific Coast League team included celebrities among their minority owners,[12] including Gene Autry, who parlayed that into ownership of the American League team that came to Los Angeles in 1961. Bob Hope and Bing Crosby, buddies in a series of *Road* movies for Paramount, were minority owners of the Indians and Pirates respectively.[13] And the Los Angeles Dons, a football team in the new All-America Conference in 1946, were named for their owner, movie star Don Ameche.

But the arrival of the Dodgers marked a new era in the marriage between sports and celebrity. Milton Berle and Doris Day could be spotted at Dodgers games. An exhibition game against Hollywood actors – started initially with the Hollywood Stars – became an even bigger deal with the Dodgers in the 1960s.[14]

And suddenly, TV roles abounded for Dodgers players in general and Koufax in particular. He played bit parts on shows like *77 Sunset Strip* and *Bourbon Street*, and played himself in cameo roles on *Dennis the Menace* and *Mister Ed*,[15] where he notably gave up a home run to the title character, a horse.[16]

Koufax had become that breed that, while common now, was rarer in the 1960s: an athlete whose fame transcended his sport. "To a gushy Hollywood columnist he is Clark Gable, Gregory Peck and William Holden rolled into one," said a 1963 *New York Times* profile that said Koufax "has the world by the tail."[17]

71

Although they both had limited roles in a variety of TV shows, Koufax and Drysdale also tried to use Hollywood as a bargaining chip during their 1966 holdout.[18] While they were waiting for a new contract, Paramount said the pitchers had signed for roles in a crime drama called *Warning Shot*. Drysdale denied the signing, but said he and Koufax were keeping their options open.[19] The two did start rehearsals for the movie, but ultimately re-signed with the Dodgers (in a deal that former Dodgers farmhand and TV star Chuck Connors helped broker[20]), and didn't take part in the film, which was released in 1967, the year after Koufax retired.

The great irony is that for as much as Hollywood took to Koufax as the Dodgers' ace, a post-playing career in television did not materialize. Following his retirement after the 1966 season, he signed a million-dollar contract with NBC, becoming host of *The Sandy Koufax Show*, a 15-minute program that aired prior to the network's *Game of the Week* on Saturday. It did not go well. "I'm not sure where it would be more accurate to say I saw Sandy go on the tube or down it," one wag said.[21] By many accounts, he improved as the years went on, but finally in 1973, the year after his Hall of Fame induction, Koufax quit NBC with four years left on his contract.[22]

"He kept saying this is the best job in the world but 'it's not for me,'" said NBC vice president Carl Lindemann.

"I'm just not suited for it," Koufax said.[23]

NOTES

1   David J. Halberstam, "Eighty years ago today, NBC experimented with the first ever telecast of a sporting event," *Sports Broadcast*

Famed comedian Milton Berle greets Sandy Koufax after the left-hander threw his perfect game against the Chicago Cubs in 1965. Courtesy of National Baseball Hall of Fame.

Journal, May 17, 2019. https://www.sportsbroadcastjournal.com/eighty-years-ago-today-nbc-experimented-with-the-first-ever-telecast-of-a-sporting-event/ The first televised sporting event in the world was the 1936 Olympics. (David J. Halberstam is not the author David Halberstam, who was noted for his writing on the Vietnam War, but who also wrote several books on sports. He was killed in an auto accident in 2007.)

2 NBC, then as now, is a tenant at Rockefeller Center, nicknamed 30 Rock. CBS's headquarters, not far away, was called Black Rock for its dark façade. The headquarters for ABC, regarded at least initially as an also-ran, was sometimes called "Little Rock."

3 Wills debuted with the Dodgers in 1959, by which time they were in Los Angeles. Both Koufax and Drysdale debuted for the Dodgers while they were still in Brooklyn, Koufax as a "bonus baby" in 1955 who signed with his hometown team, and Drysdale the following year. Drysdale was a contributor in the Dodgers' final season in Brooklyn; Koufax was seen as more of a project.

4 Jane Leavy, *Sandy Koufax, A Lefty's Legacy* (New York: Harper Collins, 2009), 382.

5 There were other reasons as well, chief among them a desire to stay out of reach of Thomas Edison's Motion Picture Patents Company. Further reading: https://www.saturdayeveningpost.com/2021/03/thomas-edison-the-unintentional-founder-of-hollywood/.

6 Leigh Allen, "Filming the 'I Love Lucy' Show," *American Cinematographer*, January 1952. https://theasc.com/articles/filming-the-i-love-lucy-show.

7 At Lucille Ball's death, it was held as an article of fact that *I Love Lucy* was always on somewhere in the world.

8 The first coast-to-coast broadcast was a speech by President Harry Truman in 1951. "This Day in History: President Truman Makes First Transcontinental Broadcast," https://www.history.com/this-day-in-history/president-truman-makes-first-transcontinental-television-broadcast.

9 Alex Marsh, "A History of Videotape, Part 1." https://blogs.library.duke.edu/bitstreams/2017/07/27/history-videotape-part-1/. The article also notes an unfortunate consequence: To save money, a lot of the tapes were reused, wiping out the earlier content. The entire first decade of Johnny Carson's stint on *The Tonight Show* (as well as much of his predecessors, Jack Paar and Steve Allen) are lost to history because of it.

10 Ralph G. Giordano, *Pop Goes the Decade: The Fifties* (Westport, Connecticut: Greenwood Publishing, 2017). Accessed online February 26, 2024.

11 Kerry Segrave, *Movies at Home: How Hollywood Came to Television* (Jefferson, North Carolina: McFarland, 1999), 35.

12 See also Stephen M. Daniels, "The Hollywood Stars," *Baseball Research Journal*, 1980. https://sabr.org/journal/article/the-holly-wood-stars/.

13 Crosby also owned minority shares in the Tigers, which he was allowed to keep with a special ruling by Commissioner Ford Frick. Kevin Reichard, "Celebrity Owners and Major League Baseball," *Ballpark Digest*, March 7, 2019. https://ballparkdigest.com/2019/03/07/celebrity-owners-and-major-league-baseball/.

14 Mark Langill, "The Movie Hollywood Stars Game," *The National Pastime*, 2011. https://sabr.org/journal/article/the-movie-hollywood-stars-game/.

15 https://www.youtube.com/watch?v=AVm-HwAkVp8&t=41s.

16 *Mister Ed* featured a cameo by Leo Durocher, who was by then on the Dodgers' coaching staff. He also made appearances on several shows in the 1960s, most notably giving Herman Munster a tryout on *The Munsters*.

17 "Man With Golden Charm: Sanford (Sandy) Koufax," *New York Times*, October 3, 1963: 40.

18 Drysdale had an even lengthier list of television credits, and he went on to a career as a broadcaster after his playing days.

19 Associated Press, "Drysdale Hints at Compromise; He, Koufax Weigh Film Pact," *New York Times*, March 17, 1966: 48.

20 Jeff Katz, "Everybody's a Star: The Dodgers Go Hollywood," *The National Pastime*, 1981. https://sabr.org/journal/article/everybodys-a-star-the-dodgers-go-hollywood/.

21 Charlie Maher, "Sandy Koufax' New Life," *Sport*, July 1967.

22 Among Koufax's difficulties, as described in his SABR biography, were imparting his knowledge to a generalized audience and his discomfort being critical of players he'd played with or against.

23 Sandy Padwe, "Koufax Leaves TV, 'Just Not Suited for It," *Newsday* (Suffolk edition), February 23, 1973: 119.

Koufax Helped Shape Future Generations of Hurlers

BY LES MASTERSON

Sandy Koufax threw his final pitch in a major-league game in 1966, but his influence could still be spotted on a mound decades later. Not in a pitch but in a stare. A death stare. Specifically, Dave Stewart's death stare.

During his years working with Dodgers pitchers in spring training and in the minor leagues, Koufax approached the young pitcher with a tip that would change his career. He didn't suggest a different arm angle or show Stewart a new grip. Koufax instead told him to pull his cap lower on his head. The Hall of Fame lefty explained doing so would lower Stewart's sight.

"And so as I kept lowering my cap, he kept asking me, 'What do you see?'" Stewart recalled. "And I said, 'At this point, all I can see is below the catcher's neck and below.' And he says 'OK, I'd like for you to start throwing with your cap like that.'"[1]

Stewart followed instructions. He pulled his hat just above his eyebrows. So low he couldn't see the catcher's face and it caused a shadow over his face, which intimidated hitters in the 1980s and 1990s.[2]

Stewart didn't find much success with the Dodgers but went on to win 20 games four straight years for the Oakland A's and won two World Series with the A's and Toronto Blue Jays.

Koufax watched Stewart's career with pride.

"I paid attention to his career after he'd been traded," the left-hander said. "His success was something I enjoyed watching because he was just a good guy."[3]

Koufax continued, "If I helped Dave at all, that's fine, but it really boils down to the man on the mound. Whatever Dave did is what Dave did. He did it. Nobody did it for him."[4]

Stewart said, "Shoot, I ran off 20-win seasons in a row, and for a lot of that, I knew Sandy was watching me on the mound or he'd hear about it."[5]

Dodgers right-hander Don Sutton talks about pitching with Sandy Koufax during spring training in 1979. Photograph by Donald Gregory Dughi.

Stewart was just one of the hurlers influenced by the Koufax. Clayton Kershaw,[6] Jerry Reuss,[7] Rick Honeycutt,[8] and Al Leiter[9] have all pointed to him as a reason for their success.

"Basically, Sandy didn't tell me anything different about fundamentals than any pitching coach I've ever had didn't tell me," recalled Reuss. "But he gave me direction. He taught me how to approach a game."[10]

After retiring in 1966, Koufax spent more than a decade staying mostly away from baseball before the Dodgers hired him as a special pitching coach in 1979. Koufax's return wasn't completely about getting back into uniform. Instead, it came down partly to finances.

"One, it was hard to stay away from the one thing I had done so well in my life. Two, the way the economy has gone, it has become tough to make ends meet. And three, I love egg rolls and I understand Tommy Lasorda has become the biggest egg roll dealer in the country," said Koufax at a press conference at Little Joe's, a Los Angeles restaurant.[11]

Koufax was living with his wife, Anne, in Paso Robles, California, a city midway between Los Angeles and San Francisco. He said other organizations had approached him with similar job offers but he turned them down. He dabbled in broadcasting and real estate and occasionally spent time at Dodger Stadium during old-timers days.[12]

Back in a Dodgers uniform, the former hurler spent the spring of 1979 working with minor- league and major-league pitchers in Vero Beach and assisted Red Adams, Dodgers pitching coach, and Ron Perranoski, Dodgers pitching instructor.

Koufax kept a low profile during his years helping Dodgers pitchers. That included not even having his name on the back of his jacket.[13]

Koufax also traveled to the Dodgers' Double-A and Triple-A teams. His time working for the organization ended officially in 1990, though he continued to visit spring training and club events.[14]

When Koufax left his job, Dodgers executive vice president Fred Claire said he wanted to spend more time traveling.[15] There were also other theories, including one that Koufax had become "weary of the job,"[16] and disagreed with the organization's player development program.[17] Another rumor was that Lasorda was jealous of the former hurler. Terry Collins, who managed in the Dodgers organization, recalled that Koufax's exit was connected to Lasorda's ego and that the manager resented the baseball legend's work with "his pitchers."[18]

Koufax stayed out of the game for a few years before being coaxed back by Texas Rangers manager Kevin Kennedy. The lefty served as a pitching consultant during spring training.[19]

Koufax worked with old friend and Dodgers teammate Claude Osteen, who was the Texas pitching coach. The one caveat was that Koufax refused to wear the Rangers jersey or cap and instead wore the Rangers blue pants and a generic hat.[20]

Koufax returned to his previous ways of staying out of the limelight and away from baseball until Mets CEO Fred Wilpon, a longtime friend, asked him to speak with his pitchers during spring training. Koufax worked informally with Mets hurlers, signed autographs, and chatted with Wilpon.

"It's so neat to have him here," said Terry Collins, the Mets manager. "It's so fun to be around him. He's so upbeat. And he wants to help. That's all he wants to do."[21]

Koufax mostly stayed away from the Dodgers, which media reports said had to do with his issues with ownership.[22]

Koufax did spend time in the Dodgers's camp, including working with young pitcher Clayton Kershaw in 2012. Koufax praised the young lefty. "How do you make up a ceiling? His only ceiling is time," Koufax said.[23]

It wasn't until 2013 that the Dodgers brought Koufax back and gave him a role as a special adviser to Chairman Mark Walter. He resumed working with pitchers in spring training and consulting during the season.[24]

"This is the only organization I've ever played in, and been in. I came here with Jackie and Gil and Duke," Koufax said. "I played with great people then, and great people with Don, Tommy, Willie, and Maury. I want to see this organization be a winner again. I don't know if I can do that much, but I'll try and help."[25]

Koufax didn't keep his adviser role for long but continued to visit Dodgers spring training in an unofficial capacity.[26] When he returned in 2014, he wore a Dodgers pullover and cap and cargo shorts.

Reporters wanted to hear from the pitching legend. Though he no longer had a defined role, Koufax said he was there to offer advice to pitching coaches Rick Honeycutt and Ken Howell or players. Koufax was asked about Kershaw, who was already being compared to him.[27]

"At 25, you don't have to adjust," Koufax said. "Talk to me when he's 35. He just has to keep doing what he's doing and every year he has gotten better. If he keeps getting better, the sky's the limit, and if he doesn't get any better, the sky's the limit. He's a great pitcher, he's special."[28]

Koufax kept a low profile as usual, but he made news that spring and it had nothing to do with pitching. An Andre Ethier line drive struck him in the head. Bloodied but otherwise OK, Koufax was driven off in a golf cart with a towel pressed to his head.[29]

Future spring trainings were not as eventful for Koufax. There were the usual articles about his arrival in camp and photos of him chatting with players and signing autographs.[30]

Koufax attended many games at Dodger Stadium though the years, especially during the postseason, where he sat in the stands and cheered for his former team. He also went to the ballpark in 2022 for the unveiling of a statue that depicts him in his famous pitching motion. During the ceremony, Kershaw praised Koufax for his help. Much like Stewart's advice, Koufax didn't fiddle with Kershaw's mechanics while helping the young pitcher reach his potential. He just gave him simple advice to "stay tall."[31]

"It was simple. It was helpful. It was also caring. It was also genuine. Those are the qualities that I admire most in you," Kershaw told Koufax.[32]

NOTES

1   Tristi Rodriguez, "How Koufax Influenced Stewart's Patented Intimidating Stare," NBCSportsBayArea.com, September 6, 2022. https://www.nbcsportsbayarea.com/mlb/oakland-athletics/how-ko-ufax-influenced-stewarts-patented-intimidating-stare/1430086/.

2   Rodriguez.

3   Alex Coffey, "How Sandy Koufax Unleashed Dave Stewart's Stare on the Baseball World," The Athletic, May 13, 2020. https://theathletic.com/1808367/2020/05/13/how-sandy-koufax-unleashed-dave-stewarts-stare-on-the-baseball-world/.

4   Coffey.

5   Coffey.

6   Fabian Ardaya, "Clayton Kershaw Finds the Words to Honor Sandy Koufax: 'No One More Deserving Than You,'" The Athletic, June 18, 2022. https://theathletic.com/3372555/2022/06/18/clayton-kershaw-finds-the-words-to-honor-sandy-koufax-no-one-more-deserving-than-you/

7   Gordon Verrell, "Positive Attitude Put Reuss on Right Road," The Sporting News, November 22, 1980: 41.

8   Gordon Verrell, "Shouldering the Burden," The Sporting News, June 1, 1987: 16.

9   Jane Leavy, Sandy Koufax: A Lefty's Legacy (New York: Harper Perennial, 2010), 289.

10 Verrell, "Positive Attitude Put Reuss on Right Road."

11 Gordon Verrell, "Recluse Koufax Steps Into the Game With Dodgers," The Sporting News, February 17, 1979: 35.

12 "Recluse Koufax Steps Into the Game With Dodgers,"

13 Marc Z. Aaron, "Sandy Koufax," SABR.org. https://sabr.org/bioproj/person/sandy-koufax/.

14 Aaron.

15   "Dodgers Say Koufax Not Severing Ties," The Sporting News, March 19, 1990: 28.

16   "Belcher Knows Value of Arbitration Value," The Sporting News, March 12, 1990: 19.

17   "Belcher Knows Value of Arbitration Value."

18   Leavy, 288.

19   T.R. Sullivan, "Texas Rangers Notes," The Sporting News, February 21, 1994: 22.

20   Leavy, 288.

21   Andy McCullough, "Sandy Koufax Makes Usual Visit to Mets' Training," NJ.com, February 19, 2011. https://www.nj.com/mets/2011/02/sandy_koufax_makes_usual_visit.html.

22   Mark Saxon, "Sandy Koufax to Advise Dodgers," ESPN.com, January 22, 2013. https://www.espn.com/los-angeles/mlb/story/_/id/8869991/sandy-koufax-advise-los-angeles-dodgers-spring-training.

23   Eric Stephen, "Dodgers Spring Training 2012: Sandy Koufax Visits Camp, Talks Clayton Kershaw," losangeles.sbnation.com, March 12, 2012. https://losangeles.sbnation.com/los-angeles-dodgers/2012/3/2/2840487/dodgers-spring-training-2012-sandy-koufax-clayton-kershaw.

24   Bruce Horowitz, "Dodgers Hope Koufax Can Still 'Bring It' as LA Readies for Spring Training," bleacherreport.com, January 23, 2013.

https://bleacherreport.com/articles/1498221-dodgers-hope-koufax-can-still-bring-it-as-la-readies-for-spring-training.

25   Eric Stephen, "Sandy Koufax Arrives at Dodgers Camp," truebluela.com, February 17, 2013. https://www.truebluela.com/2013/2/17/3998806/sandy-koufax-dodgers-spring-training.

26   Stephen, "Sandy Koufax Arrives at Dodgers Camp."

27   Eric Stephen, "Sandy Koufax Arrives in Dodgers Camp," SB Nation Los Angeles, February 17, 2014. https://www.truebluela.com/2014/2/17/5420010/sandy-koufax-dodgers-camp-clayton-kershaw-yasiel-puig.

28   Stephen, February 17, 2014.

29   Dan Zinski, "Sandy Koufax Hit in Head by Line Drive at Spring Training," Calltothepen.com, February 21, 2014. https://calltothepen.com/2014/02/21/sandy-koufax-hit-head-line-drive-dodgers-spring-training/.

30   Ken Gurnick, "No Longer Advisor, Koufax Visits Dodgers Camp," MLB.com, February 26, 2016. https://www.mlb.com/news/sandy-koufax-visits-dodgers-spring-training-c165547778.

31   Ardaya, "Clayton Kershaw Finds the Words to Honor Sandy Koufax: 'No One More Deserving Than You.'"

32   Ardaya.

Comprehending Koufax

Biographical Interpretations of an Intensely Private Man

BY CHARLIE BEVIS

Beneath the orderly reporting of baseball accomplishments that Sandy Koufax compiled in nine-inning ballgames over 162-game seasons and several World Series is a much less well-structured human narrative about the man.

Terms such as "the J.D. Salinger of baseball," "a Greta Garbo-like isolation," and more simply "reclusive" have all too often been deployed to one-dimensionally characterize Koufax, the result of his infrequent interactions with the media after his Hall of Fame enshrinement in Cooperstown in 1972. The nature of the introverted, unassuming Dodgers left-handed pitcher is much more nuanced.[1]

It is relatively easy to refute the "reclusive" label tagged on Koufax from an empirical perspective, since he was not bashful about participating in occasional public events. For instance, Koufax appeared at a White House ceremony in 2010 at which President Obama quipped, "Sandy and I actually have something in common – we are both lefties. He can't pitch on Yom Kippur; I can't pitch." It is the intellectual aspect of reclusive as a Koufax character trait that has had long-lasting impact, due to the lack of suitable substitute descriptors. This is largely because only a few biographies have examined Koufax.[2]

This article probes four aspects of the biography production relating to Koufax: (1) the 1966 autobiography ghostwritten by Ed Linn and its implicit character revelations, (2) the dearth of biography published about Koufax during the next three decades, (3) the books by Ed Gruver and Jane Leavy published at the turn of the twenty-first century that provide some understanding of the existential Koufax, and (4) the possibility of future biographies of Koufax.

Biography is the window into the character of a public figure, far more than a simple recounting of the facts of a person's life. In his seminal history of biography, Nigel Hamilton succinctly defines the essence of this literary genre as "the life and character of a distinctive human being." Another literary historian describes the biographer's most vital task as "the explanation which lies behind the facts, the interpretation which will explain the progress and decline" of the subject's life.[3]

Character assessment is the most difficult aspect of the subgenre of baseball biography, compared with its other components of life's work in the baseball industry, the person's cultural/societal impact, and the writer's quality of research evidence. Developing a subject's character is no easy task. Most biographers don't discover their subject's character as a distinct piece of the research evidence, as if the quest were a complex scavenger hunt. Biographers almost always form character traits out of tidbits of the research examined, which is more like putting together a jigsaw puzzle without all the pieces being readily available. Inevitably, character assessment is informed inference, not a definitive conclusion, and thus subject to continual debate. This is especially the case with the very private Koufax.[4]

Several of Koufax's inherent character traits, though, have been hiding in plain sight for nearly 60 years – in his 1966 autobiography that still sits on library shelves across America. Ed Linn, the ghostwriter of that book, essentially functioned as a biographer who wrote in the first-person point of view. Through his structure of the book and the depth of the particular topics covered in it, Linn reveals much about the underlying nature of Koufax.

Autobiography of Koufax

When this book was published in 1966, Koufax was not yet labeled a recluse, as he tried to navigate the brave new world of the 1960s regarding sports celebrity status. The book was published in the fall of 1966, before Koufax shocked the sports world by announcing his retirement from baseball at age 30. The one-word title *Koufax*, with no modifiers or subtitles, provides a distinct peek into the inner Koufax.

By revisiting this autobiography, four value-driven tenants of Koufax's character can be gleaned from Linn's text: (1) integrity, (2) humility, (3) craftsmanship, and (4) trusting nature. The first three characteristics are fairly straightforward interpretations. The fourth one is less obvious but is supported by recent academic research and importantly helps to explain Koufax's intense desire for privacy that has provoked so many writers to evoke the Salinger and Garbo analogies.

Linn demonstrates integrity through the handshake arrangement prior to Koufax's actual initial contract with the then Brooklyn Dodgers, a $20,000 deal consisting of a $6,000 salary and a $14,000 bonus that roughly equaled the cost of a college education. Irving Koufax, the pitcher's father and an attorney, shook hands with Dodgers owner Walter O'Malley in the interim period before a roster spot was available. Koufax could welsh on the deal and besmirch his father's reputation (his word was his bond) by taking a better offer from another team. "But *any* deal that you make for me, even if I never pitch another game in my life, I will stick by," Linn wrote about Koufax's stance. He actually turned down more money from the Pittsburgh Pirates, with whom he would have had a more immediate chance to actually pitch rather than sit on the bench.[5]

Humility is readily apparent through Linn's penning of the Koufax remarks that "I don't think ballplayers are really entertainers" or even "of any extraordinary importance in our natural life" as they "do not heal the sick or bring peace and comfort to a troubled world." Later in the book, Linn gives ample credit to several people for making Koufax a baseball success, notably statistician Alan Roth in an era well before sabermetrics. "I made the transition from thrower to pitcher and had not understood that in making the transition I had made a beginning, not an end," Linn wrote on behalf of Koufax. "You become a pitcher before you become a good pitcher." As a paean to Roth, Linn includes 18 pages of Roth's statistics in an appendix.[6]

Roth enabled Koufax to become a craftsman at his profession, a seeker of intimate knowledge about his craft, not just to excel at the strategy of the ballgame. Koufax sought also to improve his baseball output by understanding the medical aspects of his left arm. Here, he was tutored by Dr. Robert Kerlan. Linn details a number of arm injuries and recoveries plotted by Kerlan, as Koufax understood that his arm "had passed over the line between temporary change and permanent trouble," after "an arthritic change had taken place."[7]

Linn illustrates Koufax's trusting nature as the foundation of the opening chapter, where Koufax is infuriated by a *Time* magazine story published after the 1965 World Series in which the magazine "managed to gather together all the myths into one great orgy of myth-making." In the book's opening paragraph, Linn writes that Koufax wants to bury "the myth of Sandy Koufax the anti-athlete" who supposedly has "regretted – and even resented – the life of fame and fortune that has been forced upon me."[8]

Later in the book, Linn details another example of Koufax's trusting nature with his extreme dismay at the gamesmanship and deception employed by Dodgers management in his 1964 salary negotiation, a process that he terms "negotiation by ultimatum." What particularly rattled Koufax was the demand that he refrain from negotiating his salary through the newspapers, but then management did just that to push its position. Koufax was cornered into agreeing to a $70,000 salary after the Dodgers had inaccurately told the newspapers that he wanted $90,000. After the conclusion of the negotiation, Koufax (through Linn) says, "All right, I'm signing this as we agreed. But I want you to know that I'm not happy about it. It's not that I'm not happy with the money. I'm just not happy about the way it was done."[9]

The veracity of revelations in any autobiography is, of course, subject to the author being a reliable narrator. Gruver's 2000 biography provides reliability by articulating Linn's take on Koufax's motive for writing the book: "One of the reasons Koufax agreed to do his autobiography before the '66 season was because he knew he was going to hold out and didn't want to feel pressure for money." As Gruver writes about the famous

Koufax/Drysdale joint holdout in the spring of 1966, "Koufax strengthened his position by accepting $100,000 to do his autobiography with Ed Linn."[10]

Additional reliability, and support for the view of his trusting nature, comes from current-day experts who study generations. Koufax was a member of the Silent Generation, those Americans born between 1925 and 1945, which influenced the shaping of his values and motivations, i.e., his inner character traits. According to psychology professor Jean Twenge in her analysis of generational differences, Silents are "more likely to trust others, and more likely to see the good in people," in line with the those in the preceding Greatest Generation, more than the following Boomer Generation, and much more than the next subsequent Generation X grouping.[11]

Several authors have given readers a glimpse of Sandy Koufax's life and career. Courtesy of National Baseball Hall of Fame.

Besides this higher level of trust in others, Silents also "lived their young adulthood in a more collectivistic, family-oriented time in American history." However, Silents were snagged in a societal transition when "American culture began the 1960s as a collectivistic culture (focused on social rules and group harmony) and ended it as an individualistic one (focused on the needs of the self and thus often rejecting traditional rules)." From the 1970s forward, individualism trended higher with each subsequent decade.[12]

Some Silents adapted to the new individualism and the emerging celebrity culture; others like Koufax held steadfast. The celebrity life was not something Koufax inherently wanted, nor as a Silent was it something he could philosophically handle. Koufax was a man seemingly locked into the mentality of the 1940s. He was highly resistant to the societal changes of the 1960s, which were just unfolding when the Koufax autobiography was published in the fall of 1966.

The value system of many Silents was largely binary in nature, i.e., right/wrong, true/false, black/white with no gray area. Koufax, like many members of the Silent Generation, seemed to possess this mindset. Certainly, Koufax's own chosen profession reinforced this absolutist nature, with its dichotomous orientation of ball/strike, safe/out, and fair/foul. It's also reasonable to assert as an extension that Koufax would also strictly demarcate work life from nonwork life.

While Koufax's autobiography reportedly sold 32,000 copies by the end of the 1966 World Series, subsequent sales were lackluster. Three years later, only 40,000 copies had been sold, "well short of the 100,000 breakeven point" for the publisher to turn a profit. The great Dodgers pitcher, true to the underlying character traits exposed in the book, was not congenitally a star pitchman for his own book.[13]

Given the book's concealed insights into the mindset of Koufax, it's a shame that Linn's work isn't more widely available today or at least digitally accessible through GoogleBooks. Several hundred copies of the book are maintained in US libraries (according to records at the World Cat website), but the majority are housed in academic libraries generally inaccessible to the public. Public libraries have some copies, but those that have survived culling from the collection due to age or diminished borrower demand are too often in rough physical shape after six decades on the bookshelf.[14]

Dearth of Koufax Biographies

When Linn wrote the Koufax autobiography, the subgenre of baseball biography was in its infancy. Baseball biography during Koufax's 12-year major-league career was almost exclusively published as hero-worshipping books for the juvenile audience, youngsters under age 14. Koufax's ghostwritten autobiography was then state-of-the-art in life writing about baseball players.[15]

During the early 1960s, there was almost no market for baseball biography as we know it today, i.e. for adult consumption, particularly regarding living ballplayers like Koufax. Publishers were leery of potential litigation for libel since truth was then not necessarily a viable defense to many assertions of libel. The landmark 1964 US Supreme Court decision in *New York Times v. Sullivan* changed this publishing perspective, when the justices ruled that public figures must demonstrate that publishers acted in "reckless disregard" of a statement's truth or falsity. The standard of "actual malice" limited the libel risk for publishers and opened a nascent market for objective, third-party baseball biography.[16]

After Robert Creamer initiated modern baseball biography with his insightful 1974 book *Babe: The Legend Comes to Life*, sportswriter Maury Allen wrote numerous books about ballplayers and became a prolific author in the evolving craft of baseball biography. Allen, though, did not include Koufax among his multiple ballplayer subjects. Had there been an Allen-crafted biography of Koufax, readers probably wouldn't have learned much more about him, since Allen was notorious for concentrating on the baseball activities of his subjects and never delving too deeply, if at all, into character assessment.[17]

Allen likely avoided Koufax as a biographical subject due to his run-in with the pitcher back in 1963 when Allen revealed that Koufax was adopted and interviewed his biological father for an article in the *New York Post*. Demonstrating his trusting nature, Koufax believed this was not just a breach of old-school ballplayer-sportswriter journalistic etiquette, but also a violation of the work/nonwork bifurcation of his life. Although what Allen wrote was the truth, Koufax surely considered that Allen lacked integrity by divulging this fact.[18]

In part because Allen did not write a basic, baseball-oriented biography of Koufax, there was a three-decade dearth of Koufax biographies.

During the 1980s, while Allen pursued the popular approach to baseball biography, history professor Charles Alexander produced several scholarly biographies of deceased ballplayers. The efforts of Alexander and other professional historians moved the baseball biography subgenre into examining the cultural and societal impacts of ballplayers during the 1990s, as notably exhibited by the Nicholas Dawidoff biography of Moe Berg – a work that also raised the standard for character assessment – and the Arnold Rampersad biography of Jackie Robinson to mark the 50th anniversary of racial integration in professional baseball.[19]

A general market also developed in the 1990s for straight-forward biographies of Hall of Fame ballplayers, which led Ed Gruver to fill the void left by Maury Allen to research the first book-length biography of Koufax.

First Koufax Biography

The Gruver biography of Koufax published in 2000, succinctly titled *Koufax* like the Linn-ghostwritten book, is a classically written baseball biography, focused on the arc of his baseball career, in particular an in-depth look at Game Seven of the 1965 World Series. "I wanted to illuminate what I feel is Sandy's greatest game and one of the best pitched games in World Series history," Gruver recalled in 2023. "I believe I did that with the aid of recollections from his Game 7 opponents – Harmon Killebrew, Tony Oliva, Jim Kaat, et al."[20]

Gruver also contributes some insights into Koufax's character. "Gruver interviewed many of Koufax's teammates and opponents, but even as they sing the tributes in personality and achievement of the reclusive Koufax, he remains an enigma," the *New York Times* noted in its review of the book. "Although Koufax appeared to the public as reclusive and guarded, he was actually a shy, self-effacing, and private person who really didn't want the spotlight," another book reviewer described Gruver's characterization of Koufax.[21]

The book's most valuable contribution to understanding Koufax is Gruver's peek inside the mind of ghostwriter Linn, which he obtained from interviews with him before his death in 2000. "He is reclusive," Linn told Gruver. "He has tremendous integrity. He could have been the first merchant prince of baseball, but he decided he wasn't going to sell his name. He turned down massive amounts of money." Even though Koufax was forthcoming in his conversations with Linn for the book, Linn "had the feeling that Koufax was forever holding something back"; he referred to it as "a wall of amiability."[22]

Gruver also adds color to the character traits that anchored Linn's book about Koufax. In craftsmanship, Gruver delves into the role of catcher Norm Sherry in 1961 to inspire Koufax's pitching evolution. Gruver also demonstrates the trusting nature of Koufax, through his complicated relationship with the sports media from 1963 to 1966 and its sometimes casualness with the truth. Gruver shows Koufax's integrity, writing that "while patient and polite," he was "clearly uneasy" talking to the media, finding it "embarrassing" to be a craftsman thrust into the role of celebrity.[23]

Koufax's post-1966 life is covered in the Gruver biography, which obviously was not explored in Linn's book, including his retirement as a player and his stint as an NBC television broadcaster. Gruver corroborates the Linn-inspired character traits in these sections, writing about the integrity of Koufax in wanting the ability to use his left arm for the rest of his life, not more money to keep pitching, and the extent of his baseball craftsmanship as Koufax had difficulty coping with the entertainment nature of television.[24]

Second Koufax Biography

Jane Leavy's book *Sandy Koufax: A Lefty's Legacy* captures the broad essence of Koufax's character, based on her 469 interviews, which she largely confines to the book's preface rather than rigorously develop within the main text.

"Koufax spans two distinct eras in baseball and America," she presciently observes. "Koufax is the sixties before the sixties became the sixties," adding that "he is hound's-tooth, a crisp white shirt and a skinny black tie held in place by a discreet gold tie tack." Left unsaid is that his values are of another era than the 1960s we know today (or as Leavy knew in 2002); Koufax's values are from the Silent Generation that grew up in the 1940s. She also refutes the ever-present "recluse" branding of the man:

"Koufax cherishes his privacy. Yet an individual who chooses to do so, to keep an inner life inner, is deemed reclusive, enigmatic, aloof … [and] is thought odd."[25]

In post-publication interviews and articles, Leavy articulates more about her perspective on Koufax's character beyond the material included in her book.

"The myth I was deconstructing was not the usual one of hubris brought low. The revelation here was character," Leavy wrote in a *New York Times* article about her book. "We live in a culture where it is considered daring to be kind. Skepticism has purchase on our souls. What if the inside story is too good to be true? What if the lefty's legacy is one of uncommon grace and decency?" Leavy added, "The word used most often to describe him was 'gentle.' The nicer he appeared, the more miserable I got. When people asked what kind of guy he was, I was embarrassed to tell the truth. It felt almost unprofessional." She concluded: "The man is not without flaw or complication or idiosyncrasy. He can be testy, especially with fund-raisers looking to exploit his name for their own purposes. He is capable of not telling the truth, the whole truth, but is incapable of lying."[26]

"Koufax gave the impression by the way he left the game that he didn't need baseball to know who he was," Leavy told a book reviewer for the *Los Angeles Times*. "I don't think Koufax wanted to spend his life being Sandy Koufax, the public persona. I think he wanted to be himself. It was a radical thing to do. The Koufax persona seems part of a world apart from today's baseball industry." She then observed, "He was bigger than winning. He's an American icon as much for what he refused to do as what he did on the field. The defining differences of Koufax's career weren't economic. They were moral, and bound up with a sense of responsibility to his teammates and the game. In every way that matters, he offers a barometer – a way of measuring where we were and where we've come to."[27]

One interview with Leavy resulted in an article title that seemingly captures the essence of the man's character: "Koufax: The Pitcher as a Mensch." "Mensch" is the Yiddish word for "someone of consequence, someone to admire and emulate, someone of noble character" who exudes "rectitude, dignity, a sense of what is right, responsible, decorous." There is no comparable word in the English language that equates to the solemn overtones of the Yiddish term.[28]

Leavy did not pursue a more extensive character assessment in her book because she was stymied by the always contentious quandary for a biographer – the conflict between commercial element (book sales) and intellectual inquiry (exposing the soul of the subject). The thesis of Koufax as a "nice guy" wouldn't sell many books. Lacking a saleable character theme, Leavy adopted an unusual structure for her book. "This won't be so much a biography, I told Koufax, as a social history of baseball, using his career as a way to measure how much has changed. My aim, I said, is to limn the trajectory of his career and in so doing recreate that time in baseball and America when change was imminent, when a well-placed tie tack held it all at bay."[29]

She focuses on Koufax's contribution to cultural impact, an important element of baseball biography that was just emerging in the 1990s. Leavy's not-a-biography book is organized into 22 chapters. There are 12 odd-numbered chapters that are slices of Koufax's career, ostensibly cut by time periods but that also align with a variety of cultural impacts, and 10 even-numbered chapters that are slices of Koufax's perfect game pitched in September 1965, cut by pregame and the nine innings.

While Leavy didn't set out to expand upon the implicit character traits embedded within Linn's ghostwritten autobiography of Koufax, most of the dozen career-related chapters do advance beyond cultural impact to map to one of the four Linn-inspired character traits. For example, Chapter 13 focuses on the new chipmunk-style of sportswriting, but delves into his trusting nature, while Chapter 17, which focuses on Yom Kippur, also discusses integrity.

Given the challenge to adequately portray the character of Koufax, the book reviews were a mixed bag. The *New York Times* sniffed, "We scarcely know Koufax at all, but after Jane Leavy's delightful 'Sandy Koufax: A Lefty's Legacy,' we probably know him as well as anyone needs to." The academic journal *Aethlon* was more charitable: "Her book is as much a cultural commentary and a eulogy for a lost Golden Age as it is biography. If Koufax's public deeds are heroic (by our debased standards, of course, 'super' heroic), then his silence, both about those deeds and about the private man who performed them, becomes, in an Age of Blab, nothing short of Olympian."[30]

Although not the plan, Leavy did advance the world's knowledge of Koufax's character. Leavy's observations don't jump off the page at the reader, though, as the reader must think into her subtle references to paint the inner mindset of Koufax. He is a private man in a celebrity-crazed culture who never tried to capitalize on his baseball fame and wants to be just an ordinary, modest, decent person far removed from the sports spotlight.

Leavy in 2002 had the last word on Koufax. No writer in the next 20 years attempted to write another book-length biography of Koufax.

Future Koufax Biographies

There likely will never be another Koufax biography to top Leavy's work. As Mark Armour writes in his tribute to Leavy as a Chadwick Award winner in 2022, she "got as close to Koufax as we likely ever will, or will ever need to."[31]

To make a new biography viable, there would need to be the discovery of a new research source that disclosed some revelatory thoughts from Koufax (such as a diary or archive of papers) or about him (such as court records) or notes from Linn's ghostwriting conversations with Koufax. The latter approach enabled Jeff Pearlman to write his 2022 biography of Bo Jackson (another legendary athlete who avoided a public life after his baseball days) when he discovered at an Auburn University library the interview tapes used by a ghostwriter to pen Jackson's autobiography decades earlier.[32]

Barring the discovery of new research evidence, any new Koufax biography that simply focuses on his post-1966 life and activities – little remarkable there – or a deep dive into his personality or character – of marginal interest to modern-day sports fans – would probably be a poor business proposition, with not enough projected sales volume to justify the expense of such a project.

The sports world likely needs to be satisfied with the existing interpretations in the books written by Linn, Gruver, and Leavy (and thoughts in this essay) to convey a comprehension of the inner Koufax, a quintessential representative of the Silent Generation.

NOTES

1   "SI 60 Q&A: Tom Verducci on Sandy Koufax and 'The Left Arm of God'," *Sports Illustrated* website, August 25, 2014, https://www.si.com/mlb/2014/08/26/si-60-qa-tom-verducci-sandy-koufax-left-arm-god; David Kaufman, *Jewhooing the Sixties: American Celebrity & Jewish Identity* (Waltham, Massachusetts: Brandeis University Press, 2012), 46.

2   "Remarks by the President at Reception in Honor of Jewish American Heritage Month," Obama White House press release, National Archives website, May 27, 2010, https://obamawhitehouse.archives.gov/realitycheck/the-press-office/remarks-president-reception-honor-jewish-american-heritage-month.

3   Nigel Hamilton, *Biography: A Brief History* (Cambridge, Massachusetts: Harvard University Press, 2007), 26; Edward O'Neill, *A History of American Biography 1800-1935* (New York: A.S. Barnes, 1935), 8.

4   Charlie Bevis, *Baseball Biography: A Comprehensive History* (self-published web-book, 2021), chapter 7, paragraph 2. This web-book can be accessed at https://bevisbaseballresearch.wordpress.com/research-archive/baseball-biography-a-comprehensive-history/.

5   Sandy Koufax with Ed Linn, *Koufax* (New York: Viking Press, 1966), 66-67.

6   Linn, *Koufax*, 157.

7   Linn, *Koufax*, 225.

8   Linn, *Koufax*, 1, 4.

9   Linn, *Koufax*, 269, 283.

10 Edward Gruver, *Koufax* (Dallas: Taylor Publishing, 2000), 197-198, 200.

11 Jean Twenge, *Generations: The Real Difference Between Gen Z, Millennials, Gen X, Boomers, and Silents – And What They Mean for America's Future* (New York: Atria Books, 2023), 196-197.

12 Twenge, *Generations*, 56, 84.

13 Jerome Holtzman, "Supreme Test for Sandy's Arm: Inking Copies of His New Book," *The Sporting News*, October 15, 1966: 27; Marvin Kitman, "Some Serious Writers Are Ballplayers," *New York Times*, November 23, 1969: book section, 72.

14 The author thanks the Winthrop (Massachusetts) Public Library for having retained a copy of the Koufax autobiography and making it available to borrowers in other Massachusetts library systems. The book in Winthrop is a sad testament to the ravages of time. The dust jacket is long gone; the title on the spine is barely legible; the back cover hangs on literally by a few threads to the spine; the pages

are stained, dog-eared, and brown from acid deterioration; and the book tilts at a 60-degree angle. Inside the back cover, there is a flap holding an antiquated check-out card with stamped entries (last due date: August 15, 1977), with a modern bar-code label affixed above it.

15 Bevis, *Baseball Biography*, chapter 5, paragraphs 1-4. There were a few youth-oriented Koufax biographies published, which focused solely on his baseball achievements.

16 Anthony Lewis, *Freedom for the Thought That We Hate: A Biography of the First Amendment* (New York: Basic Books, 2007), 54-57; Bevis, *Baseball Biography*, chapter 5, paragraphs 17-18.

17 Bevis, *Baseball Biography*, chapter 6, paragraphs 16-17, 35-36.

18 Jane Leavy, *Sandy Koufax: A Lefty's Legacy* (New York: HarperCollins, 2002), 129-130.

19 Bevis, *Baseball Biography*, chapter 6, paragraphs 29-34, and chapter 8, paragraphs 8-12, 25-28, 35.

20 Gruver, email to author, February 27, 2023.

21 Michael Lichtenstein, "Baseball Books in Brief," *New York Times*, July 2, 2000: section 7, 15; Jim LaFollette, *Koufax* book review, *NINE: A Journal of Baseball History & Culture*, Fall 2001, 177-180.

22 Gruver, *Koufax*, 4-5.

23 Gruver, *Koufax*, 126, 172-174.

24 Gruver, *Koufax*, 212, 217.

25 Leavy, *Sandy Koufax*, xvi, xix.

26 Jane Leavy, "Tape From 1965 Easier to Find Than Ill Will Toward Koufax," *New York Times*, September 1, 2002: section 8, 6.

27 Josh Karp, "Searching for Sandy Koufax," *Los Angeles Times* website, October 20, 2002, https://www.latimes.com/archives/la-xpm-2002-oct-20-tm-crkoufax42-story.html.

28 Todd Leopold, "Koufax: The Pitcher as a Mensch," CNN website, October 18, 2002, http://www.cnn.com/2002/SHOWBIZ/books/10/18/koufax.leavy/; Leo Rosten, *The New Joys of Yiddish* (New York: Crown, 2001), 232-233.

29 Leavy, *Sandy Koufax*, xvii.

30 Allen Barra, "Artful Dodger, Damn Yankee," *New York Times*, October 13, 2002: section 7, 18; Robert Lee Mahon, *Sandy Koufax* book review, *Aethlon*, Spring 2004, 110.

31 Mark Armour, "2022 Chadwick Awards: Jane Leavy," *Baseball Research Journal*, Spring 2022, 118.

32 Jeff Pearlman, *The Last Folk Hero: The Life and Myth of Bo Jackson* (New York: Mariner Books, 2022), 435.

Sandy Koufax:
Life After Retirement

BY PAUL BROWNE

When Sandy Koufax retired on November 18, 1966, many people were surprised. Not Buzzie Bavasi – the Dodgers pitcher had told him over the phone the day before. Others within the organization probably had at least an inkling.

Dick Tracewski knew. Roommates while with the Dodgers, Koufax and Tracewski stayed, and continue to stay, close into their late 80s. Koufax had called him after the Dodgers lost the World Series to the Orioles to give him a heads-up about his pending retirement.[1]

Koufax was just 30 and had had a phenomenal year. Among other records, he led the league in ERA for the fifth consecutive year. Tracewski is pretty sure that will never happen again. "Sandy was not a stats man and he didn't know he was in line for the record," he said.[2] Former Dodgers teammate Ed Roebuck said, "I think he wanted to get out while he was on top."[3]

By the time of his retirement, every sport coat Koufax owned had two different-sized sleeves. His arthritis sometimes swelled to twice the size of his knee. While Koufax had told Bavasi that he wanted to maintain the use of his left arm, Tracewski said the pitcher's concerns were much deeper. The bottom line was cortisone and a pill. Koufax told Dick that doctors had told him taking those pills could affect his liver, and he wanted to live a long life. The pill was phenylbutazone alka. In *Koufax*, author Ed Linn says this pill could cause a depleted blood count and that could be fatal.[4] This pill is no longer approved for human use in the United States and has been linked to kidney failure in various studies. By the end of the 1966 season, Koufax had enough of risking his health, quality of life, and possibly his life itself. His decision had not been made lightly.

On the day he retired Koufax said, "Right now, I'd guess you'd have to say I'm unemployed."[5] While Koufax may have been able to live comfortably on his savings for a while, Koufax was smart enough to know he needed a job. Enter NBC. On December 30, 1966, his 31st birthday, he signed a 10-year deal for a total of $1 million. The salary of $100,000 per year was better than all but the last two years of his playing career.

Koufax's first broadcast with the *NBC Game of the Week* took place on April 15, 1967, the Dodgers playing the Cardinals in St. Louis. The retired star had a 15-minute pregame program, *The Sandy Koufax Show*, before every episode. He said in the Dodgers dugout, after the interview, "I used to think it was harder to answer questions than to ask them, now I am not sure. During my last five or six years I was never as nervous as I was for this assignment."[6] Early coverage of Koufax's work in his new career was generous, allowing him a chance to get his feet under him.

Rumors were spreading that July that NBC had offered the job to Koufax prior to his announcing his retirement. "That isn't true," Bavasi told sportswriter Bob Addie. "Sandy quit because he meant what he said about his arm. And there was no NBC contract in sight then."[7]

While playing a round of golf with a club pro in 1968, "Sandy pushed a shot badly into the rough. 'No! No!' commanded the pro. 'Get that left arm all the way around. Straighten it out.'

'If I could straighten it out,' said Koufax, 'I'd be pitching today instead of playing golf.'"[8] Golf was important to him and remained so long into his retirement.

In October 1968 it was reported that Bavasi was trying to get a deal that would allow Koufax to come to San Diego to pitch. Bavasi was now the president of the new Padres.[9] Koufax's response to another story in November put the possibility of a comeback to rest. "Ridiculous" is the way he summed up a comeback. "I have no intention of returning to baseball," he said. "Trying to pitch again would only make my arm worse. I made my decision to call it quits without a job, now I have one. It would be ridiculous for me to think of reconsidering."[10]

On New Year's Day in 1969 Koufax married Anne Widmark, daughter of actor Richard Widmark. Ed Gruver tells us that "[w]hen Koufax married Anne Widmark, the couple stepped away from public life. They lived a quiet life, splitting time between homes in Maine and California. Because he had invested wisely during his playing career, Koufax was comfortable financially."[11] The couple had bought a farm in Maine in the fall of 1971. He did much of the work on the farm, and his interests in carpentry, gourmet cooking, and fly fishing suited this rural life. While he may have been retreating from public life, he and Anne enjoyed entertaining friends and neighbors at their Maine home as well as in California.

Tracewski said there is some truth in the idea that the couple was retreating from the world when they bought their Maine property. At the time Koufax met Anne, they were both living in Malibu. They met on the beach and she didn't even know who he was.[12] Six months after meeting, he and Anne were married.

Koufax's life with Anne probably got the most coverage of his three marriages despite the couple's efforts to maintain their privacy. They divorced in 1982. Koufax married Kimberly

Francis, a personal trainer, in 1985. They remained together until 1998. He married Jane Purucker Clarke in 2008.

Golf was another part of Koufax's life in Maine where he joined Bucksport Golf Club. Koufax had played in celebrity tournaments going back to his playing days. In 1964 he played in the Bing Crosby National Pro-Amateur Tournament (or the Crosby Clambake). Play in various others continued on and off over the years.

In 1990 he started a 15-year run with golfers Billy Andrade and Brad Faxon's charity tournament in Rhode Island. Andrade had met Koufax as a college golfer in 1985, working up the nerve to introduce himself to the baseball great while they were both having lunch in Santa Barbara. After turning pro, Andrade and Koufax were both at the Dan Sullivan Pro-Am in Aspen, Colorado. They ran into each other at the driving range and Koufax said he remembered Andrade and had been following his career. Andrade invited him to play in his Rhode Island tournament. He said he could not make it in 1990 but would be there in 1991. Koufax played in two pro-am events a year and Andrade's was one of them. Echoing comments of others who have maintained long-term friendships with the supposed recluse, Andrade said, "I don't know the baseball player, I know Sandy the person. It's been a very, very special relationship."[13]

Earlier in Koufax's life, basketball had been more important to him than baseball. He played high-school basketball before he played baseball, not going out for the latter sport until his senior year. He went to the University of Cincinnati on a basketball scholarship but tried out for baseball his freshman year, attracting the attention of major-league scouts. He had a contract with Brooklyn and a $20,000 bonus before his sophomore year. Koufax continued to be a college basketball fan and became a frequent attendee at the annual Final Four Championships. This despite his conjecture that "it is far from impossible that my traumatic arthritis started when I banged my elbow into one of those iron poles (that held up the basket on the outdoor courts he played on)."[14]

One event in 1972 brought Koufax fully back into public life for a time. At the end of the required five-year waiting period, the Baseball Writers' Association of America elected Koufax to the National Baseball Hall of Fame. In his first year of eligibility, Koufax received 344 votes, finishing ahead of Yogi Berra at 339 and Early Wynn (301), the only other players reaching the required 75 percent of the 396 votes cast. At 36, Koufax became the youngest player ever elected and, up to that time, he was only the fifth elected in their first year of eligibility.

Did he expect it? Tracewski said everyone expected it, including Koufax. But some things surprised him. In his induction speech Koufax said, "I'm a little surprised I got as many votes as I did. I didn't have as many good years as some others in the Hall and I thought that might count against me."[15] This was a part of the humble tone of the speech. He said, "This is the biggest honor I've ever been given, not just in baseball, but my life."[16] Pointing out that "Mine was a career that began ingloriously,"[17] he expressed his gratitude to Joe Becker, his pitching coach

during most of his time with the Dodgers, who pushed him to work hard to become a better pitcher, and to his catchers, naming Roy Campanella and, as particularly important to his career, John Roseboro.[18]

Koufax retired from NBC and sportscasting in February of 1973. Early coverage of his new career had been somewhat of the "give the new guy a chance" variety as well as the sport and those that covered it showing respect for the pitcher's accomplishments on the field. As time went on, he improved but was never fully comfortable in his new role and it showed. His knowledge of baseball and judgment and insight about pitchers and pitching made him a good and insightful analyst but something was lacking. The consensus that he was a fish out of water became public after he almost as much as said so himself.

Tracewski had an explanation for that. Despite the phenomenal salary for the time, Koufax hated the job. While the travel is difficult for all in that field, Koufax had an added challenge. He was such a celebrity that he couldn't go anywhere, even when he and Tracewski roomed together on the road. He was a very private person, and while some stars thrive on the attention and public adulation, it was not for him. While he would have loved to go out for a private dinner or other type of outing with friends, it couldn't be done.[19] Eventually he had enough money, for a time, to explore what he wanted to do next.

In early February 1979, Dodgers President Peter O'Malley announced that Koufax would be rejoining the franchise as a

SANDY, THEN AND NOW--NBC sportscaster Sandy Koufax, the youngest player ever to be elected to the Baseball Hall of Fame, shows the grip which earned him the Cy Young Award as baseball's top pitcher during his sparkling career with the Los Angeles Dodgers. Sandy will lend his expertise to NBC Television Network's colorcast of the 43rd All-Star game on the NBC Television Network Tuesday, July 25, starting at 8 p.m. NYT. He will help describe the action, along with Curt Gowdy, Tony Kubek and Jim Simpson, from Atlanta Stadium. The game will be seen on more than 220 television stations in the United States and in Latin America and Canada.

Sandy Koufax shared his baseball insight on the NBC Game of the Week after retiring from the Dodgers. SABR: The Rucker Archive.

part-time pitching instructor. Koufax would work with both major-league and minor-league pitchers during spring training each year and then make visits to LA's Double-A and Triple-A franchises to provide additional instruction to those he had worked with in the spring. He maintained that position until 1990.

When asked why he was taking the job, Koufax gave two main reasons. "One, it was hard to stay away from the one thing I had done so well in my life"; and "Two, the way the economy has gone, it had become tough to make ends meet."[20] Koufax was 44 and it seems likely the first reason he gave was at least as much a driving force in his decision as the financial one. He was young enough to do the job but may have been old enough to start wondering how long that would be true.

Koufax's desire to teach was his motivation for becoming a coach. He said, "Pitching is a branch of learning, no doubt of it. You're part of a chain that goes back for generations passing the art along. You want to start others off further down the line than you did." When asked where he was from 1972 to 1979, Koufax said, "Wherever I wanted to be. ..."[21]

Some have speculated that Koufax did his coaching at the minor-league level after spring training because of a desire to maintain a low profile.[22] Koufax has always insisted that the recluse thing has been greatly exaggerated. At the time of taking the job, he gave his own explanation: "I'm not so presumptuous as to tell veteran pitchers how to throw. They got to the majors without me. But if I can help them develop a certain pitch, or can do the same with the young fellows, I'll be happy."[23] Koufax wanted to teach the game he had played so well. The knowledge of baseball and judgment and insight about pitchers and pitching that had been his strong point as an announcer were even greater strengths in his new job.

In 1990 Koufax resigned his position with the Dodgers. He "reportedly resigned because he said he was weary of the job. Dodger officials said he was taking a one-year sabbatical, but Koufax said there was no timeframe involved in the resignation. Sources said Koufax was upset with the Dodgers' player-development program, which had not produced many prospects in recent years. While Koufax and the Dodgers denied any hard feelings, a source said he wouldn't be surprised to see Koufax align with another team."[24]

Tracewski said Koufax didn't like the last years with the Dodgers because he couldn't teach much except about conditioning. He felt he was only a celebrity and the attention because of that made it difficult for him to teach the way he wanted to. Photographers were always taking pictures and he hated it. This made him quit earlier than he would have if he could have really taught.[25]

Koufax continued to attend major Dodgers events after his resignation as well as other baseball happenings, and did some brief periods of outside coaching of pitchers on other teams.

In March of 1999, Koufax visited the Yankees during spring training. Coach Don Zimmer "told reporters that Koufax's words carried weight" with pitchers.[26] "Pitchers who have been lucky

enough to have Koufax counsel them have said that his simplistic approach when coaching is easy to follow and understand," an observer said.[27]

Koufax's visits came to a sudden stop at the end of 2002. In March of 2004, Koufax showed up at the Dodgers' spring-training facility at Vero Beach again. His appearance sparked excitement among players and coaches alike. Koufax said he hadn't worked for the Dodgers in 12 years and wasn't working now. He was visiting friends and talking baseball. Frank McCourt, who had recently bought the team, "said he wants Koufax and other expatriate Dodgers alienated by Murdoch's crew to return to the fold."[28]

The McCourt ownership of the team ended in the franchise's bankruptcy in 2011. McCourt was able to sell the team out of bankruptcy to a group of investors led by Mark Walter that included Magic Johnson. Koufax took a job as a special adviser to Walter. Koufax would return to working with Dodgers pitchers. Clayton Kershaw was one of the pitchers to benefit from Koufax's presence with the team. Magic Johnson is reported to have been the one to open discussions with Koufax.[29]

In February 2016, Koufax made an announcement: "I'm 80 years old and I have retired. I have not quit. I'm still part of the Dodger organization and always will be as long as Mark and Kimbra Walter are a part of ownership. I will do most of what I have done in the past with no official title. I hope all the players, coaches, managers, and everyone else in the clubhouse have successful and healthy seasons with a spectacular ending. See you Opening Day."[30]

Koufax and Tracewski continued to be friends throughout the period after his retirement from baseball. Koufax's wife's family has ties in Northeast Pennsylvania, which caused him to be a frequent visitor to that area in summers. He and Tracewski would golf at the Scranton Country Club, near where Tracewski lived, at least three or four times a year until recent years. On one occasion Tracewski persuaded 1959 Masters winner Art Wall Jr. to join them in a round.[31] Wall was from Honesdale, Pennsylvania, which is close to Scranton. The Koufaxes spent their winters mainly in Vero Beach. They became frequent visitors to games at Dodgers Stadium, especially during the postseason.

Tracewski said Koufax was a special guy and conducted himself quietly and positively. He had his own ideas about how he wanted to live and did so accordingly even when he was an active player and a young man. No one pitched like him. He was his own man.

"One thing about Koufax was that he was 120 percent into pitching. He never played golf during the season because it would interfere with his readiness. Pitch, rest, prepare for his next start was his life in his playing days."[32]

Koufax brought this dedication to his craft and the Dodgers to his post-playing days' work with the team. On June 18, 2022, a statue of Koufax joined that of Jackie Robinson in the center-field plaza of Dodger Stadium, the only two players thus immortalized by the team. Clayton Kershaw, one of the speakers at the dedication, said, "Sandy, one day I hope I can impact someone the way you championed me – you really have – left-handed pitcher or not.[33]

NOTES

1   Dick Tracewski, telephone interview, September 8, 2023.

2   For a list of ERA leaders 1878-2023, see https://www.baseball-almanac.com/pitching/piera4.shtml.

3   Edward Gruver, *Koufax* (Dallas: Taylor Publishing Company, 2000), 213.

4   Sandy Koufax with Ed Linn, *Koufax* (New York: Viking Press, 1966), 237.

5   Gruver, 213.

6   Bob Hunter, "Sandy Discovers Few Kinks in Mike Delivery," *The Sporting News,* April 29, 1967: 15.

7   Bob Addie, "Addie's Atoms," *The Sporting News,* July 29, 1967: 14.

8   Dick Young, "Young Ideas," *The Sporting News,* May 11, 1968: 14.

9   "Koufax Hints at Trying for Comeback Next Year," *The Sporting News,* October 12, 1968: 18.

10 Bob Hunter, "Sandy Says Nix to Comeback Pitch by Dodgers," *The Sporting News,* October 9, 1968: 45.

11 Gruver, 217.

12 Tracewski interview.

13 T.J. Auclair, "How Over-Sleeping Led to Golfer's Lifelong Friendship with Sandy Koufax," PGA.com, October 12, 2017. www.pga.com/archive/how-oversleeping-led-golfers-lifelong-friendship-sandy-koufax.

14 Koufax with Linn, 24.

15 Gruver, 223.

16 https://www.history.com/this-day-in-history/youngest-elected-baseball-hall-of-famers-sandy-koufax.

17 Janey Murray, "Berra, Koufax Inducted Amid Star-Studded Class of 1972," baseballhalloffame.org, https://baseballhall.org/discover/inside-pitch/berra-koufax-inducted-amid-star-studded-class-of-1972.

18 Marc Z Aaron, "Sandy Koufax," SABR BioProject, https://sabr.org/bioproj/person/sandy-koufax/.

19 Tracewski interview.

20 Gordon Verrell, "Recluse Koufax Steps Back Into the Game With Dodgers," *The Sporting News,* February 17, 1979: 35.

21 Thomas Boswell, "Koufax: Hall of Famer Back in Baseball After Years of Wandering," *Washington Post*, March 21, 1979, https://www.washingtonpost.com/archive/politics/1979/03/21/koufax/3139f66f-996a-485f-8cce-8f7671152136/.

22 Tom Verducci, "The Left Arm of God: Sandy Koufax Was More Than Just a Perfect Pitcher," *Sports Illustrated's 60th Anniversary Issue*, August 29, 2014 (originally published July 12, 1999). https://www.si.com/mlb/2014/08/29/sandy-koufax-dodgers-left-arm-god-si-60#gid=ci025584b020042580&pid=sandy-koufax.

23 Melvin Durslag, "Gimmie a Handy Guy Like Sandy," *The Sporting News*, March 24, 1979: 14, 16.

24 "Baseball," *The Sporting News*, March 12, 1990: 19.

25 Tracewski interview.

26 Gruver, 243.

27 Stacie Wheeler, "Sandy Koufax Will Join Dodgers for Spring Training as Special Adviser to Mark Walter," https://dodgersway.com/2013/01/22/sandy-koufax-will-join-dodgers-for-spring-training-as-special-advisor-to-mark-walter/.

28 T.J. Quinn, "Koufax Ends Grudge, Back at Dodgertown," *New York Daily News*, March 7, 2004 https://www.goupstate.com/story/news/2004/03/07/koufax-ends-grudge-back-at-dodgertown/29708514007/.

29 Dylan Hernandez, "Dodgers and Sandy Koufax Team Up Again After Years Apart," *Los Angeles Times*, www.latimes.com, January 22, 2013.

30 "Koufax Says He Has Retired," *Los Angeles Times*, February 29, 2016.

31 Tracewski interview.

32 Tracewski interview.

33 Jacob Gurvis, "Jewish Baseball Legend Sandy Koufax Immortalized with a Statue," *Times of Israel*, June 22, 2022. https://www.timesofisrael.com/jewish-baseball-legend-sandy-koufax-immortalized-with-a-statue/#:~:text=The%20two%20statues%20were%20both,10%25%20larger%20than%20life%20size.

An Enduring Legacy

Even after his retirement,
Koufax influences Jewish ballplayers

BY CRAIG GARRETSON

Just two years after Sandy Koufax's shocking retirement from baseball, the headline in *The Sporting News* on April 20, 1968, read: "New Koufax? It Could Be Cubs' Holtzman."[1]

"Holtzman is regarded by many baseball observers as 'another Koufax,'" Edgar Munzel wrote. "This, perhaps, is the critical year for him, the year he'll prove it or not."

Ken Holtzman was left-handed, he threw hard, and he was Jewish. And while he did have some good seasons – a two-time All-Star, with 174 wins,[2] a 3.49 ERA, and two no-hitters – it turned out he was not, indeed, "another Koufax."

But then again, who could be?

Koufax set a high bar not just on the mound, but also when to be off it. Two generations earlier, famed slugger Hank Greenberg of the Detroit Tigers sat out a game on Yom Kippur in 1934. When the 23-year-old "Hebrew Hammer" walked into temple on that solemn day, he was stunned and embarrassed to receive a standing ovation.[3]

Twenty years later, Cleveland third baseman Al Rosen told his manager he couldn't play in Game Five of the 1954 World Series because of the holy day – but it was a moot point as the Indians were swept in four games by the New York Giants.[4]

But the most famous example was Koufax – "The Left Arm of God" – sitting out Game One of the 1965 World Series against the Minnesota Twins because it fell on Yom Kippur. Don Drysdale took the mound and the Dodgers lost, 8-2. (Drysdale gave up seven runs in 2⅔ innings; when the manager came to take him out,

Sandy Koufax speaks at the Baseball Writers Association of America (BBWAA) dinner in 2014. Photograph by Arturo Pardavila III from Hoboken, New Jersey.

Drysdale supposedly quipped, "Hey, skip, bet you wish I was Jewish today too.")[5]

Koufax pitched in Game Two and the Dodgers lost again, 5-1. But they won the Series in seven games, with Koufax throwing a four-hit shutout in Game Five and a three-hit shutout in Game Seven.

The following year, Koufax again sat on Yom Kippur in a game against the Cubs ... as did Holtzman, Chicago's scheduled starter. The Jewish left-handers instead faced off the following day, and Holtzman outdueled Koufax, giving up one run on two hits, while Koufax gave up two runs (one earned) on four hits in a 2-1 Cubs victory.[6]

The precedent had been set. Five years later, Mike Epstein followed in their footsteps when he sat out the Oakland A's final game of the season – September 29, 1971 – because it fell on Yom Kippur. The A's, 100-60, had a 15-game lead over the second-place Kansas City Royals. (Oakland won the game anyway, 8-7.) Billed as "a Kosher Lou Gehrig" and "Mickey Mantle bred on blintzes and gefilte fish,"[7] Epstein was an imposing, muscular 6-foot-3, 230-pound first baseman nicknamed "Superjew" after hitting a monster home run in the California League.[8] At the end of the 1971 season, Holtzman was traded to Oakland, and teammate Rollie Fingers dubbed the 175-pound Holtzman "Regular Jew."[9]

In 2022 Shawn Green recalled how more than 20 years earlier – for the first time in his career – there was a game on Erev Yom Kippur[10] and another on Yom Kippur itself.[11] And those games were against the archrival San Francisco Giants, battling with the Dodgers as they chased the Arizona Diamondbacks for the NL West title. Just to make it more interesting, Green had the longest active consecutive games streak in the majors at 415 games.[12]

To play or not to play? It was the question Koufax had asked himself prior to Game One of the 1965 World Series ... and before him, Hank Greenberg in 1938 and Al Rosen in 1954.

Now Green was wrestling with the same dilemma faced by the Jewish ballplayers who came before him. He said it was the first time in his career that Yom Kippur coincided with a game he was scheduled to play.[13]

"If I missed both games, I'd say, 'Well, I'm not super observant. So that doesn't seem right,'" Green told *Forward* in 2022. "And if I didn't sit out either game, as someone who embraced being Jewish, and being a Jewish role model, I didn't feel that was right."[14]

So Green reflected on a conversation he once had with – who else? – Koufax. "[Green's] earliest memories of Judaism are attending Passover seders at the table of his grandparents – and hearing about Koufax," Steve Springer wrote in the *Los Angeles Times* in 2001.[15]

Later, after he became a Dodger, Green got to meet the legend and asked him why he hadn't pitched that day.

"I did what I felt was right," Koufax told him.[16]

"He really set the standard for me," Green told the *Washington Post* in 2001. "He set a great example for all Jewish people. The first thing I always comment on about Sandy Koufax was that he was the great pitcher who did not pitch on Yom Kippur. It was something that always stood out for me."[17]

And ultimately Green decided to play on September 25, Erev Yom Kippur, but not on the Day of Atonement itself.

"There is nothing I would rather do than play against the Giants in a pennant race, but some things take precedence over that. I think it's important as a Jewish athlete to set an example for kids, even kids who are not Jewish, to show them that there are certain priorities in life. Baseball has been a huge part of my life. To put my religion before it I feel is a good example to set," Green said. "Whether we like it or not, we as athletes are role models."[18]

On September 25 Green went 2-for-5 with a home run in a 9-5 win, and announced he would donate that night's salary, about $70,000, to a charity assisting families affected by the terrorist attacks on 9/11.[19] The following night, it was Marquis Grissom in right field. (Grissom went 0-for-4 in a 6-4 loss.) Green wasn't at the ballpark that night, but didn't say where he would attend services, if he did. "That's personal."[20]

Of course, some Jews do play on Yom Kippur. One was Jesse Levis, a backup catcher for the Milwaukee Brewers who was sent to the plate as a pinch-hitter against the Baltimore Orioles on Yom Kippur in 1996. "It's not like I'm Sandy Koufax. I don't have that kind of leverage," Levis said. "I hope God forgives me."[21]

Levis struck out against Mike Mussina in the top of the seventh inning, then remained in the game. He grounded out twice but the Brewers won it, 8-7, in 10 innings.[22]

Norm Miller, a Jewish outfielder for the Houston Astros, was quoted by Jim Bouton in *Ball Four* as saying he'd never play on a Jewish holiday ... but not because of Koufax.

"I play on one and go 0-for-4 and the next day go 0-for-5 and that's it," Miller said. "I'll never play on a Jewish holiday again."[23]

NOTES

1   Edgar Munzel, "New Koufax? It Could Be Cubs' Holtzman," *The Sporting News*, April 20, 1968: 7. Joe Becker, the Cubs' pitching coach, who had previously coached Koufax when he had the same job with the Dodgers, said Holtzman and Koufax had similar personalities. "This young man has too much pride to settle for anything less than the best," Becker said. "In that respect, he's the same as Sandy. And the similarity doesn't end there. Because they both have such great pride, they also are inclined to fight themselves when they're out on the mound. I constantly had to remind Sandy that it's tough enough battling nine men without adding a tenth – yourself. And now I've had to use the same arguments on Ken. Both men also are in the habit of registering disgust after making a bad pitch. That's bad because it builds confidence in the hitter." In terms of stuff, Becker said, "Ken's fastball is just as good as Sandy's and he has better control of it than Koufax did at first. However, Ken's curve at this point isn't as good as Sandy's was. Ken obviously still has a good way to go to reach Sandy's top form. But he does have one advantage. When Sandy came up with the Dodgers in 1955, they were a pennant contender, and they remained one. Koufax had such poor control that we just couldn't afford to use him, and he was around for five years, until 1959, before he finally started coming. With Holtzman, it's different. He came up with a second-division team in 1966 and he immediately got the opportunity to pitch."

2   "Holtzman would end his career with 174 wins, nine more than Koufax. He also racked up 1,601 strikeouts, second to Koufax's 2,396 strikeouts among Jewish pitchers, and a 3.49 ERA." Jacob Gurvis, "Ken Holtzman, Who Had the Most Wins of Any Jewish Pitcher in MLB History, Dies at 78," *The Times of Israel*, April 16, 2024.

3   Howard M. Wasserman, "When They Were Kings: Greenberg and Koufax Sit on Yom Kippur," *Tablet*, October 11, 2016.

4   Murray Chass, "At Yom Kippur, Green Opts to Miss at Least One Game," *New York Times*, September 23, 2004.

5   Larry Stewart, "Drysdale Didn't Quite Have It This Day," *Los Angeles Times*, November 4, 2003.

6   Los Angeles Dodgers vs. Chicago Cubs box score, September 25, 1966.

7   Jason Turbow, "How Two Jewish Baseball Players Processed the 1972 Munich Massacre," *Moment*, September 7, 2017.

8   Ted Leavengood, "Mike Epstein," SABR Baseball Biography Project. His nickname appears as "Super Jew" and "Superjew" in various publications. Asked which he preferred, Epstein told *The Sporting News*: "Well, you spell Superman with one word."

9   Turbow.

10 Erev Yom Kippur is what the non-Jewish world considers to be the evening before Yom Kippur. The Jewish religion, citing biblical evidence, considers the day to begin at sunset the night before. Genesis 1:5: "And there was evening and there was morning, one day."

11 Louis Keene, "Jewish in the big leagues: Power Hitter Shawn Green Dishes at White House Event," *Forward*, May 19, 2022.

12 William Gildea, "Green Will Sit For Yom Kippur," *Washington Post*, September 26, 2001.

13 Keene. Green recalled a moment earlier in his career when he played a game a few days after Rosh Hashanah. He was with the Blue Jays, and he came to the plate while Jesse Levis was catching for the Brewers. Green greeted the Jewish catcher with the traditional Jewish New Year greeting, "Shana Tova." Not only did Levis respond, but so did the umpire, Al Clark, who also is Jewish. "It's probably the first time three Jews stood at the plate at the same time," Green said. (On a related note, according to research by SABR's Bruce Harris, the first time a Jewish pitcher faced a Jewish catcher with a Jewish batter at the plate was May 2, 1951, with the Detroit Tigers' Saul Rogovin on the mound and Joe Ginsberg behind the plate, and at bat was Lou Limmer of the Philadelphia A's.)

14 Keene.

15 Steve Springer, "Dodgers' Green Keeps the Faith," *Los Angeles Times*, September 26, 2001.

16 Springer.

17 Gildea.

18 Springer.

19 Gildea.

20 Springer

21 Merron. Levis said he did fast that day. "I was OK," he said. "I was just really thirsty."

22 Baltimore Orioles vs Milwaukee Brewers box score, September 23, 1996.

23 Merron.

In the Beginning –
Sandy Koufax Makes His
Major-League Debut

June 24, 1955: Milwaukee Braves 8, Brooklyn Dodgers 2, at County Stadium, Milwaukee

BY CRAIG GARRETSON

Ten weeks into his rookie season, Sandy Koufax finally made his long-awaited debut.

Brooklyn's $20,000 bonus baby[1] had missed most of March with a sore back,[2] and then the 19-year-old left-hander had a disastrous outing in an exhibition game against Brooklyn's Double-A affiliate, the Fort Worth Cats, on April 3.[3]

Two weeks later, before Brooklyn's fifth game of the season, Koufax sprained his right ankle during pregame warm-ups at Forbes Field in Pittsburgh,[4] and then hurt his left ankle 11 days later at Ebbets Field.[5] The Dodgers placed him on the 30-day disabled list on May 12[6] and reinstated him a month later.[7] The move came at the expense of Tommy Lasorda, who was optioned to Montreal to make room.[8] "It took the greatest left-handed pitcher in baseball history to get me off that Brooklyn club," Lasorda later joked, "and I still think they made a mistake."[9]

Dodgers manager Walt Alston wasn't in a rush to get the bonus baby into a game. Perhaps he was waiting for a lost cause in which the rookie could get his feet wet, but on the 1955 Dodgers blowout losses were few and far between. In his first two weeks after coming off the disabled list, the Dodgers went 10-4, with two of their losses by one run and another by three runs. The only opportunity came on June 12.[10] In an article in *The Sporting News* about how the Dodgers had gone 13-3 on their homestand between May 30 and June 12, Roscoe McGowen noted that they had primarily used just eight pitchers, with only two appearances given to a ninth pitcher – Karl Spooner, who been hampered by a sore shoulder since spring training.

The 10th pitcher on the roster, "the bonus southpaw kid," hadn't been used at all. Under the subhead "No Contributions by Koufax," McGowen had written:

"Koufax contributed nothing – although the kid almost got into the June 12 first game against the Cubs when it appeared the Dodgers were well beaten. With the Cubs leading, 9 to 2, Sandy was put to work in the bull pen, but when Pee Wee Reese smacked a three-run homer in the eighth inning off Jim

Davis to reduce the Bruins' margin, Jim Hughes, the Chicago fireman, was hurriedly put to work by Alston."[11]

Hughes pitched a scoreless top of the ninth, but the Dodgers lost the game, 9-5.

Koufax sat unused in the bullpen until June 24, the 10th day of a 12-day road trip. The Dodgers, riding a four-game winning streak, were comfortably in first place with a 14-game lead over their nearest pursuers, the Milwaukee Braves and Chicago Cubs. But this night, the Braves jumped ahead early on a home run by Eddie Mathews in the bottom of the first inning off Carl Erskine, then got three more in the second inning on an RBI double by Joe Adcock and a two-run home run by Del Crandall. The Dodgers finally got on the board in the top of the third on a sacrifice fly by Roy Campanella to score Jim Gilliam, but the Braves blew it open in the bottom half of the inning on a three-run home run by Henry Aaron.

Erskine was pulled after the Aaron home run and replaced by Jim Hughes, who closed out the third inning and the fourth without allowing a run. Hughes was scheduled to lead off the top of the fifth inning, but Alston sent up Johnny Podres to pinch-hit for him, and had Koufax warm up along with Clem Labine. Before this game, Alston had only warmed up Koufax as a decoy to dissuade opposing managers from sending up a left-handed pinch-hitter.[12] But in the bottom of the fifth inning of the Dodgers' 66th game of the season, in front of 43,068 fans at Milwaukee's County Stadium, Alston asked for the bonus baby.

Taking the mound to open the bottom of the fifth inning – after the Milwaukee public-address announcer pronounced his last name as "KOO-fax"[13] – Koufax's first pitch in the major leagues was a called strike to Johnny Logan. He missed with his next two pitches; Logan then blooped one off the end of the bat into right field for a base hit.[14]

The next batter was Mathews, and again Koufax got ahead with a first-pitch strike. The future Hall of Fame third baseman tapped the second pitch right back to Koufax for a tailor-made

1-4-3 double play, but instead the rookie threw the ball into center field.

Now with men on first and third, up stepped Aaron, Milwaukee's cleanup hitter. In the first of 130 matchups between the two Hall of Famers,[15] Aaron walked on four straight pitches. The bases were loaded with nobody out. Koufax fell behind the next batter, Bobby Thomson, 2-and-0, but battled back to a 3-and-2 count. He then struck out the Dodgers' 1951 nemesis on a fastball.[16] That brought up Adcock, who grounded a 2-and-1 pitch to Pee Wee Reese at shortstop for an inning-ending double play.

In the next inning, Koufax breezed through the bottom of the Braves lineup, getting Danny O'Connell to ground out to short, Crandall to fly out to center, and running the count full on Lew Burdette before ending the inning on a called strike three.

Due to lead off the top of the seventh, Koufax was pulled for pinch-hitter George Shuba, who singled to right field but was erased on a fielder's choice. Rube Walker had a two-out single to knock in Gilliam for the Dodgers' only other run of the game. Labine took over on the mound, giving up an unearned run on two walks and an error by Campanella, and Ed Roebuck pitched a scoreless eighth. Burdette went the distance for the Braves, giving up two runs on nine hits and four walks, as the Braves won, 8-2.

The first of Koufax's 397 appearances was in the books. In two innings, he had thrown 33 pitches, 16 for strikes, and struck out two batters, walked one, and gave up a bloop single, without allowing a run.

Even better days were to come.

SOURCES

In addition to the sources cited in the Notes, the author consulted Baseball-Reference.com and Retrosheet.org, and the SABR BioProject biography of Sandy Koufax written by Marc Z. Aaron.

https://www.baseball-reference.com/boxes/MLN/MLN195506240.shtml

https://www.retrosheet.org/boxesetc/1955/B06240MLN1955.htm

https://sabr.org/bioproj/person/sandy-koufax/

NOTES

1 Edward Gruver, *Koufax* (Dallas: Taylor Publishing, 2000), 84-85. Koufax was signed to a $6,000 contract with a $14,000 bonus. Under league rules in effect from 1953 to 1957, any player signed for more than a $4,000 bonus had to remain on the roster for his first two seasons. The Associated Press, in an article on December 15, 1954 in the *Brooklyn Daily Eagle,* and *The Sporting News* on December 22, 1954, both agreed that Koufax was signed for $20,000, but *The Sporting News* kept changing the figure over the next few months: It was reported as a $40,000 bonus on March 2, 1955, and a $25,000 bonus on April 13, 1955.

2 "Sandy Koufax, Dodger Bonus Kid, Shows Strikeout Pitch in Debut," *The Sporting News,* March 30, 1955: 26. "Sandy Koufax, the 19-year-old bonus baby lefthander, restored a lot of confidence in

himself one night recently in Vero Beach. The young man, who has pride – or perhaps youthful vanity – had been fretting because he had done no pitching and had a sore back." Koufax, facing "the minor league farm clubs' All-Stars," in two innings of work struck out five, walked two, and "nobody hit a fair ball off him." No date was given for the game.

3 "Fort Worth Kayoes Koufax," *The Sporting News,* April 13, 1955: 48. "Taking over in the sixth inning, the youngster gave up a run on a single, sacrifice, and wild pitch. Two more singles and a wild pitch added a counter for Forth Worth in the seventh and, in the eighth Koufax walked six batters in a row to force in three runs and Dick Williams followed with a single for two more tallies before Glenn Mickens relieved to end the inning." The 1955 Fort Worth Cats roster was studded with 11 future major leaguers, including Maury Wills, Joe Pignatano, and Dick Gray, and four future major-league managers, Sparky Anderson, Danny Ozark, Norm Sherry, and Dick Williams.

4 "Major Flashes: National League," *The Sporting News,* April 27, 1955: 25. "Sandy Koufax, Brooklyn bonus hurler, suffered an ankle sprain when he stepped in a hole chasing a long fly in pre-game drills at Pittsburgh, April 17. X-rays proved negative, but the southpaw was advised to remain off his feet for three days."

5 "Major Flashes: National League," *The Sporting News,* May 11, 1955: 23. "Sandy Koufax, Dodger bonus pitcher who twisted his right ankle when he stepped in a hole at Forbes Field, two weeks earlier, stepped in another depression at Ebbets Field, April 28, and injured his left ankle. X-rays were negative."

6 "Koufax Placed on Disabled List in Dodgers' Cut-Down," *The Sporting News,* May 18, 1955: 11. Teams were required to cut their rosters to 25 players by May 12. As a bonus baby, Koufax was required to be on the major-league roster until the end of 1956, but the newspaper reported that every day Koufax spent on the disabled list added another day to his bonus-baby status, extending it into 1957.

7 "Pale Hose Lead Swap Pace as Deadline Nears for Deals," *The Sporting News,* June 15, 1955: 9. "In other National League moves … the Dodgers released Southpaw Tommy Lasorda to their International League farm at Montreal and reinstated their bonus pitcher, Sandy Koufax, who had been on the disabled list. …"

8 Bill Plaschke and Tommy Lasorda. *I Live for This!: Baseball's Last True Believer* (San Diego: Houghton Mifflin Harcourt, 2007), 83. Lasorda said Dodgers general manager Emil "Buzzie" Bavasi asked him whom the Dodgers should cut, and Lasorda responded: "Koufax. That kid can't win up here." Bavasi evidently disagreed.

9 Joe Resnick (Associated Press), "Lasorda Remembers Being Replaced by Koufax," June 7, 2005, as quoted by Marc Z. Aaron in Koufax's SABR BioProject biography.

10 Roscoe McGowen, "Dodgers Support Rickey Dictum: '8 Pitchers Enough,'" *The Sporting News,* June 22, 1955: 7. "As things turned out, Smokey might as well have let Koufax do his first major league pitching. But, since a four-run deficit frequently means nothing to these Dodgers, Alston wasn't taking any chances."

11 Roscoe McGowen, "Dodgers Support Rickey Dictum: '8 Pitchers Enough.'"

12 Gruver, *Koufax,* 102.

13 Jane Leavy, *Sandy Koufax: A Lefty's Legacy* (New York: Harper Perennial, 2010), 74. The mispronunciation was despite *The Sporting News* on April 13, 1955, publishing a list of "uncommon names" and how they were pronounced, with Koufax's last name listed as "KO-fax." Meanwhile, according to Gruver in *Koufax* (page 83), Dodgers

scout Al Campanis thought Koufax's last name was "Kovacs," like the pioneering television comedian Ernie Kovacs.

14   Gruver, *Koufax*, 103.

15   Retrosheet.org, Selected Pitcher-Batter Matchups for Sandy Koufax. Aaron was 42-for-116 with 6 doubles, 3 triples, 7 home runs, 14 walks, and 12 strikeouts against Koufax, a .362/.431/.647 line, the best OPS of any batter with at least 18 at-bats.

16   Gruver, *Koufax*, 103.

A Wild Beginning: Sandy Koufax Makes His First Major-League Start

July 6, 1955: Pittsburgh Pirates 4, Brooklyn Dodgers 1,
at Forbes Field, Pittsburgh
(Game two of a doubleheader)

BY MARK S. STERNMAN

A two-outcome (walk or strikeout) pitcher in his first major-league start in the twilight game of a double-header, Brooklyn's Sandy Koufax pitched four shutout innings against Pittsburgh before walking in a run in the fifth and leaving the game. The Pirates gained a split by roughing up reliever Ed Roebuck to beat the Dodgers 4-1 before a crowd of 20,674 that witnessed a humble first in a historic hurling career.

Facing Vern Law, who had neither won 10 games in a season nor had an ERA lower than 4.50 in his first three big-league seasons but would have a breakout campaign in 1955, Brooklyn threatened in the top of the first. With one out, Pee Wee Reese singled. After Law fanned Duke Snider, Gil Hodges singled with two outs to put runners on the corners. Law escaped the jam by fanning future World Series hero Sandy Amoros.

With the doubleheader concluding "the last phase of [Brooklyn's] toughest schedule span – seven games in four days"[1] along with "the defections of [Johnny] Podres and [Billy] Loes and the doubt about [Russ] Meyer, young Koufax had entered … the starting picture."[2]

In a confrontation between two rookies who would star in the National League for years, Koufax first faced Roberto Clemente, who batted leadoff 55 times in 1955 but only 95 more times from 1956 to 1972. Koufax walked Clemente, which said more about the former than the latter given that Clemente drew just 18 walks in 501 plate appearances in 1955.

Koufax struck out Dick Cole swinging, and on the third strike, backup backstop Rube Walker picked off Clemente trying to steal second. The play proved critical as Koufax walked each of the next two before escaping the frame on a liner to right.

Brooklyn got its run in the top of the second. Don Zimmer doubled and scored on Jim Gilliam's single to center that turned into an out when Gilliam tried to advance on the throw home that first baseman Dale Long cut off and threw to Cole at second.

As in the bottom of first, the baserunner out loomed large as Walker followed with the third straight Dodger hit of the inning. But Koufax struck out bunting, and Don Hoak grounded out, leaving Brooklyn up just 1-0.

Koufax pitched around walks to Dick Groat and Law in the second with strikeouts of Hardy Peterson and Clemente.

The Dodgers went out in order in the third. Koufax pitched to contact in the bottom half. After a lineout, Román Mejías singled for the first Pittsburgh hit, but Frank Thomas grounded into a second-to-first double play.

Amoros tripled to lead off the top of the fourth. Impressively, Law escaped unscored on with a grounder to third by Zimmer, a swinging strikeout of Gilliam, an intentional walk to Walker, and another K of the weak-hitting Koufax.

Koufax protected the lead in the fourth, working around a one-out walk of Gene Freese.

Brooklyn went quietly in the fifth, and Pittsburgh knocked out Koufax by making him throw too many pitches. After Koufax fanned Law, Clemente and Cole knocked consecutive singles to put runners on first and second. Mejías forced Cole, putting runners on the corners with two outs. Koufax could not, however, get the final out, walking Long and Thomas, forcing in a run that tied the game and ended the pitcher's first career start.

John Drebinger of the *New York Times* wrote, "Koufax did some stout hurling to overcome a grievous lack of control."[3]

Second-year manager Walter Alston chose the rookie Roebuck to replace the rookie Koufax. In *The Sporting News*, Bob Broeg noted, "Roebuck … came up to the Dodgers from Montreal as a highly-regarded solid man of the mound and hasn't disappointed, muscling in ahead of Jim Hughes and Clem Labine as captain of the Brooklyn bull pen."[4] Still, the choice in hindsight appears curious as Roebuck had thrown 4⅓ innings on July 3, gotten two outs on July 5, and pitched two innings of relief in the first game of the doubleheader. While the Dodgers had a decimated pitching staff, Roebuck had already worked seven relief innings in a four-day span before this appearance. In the short term, Roebuck repaid Alston's faith by striking out

Freese, also a rookie, with the bases loaded to keep the game deadlocked at 1-1.

Amoros walked with one out in the top of the sixth. Amoros swiped 10 bases in 1955, but catcher Peterson threw out the Dodger attempting to steal second. The rookie Peterson threw out nearly half of the runners attempting to steal against him in 1955 and exactly half of all runners in his 65 career games behind the plate. The next 12 hitters all went out in order until Snider singled with two outs in the eighth, but Law got a groundout from Hodges to end the inning.

Pittsburgh surged ahead in the home half as Roebuck may have understandably tired. With one out, Long singled; Tom Saffell ran for him. In the first 28 appearances of his career before July 3, Roebuck had yielded two triples. Beginning that day through this doubleheader over four appearances, Roebuck gave up three triples. Over the course of their careers, Roebuck held Freese to one hit in 13 plate appearances, but that hit won a game.

Freese, "who took a third strike from Roebuck in the fifth, hit a line drive to right which bounced off the wall and past … Gilliam for a triple and a run. The Dodger infield came in, but … Groat bounced a single over … Hoak's head into left, scoring Freese."[5] One out later, Law doubled in Groat to give himself a 4-1 edge. Alston left Roebuck in to absorb blow after blow.

Law bent did not break on his way to a complete game. With one out in the ninth, he gave up singles to Zimmer and Gilliam that put the tying run at the plate. Law then got Walker to hit into a 4-6-3 twin killing to end the game.

The player of the game, Law, by capturing the nightcap, "saved the night at Forbes Field for the largest crowd since opening day [and] became a man of distinction. … Law stands … alone in the National League as the only pitcher to go the distance twice and beat the Dodgers. And he did it within the space of six days."[6] Law threw 132 pitches and gave up nine hits and two walks while tying his season high in strikeouts with 10. (He would fan 12 in 18 innings on July 19.) He improved to 5-3 for a team with a 29-53 record after its win over the 56-24 Dodgers. In 1955, Law won MVP votes for the first of four times in his career.

Koufax had walked eight while striking out four. This inauspicious first start notwithstanding, Koufax would transform his career in Los Angeles on his way to Cooperstown. More than a decade later, he recounted, "After I pitched the no-hitter in 1964, a woman wrote to ask if I could possibly be the same Koufax … whom she had seen years ago … She had felt so sorry for me … that she had almost cried. … [O]nly once did I ever walk more than I walked in half a game on my first start. That was in 1960, when I walked nine men in a thirteen-inning game."[7]

SOURCES

In addition to the sources cited in the Notes, the author consulted Baseball-Reference.com and Retrosheet.org.

NOTES

1   John Drebinger, "Roberts Scores 5-to-4 Triumph When Brooks' Rally Falls Short," *New York Times*, July 6, 1955: 31.

2   Roscoe McGowen, "Strikeout Artist Spooner Strikes Stride for Brooks," *The Sporting News*, July 6, 1955: 5. Meyer was on the 30-day disabled list after suffering a fractured shoulder in a collision with the Milwaukee Braves' Bill Bruton. "Campy and Walker Shelved; Meyer Put on Disabled List," *The Sporting News*, July 6, 1955: 5.

3   John Drebinger, "Brooks Win 10-5, Then Lose 4-1 Test," *New York Times*, July 7, 1955: 30.

4   Bob Broeg, "Cards in Front Again with Top Rookies," *The Sporting News*, July 13, 1955: 2.

5   Jack Hernon, "Bucs Whip Dodgers, 4-1, After 10-5 Setback," *Pittsburgh Post-Gazette*, July 7, 1955: 18.

6   Lester J. Biederman, "Dodgers Find Law Hasn't Changed," *Pittsburgh Press*, July 7, 1955: Section 2, 20.

7   Sandy Koufax with Ed Linn, *Koufax* (New York: The Viking Press, 1966), 99.

19-Year-Old Koufax Tosses Two-Hitter and Fans 14 to Notch First Big-League Victory

August 27, 1955: Brooklyn Dodgers 7, Cincinnati Redlegs 0, at Ebbets Field, Brooklyn

BY GREGORY H. WOLF

Brooklyn Dodgers skipper Walter "Smokey" Alston was on edge. Though his club (80-45) was in first place, leading the Milwaukee Braves by 10 games, they had been playing terribly and had lost 12 of their last 18 contests. To shake up his team, he tabbed 19-year-old Sandy Koufax to start the final contest of a four-game series with the fifth-place Cincinnati Redlegs (64-65) in front of family and friends at Ebbets Field.

It had been thus far a rough rookie season for the Brooklyn-born Koufax. Blessed with a blazing heater and devastating curve ball, the southpaw had whiffed 58 in 32 innings, including 34 in consecutive games, as a freshman the previous year at the University of Cincinnati, where he had enrolled to study architecture; however, he suffered from chronic bouts with wildness. Reds scouts, reported sportswriter Lou Smith of the *Cincinnati Enquirer*, were turned off by the teenager's lack of control and doubted he would ever develop big-league "stuff."[1] The Dodgers swooped in and signed Koufax for $20,000 (including a $6,000 salary), but were required to keep the "bonus baby" on their roster for two full seasons.[2] It was obvious that Koufax was not ready for the big leagues and many wondered if he might be better suited to Class-A ball, where he'd at least have the opportunity to pitch regularly.

Koufax's season started badly and seemed to get worse. Early on he sprained both ankles within a three-day period and then soon developed acute pain in his left wing and landed on the 30-day disabled list without yet having thrown his first regular season pitch. "All of a sudden, my arm was so sore I couldn't throw at all," he said.[3] He made his major-league debut on June 24, tossing two scoreless innings of relief. About two weeks later he was given his first start, but was pulled after 4⅔ innings having walked eight, yet yielded just a run in the second game of a double header against the Pittsburgh Pirates. Tabbed to make his second start of the season, against the Reds, Koufax had thus far walked more batters than innings (12 to 11⅔) and had not yet earned a decision. "I'd be happier if I could be

pitching regularly," he said, fully aware of his lack of experience and bonus status which had the potential to rankle veterans. "But I know I've got a lot to learn before that can happen."[4]

On a warm, summer Friday afternoon, Ebbets Field was packed with 18,133 spectators on Ladies Day, though paid admission was just 7,204.[5] "Dem Bums" were in the middle of a 16-game home stand and had their work cut out for them against skipper Birdie Tebbetts' hard-hitting squad, winners of seven of their last nine games and were making a push to finish in the first division. After Koufax quickly dispatched the first two batters, muscular Ted Kluszewski singled to right. It would be a long time before the Reds connected off the 19-year-old again.

The Dodgers, on the other hand, teed off on Reds starter Art Fowler. In his second season, the 33-year-old right-hander was 9-7 following an impressive rookie campaign (12-10), but was overmatched by Brooklyn's slugging crew. Leadoff hitter Jim Gilliam walloped a double off the scoreboard in right field. After a wild pitch sent him to third with one out, Duke Snider walked, and Roy Campanella drove home the first run on a sacrifice fly. Up stepped Carl Furillo, one of the hottest hitters in the league, batting .395 (45-for-114) and slugging .605 in his last 27 games. He sent a line drive "dozen rows back in the lower center-field stands," wrote Dodgers beat reporter Roscoe McGowen, to make it 3-0. It was the Reading Rifle's 22nd home run of the season to set a new career high.[6]

After young Sandy breezed through the second, third, and fourth innings, whiffing five more and issuing a walk to Big Klu, the Jackie Robinson show began. The 36-year-old led off the fourth by beating out a single to deep short. On successive pitches to Gil Hodges he stole second and then third base. Reds reporter Lou Smith took what might be construed as an offhanded dig at Robinson's aggressive baserunning, noting that he reached third by "nonchalantly kicking the ball out of [Rocky] Bridges hand."[7] After Hodges walked, Sandy Amoros hit a tailor-made double-play grounder to shortstop Roy McMillan, but the future two-time All-Star and three-time Gold Glove winner fumbled the ball, according to McGowen, and could only manage to force Hodges at second while Robison crossed the plate. [No error was charged]. The Dodgers tacked on another run in the next frame when the Duke and Campy walked with one out to send Fowler to the showers. Furillo greeted reliever Gerry Staley with a single to load the bases, then Robinson drew a walk to force in Snider. The Dodgers threatened to blow the game open, but Hodges' grounder to third forced out Campanella at home and then Amoros whiffed.

By the end of the fifth Tebbetts had seen enough of Koufax, who had whiffed eight. Lou Smith reported that the hard-nosed pilot instructed his batters to play a waiting game to disturb the rhythm of the young twirler. "It failed to disrupt Koufax who continued to mow 'em down with uncanny consistency," continued Smith.[8] The devious strategy nonetheless had an immediate effect. Koufax issued consecutive one-out walks to Johnny Temple and Smoky Burgess in the sixth which drew Alston to the mound for the first and only time in the game. "I thought maybe he might be trying to aim the ball," explained Alston. "I just wanted to tell him to keep throwing it as he had been doing."[9] Koufax's two-out balk sent both runners up a station, but he retired Wally Post on a soft fly to right field.

Koufax had another hiccup in the seventh, walking Bridges and McMillan with two outs before emphatically ending the frame by making Chuck Harmon his 11th strikeout victim.

The Dodgers scored their final two runs in the seventh. After McMillan flubbed Furillo's grounder for the only error of the game, Robinson sent the first pitch to him from Rudy Minarcin, the Reds fourth hurler of the afternoon, into the lower left-center-field stands for a two-run blast, his seventh of the season, for a 7-0 Dodgers lead.

Koufax punched out two more in the eighth and entered the ninth with an outside chance to tie Nap Rucker's team record of 16 strikeouts in a game, set in 1909. That quest became moot when Post grounded to third. Gus Bell, on a tear in his last 23 games, slugging .628 with seven home runs and 21 RBIs, donned the golden sombrero with his fourth strikeout. "The lad had as much stuff as any pitcher I've faced in quite a spell," gushed Bell who couldn't remember whiffing four times in a game, even in high school.[10] Sam Mele, entering the game batting .145, connected for the "hardest hit ball," according to McGowen, a line-drive double to left field.[11] Koufax retired Bridges on a popup to short to end the game in 2 hours and 37 minutes, and to record his first big-league victory and shutout.

"He had a good curve and his fast ball was good, too," said batterymate Campanella. "His control was all right. He never was wild at any time. Did not ever miss the plate by much."[12] Sportswriter Lou Smith was equally impressed by the teenager, lamenting that Koufax did not play for the Reds. "He had poise,

a smooth delivery, along with a changeup that usually takes years for a young hurler to acquire."[13]

Koufax's 14 strikeouts were the most by an NL pitcher in 1955. Combined with the nine strikeouts by Reds pitchers, the game produced 23 punchouts which tied a then-major-league record for most in a nine-inning game, matching the mark set by the Boston Braves and Reds in 1901 and matched by the New York Yankees and Washington Senators in 1914.

Continuing his season-long roller-coaster, Koufax was clubbed for five hits and four runs by the Braves in his next appearance, on August 31 at Ebbets Field, then followed that outing by blanking the Pittsburgh Pirates on five hits and fanned six on September 3. He concluded the season with a 2-2 slate and 3.02 ERA, 30 strikeouts and 28 walks in 41⅔ innings for the eventual pennant-winning Dodgers who defeated the Yankees in seven games to capture their only World Series in Brooklyn. Koufax did not pitch in that Fall Classic.

Plagued by excruciating elbow pain, Koufax retired prematurely 12 years later, after winning his third Cy Young Award in four seasons at the age of 30 with 165 wins and 40 shutouts. He was elected to the National Baseball Hall of Fame in his first year of eligibility, 1972, becoming at the age of 36 the youngest player to be enshrined.

Sandy Koufax's 14 strikeouts on August 27, 1955, were the most by any National League pitcher that season. Courtesy of National Baseball Hall of Fame.

SOURCES

In addition to the sources cited in the Notes, the author accessed Retrosheet.org, Baseball-Reference.com, Newspapers.com, and SABR.org.

https://www.baseball-reference.com/boxes/BRO/BRO195508270.shtml

http://www.retrosheet.org/boxesetc/1955/B08270BRO1955.htm

NOTES

1   Lou Smith, "Koufax Lacks Stuff, Reds Scouts Reported," *Cincinnati Enquirer* August 28, 1955: 58.

2   Instituted in 1947, the bonus rule required major-league teams to retain any player who signed a contract in excess of $4,000 on their 25-man roster for two seasons. This rule went through various iterations until it was abolished in 1965.

3   Roscoe McGowen, "Brooklyn-Bred 'Bonus Baby' Is Coming of Age," *New York Times*, August 29, 1955: 13.

4   McGowen, "Brooklyn-Bred 'Bonus Baby' Is Coming of Age."

5   Roscoe McGowen, "Koufax Is Victor," *New York Times*, August 29, 1955: S1.

6   McGowen, "Koufax Is Victor."

7   Lou Smith, "Koufax Fans 14 as Dodgers trounce Reds, 7-0," *Cincinnati Enquirer*, August 28, 1955: 55.

8   Smith, "Koufax Fans 14 as Dodgers trounce Reds, 7-0."

9   McGowen, "Koufax Is Victor."

10   Smith, "Koufax Lacks Stuff, Reds Scouts Reported."

11   McGowen, "Koufax Is Victor."

12   McGowen, "Koufax Is Victor."

13   Smith, "Koufax Lacks Stuff, Reds Scouts Reported."

Bonus Baby Sandy Koufax Pitches Five-Hit Shutout Against Pirates for Second Win

September 3, 1955: Brooklyn Dodgers 4, Pittsburgh Pirates 0, at Ebbets Field, Brooklyn

BY STEVEN C. WEINER

"Only twice in my life has my spine actually tingled. Once was when I saw the Sistine Chapel. The other was when I saw Sandy Koufax throw a fastball."

– Al Campanis scouting Koufax[1]

You're a 19-year-old pitcher, injured and sitting on the bench for more than two months before your major-league debut, a two-inning relief appearance, your team trailing by six runs. Your rookie season promises to be like a roller coaster. Shouldn't you be honing your pitching skills in the minors? Not Sandy Koufax. He was a bonus baby, a free agent signed for an estimated $20,000 under the bonus rules of 1953-1957.[2] Author Paul Dickson aptly characterized the fate of many bonus babies, noting that "their talent rusted in idleness on the bench."[3]

Koufax's performance in his first year at the University of Cincinnati unsurprisingly garnered considerable attention – 34 strikeouts in two consecutive games,[4] 51 strikeouts and 30 walks in 30 innings, and a 3-1 record.[5] The Dodgers, always reluctant to sign bonus players, knew very well that the Giants, Yankees, Pirates, Cubs, Indians, and Braves were all interested in signing Koufax.[6]

When Koufax became a Brooklyn Dodger in December 1954, he became their first and only signing under the various iterations of the bonus rules in effect from 1947 to 1965. In 1953 one bonus rule stated that "any player signed for more than a $4,000 bonus must stay two full seasons on the roster of the signing club."[7]

Opportunity knocked infrequently in this bonus baby's 1955 season – that first appearance in relief in June against the Braves, his first start in July against the Pirates, and an occasional relief inning here and there.[8] His first win came on the last Saturday in August giving us just a hint of what the future might hold. Koufax shut out the Redlegs 7-0 at Ebbets Field for his first win, pitching a two-hitter and striking out 14.[9]

The roller coaster? Four days later, Koufax's relief appearance against the Braves was a flop, four earned runs on four hits in one inning of work. As the baseball calendar turned to September, Koufax's pitching stats told various stories – two starts in eight appearances, 22 strikeouts and 17 walks in 21⅔ innings, a 2.91 ERA. But Koufax was getting another chance as the starting pitcher facing the Pirates and Bob Friend (9-8, 3.26 ERA) three days after the disastrous relief appearance.

A groundout and two strikeouts in the top of the first were a sign of good things to come for Koufax. Friend, who already owned two wins over the Dodgers in 1955, was not so fortunate in the bottom of the first. Jim Gilliam opened with a drag-bunt single and stole second before Pee Wee Reese struck out. The Dodgers led the majors in stolen bases, and their thievery paid off once again in this rally. Duke Snider lined a single to right-center scoring Gilliam for a 1-0 Dodgers lead.[10]

The best opportunity all afternoon for the Pirates came in the third inning, the only time they ever had two runners on base. With one out, Friend lined a single to left and advanced to second when Eddie O'Brien was hit by a pitch. However, Gene Freese struck out swinging and Román Mejías fouled out to Gil Hodges at first. It was the only time all afternoon that a Pirates baserunner who had gotten a hit advanced as far as second base and the opportunity went for naught.

The groundouts kept coming for Koufax, six of them for all the outs in the fourth and fifth innings. In fact, other than yielding those five harmless singles, Koufax allowed only one ball to be hit to the outfield, a short fly to Gilliam in left to end the sixth inning.[11]

But the pressure was still on Koufax because the Dodgers couldn't add to the lead against Friend until the seventh. Their best opportunity was in the fourth inning. Reese opened with a single to right and advanced to second on a passed ball, but Friend retired Snider, Roy Campanella, and Carl Furillo in order.

Friend finally yielded a second run in the seventh inning. Snider opened with a single to left, advanced to second on Campanella's sacrifice, and scored on Furillo's line single to right. The Dodgers led 2-0.

Roberto Clemente fouled out as a pinch-hitter for Friend in the eighth; it was Roy Face on the mound in relief against the Dodgers in their next turn. Singles by Gil Hodges and Don Zimmer to open the inning put runners on first and third. Hodges scored on a passed ball with Zimmer reaching third. Another bunt by Gilliam scored Zimmer for the final Dodgers run.

Koufax yielded a harmless second walk in the ninth, but retired the side without further consequence for his second victory. As noted, Hodges was kept busy fielding throws on groundouts, totaling 13 putouts for the game. Snider in center and Furillo in right never had to field a fly ball. Koufax's control was as important to his success in this game as any other factor.

Less than one month remained in the 1955 regular season and it wasn't much of a pennant race in the National League after the Dodgers won their first 10 games. Now they led the second-place Milwaukee Braves by 14 games and eventually clinched the pennant on September 8, the earliest date in league history.[12]

After the clinching, Koufax pitched ineffectively on three occasions, losing twice including in a relief appearance against the Pirates on the next to last day of the regular season.[13] Koufax's line for the season – 2-2, 3.02 ERA, 28 walks/30 strikeouts in 41⅔ innings with two brilliant shutouts.

Sometimes the stat line tells only part of the story. When manager Walter Alston had given the ball to his bonus baby in late August against the Reds, the Dodgers pitching was crippled with injuries to both Billy Loes and Don Newcombe. Koufax's brilliant shutout prompted sportswriter Roscoe McGowen to remark, "Nobody raised his hat higher to young Koufax than his manager, who certainly needed a lift."[14] Surely the shutout of the Pirates deserved an extra wave of the cap by Alston.

We can speculate that Koufax's path to dominant pitcher would have been different had he started his career in the minor leagues to learn his craft and not been subjected to the bonus-baby rules. *Baseball Almanac* notes that nine pitchers made their bonus-baby debuts during the 1954 and 1955 seasons. Only Pittsburgh's Laurin Pepper (8) made more starts than Koufax (5) in the first 50 innings of their major-league careers.[15] Give credit to Alston for using Koufax as he did and reaffirming to the press after clinching the National League pennant, "It was a 25-man job."[16]

With the last out of World Series Game Seven, the season became historic – the only World Series title ever celebrated by the Brooklyn Dodgers and their Flatbush faithful.[17] As for Koufax, he remained on the Dodgers' postseason roster in 1955 and 1956, but did not pitch in either World Series. Sometimes, greatness takes a while. When opportunity knocked in 1963, Koufax's MVP performance led the Los Angeles Dodgers to a four-game sweep of the Yankees for the World Series title.[18]

AUTHOR'S NOTES

As former Brooklyn Dodgers fans, the author and his father finally got to see Sandy Koufax pitch in 1963, an opportunity they never enjoyed at Ebbets Field. In the midst of his record-breaking 25-5 season, Koufax merely struck out 13 at the Polo Grounds and handed the hapless New York Mets their 13th consecutive loss.[19]

In his book *The Baseball 100*, author Joe Posnanski attributes the reference to Koufax and the Sistine Chapel to Dodgers executive Buzzie Bavasi.[20] Perhaps both Campanis and Bavasi uttered a similar line or maybe it makes not one bit of difference. Posnanski concludes his essay on Koufax in fitting fashion – "Baseball wouldn't be the same without Sandy Koufax, the man, the myth, the legend, and the balderdash."[21]

SOURCES

The author accessed Retrosheet.org (retrosheet.org/boxesetc/1955/B09030BRO1955.htm), Baseball Almanac (baseball-almanac.com/legendary/Bonus_Babies.shtml), and Baseball-Reference.com (baseball-reference.com/boxes/BRO/BRO195509030.shtml) for box scores/play-by-play and other data.

NOTES

1   Roger Kahn, *The Era 1947-1957 When the Yankees, Giants and Dodgers Ruled the World* (Lincoln, Nebraska: University of Nebraska Press, 1993), 327.

2   "New Pitching Prospect for Dodgers," *New York Times*, December 14, 1954: 47.

3   Paul Dickson, *The Dickson Baseball Dictionary, Third Edition* (New York: W.W. Norton & Company, 2009), 125.

4   Marc Z. Aaron, "Sandy Koufax," SABR Baseball Biography Project. Koufax pitched a four-hitter against Wayne State, striking out 16 and in his next start against Louisville, he fanned 18, a school record.

5   The *New York Times* reported that Koufax recorded a 4-0 record at the University of Cincinnati (John Drebinger, "O'Malley Replies to Brooks' Critic, *New York Times*, December 15, 1954: 44). Other sources (Sandy Koufax with Ed Linn, *Koufax* (New York: Viking Press, 1966), 43; *2022-23 Cincinnati Baseball Record Book*, gobearcats.com/documents/2022/9/22/2022-23_Baseball_Record_Book.pdf, 7.) report Koufax's one-season record, 3-1, 2.81 ERA. Koufax's record of 18 strikeouts was broken by Bill Faul, UC's first baseball All-American, who fanned 24 in a game against the Jacksonville Naval Station in 1961.

6   "Koufax, Boro Sandlot Star, Newest Dodger," *Brooklyn Daily Eagle*, December 15, 1954: 18.

7   Brent Kelley, *Baseball's Bonus Babies: Conversations with 24 High-Priced Ballplayers* (Jefferson, North Carolina: McFarland & Company, 2006), 1.

8   Mark S. Sternman, "A wild beginning: Sandy Koufax makes his first major-league start," SABR Baseball Games Project.

9   Gregory H. Wolf, "August 27, 1955: Teenage Sandy Koufax strikes out 14 in first big-league win," SABR Baseball Games Project.

10 Roscoe McGowen, "Koufax Blanks Pittsburgh; Brooks Need 7 for Pennant," *New York Times*, September 4, 1955: 5-2. McGowen notes that Snider was "still booed by one or two fans." The Dodgers lost a late August doubleheader to Cincinnati. Slowly recovering from a bout with the flu, Snider was in a 10-game homerless streak and had stranded eight runners in the doubleheader. He was loudly booed. After the second game, he blurted to reporters: "Fans! What a bunch of cruddy front-runners! They're the worst fans in the league!" He apologized the very next day. (Bill Madden, "Hall-of-Famer Duke Snider, the Last Surviving Regular of the 'Boys of Summer' Dodgers, Dead at 84," NewYorkDailyNews.com, February 28, 2011, nydailynews.com/sports/baseball/hall-of-famer-duke-snider-surviving-regular-boys-summer-dodgers-dead-84-article-1.136741).

11 McGowen, "Koufax Blanks Pittsburgh; Brooks Need 7 for Pennant."

12 Roscoe McGowen, "Record N.L. Starting Streak, Newk's Surge Highlighted Dodgers' Drive," *The Sporting News*, September 14, 1955: 5.

13 Gordon J. Gattie, "September 24, 1955: Bob Friend clinches NL ERA title for last-place Pirates," SABR Baseball Games Project. Friend won five games in September, including a shutout and three complete games, to finish the season with a 14-9 record. For the next three seasons, no one in the major leagues started more games than Bob Friend (118).

14 Roscoe McGowen, "Hats Off ... Sandy Koufax," *The Sporting News*, September 7, 1955: 19.

15 Pepper won two games during his short major-league career (1954-1957). Pittsburgh's Red Swanson also made five starts during the first 50 innings of his major-league career (1955-1957).

16 Roscoe McGowen, "'It Was 25-Man Job,' Says Smokey, Dodging Orchids," *The Sporting News*, September 14, 1955: 5.

17 Steven C. Weiner, "October 4, 1955: Brooklyn Dodgers win first World Series as 'Next Year' finally arrives," SABR Baseball Games Project.

18 The reader is directed to SABR author Andy McCue's 1963 World Series essays available on the SABR Games Project website.

19 Steven C. Weiner, "July 12, 1963: Koufax fans 13, hands Mets 13th loss in a row," SABR Baseball Games Project.

20 Joe Posnanski, *The Baseball 100* (New York: Simon & Schuster, 2021), 189. "As soon as I saw that fastball," Bavasi said, "the hair raised up on my arms. The only other time the hair on my arms raised up was when I saw the ceiling of the Sistine Chapel.'"

21 Posnanski, 196.

Koufax K's 13, Combines With Cubs Pitchers to Tie NL Game-Strikeout Record

May 16, 1957: Brooklyn Dodgers 3, Chicago Cubs 2, at Wrigley Field, Chicago

BY HOWARD ROSENBERG

On May 16, 1957, "a day after Sandy Koufax lost his bonus-baby status, meaning he could be farmed out by the Dodgers,"[1] he and two Chicago Cubs pitchers, Moe Drabowsky and Turk Lown, combined to tie the record for the most strikeouts in a National League game: 23. The record lasted until the Philadelphia Phillies played the Los Angeles Dodgers on June 22, 1959, when, in a nine-inning game, three pitchers struck out 24 batters, with Koufax again on the mound.[2]

On the 1957 date in Chicago, Koufax, 21, was pitching in his eighth game of the season but just his second start. In none of the seven previous appearances did he pitch more than four innings. It was Koufax's 17th career start and his third against the Cubs.

The Cubs had yet to win a home game in '57, this afternoon game against the Dodgers being their eighth try.

With a 7-17 record, the Cubs were already 9½ games behind the league-leading Cincinnati Redlegs and Milwaukee Braves, who shared the league lead after just 24 games, and just a half-game ahead of the cellar-dwelling Pittsburgh Pirates. In contrast, the Dodgers at 14-10 were in second place. Surprisingly, the Dodgers and Cubs had both scored 106 runs, but Brooklyn's pitching had allowed only 92 runs, while 133 opposing runners had crossed the plate against Cubs hurlers. *Chicago Tribune* reporter Edward Prell wrote that the "biggest disappointment to Manager Bob Scheffing has been failure of the pitching staff."[3]

It wasn't the pitchers, however, who failed Scheffing on May 16; it was most of the team's batters and Ernie Banks, in particular, his average dropping to .220 after the Cubs' loss.[4]

Koufax's arm heated up Wrigley Field in the 44-degree chill, though "it felt much colder," wrote *New York Times* sportswriter Roscoe McGowen.[5]

Before 3,105 spectators, the game began with Jim "Junior" Gilliam facing Moe Drabowsky, who was the same age as Koufax but in his second major-league season, one less than Koufax.[6] Gilliam grounded out. After Pee Wee Reese grounded out, Duke Snider struck out.

Bobby Morgan led off the Cubs' half of the first and flied out to center. Koufax then struck out both Bobby Del Greco and Ernie Banks.

After Carl Furillo opened the top of the second with a walk, Drabowsky struck out Gil Hodges, Sandy Amorós, and Don Zimmer, the first two looking. (In 1957 Drabowsky fanned the sixth-most batters in the majors and more than any Dodgers pitcher.)[7]

The Cubs second began with the game's first hit, Lee Walls getting a double on a blooper to right. Walls, a .271 hitter, had a .458 slugging percentage against Koufax in their 68 career matchups. Koufax matched Drabowsky, striking out two of the next three batters, Jim Bolger on four pitches and Dale Long on three. Between them, Jack Littrell fouled out.

Drabowsky set down the Dodgers one-two-three in the third, Rube Walker and Koufax both whiffing.

In the bottom half, Koufax walked Cal Neeman and then retired the side, striking out Del Greco for the third out.

In the top of the fourth, the Dodgers broke the scoreless tie. It was the first half-inning in which no batter struck out. Reese started the action with a walk. After Snider flied out, Reese stole second, and Furillo drove him home with a double. Hodges' single placed runners on the corners. Amorós hit into a force out to second baseman Morgan that removed Hodges from the bases and allowed Furillo to score. Zimmer's grounder to short forced Amorós at second, ending the inning with the Dodgers ahead by two.

In the Cubs' fourth, Koufax struck out Banks for the second time, the Cubs' shortstop again swinging at strike three. Walls walked on a full count, but the Cubs stranded him on first when both Bolger and Littrell flied out.

The fifth inning started with a lineout to short and a strikeout. Drabowsky walked Gilliam, who stole second. Reese grounded out.

The Cubs' turn at the plate in the fifth produced a run without a hit. Koufax struck out Long and walked Neeman.

Drabowsky watched the third strike end his time in the batter's box. After Morgan walked, Jim Fanning pinch-hit for Del Greco and reached first when Reese muffed his bouncer to short.

Dick Young wrote, "Reese scooped the ball, then lost the handle. The ball seemed caught up in a vacuum above his glove, Reese made another stab at it – and another miss. Finally, he clutched it and threw to first – just too late."[8]

The error seemed to disconcert Koufax. His first two pitches to Banks landed outside the strike zone. Manager Walter Alston visited the mound but didn't call for a new pitcher. Koufax threw two more balls, walking Banks on four pitches and forcing Neeman home. The run was unearned but still cut the Brooklyn lead in half. A fly ball to center by Walls ended the frame.

On a 1-and-2 count in the sixth, Snider doubled the Dodgers lead, lining his fifth homer of the season into the right-field bleachers and "into a strong wind."[9] The next three batters failed to get on base.

In the bottom of the sixth, despite Bolger's single and Long's base on balls, Koufax prevented the Cubs from closing the gap, getting two swinging strikeouts and a force-play grounder.

Turk Lown replaced Drabowsky on the mound in the seventh and threw just nine pitches to end the inning one-two-three.

After the seventh-inning stretch, Koufax shut down the top of the Cubs lineup. After Morgan flied out to right, Koufax struck out Walt Moryn and Ernie Banks, the latter for the third time. Only one right-handed batter was struck out more during a career by Koufax than Banks's 31 times: Wally Post, who fanned 32 times.

Though Snider and Furillo both singled in the eighth with two outs, Brooklyn couldn't increase its lead, Hodges' groundout to third ending the threat.

The Cubs scored their other unearned run in the bottom of the eighth on Walls' "high fly to left-center" when "Amorós cut in front of Snider, who could have caught the ball" but dropped it for a two-base error.[10]

Walls took third on Bolger's single and scored on Littrell's fly ball. Down just a run, Long ended the Cubs' threat by grounding into a double play.

In the Dodgers' ninth, Lown prevented the ball from leaving the infield, getting Brooklyn's 6-7-8 batters to ground out.

In the game's last half-inning, after Koufax recorded his 13th strikeout by fanning Cal Neeman, he walked Casey Wise on four pitches. The Cubs mounted another threat when, as the *Times*'s McGowen wrote, "Bobby Morgan slashed a ball a little to Koufax's right. Sandy tried to field the ball, which was headed toward Reese, who could have handled it perhaps for a double play. Koufax slowed the ball, then chased it and couldn't pick it up. It went for a hit."[11]

Morgan's infield single put runners on first and second. Moryn, though, fouled out to third and Banks lifted a fly ball to left-center that shortstop Reese caught, giving Koufax his second win of the season. It was the third complete game of his career and his first since September 3, 1955.

Koufax struck out 13, the second time in his career that he had double-digit strikeouts in a game. On August 27, 1955, he fanned 14.

The Cubs batters weren't the only ones to struggle against Koufax. "Hitting against Sandy Koufax," said Pirates slugger and future Hall of Famer Willie Stargell, "is like drinking coffee with a fork."[12]

ACKNOWLEDGMENT

The author would like to thank Mike Emeigh for providing the information about this game and record-setting games on August 27, 1955, and May 22, 1901.

SOURCES

In addition to the sources cited in the Notes, the author consulted Baseball-Reference.com, Stathead.com, and Retrosheet.org for player, team, and season data.

https://www.baseball-reference.com/boxes/CHN/CHN195705160.shtml

https://www.retrosheet.org/boxesetc/1957/B05160CHN1957.htm

NOTES

1   Dick Young, "Koufax 'Manhandles' Cubs, 3-2, Fans 13; Duke HRs," *New York Daily News*, May 17, 1957: C24. Drabowsky, also a bonus baby, was still affected by the bonus-baby regulations.

2   Koufax also pitched in a game on August 27, 1955, in which the 23-strikeout record, set on May 22, 1901, by the Cincinnati Reds and the Boston Beaneaters, was matched for the first time.

3   Edward Prell, "Cubs Play Dodgers Today," *Chicago Tribune*, May 16, 1957: D1.

4   Edward Prell, "Dodgers Beat Cubs; 23 Fan, Tie Record!" *Chicago Tribune*, May 17, 1957: 51.

5   Roscoe McGowen, "Brooks Down Chicago, 3 to 2, As Koufax Fans Thirteen Men," *New York Times*, May 17, 1957: 41.

6   In a baseball rarity, both teams' starters were Jewish. In the book, *The Baseball Talmud: The Definitive Position-by-Position Ranking of Baseball's Chosen Players*, Koufax is ranked as baseball's greatest left-handed starter; however, Drabowsky is not included among its right-handed starters although he won 88 games with a 3.71 ERA. Howard Megdal, *The Baseball Talmud: The Definitive Position-by-Position Ranking of Baseball's Chosen Players* (New York: HarperCollins, 2009), 195-216.

7   In both 1955 and 1956, Koufax ranked ninth among Dodgers pitchers in strikeouts. In 1957 he jumped to second place – only Don Drysdale struck out more batters.

8   Dick Young, "Koufax Whiffs 13, Edges Cubs, 3-2; Duke Homers," *New York Daily News*, May 17, 1957: 59.

9   McGowen.

10   McGowen.

11   McGowen.

12   Thomas Lawrence, "Koufax Calls It Quits," National Baseball Hall of Fame, accessed February 14, 2023, https://baseballhall.org/discover-more/stories/inside-pitch/koufax-calls-it-quits.

Koufax Sets a Night Game Whiff Record and Meets Saint Benny

June 22, 1959: Los Angeles Dodgers 6, Philadelphia Phillies 2, at Los Angeles Memorial Coliseum

BY LUIS A. BLANDÓN

Sandy Koufax was a 23-year-old hurler in his fifth season as a Dodger, and was off to an abysmal start: "My own start in 1959 had to be seen to be believed."[1] He feared receiving a one-way ticket to the Los Angeles Dodgers' Triple-A affiliate in Spokane from Dodgers general manager Buzzie Bavasi.[2]

Expectations of Koufax were high since he signed with Brooklyn at 18 in 1954. His inconsistent flashes of brilliance frustrated the Dodgers and Koufax. He once told the media he "wasn't sure whether he was a shlemiel or a shlemazel."[3]

Koufax failed to survive the fourth inning in his first four starts in 1959. Nonetheless, Dodgers manager Walter Alston was convinced Koufax had promise. Koufax doubted his sincerity.[4] After losing to the San Francisco Giants on May 26, Koufax won three starts.[5] "The "$20,000 bonus baby looked like he was finally coming of age," a Dodger beat writer commented.[6]

On Monday evening, June 22, 1959, Koufax was starting against the cellar-dwelling Philadelphia Phillies at the Los Angeles Memorial Coliseum in the first of a four-game series. Facing Koufax was 25-year-old righty Jim Owens.[7] The Coliseum was so huge that "in the far reaches of the vast arena … the game resembled a pantomime."[8] It seated 92,500 for baseball.[9] Not this night. Only 10,290 attended.[10]

Sandy Koufax allowed 10 hits but struck out 16 Phillies batters on June 22, 1959. SABR: The Rucker Archive.

Koufax dominated the top of the first, striking out the side. The Dodgers grabbed the lead in the home half. Jim Gilliam beat out a grounder to second for a single. Owens walked Charlie Neal on a 3-and-2 count. Wally Moon loaded the bases with a single to left.[11] Owens prevented an onslaught, allowing one tally. Gil Hodges made the first out with a well-hit sacrifice fly to right to drive in Gilliam, giving the Dodgers a 1-0 lead. Owens stranded the two baserunners when Don Demeter stared at a third strike and John Roseboro hit a tapper back to Owens.

Harry Anderson tied the contest in the Phillies' second with his eighth home run of the season.[12] Unfazed, Koufax struck out two in the second inning and one in third. After four innings, Koufax had eight strikeouts.

The Phillies took a 2-1 advantage in the fifth. Leading off, Joe Koppe beat out a slow grounder to third. Richie Ashburn dropped a popup into center for his third consecutive single. With runners on first and third, Roseboro let Koufax's first pitch to Dave Philley skip by him for a passed ball and Koppe scored an unearned run. Koufax walked Philley but struck out Wally Post and Anderson, giving him 10 K's. Gene Freese flied out to end the inning.

"Owens' compass went blooey" in the Dodgers' fifth.[13] He walked the bases loaded to start the frame. Hodges drove in Gilliam and Neal with a sizzling single to left.[14] With runners at first and second, Demeter attempted to sacrifice the runners. Rising from his catcher's stance, Valmy Thomas noticed Moon wandering off second and chased him down for an out.[15] Demeter flied out. With two outs, Roseboro "lobbed" an Owens delivery for a bloop single scoring Hodges from second.[16] Roseboro was thrown out trying to steal second. The Dodgers led 4-2.

In the sixth, Koufax allowed a walk but struck out each Philly looking. With 13 strikeouts, Koufax had tied the National League 1959 season high.[17] Owens continued to dole out walks at a dizzying pace, enabling the Dodgers to extend their lead in the seventh. Gilliam walked and was sacrificed to second by

Neal. Moon earned another free pass on four pitches. With Hodges batting, Moon and Gilliam pulled off a successful double steal. Hodges struck out swinging for the first out. Demeter was up again with another chance to drive in runs. "The rangy Oklahoman" was successful with a two-run single, taking second on Ashburn's throw home.[18] Roseboro grounded to first to end the inning. The Dodgers had a reassuring 6-2 lead.

The Phillies were still swinging at shadows in the eighth, failing to score. With one out, Freese singled. Jim Bolger, batting for Sparky Anderson, walked.[19] Thomas went down swinging. Pinch-hitting for Owens, Bob Bowman was the 16th victim and third out as "Koufax cooled him with a fast ball on a full count."[20] Koufax's strikeout tally was one behind the National League record held by Dizzy Dean and two from matching Bob Feller's major-league record of 18.[21] Koufax also "establish[ed] a new arclight record" for strikeouts.[22] Koufax tied the Dodgers record set by Nap Rucker in 1909, and tied the record for most whiffs by a left-hander.[23]

Relieving Owens in the Dodgers' eighth, Humberto Robinson gave up a leadoff single to Carl Furillo, who was forced out by a Maury Wills grounder.[24] Wills tried to steal second and was thrown out in a double play as Koufax struck out looking. With Owens' seven punchouts and Koufax's 16 whiffs to go along with one from Robinson, the teams tied the major-league record for most strikeouts in a game, set at 24 on May 19, 1956, by the Washington Senators and Cleveland Indians.[25] With Koufax pitching, the Dodgers had been involved in four of the five games that tied the previous NL record of 23.[26] "I did it on purpose. I was tired of tying [that] record and wanted to break it," Koufax said about his whiff.[27]

As the ninth approached, the sparse crowd evolved into "an echo chamber of cheers."[28] The fans knew that Dean's record and perhaps Feller's were in Koufax's grasp. Koufax "didn't realize he was making horsehide history" until, he said, "I heard somebody in the stands yell something about it."[29]

The ninth was the one inning in which Koufax did not register a strikeout despite having chances. Koufax had two strikes on each batter he faced. The home crowd booed Demeter when he caught the fly balls hit by Koppe and Ashburn for the first two outs. The fans "yell[ed] for [Demeter] to drop the two fly balls hit to him, hoping against hope."[30] Koufax delivered a fastball on a 2-and-2 count to Philley, who hit a single toward Demeter. Philley attempted "to obtain extra mileage on a single," but Demeter threw him out at second.[31] A cacophony of fan anger descended, convinced Philley had intentionally run into the out to prevent Koufax from setting any records. On deck was Post, who had already struck out four times in the game. Later, Koufax said, "[W]hen I didn't fan their lead-off, Joe Koppe, I felt I wouldn't get any more."[32]

The Dodgers at 37-33, winner of five of seven games, leap-frogged by Pittsburgh into third place, three games behind first-place Milwaukee.[33] Philadelphia at 25-39 was mired in last place, where they remained. With his fourth straight win, Koufax was 4-1 with two straight complete-game victories and 64 strikeouts in 61 innings. Pitching coach Joe Becker said Koufax threw 147 pitches, of which 103 were fastballs, 42 were curves, and 2 were changeups.[34] "I got the majority of the third strikes on a fast ball," Koufax said.[35] Koufax himself sat down on strikes three times.

Afterward, "sweat matting his coal-black hair," Koufax listened to Demeter apologize.[36] "I'm sorry I threw that guy out."[37] Koufax assuaged Demeter: "No. No. I didn't want to pitch to Post. I wanted it to end right there."[38]

"Sure I'd like to have had the record, but as bad as I was going early in the year, … I'm glad to be pitching here instead of Spokane," Koufax said.[39] It was not his best game: "I think my best one was my first complete game against Cincinnati in 1955 when I struck out 14."[40] Why was he pitching better? "Throwing strikes."[41]

Adding to the heightened excitement of the game had been the sudden appearance of Benny Stone in the top of the eighth. Short, balding, and kindhearted, Stone was intent on winning a bet. The "self-styled philanthropist" for the Casa de Cuna Orphanage in Tijuana, Mexico, climbed over the third-base railing onto the field, blowing a whistle to halt action.[42] Ambling to the mound, he chatted with Koufax, who "shook his head" no.[43] "He said something about having a $500 bet – but when I heard that word 'bet,' I wanted no part of him," Koufax said.[44]

Stone offered his business card to Koufax, who refused it. Roseboro snatched it forcefully from Stone "to get rid of the guy."[45] Walking to the first-base bag, Stone blew his whistle to start play again. A policeman grabbed him but Stone managed to escape his clutches. Magically, Stone appeared in the press room after the game, holding court. "Saint Benny" pulled out a cache of clippings praising his charitable work.[46] Stone had gone on the field to meet Koufax to win a bet he made with vendors and planned to donate the proceeds to the orphanage.

Koufax said he was amused watching Stone standing at first base blowing his whistle. Koufax also said it might not have been uproarious "if it had some crackpot with a gun."[47] The police tracked down Stone. Saint Benny spent the night with the law.

SOURCES AND ACKNOWLEDGMENTS

Many thanks to the Black Lion Cafe in Travilah, Maryland where I researched, conceived, and wrote several iterations of this article.

In addition to the sources cited in the Notes, the author consulted the Baseball Hall of Fame Giamatti Research Center, Baseball-Reference.com, retrosheet.org, the Spokane Public Library, YouTube.com, the Library of Congress, and mlb.com.

https://www.baseball-reference.com/boxes/LAN/LAN195906220.shtml

https://www.retrosheet.org/boxesetc/1959/B06220LAN1959.htm

NOTES

1   Sandy Koufax with Ed Linn, *Koufax* (New York: Viking Press, 1966), 133. Koufax didn't win his first game until May 31, and had an ERA over 12.00 on May 15.

2   Spokane was a member of the Pacific Coast League. Built upon its namesake river in eastern Washington, Spokane was the birthplace of Father's Day and where Bing Crosby was raised.

3   Jane Leavy, *Sandy Koufax – A Lefty's Legacy* (New York: HarperCollins Publishers, 2002), 92. Americans of a certain age may recall the catchy theme song that opened the 1976 to 1983 ABC television show *Laverne & Shirley*, in which the lyric "shlemiel and shlemazel (or shlimazel)" was featured. The two words are Yiddish terms normally used in a comical tone with a twinge of sardonic humor. Merriam-Webster defines shlemiel as an Yiddish word meaning a bungler or chump or an inept clumsy person. Shlemazel is a habitually unlucky person. There is a Yiddish saying that places the similar-sounding words in context: "A shlemiel is somebody who often spills his soup and a shlemazel is the person it lands on."

4   *Koufax*, 134.

5   In addition, Koufax came in a relief for a game and picked up a save.

6   Dave Siddon, "Lefty Fans 16 Phils; McDevitt Hurls Tonight," *Valley Times* (North Hollywood, California), June 23, 1959: 8.

7   Jim Owens' 1959 season was by far his best major-league season, with an ERA of 3.21 and a 12-12 record for a last-place team, with 11 complete games and 135 strikeouts in 221⅓ innings of work.

8   Al Wolf, "Players Complain but Fans Happy," *Los Angeles Times*, April 19, 1958: Part II, 1.

9   In 1959 the dimensions at the Coliseum were 250 feet to left, 420 feet to straightaway center, 330 feet to the spot where the fence met the wall, and 300 feet to right.

10   The game was the smallest Coliseum crowd of the season until the 10,201 who attended the Dodgers 4-3 victory over the Phillies on August 2, 1959. See: https://www.baseball-reference.com/boxes/LAN/LAN195908020.shtml.

11   Moon hit in his 15th straight game. It was the Dodgers' longest hitting streak since and matching Gil Hodges 15-game streak in 1957. The single kept Moon in the National League top 10 in hitting with his .333 average.

12   Harry Anderson's home run was the only extra-base hit of the contest.

13   Frank Finch, "Koufax Fans 16, L.A. Wins," *Los Angeles Times*, June 23, 1959: Part IV, 3.

14   Hodges drove in three runs in the game and extended his hitting streak to seven games.

15   In 1957 Valmy Thomas became the first major leaguer from the U.S. Virgin Islands.

16   Allen Lewis "Lefty Sets Night Mark, Just Misses NL Record," *Philadelphia Inquirer*, June 23, 1959: 35.

17   Koufax's teammate Don Drysdale struck out 13 Milwaukee Braves to set the National League season high a few days earlier on June 15, 1959. See https://www.baseball-reference.com/boxes/LAN/LAN195906150.shtml. Whitey Ford of the New York Yankees held the 1959 major-league high at the time with 15 achieved on April 22, 1959, against the Washington Senators. See https://www.baseball-reference.com/boxes/WS1/WS1195904220.shtml.

18   Finch.

19   George Anderson, the Phillies' starting second baseman, is better known as the Hall of Fame manager Sparky Anderson of the Cincinnati Reds and Detroit Tigers. The 1959 campaign was Anderson's only season in the majors as a player.

20   Charlie Park, "Sandy Sets Night Mark by Whiffing 16 Phillies," *Los Angeles Evening Mirror News*, June 23, 1959: Part III, 4.

21   Dizzy Dean of the St. Louis Cardinals struck out 17 Chicago Cubs on July 30, 1933. The Cleveland Indians' Bob Feller fanned 18 Detroit Tigers on October 2, 1938.

22   "16 Phils Fan, Dodgers Win," *Philadelphia Inquirer*, June 23, 1959: 1. Koufax broke the record of most strikeouts for a night game previously held by Johnny Vander Meer, Sam Jones, Bob Feller, and Bob Turley with 14. See Finch and also George Lederer, "Big 'K' Night for "Ko Koofoo' Koufax!," *Press-Telegram*, (Long Beach, California), June 23, 1959: 17.

23   The record was held jointly at the time by Noodles Hahn, Rube Waddell, Nap Rucker, Jack Harshman, and Herb Score. See Lederer.

24   Owens pitched seven innings, allowing six runs, all earned, with seven strikeouts and the damaging seven walks.

25   Lederer. See https://www.baseball-reference.com/boxes/CLE/CLE195605190.shtml.

26   Most recently against St. Louis on May 31, 1959. See https://www.baseball-reference.com/boxes/LAN/LAN195905310.shtml.

27   Lederer.

28   Lederer.

29   Al Wolf, "Didn't Press in Last Inning, Just Tired, Explains Sandy," *Los Angeles Times*, June 23, 1959: Part IV, 3. Charles Maher (Associated Press), "Dodgers Fans Yell for Fielders to Drop 'Em," *Rock Island* (Illinois) *Argus*, June 23, 1959: 14.

30   Siddon.

31   Finch.

32   Wolf.

33   After they tied for first place with records of 86-68, Los Angeles swept Milwaukee, 2 games to none, in a best-of-three tiebreaker playoff series to decide the winner of the National League pennant. The Dodgers proceeded to defeat the Chicago White Sox in six games to win the City of Los Angeles' first World Series championship.

34   "Koufax Simply Glad He Beat Phils," *Los Angeles Evening Citizen News*, June 23, 1959: 10. Baseball Reference indicates that Koufax threw 158 pitches. See https://www.baseball-reference.com/boxes/LAN/LAN195906220.shtml.

35   Park, "Sandy Sets Night Mark by Whiffing 16 Phillies."

36   Park, "16 Whiffs Set League Night Mark," *Los Angeles Evening Mirror News*, June 23, 1959: Part III,1.

37   Park, "Sandy Sets Night Mark by Whiffing 16 Phillies."

38   Park, "Sandy Sets Night Mark by Whiffing 16 Phillies."

39   Park, "16 Whiffs Set League Night Mark."

40   "Koufax Simply Glad He Beat Phils." Post played for the Reds in the game. He did not strike out against Koufax. The 14 strikeouts were Koufax's career high until he achieved 16. See https://www.baseball-reference.com/boxes/BRO/BRO195508270.shtml.

41   Park, "Sandy Sets Night Mark by Whiffing 16 Phillies." On August 31, 1959, Koufax struck out 18 San Francisco Giants batters at home, setting a new National League record and tying the major-league

record for the most strikeouts in a game. See https://www.base-ball-reference.com/boxes/LAN/LAN195908310.shtml.

42 Associated Press, "Fan Approaches Koufax on the Hill," *Daily News-Post,* (Monrovia ,California), June 23, 1959: 6.

43 Charlie Park, "Koufax Not Annoyed at Whistler's Intrusion," *Los Angeles Evening Mirror News,* June 23, 1959: Part III, 3.

44 Wolf. Other accounts indicated it was a $200.00 wager. See George Lederer, "Fan Visits Koufax 'Wins' $200 Bet," *Press-Telegram* (Long Beach, California), June 23, 1959: 7.

45 Park, "Koufax Not Annoyed at Whistler's Intrusion." Buzzie Bavasi marveled at John Roseboro's steadiness and leadership calling him the Dodgers' "Rock of Gibraltar." See Ken Lazabnik, *Buzzie & The Bull,*" (Lincoln, Nebraska: University of Nebraska Press, 2020): 90

46 Paul V. Coates, "Confidential File: Saint Benny and the Sad People," *Los Angeles Evening Mirror News,* August 29, 1956: Part I, 2. The *Mirror News* tagged him as "Saint Benny."

47 Park, "Koufax Not Annoyed at Whistler's Intrusion."

Sandy Koufax Strikes Out 18 Giants, Ties Major-League Record

August 31, 1959: Los Angeles Dodgers 5, San Francisco Giants 2, at Los Angeles Memorial Coliseum

BY GLEN SPARKS

Sandy Koufax's devastating mix of fastballs and curveballs fooled San Francisco Giants batters at a furious pace on August 31, 1959. Koufax, a talented but erratic left-hander for the Los Angeles Dodgers, broke the National League single-game strikeout record by one and tied the major-league mark. Wally Moon hit a three-run home run in the bottom of the ninth inning to give the Dodgers a 5-2 victory.

"That was the biggest game I've ever won," Koufax told reporters. "My top thrill. We've got a chance to go all the way, and I'm glad to do my share."[1]

Koufax struck out 18 batters, one more than St. Louis Cardinals great Dizzy Dean fanned on July 30, 1933, and the same number that Cleveland Indians fireballer Bob Feller rang up on October 2, 1938.[2]

Every Giants starting player struck out at least once. Koufax struck out the side three times. "I didn't count the strikeouts," he said, "but I sensed in the seventh inning that I was close to a record. I knew I had a few. The crowd was terrific. They were with me on every pitch."[3]

"A whooping, whooping"[4] gathering of 82,794 (60,194 paid) watched the action. Maxwell Stiles of the *Los Angeles Mirror* noted that in the bottom of the ninth inning, fans stood "screaming … in noisy tribute to Sandy Koufax when he came to bat with one out."[5]

Koufax, who struck out 13 batters in his previous start, on August 24 against the Philadelphia Phillies at Connie Mack Stadium, also broke Feller's record from 1938 of 28 combined punchouts in consecutive games.

Stiles wrote that the game would rank "among the great athletic contests that have been held (at the Coliseum) – for thrills, drama, record-setting performance, and the happy ending."[6]

The Dodgers began the day 71-59 and in second place, two games behind the Giants. Two years removed from Brooklyn, they had rebounded from a difficult first year in Southern California, when they finished in seventh place – next to last.

Koufax got off to a wobbly start in 1959. Through his first eight games, he had an ERA of 8.06 with 22 walks in 22⅓ innings. Finally, on May 31, he earned his first win, striking out nine St. Louis Cardinals and walking five over six innings. He gave up three runs. "I thought I'd never win a game," Koufax said. "I was losing my appetite, and I wasn't able to sleep well from worrying."[7] He entered this game vs. the Giants with a 7-4 record and a 3.89 ERA.

Willie Mays led a powerful San Francisco offense that also featured the hard-hitting Orlando Cepeda, in his second season, and talented rookie Willie McCovey. Manager Bill Rigney had led the Giants to an 80-74 record and a third-place finish in 1958.

This was the finale of a three-game series. The Giants won the opener, 5-0, behind Sam Jones. After an offday, the Dodgers won the second game, 7-6, scoring two runs in the bottom of the ninth. Rigney sent right-hander Jack Sanford (12-10, 3.24) out to win the rubber game. San Francisco had traded for Sanford over the offseason.

The Giants took a 1-0 lead in the first inning. Koufax struck out Jackie Brandt and McCovey swinging before giving up a double to Mays. Cepeda followed by lining another double, driving in the run. Felipe Alou grounded out to end the frame.

LA got even in the bottom half of the first. Jim Gilliam drew a leadoff walk and stole second base with Moon at bat. After Moon struck out, Sanford threw a pitch to Norm Larker that eluded catcher Bob Schmidt. Gilliam scooted to third base on the passed ball. Larker walked and was forced out when Duke Snider hit a groundball that scored Gilliam. Gil Hodges got the Dodgers' first hit, a single that loaded the bases. Charlie Neal, though, grounded out to end the inning. Sanford gave up just one hit, a single to Snider, over the next three frames. Koufax, meanwhile, allowed two walks and two hits in innings two through four. He also added three more strikeouts. He now had five.

Brandt struck out to begin the San Francisco fifth. McCovey stepped to the plate. From Mobile, Alabama, McCovey made his big-league debut just a month earlier, on July 30, and went 4-for-4 against Philadelphia Phillies ace Robin Roberts. McCovey came into this game against the Dodgers with a robust .396 batting average and a .698 slugging percentage. He drove a curveball deep into the right-field seats, giving the Giants a 2-1 lead.

"I was scared that one bad pitch was going to beat us," Koufax said afterward. "I guess I aimed it. I wanted it low and outside. He hit it good."[8] Mays and Cepeda struck out to end the inning.

Maury Wills singled to begin the Dodgers' half of the fifth. Koufax, a notoriously bad hitter, whiffed, bringing up Gilliam. Wills, a 26-year-old rookie known for his speed, strayed a bit too far off first base, and Sanford picked him off for the second out. Gilliam reached base on an error and stole second, but Moon went down swinging.

Koufax struck out the side in the sixth inning and fanned two more Giants in the seventh, including McCovey to end the frame. Koufax said, "It was a curve, high and inside, and I debated a long time before I threw the pitch."[9] He was up to a dozen strikeouts.

Dodgers manager Walter Alston nearly pulled Koufax for a pinch-hitter in the bottom of the seventh. John Roseboro led off by driving a base hit into right field. Wills came to bat with instructions to sacrifice, but the attempt failed, and Roseboro was forced at second. Alston let Koufax hit. "Since the bunt failed, I had to go with my pitcher," Alston said.[10] Koufax laid down the bunt, advancing Wills to second. Roseboro, though, grounded out to end the threat.

Mays took a called third strike to start the Giants' eighth; Cepeda also fell victim to Koufax's excellence. Alou singled, but Schmidt lifted a fly ball to left field that settled into Larker's glove.

Moon drew a walk to begin the Dodgers' half of the eighth, and Larker sacrificed him to second base. Sanford unfurled a wild pitch with Snider at bat, and Moon took off for third. Sanford threw another wild pitch on ball four to Snider, and Moon rushed home, tying the score, 2-2. Hodges reached base on an error, but Neal and Roseboro made outs.

Koufax entered the ninth inning with 15 strikeouts. Leadoff batter Eddie Bressoud went down swinging. Danny O'Connell followed and took a called third strike. Next, Sanford came to bat. No match for Koufax, he swung and missed on strike three.

Wills grounded out to start the bottom of the ninth. Koufax sent a groundball to left field for a single, and Gilliam followed by lining a hit to left field, putting runners on first and second. That ended Sanford's evening. Rigney brought in right-hander Al Worthington.

Moon and Larker, the next two batters, watched as Worthington stepped toward the mound. Moon turned to his teammate and said, "Here comes Worthington. Let's get him." Larker said, "If you don't, I will." Moon, traded from the St. Louis Cardinals to the Dodgers after the 1958 season, said, "You can take a seat, Larker."[11]

On a 1-and-1 pitch, Moon smashed a Sanford slider the opposite way over the left-field screen and "pandemonium broke loose."[12] Fans cheered and "mobbed"[13] Moon as he touched home plate. "One of the first to greet him, of course, was the equally heroic Koufax," Mal Florence wrote.[14]

According to a pitching chart, Koufax delivered 92 fastballs, 45 curveballs, and four changeups. Roseboro, the Dodgers' catcher, said, "He had great stuff. He kept them looking for that high, hard hummer and then he slipped his curve over. This was something I'll remember all my life."[15]

Koufax finished the season with an 8-6 record and a 4.05 ERA. He struck out 173 batters, third most in the National League. He walked 92, fourth most. The Dodgers won the NL pennant with a mark of 88-68. (The Giants finished 83-71, in third place.) LA beat the Chicago White Sox in the World Series. Koufax pitched in two games and lost one. Over nine innings, he gave up just one run, while striking out seven and walking only one.

He was still a few years away from his epic run of greatness, when he won three Cy Young Awards and five ERA titles en route to a spot in the National Baseball Hall of Fame. On a late summer night in 1959, while pitching at the vast LA Coliseum, he gave fans a glimpse of the glorious future. Moon, who watched it all, said, "That was the most beautiful game I ever saw anyone pitch."[16]

SOURCES

In addition to the sources cited in the Notes, the author consulted Baseball-Reference.com and Retrosheet.org.

https://www.baseball-reference.com/boxes/LAN/LAN195908310.shtml

https://www.retrosheet.org/boxesetc/1959/B08310LAN1959.htm

NOTES

1   Charlie Park, "Bad Bunt Leaves Sandy in Classic," *Los Angeles Mirror*, September 1, 1959: 23.

2   Dean and the Cardinals beat the Chicago Cubs, 8-2, at Sportsman's Park in St. Louis. Feller and the Indians lost to the Detroit Tigers, 4-1, at Cleveland Stadium.

3   George Lederer, "Bungled Bunt Saved Koufax," *Long Beach* (California) *Press-Telegram*, September 1, 1959: 21.

4   Lederer.

5   Maxwell Stiles, "Koufax Classic Rates with Best in History," *Los Angeles Mirror*, September 1, 1959: 24.

6   Stiles.

7   United Press International, "Strikeout Champion Sandy Koufax Started 1959 in Slow Style," *Pomona* (California) *Progress-Bulletin*, September 15, 1959: 35.

8   Park, "Bad Bunt Leaves Sandy in Classic."

9   Mal Florence, "'Best Game and Luckiest I Ever Pitched,' Says Koufax," *Los Angeles Times*, September 1, 1959: 65.

10   Lederer, "Bungled Bunt Saved Koufax."

11   Sid Ziff, "A Baseball Classic," *Los Angeles Mirror*, September 1, 1959: 23.

12   Park, "Bad Bunt Leaves Sandy in Classic."

13   Park, "Bad Bunt Leaves Sandy in Classic."

14   Florence.

15   Park, "Bad Bunt Leaves Sandy in Classic."

16   Park, "L.A. Begins September Push Against Cards," *Los Angeles Mirror*, September 1, 1959: 24.

Koufax Stops First-Place Pirates With One-Hitter

May 23, 1960: Los Angeles Dodgers 1, Pittsburgh Pirates 0, at Forbes Field, Pittsburgh

BY JOHN FREDLAND

Sandy Koufax was on the fringes of the Los Angeles Dodgers' pitching staff early in the 1960 season, his sixth in the majors. Shaky control and hard luck left him with a 0-4 record and a 5.16 earned-run average entering his May 23 start against the Pittsburgh Pirates. Facing the hot-hitting, rally-prone, championship-bound Pirates, however, Koufax hinted at the superstardom to come, as he limited Pittsburgh to one hit – a second-inning single by mound opponent Bennie Daniels – and struck out 10 in the Dodgers' 1-0 victory at Forbes Field.

Dazzling, dominant moments were scattered through Koufax's first five big-league seasons, at times validating the Dodgers' wisdom in signing him to a $14,000 bonus in 1954.[1] Striking out batters at a rate nearly unrivaled among major-league pitchers,[2] Koufax broke the record for strikeouts in a National or American League night game in one 1959 start[3] and tied Bob Feller's post-1900 record for a nine-inning game in a subsequent appearance.[4] In a spot start in Game Five of the 1959 World Series, he allowed just one run in seven innings.[5]

But overall Koufax had won about as many games (28) as he had lost (27), seldom securing a regular place in the starting rotation.[6] Through three seasons in Brooklyn and two more after the Dodgers moved to Los Angeles in 1958, his 4.16 lifetime ERA was exactly average for his ledger of clubs, years, and ballparks.[7]

As 1960 opened, Koufax's role with the Dodgers reflected his middling record. He made just three appearances for the defending World Series champions in the season's first three weeks. In his only start, on April 22, the St. Louis Cardinals drove him from the mound before he recorded an out.[8] Koufax did

Although he posted just an 8-13 won-loss record in 1960, Sandy Koufax had more strikeouts than innings pitched. SABR: The Rucker Archive.

not pitch again until eight days later, when he walked three straight San Francisco Giants and threw 11 balls in a row in relief, causing manager Walter Alston to pull him from the game.[9] Newspapers reported Koufax pitching batting practice to regain his control[10] and confronting general manager Buzzie Bavasi over his lack of playing time.[11]

Roger Craig's broken collarbone on May 2 gave Koufax a chance in the rotation,[12] and the 24-year-old left-hander's next four starts were a mix of mastery and misfortune. Koufax fanned 15 Philadelphia Phillies on May 6 but lost on a five-run 10th.[13] Five days later, the Pirates, down 3-1 with two outs and nobody on base in the eighth inning, rallied for a 6-3 win.[14] A rainout in Milwaukee washed away three first-inning strikeouts on May 16.[15]

On May 19 Koufax was one pitch from a 10-strikeout, 1-earned-run complete game against the Cincinnati Reds before ninth-inning hits by Eddie Kasko and Vada Pinson occasioned another defeat.[16] The *Los Angeles Times* labeled him "the snake-bitten southpaw."[17]

Koufax's next shot was in the Monday opener of a three-game series against Pittsburgh, one of the clubs the Dodgers had outmaneuvered to sign him.[18] Two come-from-behind, extra-inning wins over the Giants had increased the first-place Pirates' lead to 1½ games;[19] the fifth-place Dodgers were already 8½ games out. Pittsburgh's team batting average and total runs scored led the majors by large margins.[20] Six of the Pirates' 23 victories had come after they had trailed in the seventh inning or later, including Koufax's May 11 start at the Los Angeles Coliseum.

Pittsburgh's Daniels – who had grown up near Los Angeles in Compton and made his major-league debut as the Pirates starter in the Dodgers' final game in Brooklyn in September 1957[21] – took the mound on a night the *Los Angeles Mirror* described as "cold [and] damp."[22] A dog ran among Pittsburgh's outfielders, delaying the first pitch for about five minutes.[23] The 27-year-old Daniels, in his fifth start of the season,[24] pitched around Wally Moon's two-out walk for a scoreless first.

Koufax began his outing by walking .351-hitting Bob Skinner on a full-count pitch,[25] then striking out .307-hitting Dick Groat. Skinner stole second while .382-hitting Roberto Clemente batted, but Koufax fanned Clemente. After Dick Stuart walked, Don Hoak took a called third strike.

Two quick Pirate outs in the second were followed by more control troubles. Eighth-place hitter Bill Mazeroski walked on four pitches. Koufax got ahead of Daniels 1-and-2 but left a curveball hanging high and inside,[26] and the lefty-swinging Pirate pitcher lined a single to left.[27]

When Skinner took a 3-and-1 pitch for ball four, Pittsburgh had its fourth walk of the game, and the bases were loaded. But Groat grounded to shortstop Maury Wills, who threw to Charlie Neal at second for the inning-ending force.

The Dodgers threatened against Daniels in the third. Jim Gilliam drew a one-out walk and took second on Neal's ground-out. Moon hit a grounder up the middle; Mazeroski fielded it behind second, too late to get the out at first. Gilliam rounded third, stopped, and broke for home. Mazeroski – headed for his second of eight Gold Gloves at second base – fired to catcher Hal Smith, who tagged Gilliam on the arm for the third out.

Hoak walked with two outs in the third, but Koufax was finding his groove. Smith struck out to end the inning; he was the first of nine straight Pirates set down until a harmless two-out walk to Smith in the sixth.

"After the first two innings, he really started to pump [his fastball]," Dodgers catcher John Roseboro said of Koufax. "It was the best I've seen him because his control was so good."[28]

Daniels, whose curveball drew postgame praise from Alston,[29] was matching Koufax with scoreless innings, putting up clean frames in the fourth, fifth, and sixth. He took a two-hitter into the top of the seventh.

Los Angeles first baseman Norm Larker led off the seventh with a double to left-center. Right fielder Frank Howard, a 6-foot-7-inch, 23-year-old power-hitting prospect who had been called up from Triple-A Spokane earlier in May,[30] hit a first-pitch grounder to short, and Larker held at second. Roseboro also swung at the first pitch, lining it to right; Clemente saved a hit and kept the game scoreless with a sliding catch on his knees.[31]

Daniels got ahead of 21-year-old center fielder Tommy Davis – like Koufax, a Brooklyn native – with a strike, then threw an outside slider. Davis, hitless in his past 24 at-bats, drove it against the screen near the light tower in left-center, about eight inches short of a home run.[32] Larker scored on the double for a 1-0 Dodgers lead.

Now ahead, Koufax cruised through the seventh, retiring Mazeroski on a foul pop to Roseboro and striking out pinch-hit-

ter Gene Baker and Skinner. Groundouts by right-handed hitters Groat, Clemente, and Stuart finished the Pittsburgh eighth.

Elroy Face, in relief of Daniels,[33] had pitched two scoreless innings, aided by Stuart's diving stop of Moon's grounder with Gilliam at second in the eighth.[34] It remained a one-run game heading to the bottom of the ninth. What the *Los Angeles Times* called a "big and noisy crowd" of 15,936 waited for another rally.[35]

Koufax began the ninth by catching Hoak looking for his 10th strikeout.

"He was getting his curveball over," said Hoak, Koufax's Dodgers teammate in 1955. "That's what made his fastball so effective."[36]

Smith grounded out, and defensive replacement Don Demeter hauled in former Dodger Gino Cimoli's deep drive near the exit gate in right-center.[37] The partisan Pittsburgh crowd gave a cheer for Koufax,[38] who had a one-hit shutout on 135 pitches and his first victory in 13 regular-season outings since August 1959.[39]

"I've never been a better pitcher than this year," Koufax said afterward. "To be perfectly honest, I was looking forward to my best year at the beginning of the season. Then, I lost four in a hurry."[40]

"Now, I'm still looking forward to my best year."[41]

Koufax followed up his gem in Pittsburgh with a display of dominance, stamina, and hard luck, pitching into the 14th inning, striking out 15 Chicago Cubs, and allowing just three hits – but again taking the loss.[42] The next time he faced the Pirates, on June 19, he failed to make it through the fifth inning despite a five-run lead, a performance the *Los Angeles Times* summarized as "tottering [and] unpredictable."[43] In July, Koufax spent time pitching out of the bullpen.

He finished 1960 with more strikeouts per nine innings than anyone else in the NL,[44] but his record for the fourth-place Dodgers was 8-13 and his ERA was just slightly better than league average at 3.91 (101 ERA+). He had reached a career crossroads.

"By the end of 1960, Koufax was ready to quit," biographer Jane Leavy wrote. "After the Dodgers' final game … he tossed his gloves, his spikes, and his dreams into the trash can, keeping one mitt in case he wanted to play softball in the park on a Sunday afternoon."[45]

ACKNOWLEDGMENTS

SABR members Gary Belleville, Kurt Blumenau, and Jacob Pomrenke provided insightful comments on an earlier version of this article.

SOURCES

In addition to the sources cited in the Notes, the author consulted Baseball-Reference.com and Retrosheet.org for pertinent information, including the box score and play-by-play. He also reviewed game coverage in the *Los Angeles Mirror*, *Los Angeles Times*, *Pittsburgh Post-Gazette*, and *Pittsburgh Press* newspapers.

https://www.baseball-reference.com/boxes/PIT/PIT196005230.shtml

https://www.retrosheet.org/boxesetc/1960/B05230PIT1960.htm

NOTES

1 Jane Leavy, *Sandy Koufax: A Lefty's Legacy* (New York: Harper Collins, 2002), 52-57.

2 From 1955 through 1959, Koufax averaged 8.5 strikeouts per nine innings in 516⅓ innings pitched. The only major-league pitchers active during that period who pitched at least 50 innings and averaged more strikeouts per nine innings were Ryne Duren (10.2 strikeouts per nine innings in 195 innings pitched), Herb Score (9.3 strikeouts per nine innings in 714⅓ innings), and Marshall Bridges (9.0 strikeouts per nine innings in 76 innings). Only four other pitchers with at least 50 innings pitched reached 7.5 strikeouts per nine innings: Sam Jones (7.6 strikeouts per nine innings in 1133⅓ innings), Juan Pizarro (7.6 strikeouts per nine innings in 329⅔ innings), Bob Blaylock (7.6 strikeouts per nine innings in 50 innings), and Jack Meyer (7.5 strikeouts per nine innings in 428 innings).

3 Koufax struck out 16 Philadelphia Phillies on June 22, 1959. Frank Finch, "Koufax Strikes Out 16, Dodgers Win: Night Tilt Record Set by Sandy," *Los Angeles Times*, June 23, 1959: IV, 1. The previous record for strikeouts in a night game was 15 by Whitey Ford of the Yankees, in a 14-inning game in April 1959. Through 2023, two pitchers – Roger Clemens twice, in 1986 and 1996; and Max Scherzer in 2016 – have struck out 20 batters in nine-inning night games.

4 Koufax struck out 18 San Francisco Giants on August 31, 1959. "Koufax Fans 18 for Record; L.A. Wins: Moon's Homer Beats Giants in 9th, 5-2," *Los Angeles Times*, September 1, 1959: IV, 1. Feller had struck out 18 Detroit Tigers in 1938; Koufax repeated the feat against the Chicago Cubs in 1962. In the nineteenth century, Hugh Daily and Charlie Sweeney each recorded 19 strikeouts in nine innings, a mark not reached in the twentieth century until Steve Carlton against the New York Mets in 1969. Through the 2023 season, the record for a nine-inning game is 20 strikeouts, shared by three pitchers (Clemens in 1986 and 1996; Kerry Wood in 1998; and Scherzer in 2016.)

5 Braven Dyer, "Dodgers Lose Tense Struggle, 1-0, Before Record Throng of 92,706," *Los Angeles Times*, October 7, 1959: IV, 1. The White Sox won Game Five, 1-0, but the Dodgers went on to win the World Series in six games.

6 From 1955 through 1959, Koufax started 77 games and appeared 60 times in relief.

7 Koufax's Adjusted Earned Run Average, a metric known as "ERA+" that compares a pitcher's ERA with park factors and league opponents, was 100 through the 1959 season. "Adjusted Earned Run Average (ERA+)," MLB.com, accessed February 27, 2024, https://www.mlb.com/glossary/advanced-stats/earned-run-average-plus.

8 Frank Finch, "Cards Belt Six Dodger Hurlers, 11-7: St. Louis Scores Five in First," *Los Angeles Times*, April 23, 1960: II, 1.

9 Walter Judge, "Giant Homers Crush LA, 6-3: 85,065 Watch McCovey Hit 2 off Drysdale," *San Francisco Examiner*, May 1, 1960: III, 1.

10 Wells A. Twombly, "Cincy Hurling Flops," *Valley Times* (San Fernando Valley, California), May 3, 1960: 12.

11 Leavy, 93-94.

12 Craig, who had gone 4-0 with two shutouts and a 0.90 ERA in five September starts during the 1959 pennant race, was injured in a collision with Vada Pinson of the Cincinnati Reds. He did not return until June 20. "Craig, Neal out of Action: L.A. Loses Hurler for Two Months," *Los Angeles Times*, May 4, 1960: IV, 1.

13 Frank Finch, "Phils Win in Tenth, 6-1, Koufax Fans 15: Freak Hit off Dodger Ace Starts 5-Run Rally," *Los Angeles Times*, May 7, 1960: II, 2.

14 Frank Finch, "Pirates Rally to Beat Dodgers, 6-3: 27,926 See Face Notch Relief Win," *Los Angeles Times*, May 12, 1960: VI, 1.

15 Frank Finch, "Rain Douses Braves-L.A.; Drysdale, Buhl Go Tonight," *Los Angeles Times*, May 17, 1960: VI, 1.

16 Frank Finch, "Reds Defeat Dodgers in Ninth, 5-4: Koufax One Strike Away From Win," *Los Angeles Times*, May 20, 1960: IV, 1.

17 Finch, "Reds Defeat Dodgers in Ninth, 5-4."

18 The Yankees, Giants, and Milwaukee Braves also scouted Koufax. The Pirates offered a $15,000 bonus; the Braves offered $30,000 after Koufax and the Dodgers had reached an agreement. Leavy, 52-57.

19 Lester J. Biederman, "Bucs Still Have Magic Touch: Hoak, Groat, Clemente Spike Giants," *Pittsburgh Press*, May 21, 1960: 6; Lester J. Biederman, "Bucs Take On Dodgers After Rocking Giants," *Pittsburgh Press*, May 23, 1960: 24.

20 The Pirates were batting .283 through May 22; the second-best team average was the Reds' .266. Pittsburgh's 189 runs scored were 21 more than the Reds.

21 Davis J. Walsh, "He Attended Wake at Dodgers' Park," *Pittsburgh Sun-Telegraph*, September 25, 1957: 24.

22 Charlie Park, "Elated Koufax Sees Biggest Year Yet," *Los Angeles Mirror*, May 24, 1960: III, 2.

23 Lester J. Biederman, "Pirates Agree – Koufax Can Fire: Dodger Ace Gives Bucs Just One Hit to Gain 1-0 Verdict," *Pittsburgh Press*, May 24, 1960: 27.

24 Daniels took a regular turn in the Pirates' rotation during April 1960 but had a 9.49 ERA in three starts. He had made only one appearance in May before this game, a start in the second game of a May 15 doubleheader against the Braves. He allowed four runs in seven innings and was charged with the loss in that game.

25 This article uses pitch-count data collected by Dodgers statistician Allan Roth, as found in Baseball-Reference.com's play-by-play of this game. "Data Coverage," Baseball-Reference.com, accessed February 27, 2024, https://www.baseball-reference.com/about/coverage.shtml.

26 Park, "Elated Koufax Sees Biggest Year Yet."

27 Daniels batted .310 with a .552 slugging percentage in 29 at-bats in 1959. His hit against Koufax was his third hit in 10 at-bats in 1960. He batted .188 in 16 at-bats in 1960 and .170 in 300 lifetime at-bats.

28 Park, "Elated Koufax Sees Biggest Year Yet."

29 Biederman, "Pirates Agree – Koufax Can Fire."

30 Frank Finch, "Dodgers Recall Frank Howard," *Los Angeles Times*, May 13, 1960: IV, 1.

31 Park, "Elated Koufax Sees Biggest Year Yet."

32 Park, "Elated Koufax Sees Biggest Year Yet."

33 Daniels allowed four hits and one run in seven innings. He made only one more start for the Pirates, who acquired veteran Vinegar Bend Mizell in a trade with the St. Louis Cardinals five days after this game, on May 28. Daniels was sent to Triple-A Columbus on June 28 and remained there for the rest of the season. He was traded to the expansion Washington Senators in a four-player deal in December 1960. He made 230 appearances in nine major-league seasons with the Pirates and Senators. Jack Hernon, "Bucs Trade Ben Daniels, Two Others," *Pittsburgh Post-Gazette*, December 17, 1960: 14.

34 Jack Hernon, "Koufax Stops Pirates on One Single, 1-0: Daniels Only Buc to Hit Dodger Ace," *Pittsburgh Post-Gazette*, May 24, 1960: 22. Face was pitching for the fourth consecutive game. His 68 appearances led the NL in 1960.

35 Frank Finch, "Different Hero for Each Game Secret for Success of Pirates," *Los Angeles Times*, May 24, 1960: IV, 2.

36 Park, "Elated Koufax Sees Biggest Year Yet."

37 Biederman, "Pirates Agree – Koufax Can Fire."

38 Frank Finch, "Koufax's One-Hitter Blanks Bucs, 1-0: Strike-Out Ace Whiffs 10 Batters," *Los Angeles Times*, May 24, 1960: IV, 1.

39 Koufax, who went on to pitch four no-hitters in his career, had one other complete-game one-hitter: against the New York Mets in June 1965.

40 Park, "Elated Koufax Sees Biggest Year Yet."

41 Park, "Elated Koufax Sees Biggest Year Yet."

42 Frank Finch, "Zimmer's' Hit in 14th Beats L.A., 4-3: Koufax Fans 15, But Loses Heart-Breaker as Cubs Snap Dodgers' Five-Game Streak," *Los Angeles Times*, May 29, 1960: D2.

43 Frank Finch, "Dodgers Fight Off Pirates for 8-6 Victory: L.A. Gets Six Runs in Third," *Los Angeles Times*, June 20, 1960: IV, 1.

44 Koufax struck out 10.1 batters per nine innings in 175 innings in 1960. The only pitcher with a higher rate and more than 10 innings pitched was the Yankees' Ryne Duren, who struck out 12.3 batters per nine innings in 49 innings.

45 Leavy, 95. In 1961 Koufax had a breakthrough season, winning 18 games and recording his first of four strikeout titles. From 1961 through his retirement in 1966, he won 129 games against 47 defeats, topped the NL in ERA for five years in a row, and received three Cy Young Awards and the 1963 NL MVP Award. He was inducted into the National Baseball Hall of Fame in 1972.

Sandy Koufax Outduels Bob Gibson in 1-0 Dodgers Victory

May 25, 1961: Los Angeles Dodgers 1, St. Louis Cardinals 0, at Busch Stadium I, St. Louis

BY TIM ODZER

On May 25, 1961, the same day President John F. Kennedy set a goal for the United States of landing a man on the moon before the end of the decade, two future Hall of Famers beginning their ascents to stardom showcased the prodigious talents that would dominate National League hitters throughout the 1960s.

Entering the 1961 season, Sandy Koufax was a career 36-40 pitcher, regarded around baseball as a serviceable fireballing lefty who lacked control. Signed by the Dodgers as a bonus baby, Koufax never spent a day in the minor leagues.[1] He made his major-league debut at 19 and spent the first six years of his career trying to harness his overpowering stuff. The winter of 1960-61 had been a transformative time for Koufax as he started to take his craft more seriously. "That winter was when I really started working out. I started running more. I decided I was really going to find out how good I can be."[2] That was not Koufax's only change. At the suggestion of Dodgers catcher Norm Sherry, who pointed out that the harder the left-hander threw, the wilder he became, Koufax eased up, incorporated his curveball and changeup, and stopped trying to blow away hitters with every pitch. The changes had worked out okay for Koufax during his first nine starts in 1961 as he pitched to a 4-2 record with a 4.08 ERA.

The youngest of seven children, Bob Gibson was raised in Omaha, Nebraska. Gibson's father died three months before he was born, and his mother worked at a laundromat and cleaned houses. Growing up in a housing project, Gibson faced racism as part of daily life. But sports provided an outlet for Gibson and earned him a scholarship to Creighton University, where he starred in basketball and baseball. Gibson preferred basketball and even played hoops for the Harlem Globetrotters in 1957.[3] Yet the St. Louis Cardinals, who had tried to sign him out of high school, ultimately persuaded Gibson to focus solely on baseball. After making his major-league debut against the Dodgers as a reliever in 1959, Gibson shuffled back and forth the next two years between St. Louis and the Cardinals' Triple-A clubs in Omaha and Rochester, New York. At the outset of 1961, Cardinals manager Solly Hemus used Gibson out of the bullpen and as a spot starter.

In late May the Cardinals and Dodgers connected for a quick two-game set in St. Louis. Los Angeles arrived in St. Louis with a record of 23-15, having just split two games with the Reds at Cincinnati's Crosley Field.[4] The Cardinals, meanwhile, had not yet found their stride, and were 14-18. In the series opener, the St. Louis offense erupted for seven runs en route to a 7-2 victory.

The Thursday evening finale pitted Koufax against Gibson in front of a small crowd of 6,878. Both hurlers came into this contest on the heels of strong outings: Koufax had twirled a four-hit complete-game victory against Willie Mays and the San Francisco Giants on May 21, retiring the last 16 men in a row, while Gibson pitched a shutout (with 11 strikeouts) against Ernie Banks and the Chicago Cubs.

The first hit of the May 25 game came in the top of the second, a single off the bat of the Dodgers' veteran outfielder Duke Snider, who advanced to second with two outs on a hit by left fielder Ron Fairly. With two men on and two out, Gibson struck out Dodgers catcher John Roseboro to strand the runners.

With one out in the bottom half, Stan Musial singled off Koufax. "The Man," who had made his major-league debut when Koufax was a 5-year-old boy, had hit Koufax well coming into the game: a .321 batting average in 32 plate appearances. Koufax quickly induced a groundball double play off the bat of shortstop Daryl Spencer to retire the Cardinals. Koufax did not allow another hit until the ninth as he and Gibson matched zeroes through the first six frames.

The Dodgers took a 1-0 lead in the seventh on a home run by third baseman Tommy Davis. A second-year player who grew up a Dodgers fan in Brooklyn, Davis had struck out in his two previous at-bats against Gibson. After taking the first pitch for a ball, Gibson challenged Davis with a high fastball. Davis turned on it and hit the ball into the left-center-field bleachers. It was Davis's eighth home run of the season. "The pitch Davis hit wasn't even a strike," Cardinals backstop Hal Smith told the *St. Louis Post-Dispatch* after the game. "We tried to get the ball away from him but didn't."[5] Davis's blast was the lone damage against Gibson, who went eight innings, allowing five hits and striking out eight.

Koufax maintained his one-hitter until the ninth inning, when Curt Flood hit a leadoff single. The next man up, Joe Cunningham, twice tried to bunt Flood to second base and twice failed. With the count 2-and-2, Koufax induced a fly out to left fielder Fairly. Although left-handed-hitting Cardinals first baseman Bill White had already struck out twice against Koufax, Hemus stuck with him. White rewarded Hemus's faith by singling to left and advancing Flood to second.

That brought up Cardinals star third baseman Ken Boyer. A Missouri native who was named a National League All-Star in 1959 and 1960, Boyer came into the game slashing .297/.378/.827 with five home runs. Koufax had struck out Boyer twice so far in the game. That must have played into LA manager Walter Alston's decision to allow Koufax to face him. After the game, Alston said he had considered bringing in right-hander Turk Farell.[6] After taking Koufax's first offering, Boyer hit a low liner to right. Flood took off. "There was no doubt in my mind that it was going to be a base hit," said Flood.[7]

But Snider, a longtime center fielder who had begun playing more in right field in 1959 as a way to take stress off his knees, caught the ball and tossed it to second baseman Jim Gilliam to double off Flood, who had already rounded third, and end the game. Koufax allowed only three hits and struck out eight for his fifth victory of the campaign.

Afterward, Alston praised pitching coach (and native St. Louisan) Joe Becker for his work with Koufax. "Becker has worked with Koufax continually, has shown lots of patience and has never given up on him," said Alston.[8]

"Koufax's biggest problem was fighting himself," said Becker. "He has [had] a good curve ball to go with his great fast ball for some time now, but he couldn't control his pitches. Finally, after six years of trying, he's putting all of his baseball abilities together."[9]

How did Koufax explain his successful start in '61? "[I]t's because I'm not trying to throw so hard. I'm getting my curve over the [plate] now and that makes all the difference in the world. This makes two complete games in a row – I hope I'm on my way."[10]

Whatever Koufax found continued to work for the rest of the season. In July he was named to his first All-Star team. By season's end, he had broken Christy Mathewson's National League single-season strikeout record, having fanned 269 batters.[11]

On July 6, with a 33-41 record, the Cardinals fired Hemus and replaced him with Johnny Keane. Gibson flourished under Keane

and made his first All-Star team in 1962. Two years later in the World Series against the Yankees, Gibson became a bona fide star after pitching complete-game victories in Games Five and Seven to help bring St. Louis its first championship since 1946.

SOURCES

In addition to the sources cited in the Notes, the author consulted Baseball-Reference.com and Retrosheet.org for pertinent information, including the box score and play-by-play. The author also relied on game coverage in the *St. Louis Post-Dispatch* and *Los Angeles Times* and SABR BioProject biographies for several players involved in the game, especially Terry Sloope's biography of Bob Gibson.

https://www.baseball-reference.com/boxes/SLN/SLN196105250.shtml

https://www.retrosheet.org/boxesetc/1961/B05250SLN1961.htm

NOTES

1   The major leagues instituted the bonus rule in 1947. It stipulated that when a team signed a player to a contract with a signing bonus greater than $4,000, the team was required to keep him on their 25-man active roster for two full seasons. Failure to keep the player on the big-league team would cause the team to lose rights to the player, and the player would then be exposed to the waiver wire.

2   Jane Leavy, *Sandy Koufax: A Lefty's Legacy* (New York: HarperCollins Publishers, 2002), 101.

3   In fact, the *Los Angeles Times* game summary for the game described Gibson as "the former Harlem Globetrotters' melon manipulator." Koufax also excelled at basketball and played on the University of Cincinnati's freshman team in 1954. Frank Finch, "Dodger Boots Aid Cards, 7-2," *Los Angeles Times*, May 25, 1961: IV-1.

4   This turned out to be a matchup of the National League's two top teams in 1961. The Reds won the 1961 National League pennant but lost the World Series to the New York Yankees. The Dodgers finished second in the National League, four games behind Cincinnati.

5   Neal Russo, "St. Louisan Joe Becker Helps Koufax Snap Cardinal Jinx, 1-0," *St. Louis Post-Dispatch*, May 26, 1961: 9B.

6   Russo.

7   Russo, 4.

8   Russo.

9   Russo.

10 Associated Press, "Control Found, Koufax Wins," *Monrovia* (California) *Daily News-Post*, May 26, 1961: 10.

11 Mathewson struck out 267 batters in 1903.

Hurricane Sandy Strikes the West Coast

September 20, 1961: Los Angeles Dodgers 3, Chicago Cubs 2 (13 innings), at Los Angeles Coliseum

BY KEVIN LARKIN

As people awoke on Wednesday, September 20, 1961, and settled down for their morning coffee, some saw a front-page headline much like the one in the *New York Daily News:* "Esther Due Thursday."[1]

But the baseball fans on the West Coast had been dealing with their own "hurricane" since the start of the 1961 season.

For the first six seasons of his major-league career, Sandy Koufax had a rather nondescript statistical line of 36 wins, 40 losses, and a 4.10 earned-run average. Then at the start of the 1961 National League season, the left-hander from Brooklyn, New York, found something in his pitching that would turn him into one of the most feared pitchers in baseball.

After spending their first four years in Los Angeles playing at the Los Angeles Coliseum, the Dodgers began the 1962 season at brand-new Dodger Stadium. For their last game at the Coliseum in 1961, Koufax was the starting pitcher, and he pitched all 13 innings, throwing a remarkable 205 pitches, as the Dodgers escaped with a walk-off victory, one that a Los Angeles sportswriter said they eked out "the hard way."[2]

The crowd of 12,068 boosted the season's home attendance to over 1.8 million, but there was no victory celebration since first-place Cincinnati won again to protect its commanding five-game lead.[3] In 77 games at the Coliseum in 1961, the Dodgers had 45 wins and 32 defeats.

Koufax entered the game with a record of 17 wins and 11 losses with a 3.73 earned-run average. The Dodgers entered the game with 83 wins and 61 losses and trailed the first-place Reds by five games. The Dodgers had lost the first two games of the series with Chicago, 5-3 and 7-3.

Chicago was in the first year of its two-year experiment with a College of Coaches replacing the traditional manager. Lou Klein was at the helm, the fourth Cubs "head coach" after Vedie Himsl, Harry Craft, and El Tappe. As his starter, Klein chose left-hander Dick Ellsworth, who was in his third major-league season. Ellsworth was 8-11 with a 4.12 earned-run average.

Richie Ashburn led off the game with a single for the Cubs. Koufax struck out Don Zimmer and Ernie Banks. Ashburn stole second base but was left stranded as George Altman fouled out to end the inning.

In the bottom of the inning, Wally Moon walked with two out but Ellsworth struck out Gil Hodges to end the first inning.

Koufax allowed a two-out single to André Rodgers in the second inning but struck out Cuno Barragan. For the Dodgers, Ron Fairly and Gordie Windhorn singled. Fairly took third when Charlie Neal's groundball forced Windhorn at second base, and scored on catcher Norm Sherry's grounder to third. Koufax's groundout ended the inning with the Dodgers leading 1-0.

In the third inning, Koufax gave up a one-out single to Ashburn and Ellsworth allowed a one-out single to Jim Gilliam, but there was no scoring. In the Cubs' fourth, Billy Williams was hit by a Koufax pitch and Ron Santo followed with a two-run blast over the left-field screen to put Chicago ahead 2-1.

Over the next four innings Ellsworth surrendered just a single to Neal and a walk to Gilliam while Koufax allowed a two-out single to Zimmer in the fifth and a single to Barragan in the seventh, while adding four strikeouts which gave him a total of 10 whiffs after seven innings.

In the top of the eighth, Altman singled with two outs and went to second on Koufax's wild pitch with Billy Williams batting, but Koufax struck out Williams to end the inning.

Sherry's 251-foot home run down the oddly shaped (for baseball) Coliseum's left-field foul line leading off the Dodgers eighth tied the game, 2-2. Neither team scored in the ninth inning, and it was on to extra innings. Don Elston had replaced Ellsworth on the mound in the bottom of the ninth inning; Koufax continued to toe the rubber for the Dodgers.

Koufax struck out Altman and Williams in the 11th inning and got Santo to pop up to second. The Dodgers' 11th inning began with a single by Gilliam, who was sacrificed to second base by Moon. Norm Larker pinch-hit for Hodges and was intentionally walked. Fairly singled to right field, and Altman's strong throw home nailed Gilliam trying to score. Larker and Fairly each moved up a base on the throw. After Duke Snider was intentionally walked, Elston retired Neal on a fly ball to right, ending the Dodgers's threat.

Al Heist pinch-hit for Elston with one out in the Cubs' 12th; Koufax struck him out, his 15th whiff of the game. Catcher Sherry pounced on a ball hit in front of the plate by Dick Bertell and threw him out at first, ending the half-inning. New Cubs pitcher Barney Schultz walked the Dodgers' Maury Wills with two outs in the Los Angeles 12th, but Wills was caught stealing. In the top of the 13th inning, the Cubs got two walks (one intentionally, but couldn't get a run across.

Schultz struck out Gilliam leading off the Dodgers 13th. The next batter, Moon, singled to center field and reached second on Larker's grounder back to the pitcher. With Fairly batting, a passed ball by catcher Bertell allowed Moon to advance to third base. Then, on a 1-and-2 count, Fairly grounded a single past Schultz into center field, giving the Dodgers a walk-off 3-2 victory.

Fairly led the Dodgers' offense with three hits with Sherry and Gilliam each adding a couple of hits. In gaining his 18th win of the season Koufax allowed seven hits while walking three and striking out 15.

Over the next six seasons Koufax put together one of the greatest stretches of pitching in major-league history. During that time, he had a record of 129 wins and 47 losses with a 2.19 earned-run average. He pitched four no-hitters, including a perfect game, and won three Cy Young Awards and one Most Valuable Player Award.

Koufax's triumph had not been over more than a minute before workmen had pried the pitching slab loose from the mound in the first step toward dismantling the baseball fixtures that had transformed the Coliseum, designed for watching football, into a baseball venue.[4]

The Coliseum drew two very large crowds for exhibition games. Though he never played for the Dodgers in Los Angeles, on May 7, 1959, there was a benefit game held for Roy Campanella, who had been paralyzed in an automobile accident January 28, 1958. The Yankees defeated the Dodgers, 6-2, with 93,103 fans in attendance. On March 29, 2008, the Los Angeles Dodgers hosted the Boston Red Sox in an exhibition game, drawing a reported 115,300 fans who saw the Red Sox win, 7-4.[5]

The Dodgers finished the 1961 season 89-65, in second place, four games behind the pennant-winning Cincinnati Reds. As for their record at the Los Angeles Coliseum, they were 39-38 in 1958, 46-32 in 1959, 42-35 in 1960, and 45-32 for an overall record of 172 wins and 137 losses.

SOURCES

In addition to the sources listed below, the author used data from Baseball Reference.com and Retrosheet.org.

https://www.baseball-reference.com/boxes/LAN/LAN196109200.shtml

https://www.retrosheet.org/boxesetc/1961/B09200LAN1961.htm

NOTES

1   "Esther Due Thursday," *New York Daily News*, September 20, 1961: 1.

2   Frank Finch, "Dodgers Beat Cubs in 13th, 3-2," *Los Angeles Times*, September 21, 1961: C1.

3   Finch.

4   "Dodgers Beat Cubs in 13, 3-2," *Chicago Tribune*, September 21, 1961: D1.

5   Associated Press, "Red Sox Beat Dodgers 7-4 Before 115,300 Fans at Los Angeles Coliseum," foxnews.com, March 30, 2008. https://www.foxnews.com/story/red-sox-beat-dodgers-7-4-before-115300-fans-at-los-angeles-coliseum.

Koufax Sets NL Strikeout Record in Breakout Season

September 27, 1961: Philadelphia Phillies 2, Los Angeles Dodgers 1, at Connie Mack Stadium, Philadelphia

BY RICHARD CUICCHI

When Sandy Koufax started his seventh major-league season, in 1961, the verdict was still out on whether he should keep a spot in the Los Angeles Dodgers' rotation. He had struggled with control issues since the time he was signed as a 19-year-old bonus baby from the University of Cincinnati by the Brooklyn Dodgers. His 1961 season changed all that. His performance set him on a course of dominance in the major leagues for the five ensuing seasons. He gained the attention of the national baseball community that year by breaking Christy Mathewson's National League single-season record for strikeouts.

With an 8-13 record (.381), Koufax's 1960 season was one of his worst from the standpoint of a won-lost percentage, although he led the league in strikeouts per nine innings (10.1). By June 10 of that season, his record was 1-8. Because of his erratic control, he was relegated to the bullpen for most of July. When he did get into games, it looked as if he was trying to strike out every batter. Whenever he issued a walk or gave up a hit, he allowed his emotions to take over, which often got him into further trouble.[1]

At one point during the 1960 season, Koufax doubted the Dodgers' confidence in him and asked to be traded. "I want to pitch," he told Dodgers President Buzzie Bavasi, "and I'm not going to get a chance here." Bavasi's pushback was that Koufax wasn't getting batters out. Koufax countered, "If I can't do the job for you, why don't you send me somewhere where I can get a fresh start?" He considered walking away from the game but decided to give himself one more chance in 1961.[2]

The Dodgers signed Koufax in December 1954. By the rules then in effect for so-called bonus babies, the team was obligated to put him on its major-league roster.[3] Not having played in the minors, he never had the opportunity to work on control issues, which plagued him during his first few years.

After the 1960 season, Koufax worked on his delivery with Dodgers pitching coach Joe Becker. The goal was to tighten his windup and alter his grip on the curveball in order to make it more effective against left-handers. Dodgers scout Kenny Myers helped him improve pitching to spots. Then during spring training, catcher Norm Sherry worked diligently with Koufax to "try not throwing so hard." According to Sherry, the result was that Koufax started throwing harder when he was not trying.[4]

Three weeks into the start of the 1961 season, Koufax's improved mechanical and mental approach began to show positive results. Dodgers manager Walt Alston attributed Koufax's success to improving his control. In May Alston said, "He has reached the stage where he can get his curve ball over the plate consistently and he has come up with a pretty good change of pace."[5]

Between May 7 and June 20, Koufax compiled a 9-2 record, with 7 complete games in 11 starts. His ERA was 2.34, and he averaged one strikeout per inning. This was Koufax's best consecutive-game stretch so far in his career. He was hitting on all cylinders by this time, effectively using his fastball and curve to baffle hitters.[6]

By July 11, the day of the first All-Star Game in 1961, Koufax sported an 11-5 record with a 3.32 ERA and 141 strikeouts. He was named to his first All-Star team and pitched in relief in both games, on July 11 and July 31.

After Koufax's impressive 15th win on August 29, when he carried a no-hitter into the seventh inning and struck out 12,[7] Alston reiterated his belief expressed earlier in the season about Koufax's success. He said, "Where it's helped him the most is with his curve ball. He throws as hard as anybody in the league, but now he can come in with the curve ball if he has to."[8]

However, Koufax seemed to downplay his turnaround. He said, "[It's] just something that happened."[9]

With 18 wins under his belt, Koufax made his final regular-season start on September 27 against the Philadelphia Phillies.[10] The Dodgers and Reds had been in a back-and-forth battle for first place for most of the season. But by this time, the Reds had clinched the pennant, and the Dodgers turned their attention toward retaining second place over the San Francisco Giants.

With a 46-104 record, the Phillies were suffering through one of their worst seasons in franchise history. In his first season as manager, Gene Mauch suffered from a weak roster that was the worst in the league in runs scored and second worst in runs allowed.

The 27-year-old right-hander Jim Owens, who had joined the Phillies in late June, drew the starting assignment for Mauch.[11]

In the top of the first inning, Maury Wills led off with a double and Jim Gilliam walked. Ron Fairly doubled. The speedy Wills scored easily, but Gilliam was thrown out at the plate on a relay from shortstop Ruben Amaro.

Koufax gave up a single to Lee Walls in the second inning. In the third, the Phillies took the lead. Amaro led off with a single and went to second when shortstop Wills mishandled Clay Dalrymple's groundball. Jim Owens advanced the runners on a sacrifice. After Koufax struck out Bobby Malkmus, Tony Taylor's line-drive double produced two unearned runs as Amaro and Dalrymple crossed the plate.

After yielding three hits through three innings, Koufax held the Phillies scoreless for the rest of the game, yielding only three baserunners on walks. Owens, after giving up the first-inning run, blanked the Dodgers through the next six innings, despite having runners in scoring position in four of the innings. (In the seventh inning, the Dodgers put runners on first and second on singles by Gilliam and Fairly, but Wally Moon grounded out to end the threat.)

Jack Baldschun relieved Owens in the eighth and walked John Roseboro, who stole second on Daryl Spencer's swinging strikeout. But Baldschun squelched the threat by picking Roseboro off second.

The Phillies claimed the victory, 2-1, after Baldschun retired the Dodgers in order in the final frame.

Despite his impressive performance, Koufax took his 13th loss of the season against 18 wins. He struck out Pancho Herrera in the sixth to break Mathewson's National League record of 267 strikeouts set in 1903. Koufax's seven strikeouts for the game gave him 269 for the season. Sportswriters were quick to note that Koufax broke the record in 255⅔ innings pitched compared with Mathewson's 366⅓ innings.[12] A gloomy Koufax said of the record after the game, "Sure, it's nice to have, but I'd trade it in for a win."[13] He was referring to the late-season attempt by San Francisco to take over second place.

Owens recorded his fifth win of the season against 10 losses. He gave up nine hits, including three to Fairly.

Koufax's strikeout record was largely overshadowed by Roger Maris's chase of Babe Ruth's single-season home-run record. Maris had tied Ruth the day before with number 60, so most of the nation was focused on the slugger's effort to break the record.

The Dodgers led the NL in strikeouts on the arms of Koufax and his teammates Stan Williams (205) and Don Drysdale (182), who were second and third.

Koufax's next five seasons (1962-66) were one of the most spectacular pitching stretches in baseball history. In addition to breaking his own strikeout record twice – in 1963 (306) and 1965 (382) – he led the NL in ERA in all five seasons. He was a three-time Cy Young Award winner (1963, 1965, and 1966), when he won 25 or more games in each season.

Sandy Koufax broke Christy Mathewson's National League single-season record for strikeouts in 1961. SABR: The Rucker Archive.

SOURCES

In addition to the sources cited in the Notes, the author consulted Baseball-Reference.com and Retrosheet.org for pertinent information, including the box score and play-by-play.

https://www.baseball-reference.com/boxes/PHI/PHI196109270.shtml

https://www.retrosheet.org/boxesetc/1961/B09270PHI1961.htm

The author also consulted the following:

Leavy, Jane. *Koufax: A Lefty's Legacy* (New York: HarperCollins Publishers, 2002).

NOTES

1   Edward Gruver, *Koufax* (New York: Taylor Publishing: 2000), 123.

2   Gruver.

3   Marc Z. Aaron, "Sandy Koufax," SABR BioProject, https://sabr.org/bioproj/person/Sandy-Koufax/. Accessed May 11, 2023.

4   Gruver, 124-127.

5   George Lederer, "It's a Bright, New World for Koufax," *Long Beach* (California) *Press-Telegram*, May 26, 1961: D-1.

6   During this stretch, Koufax delivered several performances representative of his improvement. On May 29 against the St. Louis

Cardinals, his 13-strikeout game was the third of the season in which he posted double-digit strikeouts. He gave up only three hits. Three weeks later, on June 20, Koufax hurled a two-hitter against the Chicago Cubs for his 10th win. He carried a no-hitter into the seventh inning, and his 14 strikeouts gave him 111 for the season.

7   Coming off the Dodgers' doubleheader losses to league leader Cincinnati on August 27, which dropped them to 3½ games behind the Reds, Koufax collected his 15th win, against the Chicago Cubs on August 29. He flirted with a no-hitter, going into the seventh inning with two outs before Dick Bertell singled over shortstop Maury Wills's outstretched arm into short left field. Koufax struck out 12 and raised his total to 212 for the season.

8   John Kuenster, "Koufax peps up Dodgers," *Chicago Daily News*, August 30, 1961: 42.

9   "Koufax Peps Up Dodgers."

10   A week earlier, on September 20, Koufax had his best performance of the season, striking out 15 batters as he pitched all 13 innings in a 3-2 win over the Cubs. It was his 18th win of the season. He made another start on September 24 against the Cardinals but lasted only three innings while taking his 12th loss.

11   Owens made his first appearance of the season on June 23. He had been placed on the disqualified list at the beginning of the season by Phillies general manager John Quinn in a dispute about his role on the pitching staff.

12   As of 1961, the major-league strikeout record was held by the Philadelphia Athletics' Rube Waddell with 349 in 1904.

13   Stan Hochman, "Sandy's New Strikeout Mark Nice, but No Substitute for Victory," *Philadelphia Daily News*, September 28, 1961: 64.

"The Human Strikeout Machine": Koufax Fans 18 in the Windy City

April 24, 1962: Los Angeles Dodgers 10, Chicago Cubs 2, at Wrigley Field

BY GREGORY H. WOLF

"I lost track," replied Sandy Koufax when asked if he knew how many batters he struck out. "[I] didn't know I'd tied the record until everybody came off the bench to shake my hand."[1] Koufax fanned 18 to equal Bob Feller's nine-inning record set in 1938 and match his own personal best three seasons earlier.[2] "Strikeouts are nice to have, particularly in a jam, and they are going to come to a pitcher who throws hard," noted Koufax, "but I wouldn't trade a 20-game season for all the strikeout records in the books."[3]

Skipper Walter Alston's fourth-place Dodgers (8-5) were looking for some momentum when they arrived in Chicago for a three-game set to conclude a 10-game road swing. The Cubs, who at 3-9 were tied with the Milwaukee Brewers and better only than the winless, expansion New York Mets, seemed like the perfect victim. The North Siders were in the second campaign of club owner Philip K. Wrigley's bizarre experiment with the college of coaches and its revolving "head coach," a position currently occupied by El Tappe.

By the start of the 1962 season, Koufax had long been known as one of the hardest throwers in baseball history, but he was not yet the consistently dominating pitcher who combined power with control. "[S]ometimes erratic and sometimes unbeatable," according to the *Pasadena Independent*, the 26-year-old Koufax had a pedestrian 54-53 record in parts of seven seasons, but had averaged more than a strikeout an inning.[4] The southpaw whom sportswriter Frank Finch of the *Los Angeles Times* lauded as the "human strikeout machine" was coming off a breakout season.[5] In 1961 he won 18 games, whiffed an NL-record 269 batters, and set another standard by fanning at least 10 batters in a game 11 times to bring his career total to 31. Koufax's success could be attributed to his newfound control, his hitherto most glaring weakness. On backup catcher Norm Sherry's recommendation, Koufax began throwing more changeups, which made his heater seem even faster and his knee-buckling curve even more devastating.[6] Koufax had emerged victorious in two of his first three starts in '62, but seemed to suffer from fatigue late in games. "I

never pace myself," said Koufax about his approach. "I pitch as strong as hard as I can. If I run into trouble, I know there are a few guys in the bullpen who can come in and do the job."[7]

A crowd of only 8,938 patrons made its way to the intersection of Clark and Addison to take in an afternoon of baseball on a cool yet sunny Tuesday afternoon at Wrigley Field. After one inning, it looked as though it could be a long afternoon for both clubs' hitters. Cubs right-hander Don Cardwell, who had posted a 15-14 record and by some modern metrics was the best pitcher in baseball in 1961, fanned two in a 1-2-3 inning while Koufax fanned the side.[8]

Cardwell, who had lost all three of his starts with a 7.62 ERA thus far in '62, came undone in the second. Duke Snider, the 35-year-old gray-haired former Brooklyn icon, led off with a walk, moved up on a wild pitch, and scored on Tommy Davis's single. After Johnny Roseboro stroked a double that center fielder Lou Brock lost in the sun, Willie Davis's sacrifice fly gave the Dodgers a 2-0 lead.

Koufax continued his pitching clinic the next few frames. He fanned nine of the first 10 batters he faced, and had registered 10 strikeouts by the end of the fourth. Ron Santo collected the Cubs' first safety, a fourth-inning double. "Sandy's curve was marvelous in the early innings," said All-Star batterymate Roseboro. "But as the shadows came along, we started going more with the fastball."[9]

Meanwhile the Dodgers continued to whack Cardwell. After Wally Moon reached on a wind-aided single with two outs in the third, Snider hit a liner that eluded right-fielder Bob Will's shoestring attempt, and Moon scored. The Dodgers added another run, in the fourth, on Andy Carey's line drive round-tripper to left field, his first as a Dodger after spending his first 10 seasons in the AL. Los Angeles blew the game open in the fifth when Tommy Davis, en route to leading the NL in RBIs with 153, belted a three-run home run with Jim Gilliam and Moon on base via singles for a seemingly insurmountable 7-0 lead.

Koufax hit a bump in the fifth. Billy Williams reached second when his deep fly bounced off center fielder Willie Davis's glove. The play was generously ruled a double and not an error. Koufax loaded the bases on walks to Will and Elder White, then fanned Moe Thacker and pinch-hitter André Rodgers. One pitch from escaping the jam, Koufax issued his third free pass of the inning, to Brock, to force Williams across the plate. "I was afraid in the fifth that I might be tiring," said Koufax after the game.[10] He was obviously laboring and admitted that he started "aiming the ball."[11]

The Dodgers made it 8-1 in the seventh when Tony Balsamo, who had relieved Cardwell to start the sixth, balked with bases loaded, forcing Wills home. Tappe protested the ruling and was ejected. Sportswriter Richard Dozer of the *Chicago Tribune* noted that Balsamo had Wills picked off at third; however, first-base umpire Stan Landes overruled the decision with his balk call.[12] The Dodgers' scoring explosion culminated in the ninth when Snider walloped a two-run homer after Moon had singled.

After his hiccup in the fifth, Koufax was much less overpowering in the next three frames, yielding two singles, issuing a walk, and fanning three. Slugger Billy Williams, whose 25 homers in '61 catapulted him to the NL Rookie of the Year Award, led off the final inning with a solo home run for the Cubs' second run. "It was a good pitch to a left-hander's strength," joked Koufax after the game. "A high inside curve, and he hit it good. If I could take two pitches back, I'd take that one and the ball to Brock [in the fifth]."[13]

The Dodgers bullpen remained silent in the ninth. It was the Brooklyn native's game to complete. No doubt Alston also knew that his prized southpaw still had a chance to tie his own record for most strikeouts in a game. Koufax punched out Will and White to raise his strikeout total to 17 and tie Dizzy Dean (1933) and Art Mahaffey (1961) for the most strikeouts in a day game in the NL. Thacker followed with what appeared to be a routine pop fly to first baseman Tim Harkness, who had replaced Moon to start the frame. Playing first for just the ninth time in his big-league career, Harkness lost the ball in the swirling wind coming off Lake Michigan, one mile to the east, and watched the orb drop in fair territory just feet away him for a single. Koufax unexpectedly had another shot at the record. To the plate stepped rookie Moe Morhardt, who had led the Class-B Northwest League in hitting with a .339 average the previous year. Koufax struck him out looking to end the game in 2 hours and 41 minutes.

As expected, teammates euphorically congratulated Koufax, who yielded six hits and walked four to go along with his 18 strikeouts. "I was trying to make them hit it," he said. "I just wanted to get the game over."[14] Frank Finch of the *Times* reported that Koufax threw 144 pitches, including 96 for strikes.[15] Koufax seemed unconcerned by that number, claiming that the total was "not high" for a fastball pitcher, while he soaked his bulging, swollen elbow in ice after the game.[16]

Koufax's record-tying strikeout performance quieted detractors who had claimed that his 18 punchouts in a complete-game,

seven-hit victory over the San Francisco Giants on August 31, 1959, were the product of the "lousy" lights and poor visibility at the L.A. Coliseum, where the Dodgers played their home games from 1958 through 1961.[17] Koufax himself scoffed at comparing the games, noting only that there were more than 60,000 spectators in L.A. cheering for the Dodgers while fewer than 9,000 fans were at Wrigley Field.

Koufax suffered a career-threatening injury, not to his elbow or shoulder, but to his index finger, in his next start, on April 28, against the Pirates. In his BioProject bio on Koufax, SABR member Marc Z Aaron writes how Koufax was hit by a pitch on his left index finger, causing a trauma that developed into Raynaud's phenomenon, a circulatory condition.[18] Koufax played through the numbness and even tossed his first of four no-hitters, on June 30. But the pain proved too intense. Koufax ultimately landed on the DL in mid-July and missed nine weeks. He returned in late September, but pitched ineffectively as the Dodgers lost to the San Francisco Giants in a three-game playoff for the pennant. Koufax finished with a 14-7 slate, and led the NL in ERA (2.54) for the first of five consecutive seasons.

SOURCES

In addition to the sources cited in the Notes, the author accessed Retrosheet.org, Baseball-Reference.com, SABR.org, and *The Sporting News* archive via Paper of Record.

https://www.baseball-reference.com/boxes/CHN/CHN196204240.shtml

https://www.retrosheet.org/boxesetc/1962/B04240CHN1962.htm

NOTES

1 United Press International, "Trying to Make 'Em Hit – Koufax," *Los Angeles Times*, April 25, 1962: III, 3.

2 Warren Spahn also struck out 18 batters, but those came in 15 innings in a route-going loss, 3-1, to the Cubs as a member of the Boston Braves on June 14, 1952, at Braves Field.

3 Frank Finch, "Koufax Whiff Pace Fastest in History," *The Sporting News*, May 23, 1962: 6.

4 "Koufax Fans 18 For Record," *Pasadena Independent*, April 25, 1962: 16.

5 Frank Finch, "Koufax Fans 18 Cubs, Equals Record," *Los Angeles Times*, April 25, 1962: III, 1.

6 Finch, "Koufax Whiff Pace Fastest in History."

7 UPI, "Sandy Aimed It in Bad 5th Inning," *Pasadena Independent*, April 26, 1962: 54.

8 In his fifth big-league season, Cardwell posted a 15-14 record in 1961 which improved his career record to 40-54. He also logged 259⅓ innings and led the NL with 38 starts. By one contemporary metric, WAR (wins above replacement, which attempts to quantify the value of a player by measuring the number of wins the player added to his team compared with what a replacement player would add), Cardwell was the most valuable pitcher in baseball with a 6.1 WAR. Jack Kralick of the Minnesota Twins also had 6.1 WAR.

9 UPI, "Sandy Aimed It in Bad 5th Inning."

10   UPI, "Sandy Aimed It in Bad 5th Inning."

11   UPI, "Trying to Make 'Em Hit – Koufax."

12   Richard Dozer, "Koufax Fans 18 Cubs to Tie Own Mark," *Chicago Tribune*, April 25, 1962: IV, 1.

13   UPI, "Sandy Aimed It in Bad 5th Inning."

14   UPI, "Trying to Make 'Em Hit – Koufax."

15   Finch, "Koufax Fans 18 Cubs, Equals Record."

16   UPI, "Trying to Make 'Em Hit – Koufax."

17   Finch, "Koufax Whiff Pace Fastest in History."

18   Marc Z. Aaron, "Sandy Koufax," BioProject, Society for American Baseball Research. sabr.org/bioproj/person/e463317c.

Koufax Shines on Mound and At Dish

May 26, 1962: Los Angeles Dodgers 6, Philadelphia Phillies 3, at Dodger Stadium, Los Angeles

BY BRIAN WILLIAMS

Through mid-May of 1962, Sandy Koufax owned a modest 4-2 record, not having dented the win column since the previous month. But after an 18-win 1961 season while striking out 269 batters in 255⅔ innings, Koufax sported "the best strikeout average of any pitcher who ever lived."[1]

A 4-1 April with three complete games appeared promising. However, May began with a 3-1 loss to the Chicago Cubs. (Two of the Cubs' runs were unearned.) Koufax lasted no more than six innings without any decisions in his next three starts.

The Dodgers faced their biggest rivals, the first-place San Francisco Giants, on May 21. Koufax spun his first complete game and his first victory in three weeks (since April 28). The mojo returned as the left-hander allowed only five hits while striking out 10.

LA pummeled the Mets, 17-8, on Friday evening, May 25, to complete a three-game sweep. The Dodgers had won five in a row and looked to feast on the Philadelphia Phillies, who had just dropped two of three to the Giants. The Phillies were sputtering at 16-23, ahead of only the Houston Colt .45s, the expansion Mets, and the cellar-dwelling Cubs. Meanwhile the Dodgers were nipping at San Francisco's heels for first place in the National League.

With 18,071 in attendance at Dodger Stadium, Tony Taylor got the Phillies off to a positive start with a line double to left. Koufax settled in to retire the next two hitters. His first K was on a swing and miss by rookie Ted Savage, who enjoyed his best NL season in 1962; however, this wasn't his day against Koufax.

With Taylor still on second, cleanup hitter Roy Sievers slammed a two-run shot to deep left, his third home run of

Sandy Koufax struck out 16 Phillies batters on May 26, 1962. SABR: The Rucker Archive.

the young season. Koufax recovered to get third baseman Mel Roach on a swinging strike to end the inning.

Dennis Bennett, 22 years old, got the pitching nod for the visiting Phillies, his third start and the fourth major-league appearance of his rookie season. The lefty battled leadoff hitter Maury Wills to a full count before issuing a free pass. Bennett temporarily lost the strike zone and also walked Jim Gilliam on four pitches. Willie Davis grounded out to first baseman Sievers as both runners advanced. Tommy Davis tied the game by lacing a two-run double to right field and increasing his season RBI total to 45, trailing only Orlando Cepeda. Bennett continued to struggle from the stretch after hitting Ron Fairly and walking Larry Burright, but got Doug Camilli on a called strike three to avoid additional damage.

After a long half-inning in the dugout, Koufax seemed stronger against the bottom of the Phillies' lineup. He struck out young Cuban center fielder Tony González to start the inning and shortstop Bobby Wine to end the one-two-three frame. Both went down swinging as Koufax threw only three pitches out of the strike zone in the inning.

Koufax led off the bottom half and struck out swinging. Bennett allowed yet another walk to Gilliam but preserved the 2-2 tie.

Bennett flied out to center on the first pitch of the third. Tony Taylor reached on LA second baseman Burright's error, swiped second on the first pitch to Johnny Callison, and scored on Callison's single to right. (Callison took second on the throw to the plate.) Koufax got a pop fly to Burright at second and a liner to Fairly at first to get back into the dugout.

With the Phillies leading 3-2, Bennett issued another lead-off walk in the third inning, this time to Tommy Davis, who motored to third on Frank Howard's ground single to left. That brought up Fairly, who had been on fire, hitting .542 over his past eight games. He recorded an RBI ground single to right field. After Burright popped out and Doug Camilli walked, Dallas Green relieved Bennett and got the two final outs of the inning.

Koufax mowed down the Phillies in the fourth for his second one-two-three inning. His efficient 14-pitch inning included two groundouts and a swinging strike three by Sammy White in what became White's final professional season. That was the fifth K for Koufax. Green also retired the Dodgers in order in the fourth.

Koufax responded very well to the quick return trip to the mound by striking out the side in the fifth. Wine, Green, and Taylor saw a total of 11 pitches, all but two for strikes. Koufax now had eight K's through five innings. Green blanked the Dodgers again in the bottom half.

The heart of the Phillies order was due in the sixth inning of a tie game. Callison went down on three pitches, the last a swinging strike. Savage struck out swinging on a 2-and-2 pitch. That made it six consecutive strikeouts for Koufax. Sievers broke the string, lining out to center as Koufax completed a 10-pitch inning and now had 10 strikeouts.

Green struck out Koufax looking to start the bottom of the sixth inning and held the Dodgers scoreless as the score remained 3-3.

Mel Roach, leading off the Phillies' seventh, whiffed on a 2-and-2 pitch, Koufax's 11th strikeout. González touched Koufax for a ground double to right. White flied out to right on a two-strike pitch. Manager Walter Alston called for an intentional walk to Wine, the number-eight hitter.

The Phillies allowed Green to hit for himself with the go-ahead run at second base. Before the game, Phillies manager Gene Mauch admitted to the press, "The bullpen isn't up to snuff." He said, "We've blown six games in which we had the lead going into the seventh, eighth or ninth innings."[2] Koufax struck out Green looking for the second time to snuff out the threat.

The Dodgers responded with three singles and a walk off Green to take the lead. The tiebreaking hit was a single by Wally Moon, batting for Burright with one out. After another out, a bonus run came home courtesy of none other than the day's starting pitcher. Koufax, "who had struck out three straight times and is rated one of the worst hitting pitchers in baseball,"[3] had struck out in 24 of 33 plate appearances so far in the season. When it counted with a razor-thin lead, Koufax bopped a 2-and-1 pitch into the grass in short right field to plate Frank Howard.

With a 5-3 lead, Alston's defensive changes paid dividends. Fairly caught Taylor's line drive to right field to start the eighth. Callison grounded out to Gilliam, who was now at second base. Savage went down on strikes for the third time, giving Koufax

13 K's through eight frames. It only took the southpaw 11 pitches to finish another efficient one-two-three inning.

In the bottom half of the inning, Willie Davis brought the crowd to its feet by tacking on a solo home run, his sixth of the year, to widen the Dodgers advantage to 6-3.

Sievers walked on four pitches to lead off the Phillies' ninth. Roach legged out an infield hit to Wills at short. Suddenly the tying run was at the plate with no outs.

Koufax bore down. González walked back to the dugout after looking at strike three. Pinch-hitter Jacke Davis, playing in his only major-league season, swung and missed on a full-count pitch for the second out. Don Demeter grabbed a bat and strode toward the plate as the Phillies' last hope. Mauch had hoped to start the former (Brooklyn) Dodger, but a hamstring injury forced Demeter into a pinch-hitting role. Koufax induced strike three swinging to end the game, 6-3, stranding both Phillies baserunners.

Dodgers broadcaster Vin Scully couldn't even credit Koufax for the most strikeouts in a game that season, commenting: "Sandy Koufax ran out of victims before he could equal the major-league strikeout record of 18 he shares with Bob Feller."[4] Back on April 24, Koufax had already struck out 18 Cubs in a 10-2 Dodgers victory.

On this Saturday afternoon, Koufax allowed only five hits and struck out 16 Phillies – the last to end the game – and recorded his 100th strikeout of the season (in 83 innings pitched). He also had mowed down six consecutive Phillies in the middle innings. As noted in the *Philadelphia Inquirer*, "Sievers was the lone Phil regular who did not strike out against the blazing fast ball and sharp-breaking curve of Koufax."[5]

The feat this day was nothing new to Koufax, Frank Finch wrote: "He'd previously baffled that many Phillies in a Coliseum night game, June 22, 1959."[6] Overall, this was Koufax's 34th time reaching double-digit strikeouts in his career.

Although he tallied double-digit strikeouts six more times in 1962, none matched his two incredible early-season feats against the struggling Cubs and Phillies. Koufax improved his record to 6-2 while the hot second-place Dodgers had won 14 of their last 18 contests.

SOURCES

In addition to the sources cited in the Notes, the author consulted Baseball-Reference.com, Retrosheet.org, and the following:

Lederer, George. "Koufax Whiffs 16 Phils," *Long Beach* (California) *Independent*, May 27, 1962: 21.

United Press International. "Koufax Strikes Out 16 Phillies, as Dodgers Win, 6-3, for Sixth Straight," *New York Times*, May 27, 1962: S3.

Associated Press. "Koufax Whiffs 16, Wins 6-3," *San Bernardino County* (California) *Sun*, May 27, 1962: 27.

https://www.baseball-reference.com/boxes/LAN/LAN196205260.shtml

https://www.retrosheet.org/boxesetc/1962/B05260LAN1962.htm

NOTES

1   Allen Lewis, "Koufax Fans 16 Phils as Dodgers Win, 6-3,"
    Philadelphia Inquirer, May 27, 1962: 97.

2   Frank Finch, "Phillies Pitching Poses Problem," *Los Angeles Times*,
    May 27, 1962: G5.

3   Lewis.

4   Finch.

5   Lewis.

6   Finch.

Sandy Koufax Hits First Home Run to Beat Warren Spahn, 2-1

June 13, 1962: Los Angeles Dodgers 2, Milwaukee Braves 1, at County Stadium, Milwaukee

BY TIM OTTO

After a breakout 1961 season during which he won 18 games and struck out a National League modern-day record 269 batters,[1] Sandy Koufax was even better during the first months of the 1962 campaign. Prior to a Dodgers' mid-June three-game series in Milwaukee, the 26-year-old had compiled an 8-2 record (3.02 ERA), with 131 strikeouts in 107⅓ innings, including an 18-strikeout effort against the Chicago Cubs on April 24.

In a pitching matchup of the NL's premier southpaws, Koufax faced Warren Spahn on June 13 in the second game of the series against the Braves.[2] In 1961, at the age of 40, Spahn recorded his sixth straight 20-win season (the 12th of his career), and his 3.02 ERA was the NL's best. A 3-2 loss at Houston in his last start dropped Spahn's 1962 record to 6-6 (3.22 ERA) and was his fourth one-run loss of the season.

Despite the cold evening temperatures that saw fans at Milwaukee's County Stadium huddling under blankets,[3] the Wednesday night crowd of 14,913 was Milwaukee's largest since 30,001 turned out on Opening Day. After losing to the Braves 15-2 the night before, Los Angeles (43-20) held a one-game lead over the second-place San Francisco Giants. The sixth-place Braves (28-31) trailed the Dodgers by 13 games.

Each pitcher retired the side in order in the first inning. Leading off the top of the second, Tommy Davis singled on a grounder just out of Eddie Mathews' reach at third. One out later, he advanced to third base on Ron Fairly's line-drive single to right field. Daryl Spencer's groundball single through the hole between short and third gave the Dodgers a 1-0 lead.[4]

Del Crandall's two-out single, followed by a passed ball and a walk, put runners

Never much of a hitter, Sandy Koufax batted just .097 lifetime and hit two home runs. SABR: The Rucker Archive.

at first and second for the Braves in the bottom of the second inning. Shortstop Maury Wills' leaping catch of Frank Bolling's line drive ended the scoring threat.[5]

Koufax appeared to slip on the mound while delivering one of his pitches to Bolling. "The pain was fairly sharp and I thought I might have pulled a muscle in the upper chest," Koufax said after the game. "However, I got Bolling out and then I seemed to loosen up starting the third. I didn't feel any pain again."[6]

Hank Aaron lined a single to right leading off the bottom of the fourth inning. One out later, he stole second base. On the play, catcher John Roseboro's high throw to second sailed into center field. Willie Davis retrieved the ball as Aaron headed for third, but his throw was over third baseman Spencer's head. Aaron turned toward home, but could not advance because Koufax backed up the throw from Davis.[7] A popup to the shortstop and a line drive caught by second baseman Jim Gilliam left Aaron stranded at third.

Koufax, on deck for the start of the fifth inning, had begun the season with a career .089 batting average. Normally a right-handed batter, on April 28 he tried hitting from the left side of the plate against Pittsburgh in order to protect his throwing arm from potentially getting hit. He was jammed with a pitch that struck both the bat and his pitching hand. After that, Koufax switched back to batting right-handed.[8] Before his start against the Braves, he had only four singles in 42 at-bats during the season, and had struck out 28 times.

With one out and the bases empty, Koufax lined the first pitch from Spahn into the left-field bleachers at the 360-foot mark.[9] "I don't ever remember hitting a home run, although maybe I did in sandlot ball," he said after the game. "I know I hit one in high school. I played a little first base at Lafayette High in Brooklyn, but I never was a good hitter. That's the reason I wound up pitching."[10]

Spahn didn't hide his frustration at giving up a home run to the weak-hitting Koufax. As described by baseball author Jane Leavy, "Spahn slammed his glove to the ground, yelling at Koufax as he giddy-yapped around second base."[11]

"The pitch to Koufax was a screwball that didn't do a thing and came inside," said Spahn of the unlikely homer that increased the Dodgers' lead to 2-0.[12]

Koufax set the Braves down in order in the bottom of the fifth inning. Willie Davis and Tommy Davis started the sixth for the Dodgers with bunt singles. Willie moved to third base on Frank Howard's lineout to center. Spahn retired the next two batters on a strikeout and a groundout, keeping Milwaukee's deficit at two runs.

Leading off the bottom of the sixth, Roy McMillan hit a 0-and-1 pitch on a line into the left-field bleachers for his sixth homer, cutting the Dodgers' lead in half. With a one-run lead, Koufax retired the final 12 Milwaukee batters in order. Tommie Aaron's eighth-inning line drive, caught by a retreating Willie Davis in deep center field, was the closest any Braves batter came to getting a hit after McMillan's home run.[13] The Dodgers' 2-1 victory increased their lead over the Giants to two games.

Koufax's eighth complete-game win of the season improved his record to 9-2 and lowered his ERA to 2.86. He walked two Braves and scattered three hits: singles in the second and fourth innings and McMillan's solo homer in the sixth. Koufax struck out six, fewer than his usual number for a complete game, but those strikeouts brought his league-leading total to 137.[14]

Koufax took a fair amount of ribbing from his teammates about his newfound hitting prowess.[15] Eight bats were stacked in his locker after the game. "Only 60 behind Maris," quipped one player, referring to the home run record set by Roger Maris in 1961.[16]

Spahn's fifth one-run loss of the year dropped his record to 6-7. Of the seven hits he allowed over his eight innings of work, three were bunt singles.[17] He struck out seven and walked only one batter. "I've been getting progressively better this season. Tonight, I was sharp, making good pitches – except the one to Koufax," said Spahn of his performance. "I'll win my share of the close ones before the year is out if I keep throwing the way I have been."[18]

Koufax continued to pitch well during June, capping the month off with a no-hitter against the New York Mets on June 30. During the month, he posted a 4-2 record, with a 1.24 ERA and 74 strikeouts in 58⅓ innings. He was named National League Player of the Month for June.[19]

The Dodgers placed Koufax on the disabled list two days after he exited his July 17 start against Cincinnati in the first inning.[20] Suffering from what was described in some press reports as Reynaud's phenomenon, an arterial blockage causing numbness in the fingers, he was treated with drugs to expand the restricted artery causing the loss of feeling in his left index finger.[21]

Koufax returned to start a game in St. Louis on September 21 but was relieved in the first inning after giving up four runs. Ineffective in three other appearances, including a start in the first playoff game against the Giants,[22] he finished the season with a 14-7 record and a league-best 2.54 ERA.

Fully recovered by the following spring, Koufax attributed the injury, which cost him half of the 1962 season and likely cost the Dodgers the pennant, to his left-handed-batting experiment against the Pirates. "Early last season I decided to bat lefty because that way my right arm would be nearer to the pitcher than my left, and if I was going to get hit by a pitch, I'd rather have it hit my right arm than my left," he explained. "So, I batted lefty and I got jammed by a pitch right on my hands, and I think that's when the trouble started."[23]

When asked if batting righty was his natural way to hit, Koufax replied, "I have no 'natural' way to hit. Nothing about my batting can be described as natural!"[24] Batting solely from the right side until his retirement after the 1966 season, he remained a weak hitter. He did hit one other career home run, also in Milwaukee against the Braves. It was hit 13 months after this one, on July 20, 1963, a three-run homer off Denny Lemaster in a 5-4 win. Koufax finished his career with a .097 batting average and 28 RBIs.[25]

"About my hitting, the less said the better," Koufax joked in a *Sports Illustrated* interview after being named's *SI*'s Sportsman of the Year for 1965.[26] He did manage to get a hit in the fifth game of the 1965 World Series. With two outs and a runner at second in the seventh inning, Minnesota's Jim Perry intentionally walked Roseboro to pitch to Koufax. As described by the *Los Angeles Times*, "Sandy slugged a solid single" to left-center, driving in a run in the Dodgers' 7-0 victory over the Twins.[27] It was his only hit in 19 career at-bats in the fall classic.

SOURCES

The author accessed Baseball-Reference.com and Retrosheet.org. for box scores/play-by-play information, player, team, and season pages, pitching and batting game logs, and other data:

https://www.baseball-reference.com/boxes/MLN/MLN196206130.shtml

https://www.retrosheet.org/boxesetc/1962/B06130MLN1962.htm

Thanks to Bill Pruden for providing additional information.

NOTES

1   Christy Mathewson struck out 267 batters in 1903 to set the post-1900 NL record. From 1883 through 1899, eleven NL pitchers recorded 270 or more strikeouts in 21 seasons. Old Hoss Radbourn's 441 strikeouts in 1884 were the most of any pitcher during this period. Radbourn, playing for Providence, worked 678⅔ innings while completing 73 of his 75 starts.

2   The future Hall of Famers had faced each other as starting pitchers four times before 1962. Spahn won their first encounter on July 30, 1958, with a complete game, 4-3 win. Koufax evened things up on June 17, 1959, going the distance in the Dodgers' 10-2 win. They

next met twice in September of 1961. Spahn tossed a shutout in the Braves' 4-0 win on September 2. Koufax beat the Braves, 11-2, with a complete-game effort on September 15. Their final pairing occurred in June of 1965 when Spahn was with the New York Mets and in his final season. Spahn allowed two runs in seven innings, but lost to the Dodgers, 2-1, as Koufax improved his record to 4-2 against Spahn.

3   Jane Leavy, *Sandy Koufax: A Lefty's Legacy* (New York: Harper Collins, 2002): 117.

4   Dave O'Hara, "Braves' Bats Fail; Spahn Beaten, 2 to 1," *Capital Times* (Madison, Wisconsin), June 14, 1962: 36.

5   Frank Finch, "Koufax Homer Gives Dodgers 2-1 Triumph," *Los Angeles Times*, June 14, 1962: 48.

6   "Strikeout King Turns 'Slugger'," *Kenosha* (Wisconsin) *News*, June 14, 1962: 35.

7   AP Photo caption, *Capital Times*, June 14, 1962: 36.

8   Jack Olsen, "Koufax on Koufax," *Sports Illustrated*, December 20, 1965: 41. Koufax remained in the contest and recorded a complete-game, 2-1 win. He continued to take his regular turn in the pitching rotation after the April 28 victory against Pittsburgh. He pitched four straight complete-game wins with 10 or more strikeouts from May 21 through June 4, including a 16-strikeout effort against the Phillies.

9   "Braves' Bats Fail; Spahn Beaten, 2 to 1."

10   "Strikeout King Turns 'Slugger.'"

11   Leavy, 117.

12   "Strikeout King Turns 'Slugger.'"

13   "Koufax Homer Gives Dodgers 2-1 Triumph."

14   "Koufax Halts Braves, 2 to 1," *Chicago Tribune*, June 14, 1962: 89.

15   Frank Finch, "Drysdale Opens 20-Game Home Stand Against Colts Tonight," *Los Angeles Times*, June 15, 1962: 44.

16   "Strikeout King Turns 'Slugger.'" Koufax was kidded about his hitting throughout his career. After his no-hitter against the Mets at the end of June, a photo in *The Sporting News* (July 14, 1962: 5) shows Koufax, Walter Alston, and Maury Wills all smiling while looking at the clubhouse blackboard. On it is the score, date, and the words "No-Hitter." Alston is pointing below that, where "Koufax (0 for 4)" is written.

17   Joe Torre pinch-hit for Spahn in the bottom of the eighth inning, and Hank Fischer relieved to pitch the ninth for the Braves.

18   "Strikeout King Turns 'Slugger.'" Spahn finished 1962 with an 18-14 record and a 3.04 ERA. In 1963, at the age of 42, he was 23-7 with a 2.60 ERA. It was his 13th and last 20-game-win season.

19   "Sandy Outpolls Hank Aaron as N.L. 'Player of Month,'" *The Sporting News*, July 21, 1962: 19.

20   Bob Hunter, "Dodger High-Balling Flag Express Slowed by Walking Wounded," *The Sporting News*, July 28, 1962: 16.

21   Melvin Durslag, "Ailing Hill Ace Koufax Victim of 1,000-1 Shot, *The Sporting News*, August 11, 1962: 12. In his book *Koufax*, co-authored with Ed Linn, Koufax states that he had symptoms that were the same as Reynaud's phenomenon, but did not actually have the condition, as had been reported by some members of the press.

22   Los Angeles had been in first place since Koufax's win against San Francisco on July 8. However, the Giants caught the Dodgers on the last day of the season to force a best-of-three-game tiebreaker. San Francisco won the first game, 8-0, as Koufax gave up two homers and three runs in one-plus innings. The Dodgers rallied from a five-run deficit to win the second game, 8-7. The Giants won the pennant with a 6-4 win in the deciding game, scoring four runs in the top of the ninth inning for the comeback victory.

23   Robert Creamer, "An Urgent Matter of One Index Finger," *Sports Illustrated*, March 4, 1963: 22.

24   Olsen, 41.

25   Although Koufax hit his only two home runs at Milwaukee's County Stadium, his .111 batting average (4 hits in 36 at-bats) at that location wasn't much better than his career average.

26   Olsen, 36.

27   Frank Finch, "Dodgers Take Lead in Series, Move In for the Kill," *Los Angeles Times*, October 12, 1965: 32.

Sandy Koufax Beats Bob Gibson, 1-0; Tommy Davis Hits Walk-Off in 9th

June 18, 1962: Los Angeles Dodgers 1, St. Louis Cardinals 0, at Dodger Stadium, Los Angeles

BY THOMAS J. BROWN JR.

Right-hander Bob Gibson and left-hander Sandy Koufax, both 26 years old, faced each other for the first time on May 25, 1961, at Busch Stadium in St. Louis. Tommy Davis's leadoff home run in the seventh inning was the difference in the Dodgers' 1-0 win that day. Both men struck out eight batters with Koufax going the distance to earn his fifth win of the season. Gibson took the loss, his first in five starts.

Now both pitchers were scheduled to face each other again on June 18, 1962, when the Cardinals arrived in Los Angeles for a three-game series.

The Dodgers held a one-game lead over the San Francisco Giants in the National League. St. Louis was in fourth place, 7½ games out of the lead, after losing two games to the Giants. Los Angeles saw its lead drop to one game after losing two of three to the Houston Astros. The Dodgers won the finale, 6-2, sparked by Davis's three-run homer.

A crowd of 33,477 showed up at Dodger Stadium to see Koufax take the mound. The 26-year-old entered the game with a 9-2 record, having won five of his previous eight starts. He even earned a rare save when he finished a suspended game on June 6 to give the Dodgers an 8-3 victory over the Pittsburgh Pirates.[1]

Koufax retired the Cardinals on three groundouts in the first. After Koufax struck out leadoff batter Ken Boyer in the second, Stan Musial singled to center field. "I was pitching Musial low and outside all night. I was willing to concede him a base hit with nobody on base. It's not easy to hit one out of this park," said Koufax after the game.[2] Musial did not advance as Koufax got the next two batters out on a foul pop and a groundout.

Koufax struck out the first two batters in the third before Julián Javier singled to left. Javier stole second but Koufax struck out Charlie James to end the frame. "I made just one pitch that I wished later I could have taken back," said Koufax after the game. "That was in the third inning when Julián Javier singled to left. I had planned to use a curve, and at the last minute I changed it to a fast ball."[3]

Koufax faced the Cardinals second baseman for the third time in the sixth. Javier singled again, this time to center field, but was forced at second on Charlie James's groundball. Curt Flood grounded out for the third out. Musial singled again in the seventh but was forced out on Gene Oliver's grounder. Bill White's groundout ended the frame.

Dodgers manager Walter Alston said after the game that Koufax was not trying to strike out every batter as in the past' "He's a better pitcher this way," the skipper said. "He has better control. He doesn't make many pitches that he doesn't want to make."[4]

Koufax breezed through the eighth, striking out the side for the first time. With two outs in the St. Louis ninth, Boyer hit his second single, the Cardinals' fifth hit. Musial came up to bat "but he never got a chance to be a hero because catcher Doug Camilli threw out Boyer on an attempted steal, with Maury Wills making a nifty tag."[5]

Koufax said, "In a way I hated to see Boyer trying to steal because if he was safe, it would have been really tough to pitch to Musial. I might not have walked Musial intentionally, but I wouldn't have given him anything good to hit. Frankly, I didn't want to go out there for a tenth inning."[6]

As Koufax kept the Cardinals in check, Gibson was doing the same to the Dodgers. He entered the game with an 8-4 record after winning his previous two starts. In his last start, on June 13, he had struck out 12 batters in the Cardinals' 6-1 win over the Philadelphia Phillies.

In the first inning Gibson walked leadoff batter Wills, who stole second base as Jim Gilliam struck out. It was Wills's 36 steals on the way to a season total of 104. He moved to third on Willie Davis's groundout but failed to score when Ron Fairly flied out to center.

Gibson gave up two more two-out walks over the next two innings but retired the next Dodgers batter to end each frame. Wally Moon got the first hit off Gibson in the fourth, a two-out single. Gibson, though, struck out Camilli for the third out and his fourth strikeout of the game.

Gibson retired the next seven Dodgers batters before Moon singled again in the seventh. Moon, a former Cardinal, stole second as Gibson struck out Camilli. Instead of facing another former Cardinal, Daryl Spencer, Gibson gave him an intentional pass so he could face the weak-hitting Koufax.[7] Gibson ended the frame when Koufax swung and missed, giving Gibson his seventh strikeout.

Gibson pitched a one-two-three eighth inning. He got Fairly to fly out to center field to start the ninth. That brought Tommy Davis to the plate.

Davis had grounded out and struck out twice. "He'd been particularly deadly to Tommy Davis, striking him out twice and making him look bad each time," a sportswriter noted. "So once more Gibson called on his fastball, and Davis met it squarely. When last seen it was bouncing out of sight far into the Dodger bullpen beyond left field."[8] The home run gave the Dodgers a 1-0 win and "a heart-breaker for Gibson to lose – undoubtedly the finest three-hitter loss by any pitcher this season."[9]

"I was looking for a fast ball because he was behind on me (one ball and no strikes)," Davis said. "Gibson had been getting me out on breaking stuff. He was throwing the fast ball when he got behind."[10] It was Davis's 13th home run of the season and raised his RBI total to 69, the most by far for any slugger in either league.

Gibson was less than pleased with himself. "I don't know why I threw Davis that high fast ball," he mourned. "I had been keeping the ball down and away from him, and then I got a wild idea and came in with a high inside fast ball, and that was it."[11]

A happy Koufax said, "I'd have to say that was the most satisfying game I've ever pitched. My best pitch was my curve ball, not my fast ball. And all the grounders they hit were on curve balls." Alston echoed his pitcher's thoughts, saying, "It was one of his best pitching performances."[12] This was the first shutout Koufax threw without giving up a walk. (Koufax threw to two different catchers this day. The starting backstop, John Roseboro left the game in the fourth when Boyer's foul tip "caught him just above the right knee and he went down like a shot."[13] Doug Camilli replaced him behind the plate.)

Asked if he thought the win was even better than his 18-strikeout performance on April 24, Koufax said, "Yeah, that night I had plenty of runs and could coast. But in this game I had to bear down on every pitch. And I had better stuff tonight than I've had all season. My curve ball was working real good. It was my best pitch. And I could put the ball right where I wanted."[14]

Koufax complimented Gibson's effort, saying, "I could easily have lost the same way Gibson did. I feel sorry for the guy. He sure pitched a game."[15] Neal Russo of the *St. Louis Post-Dispatch* wrote, "Both Koufax and Gibson once accepted college basketball scholarships. The way they have been pitching, the batters wish they had stuck to jump shots and free throws."[16]

The win was the Dodgers' first shutout of the season. It was also the third time Tommy Davis had homered to give Koufax a win. The first time was in 1960 when the Dodgers beat Benny Daniels and the Pirates 1-0. The second came in the May 25, 1961, game.

Koufax raised his record to 10-2, while Gibson fell to 8-5. Koufax ran his major-league strikeout total to 146 in 125⅓ innings. He would finish the season with 216 strikeouts, second only to his teammate Don Drysdale.[17]

Koufax and Gibson faced each other twice more. Koufax won both games, a 5-0 shutout on July 3, 1963, and a 4-2 victory on April 26, 1966, with both pitchers going the distance.

SOURCES

In addition to the sources cited in the Notes, the author used the Baseball-Reference.com and Retrosheet.org websites for box-score, player, team, and season pages, pitching and batting logs, and other material.

https://www.baseball-reference.com/boxes/LAN/LAN196206180.shtml

https://www.retrosheet.org/boxesetc/1962/B06180LAN1962.htm

NOTES

1   The game was suspended in the top of the ninth on June 5 with the score 7-3 and finished on June 6 with Koufax pitching in the ninth for Don Drysdale. Koufax struck out two of the three Pirates he faced.

2   Neal Russo, "Dodgers Mr. Lightning, T. Davis, Strikes Bob Gibson Again," *St. Louis Post-Dispatch*, June 19, 1962: 26.

3   Coy Williams, "Davis-Koufax Act Proves Dazzling," *Hollywood Citizen-News*, June 19, 1962: 16.

4   Williams.

5   Frank Finch, "Sandy, Tommy Double Deal Cards 1-0," *Los Angeles Times*, June 19, 1962: 36.

6   Russo.

7   Koufax was hitting .111 on June 13 while Spencer was hitting .268.

8   Williams.

9   Williams.

10 Russo.

11 United Press International, "Tommy D's Lightning Wins for Koufax, 1-0," *San Pedro* (California) *News-Pilot*, June 19, 1962: 10.

12 "Tommy D's Lightning."

13 Williams.

14 Williams.

15 Williams.

16 Russo.

17 Gibson finished third in the National League with 208 strikeouts.

Sandy Koufax's First No-Hitter

June 30, 1962: Los Angeles Dodgers 5, New York Mets 0, at Dodger Stadium, Los Angeles

BY MARC Z AARON

The Los Angeles Dodgers (50-29), in second place a half-game behind the San Francisco Giants, were eager to host the last-place New York Mets at Dodger Stadium. The Mets, in their inaugural season, had won just 20 games and lost 52.

The last time the Dodgers' starting pitcher, Sandy Koufax, faced the Mets was Memorial Day at the Polo Grounds. Koufax went the distance as the Dodgers won, 13-6. The Mets had come up with 13 hits that day, one of them a home run by Gil Hodges. Hodges would not be facing Koufax on this day; he was out with an injured foot.

Koufax (10-4, 2.48 ERA) did not waste any time in getting down to business. Nine pitches were all he needed to set down the first three Mets hitters – Richie Ashburn, Rod Kanehl, and Félix Mantilla – on strikes. Mantilla took his looking. You could have heard each of them muttering some expletives as they left the batter's box.[1] As Koufax walked to the dugout, he received a standing ovation from the fans behind the Dodgers dugout.[2] Mets third-base coach Solly Hemus was good-naturedly needling Koufax, yelling, "It isn't really that easy, is it?" Koufax could be heard responding, "No, it surely isn't."[3]

Relief pitcher Ron Perranoski, sitting in the Dodgers bullpen, could see that Koufax had wicked stuff going. He later said, "From my angle back there … his curveball used to break from the first deck, it looked like. And all of a sudden it's breaking from the second deck."[4]

In the bottom half of the first inning, the Dodgers exhibited their appreciation and support of what Koufax had just done. Bob Miller (0-5, 4.46 ERA) was on the mound for the Mets.

Sandy Koufax struck out 13 and walked five in his first career no-hitter.
SABR: The Rucker Archive.

With two out, Willie Davis tripled to left-center and then scored on a single that gave Tommy Davis his 81st run batted in and 108th hit of the season, both of them tops in the majors. On the first pitch to Ron Fairly, Davis stole second. Fairly then drew a four-pitch walk, bringing big Frank Howard to the plate. Howard had homered in the previous night's loss to the Mets. With a one-ball count, Howard delivered a groundball single up the middle that scored Davis. John Roseboro smacked a long line drive to right field that went off the fence. Fairly and Howard scored as Roseboro moved easily into second with a double. The Dodgers led 4-0 and after the next batter, Larry Burright, singled, that was it for the starter Miller. Montreal native Ray Daviault, a rookie with a 7.97 ERA, relieved and retired Koufax on a foul pop, ending the inning.

In the top of the second, Frank Thomas swung on the first pitch and smashed a ball into the hole between third and short that looked as though it might get through, but Maury Wills got to the ball moving to his right, made a backhand stop, and threw Thomas out.[5] First baseman Ron Fairly made a sweeping catch of the tough hop on the long, hurried throw by Wills.[6] The next two batters, Cliff Cook and Jim Hickman, took called third strikes.

In the third, Koufax went to a full count on Elio Chacón but got him swinging. Chris Cannizzaro, the Mets catcher, also worked a full count before flying out to center. (He was the third batter in a row who had gone to 3-and-2; by the end of the game Koufax had gone to full counts on nine batters.) Pitcher Daviault went down swinging on three pitches. Koufax had now fanned seven and was perfect through three innings.

Leading off the fourth, Richie Ashburn became the first Mets baserunner as he walked.

In the fifth inning two Mets reached the outfield. Cook flied out to left and Hickman flied out to center.

In the sixth, on another full count, Cannizzaro went down swinging; Daviault swung and missed on the final pitch of his at-bat. That gave Koufax 11 strikeouts and marked the 39th time in his career and eighth time in the 1962 season that he had reached double figures. Looking for his 12th strikeout and third of the inning, Koufax had two strikes on Ashburn. But Ashburn struck a curving liner that Tommy Davis appeared to have momentarily lost in the lights. Davis snared the ball on the run to keep the no-hitter alive. Koufax had abandoned his changeup at the start of the fifth inning, and was relying on his fastball and curve.

Each time Koufax passed Hemus as he walked off the mound, Hemus would heckle Koufax by reminding him that he still had a no-hitter going.[7]

With one out in the bottom of the seventh, Daviault threw a slow curve that Frank Howard lined into the left-field bleachers, 374 feet away. It was his second home run in two games and his eighth of the season. The Dodgers now led 5-0.

When Koufax stepped to the plate to lead off the eighth, the crowd uttered quiet hoorays and hurrahs.

The Dodgers made two defensive replacements in the top of the ninth. Ron Fairly moved from first base to right field, replacing Howard, and Tim Harkness replaced Fairly at first. Daviault, who was still pitching for the Mets, was scheduled to lead off, and Gene Woodling – who rarely hit against a lefty – pinch-hit for him. After the game the 16-year major-league veteran said manager Casey Stengel had told him to "grab a bat, this will be a new experience for you."[8] Woodling walked. Joe Christopher ran for him. The spectators then held their breath as Ashburn again hit a liner toward left that Tommy Davis had no chance to snare. But it landed foul by about six feet. With a runner at first, Koufax got three groundballs in a row. Ashburn grounded to shortstop, forcing Christopher at second. Kanehl's grounder to third forced Ashburn at second, and on a 2-and-1 count Mantilla grounded to short, forcing Kanehl at second.

Game over! It was the first no-hitter of the season in the National League and the first for Koufax.

After the final out a message flashed on the scoreboard, reading, "Koufax, report to Buzzie Bavasi and have your con-tract torn up."[9] Sandy was engulfed by his teammates and Solly Hemus, under his breath, congratulated him.[10]

When it was all over the Mets had hit only five balls out of the infield – Cannizzaro, Cook, Ashburn, and Hickman (twice). Koufax had struck out 13 Mets.

Looking back at the great fielding plays of the game and the five walks issued, Koufax attributed luck playing a big part in pitching a no-hitter. Koufax was quoted as saying "In essence, every pitcher takes the mound trying to pitch a no-hitter. The main idea is to keep the batter from getting a base-hit, isn't it? But you have to be lucky to keep 27 batters from dunking one in or hitting one on the nose."[11]

SOURCES

In addition to the sources cited in the Notes, the author consulted Baseball-Reference.com and Retrosheet.org.

https://www.baseball-reference.com/boxes/LAN/LAN196206300.shtml

https://www.retrosheet.org/boxesetc/1962/B06300LAN1962.htm

NOTES

1   Dick Young, "A Wing for Sandy's Motel?" *New York Daily News*, appearing in *San Francisco Chronicle*, July 6, 1962: 38.

2   Frank Finch, "13 Mets Strike Out in Classic," *Los Angeles Times*, July 1, 1962: E1.

3   Bob Hunter, "Dazzling Dodger Southpaw Fans 13 Mets, Walks Five," *The Sporting News*, July 14, 1962: 5.

4   Jane Leavy, *Sandy Koufax, A Lefty's Legacy* (New York: HarperCollins, 2002), 119.

5   Joe McDonnell, "Dodger Stadium's Most Memorable Moments … Koufax's Three No-Hitters," *1987 Dodger Scorebook*, 5.

6   Young.

7   Sandy Koufax with Ed Linn, *Koufax* (New York: Viking Press, 1966), 188.

8   Sandy Koufax with Ed Linn, 188.

9   Leavy, 119.

10 Leavy, 119.

11 Finch.

Sandy Koufax's Second No-Hitter

May 11, 1963: Los Angeles Dodgers 8, San Francisco Giants 0, at Dodger Stadium, Los Angeles

BY MARC Z AARON

It was a great pitching match-up as the fifth-place Los Angeles Dodgers (15-15) hosted the National League-leading San Francisco Giants (19-11) on May 11. It was a great pitching match-up: Juan Marichal (4-2) and Sandy Koufax (3-1).

Koufax had missed two weeks at the end of April into May with stiffness in his shoulder. A couple of weeks later, he said, "Guess I'm getting old. I'm just falling apart, piece by piece."[1]

In Koufax's first no-hitter, the season before, the Dodgers supported him with four runs in the first inning. Koufax had not had great control, going to full counts on nine New York Mets batters and walking five while striking out 13.

This game was a much different story. Going to the bottom of the sixth inning, the score was 1-0 in favor of the Dodgers. The lone run was produced by a Wally Moon fly-ball home run down the right-field line. Koufax had not yet walked a batter. He only had one three-ball count – in the first inning to Willie Mays, who then flied out to center. Koufax was perfect through six. The only close play came in the fifth when Orlando Cepeda hit a slow roller that shortstop Dick Tracewski barehanded to throw out Cepeda at first.

In the bottom of the sixth, Junior Gilliam lined a single to right to open the inning. Ron Fairly tried to advance Gilliam with a bunt but popped it to first base for the first out. Tommy Davis singled to right and then Wally Moon lined a run-scoring single to right and advanced to second on the throw from the outfield. With runners on second and third and one out, Frank Howard was intentionally walked. John Roseboro, with a career average under .200 against Marichal, lined a single to center, scoring

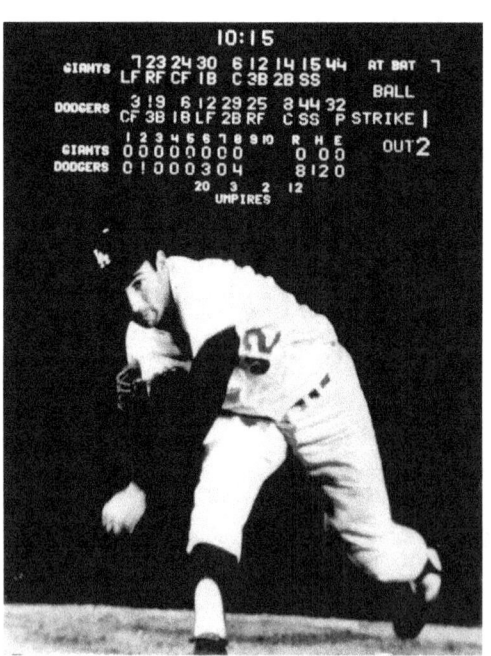

Sandy Koufax struck out just four batters in his no-hitter against the Giants. SABR: The Rucker Archive.

Davis and Moon. After an infield hit by Tracewski loaded the bases, Marichal was replaced by John Pregenzer, who struck out Koufax and got Willie Davis on a groundball.

At the start of the seventh, Nate Oliver went in to play second base. Second baseman Gilliam moved to third and Tommy Davis switched from third base to left field, replacing Wally Moon, who came out of the game.

This turned out to be a key move. Koufax ran into lady luck in the seventh inning when Harvey Kuenn smashed a liner to right, but squarely into the mitt of Frank Howard. Felipe Alou, the league's leading hitter, then sent a high, hard shot to left. Tommy Davis took it about two feet short of the stands. Next, Willie Mays cracked a blistering liner that Jim Gilliam stabbed behind the third base bag."[2] When Davis caught Alou's ball, the bullpen kept yelling, "You got room, you got room."[3]

Don Larsen, the last man to pitch a perfect game, was watching from the San Francisco bullpen.[4]

None of the players on the bench said anything about the possible no-hitter but Koufax was aware all the time and knew he was close to a perfect game.[5]

Leading off the eighth, Orlando Cepeda hit a hot shot off Koufax's glove to second baseman Nate Oliver, who threw out Cepeda by a step.[6] The next man up was catcher Ed Bailey. Bailey had not much success previously against Koufax. Bailey took three balls, then two hard, straight fastballs for strikes before fouling one off. The pressure was agonizing.[7] "Finally, he threw one I couldn't reach," Bailey said later, "and he walked me."[8] Koufax, aware of the no-hitter all the way, kicked the mound and thumped his glove as the perfect game got away.[9] Then Bailey was taken off the basepaths as Jim Davenport grounded into a double play.

It was ladies night at Dodger Stadium. The crowd of 55,350 (49,807 paid) was the largest of the season thus far in the major leagues.[10] From the sixth inning on, fans were aware of the no-hitter and a possible perfect game. They applauded every time Koufax retired a batter.[11]

In the bottom of the eighth with one out, Roseboro and Tracewski singled. As Koufax approached the plate he received a standing ovation from the crowd.[12] He drew a walk and scored the sixth run of the game on a double by Ron Fairly.

In the ninth Joe Amalfitano popped out to first baseman Fairly. José Pagán flied out to Willie Davis in deep center. Willie McCovey pinch-hit for Pregenzer and walked on four pitches. Koufax got one strike on Kuenn, who hit a bouncer right back to him. Koufax carefully lobbed the ball over to Fairly after running almost to first for the putout.

Koufax was mobbed by his teammates as the crowd roared and sent a shower of seat cushions onto the field.[13] Koufax could be seen anxiously looking for his parents, who had recently relocated to the West Coast, but they were not to be seen as Koufax had forgotten to leave them tickets.[14]

Koufax believed that in his first no-hitter he had exceptional stuff, but did not think he had overpowering stuff this night. It was good but not great. Strikeouts tell the story. In his first no-hitter he had 13, but against the Giants only four, and none after the sixth inning.[15] He threw 111 pitches, relying more on breaking balls.[16]

When it was all over, Koufax had become the only active pitcher other than Warren Spahn with two no-hitters. He also joined Carl Erskine as the second pitcher in Dodgers history to pitch two no-hitters. It was the third no-hitter pitched at Dodger Stadium.[17]

Notably, Koufax had not yet allowed a run at Dodger Stadium in 1963 after having pitched 24⅔ innings.

The victory was the second and final time Koufax beat Marichal.

NOTES

1   Bob Hunter, "Koufax' No-Hit Voodoo Kayoes Injury Hex," *Los Angeles Herald-Examiner*, May 25, 1963: 5.

2   Frank Finch, "Sandy's Finger, Arm OK ---And How!! Dodger Lefty Retires First 22 Batters in 8-0 L.A. Win," *Los Angeles Times*, May 12, 1963: 11.

3   United Press International, "Koufax Triumphs on No-Hitter, 8-0," *New York Times*, May 12, 1963: S1.

4   Melvin Durslag, "Perfecto Larsen Viewed Sandy's Classic Curving," *Los Angeles Herald-Examiner*, May 25, 1963: 4. Larsen was a relief pitcher for the Giants in 1963.

5   "Koufax Rates 2nd No-Hitter First," *New York Times*, May 13, 1963: 52.

6   Joe McDonnell, "Dodger Stadium's Most Memorable Moments ... Koufax's Three No-Hitters," *1987 Dodger Scorebook*; Durslag.

7   Durslag.

8   Jane Leavy, *Sandy Koufax, A Lefty's Legacy* (New York: HarperCollins, 2002), 123.

9   Hunter.

10 Finch.

11 "Koufax Rates 2nd No-Hitter First."

12 Finch.

13 Finch.

14 Leavy, 122.

15 Sandy Koufax with Ed Linn, *Koufax* (New York: Viking Press, 1966), 181-183.

16 "Koufax Rates 2nd No-Hitter First."

17 Bo Belinsky pitched a no-hitter for the Los Angeles Angels in Dodger Stadium on May 5, 1962.

Sandy Koufax Fans 12 Phillies in 12 Innings, Allows 0 Walks

May 15, 1963: Los Angeles Dodgers 3, Philadelphia Phillies 2 (12 innings), at Dodger Stadium, Los Angeles

BY BRUCE HARRIS

The Philadelphia Phillies were a year away from their infamous 1964 season when they arrived at Dodger Stadium in mid-May for a two-game series with the Los Angeles Dodgers. Gene Mauch's team had a mediocre 15-16 National League record, four games behind the first-place San Francisco Giants. However, the Phillies had reason for optimism. They were riding a four-game winning streak, which included a Sunday doubleheader sweep of the Milwaukee Braves in Connie Mack Stadium.[1]

The Phillies defeated Don Drysdale, 5-1, in the series opener. It was their first win ever at Dodger Stadium. They had lost all nine games there in 1962. Starting pitcher Chris Short, 2-1 against the Dodgers in 1962, gave Phillies fans even more hope for a series sweep. "Short won 135 games in his major-league career," notes Short's SABR biography. He pitched 15 big-league seasons and was arguably the National League's second-best left-hander in the 1960s after Sandy Koufax."[2] It wasn't going to be easy. Short's mound opponent was Koufax, who had gone 3-0 against the Phillies in 1962.

The Dodgers' 17-16 record on May 15 did not portend the success they would achieve that season.[3] The year would also prove momentous for the Dodgers' future Hall of Fame lefty. Mauch, when once asked if Koufax was the best left-hander he had ever seen, responded, "The best righty, too."[4]

A Dodger Stadium crowd of 20,512 settled into their seats on a Wednesday evening to watch the two talented pitchers. Koufax started the game with a 4-1 record. In his previous outing, four days earlier versus the Giants, he had thrown a no-hitter.[5] Against the Phillies, he retired the first six batters he faced, including striking out the side in the second inning. The no-hit streak ended when Johnny Callison led off the third by beating out a slow roller to second base. Bob Oldis lined into a double-play and Short struck out to end the inning.

The Dodgers opened the scoring in their half of the third. Koufax struck out looking. Maury Wills walked. Pitching from the stretch, Short failed to come to a complete stop. A balk was called, and Wills went to second. Interestingly, the balk rule had officially changed the day before. United Press International reported, "The one-second-stop-requirement, which created the pitching balk furor in the major leagues this spring, was officially deleted from the rules of baseball Tuesday [May 14, 1963]. ... Pitchers [are] required simply to pause after making their stretch with men on the bases, instead of stopping for 'at least one second.'"[6] The balk was costly. Ron Fairly lined a two-out double to left, scoring Wills.

Two innings later, the Phillies got even. Roy Sievers started the fifth with a line-drive single to center. Knowing runs would be scarce, Bobby Wine sacrificed Sievers to second. The strategy paid off. Callison's ground single to right, his second hit of the game, drove in Sievers. Frank Howard's throw home was not in time.

In the bottom of the fifth inning, the Dodgers went ahead again. Wills opened with a double, then stole third base. Jim Gilliam hit a line drive back to the mound that glanced off Short's right foot. The ball rolled to third baseman Don Hoak, but he had no play on Gilliam at first. Wills held. The Dodgers had runners on the corners with no outs. Play was delayed while Short shook it off. He retired Fairly on an infield popup for the first out. Tommy Davis followed with a ground single to center field, scoring Wills and putting the Dodgers ahead, 2-1. With the count 2-and-0 on Bill Skowron, Short could not continue. He was replaced by Jack Baldschun. Baldschun struck out Skowron, then retired Howard on a groundout, ending the inning.

The Dodgers took the 2-1 lead into the ninth inning, but Koufax found himself in immediate trouble. Ex-teammate Don Demeter opened things by doubling off the left-field wall. He advanced to third on Jim Lemon's groundout to second. Sievers beat out a grounder to third, but Demeter had to hold. With runners on first and third and one out, "[Demeter] scored as Wine laid a squeeze bunt down the first-base line and beat it out for a hit."[7] The Phillies tied the score and had a chance to go ahead, but Koufax settled down, retiring Callison and striking out Oldis.

The game went into extra innings. The Phillies had won their previous four extra-inning games.[8] Koufax was still on the mound. Oldis opened the 12th with an infield single. He took second on John Roseboro's wild pickoff throw to first base. Johnny Klippstein, another former Dodgers teammate of

Koufax's, came up to bunt. (Klippstein had taken over the mound duties, replacing Baldschun in the eighth inning.) Klippstein attempted to sacrifice Oldis to third but struck out. During that at-bat, Dodgers manager Walter Alston was tossed out of the game by home-plate umpire Al Forman for arguing a strike call. Oldis was stranded on second after Koufax retired Hoak and Cookie Rojas.

Klippstein, who had retired all 12 Dodgers he faced in his first four innings, retired the first two batters he faced in the bottom of the 12th inning, extending his no-hit performance to 14 batters. But with two outs, Gilliam singled to right. Then, with a 2-0 count on Fairly, "Klippstein threw a fastball that seemed to tail in at the last moment. Fairly jumped out of the way and the ball thumped off Oldis' glove and back to the screen."[9] Gilliam went to second on the passed ball. Mauch had a decision to make. Should he intentionally walk the left-handed Fairly and pitch to Davis? Going into the game, Fairly was tied with the Phillies' Wes Covington with a league-leading 27 RBIs.[10] His double in the third inning had driven in the Dodgers' first run. The Phillies pitched to Fairly. He promptly lined a single to right, scoring Gilliam from second and giving the Dodgers a 12-inning, 3-2 victory.

Koufax went the distance, throwing 165 pitches. He was tough when he had to be. The Phillies were 3-for-17 with runners in scoring position. Koufax allowed 11 hits but struck out 12 and did not walk anybody. Sportswriter Frank Finch wrote, "Fanning Phillies is Koufax's forte; his career performance against them shows 210 K's in 175 innings."[11] It was the fifth win of what turned out to be a magical season for Koufax. He finished the year 25-5 with a 1.88 ERA. He tossed 11 shutouts, pitched 20 complete games, and struck out 306 batters in 311 innings. His league-leading numbers earned him MVP honors and the first of three Cy Young Awards.

SOURCES

In addition to the sources cited in the Notes, the author consulted Baseball-Reference.com, Retrosheet.org, and Newspapers.com.

https://www.baseball-reference.com/boxes/LAN/LAN196305150.shtml

https://www.retrosheet.org/boxesetc/1963/B05150LAN1963.htm

NOTES

1 That was on May 12. The Phillies won the first game, 4-3, in 11 innings and the second game, 6-5, in 12 innings.

2 Andy Sturgill, Chris Short SABR biography, https://sabr.org/bioproj/person/chris-short/.

3 The Dodgers finished in first place with a record of 99-63-1. They swept the New York Yankees in four games in the World Series.

4 Jane Leavy, *Sandy Koufax, A Lefty's Legacy* (New York: Harper Collins, 2002), 2.

5 It was the second no-hitter of Koufax's career. He tossed his first on June 30, 1962, against the New York Mets. After the San Francisco game, he went on to pitch a no-hitter against the Phillies (June 4, 1964) and a perfect game vs. the Chicago Cubs (September 9, 1965).

6 United Press International, "No More Balk Talk, Stormy Rule Deleted," *Los Angeles Times*, May 15, 1963: III, 5.

7 Allen Lewis, "Dodgers, Koufax Beat Phillies in 12th," *Philadelphia Inquirer*, May 16, 1963: 39, 41.

8 In addition to the May 12 sweep of the Braves, the Phillies defeated the St. Louis Cardinals 4-3 in 10 innings (April 14, 1963) and they beat the Cardinals again, 4-3 (on April 21) in 10 innings.

9 Stan Hochman, "Veterans Klippstein, Oldis Seem Incompatible," *Philadelphia Daily News*, May 16, 1963: 60, 62.

10 Fairly finished the 1963 season with 77 RBIs. Covington finished with 64.

11 Frank Finch, "Dodgers Edge Phillies, 3-2, in 12th," *Los Angeles Times*, May 16, 1963: III, 2, 6. It was actually 175⅓ innings.

Koufax Meets a Milestone, Wins 20th

August 29, 1963: Los Angeles Dodgers 11, San Francisco Giants 1, at Dodger Stadium, Los Angeles

BY JEFF ALLAN HOWARD

A 20-win season is the goal of any major-league pitcher. On a hot August night in Houston, Texas, Sandy Koufax improved his season record to 18-4 when the Dodgers beat the fledgling Colt .45s 2-0 on Saturday, August 3, 1963, at Colt Stadium before the largest local crowd of the season.[1] It was the first stop of a 16-game, five-city road trip for the Dodgers. Meeting the magical milestone for the first time seemed imminent.

However, it took two more weeks and four starts for Koufax to get his 19th win, at the Polo Grounds in New York on August 17 against the Mets (the other expansion team in the league). It was the last stop of the road trip.

Hovering on the brink of 20, Koufax returned home but failed to reach the mark while doing yeoman's work four days later against the St. Louis Cardinals on August 21. It was a no-decision for Koufax, who threw 164 pitches in 12 innings and left the game with the score tied 1-1. The Dodgers ultimately won, 2-1 in 16 innings.[2]

Koufax's next start was in LA again on August 25 against the Milwaukee Braves. He carried a 1-0 shutout into the ninth inning, and a win looked promising, but the Braves began hitting deep fly balls. Two of them were caught, two landed for doubles. When the second double tied the game, Koufax was lifted by manager Walt Alston after 8⅔ innings. Bob Miller came on in relief, walked a batter, induced a groundout, and was credited with the victory when the Dodgers won 2-1 in walk-off fashion in the bottom of the ninth.[3]

Koufax still remained one win shy of the coveted mark on August 29 when the left-hander took the mound against the Dodgers' former crosstown, now interstate rival San Francisco Giants at Dodger Stadium. A record crowd of 54,978 showed up for the Thursday evening game at the two-year-old venue,

Sandy Koufax won at least 20 games three times in his career. SABR: The Rucker Archive.

hoping to witness history with Koufax seeking win number 20 during a hotly contested pennant race.[4] It was his eighth start in August, a month that saw him throw 61⅔ innings.[5]

Koufax got through the first inning unscathed, striking out Willie McCovey and Willie Mays in the process.

Bob Bolin, a right-hander in his third season with the Giants, started for the Giants and had a rocky first inning, allowing a leadoff walk to Maury Wills, who moved to second base on a wild pitch. Bolin walked Jim Gilliam and both runners advanced on Wally Moon's groundout to first base. A single to center field scored Wills, but Gilliam was thrown out at the plate in an attempt to add another run by challenging the arm of Willie Mays. Bolin survived giving up just a run.

In the second inning, the Giants responded with a leadoff home run to left field off the bat of Orlando Cepeda to tie the score, 1-1. It would be the only tally of the night for the Giants.

After a leadoff walk to Frank Howard in the Dodgers' half of the second inning, Giants manager Alvin Dark went to the bullpen early, bringing in Billy Pierce and hoping for long-relief help from the 17-year-veteran. Pierce gave up a single to John Roseboro and escaped the inning without further damage. Such would not be the case the next inning.

In the bottom of the third inning, the Dodgers sent 11 batters to the plate. Six hit safely (all of them off Pierce) and five scored. The big blows were a two-run single to center by Ron Fairly and a 400-foot home run to left-center by Howard that drove in Fairly. It did not stop there. Roseboro popped up to left field but Willie Davis followed with a double to left. Then Pierce walked Koufax. Wills followed with a run-scoring groundball single to right field. Pierce was lifted for Jack Fisher, who got the third out. But the Dodgers would get to him later.

In their next turn at bat, the Dodgers scored again to extend the margin to 7-1. They did it the old-fashioned way. Tommy Davis walked. Fairly moved Davis ahead, hitting behind the runner on a groundout to second base. Howard lined a single to center field to score Davis.

The Dodgers teed off on Fisher in the bottom of the fifth and batted around again. It started harmlessly enough as Fisher retired the first two batters of the inning. The damage began after that. Wills singed and Gilliam walked. Consecutive base hits by Moon, Willie Davis, and Fairly followed. Wills, Gilliam, and Moon scored. When the dust settled, the Dodgers had pushed home three more runs and led 10-1.

With the game just half over, Koufax needed no more support, but the Dodgers gave him another old-school run in the sixth inning on Willie Davis's double, a sacrifice by Koufax, and a sacrifice fly by Maury Wills.

Meanwhile, Koufax masterfully moved through the powerful Giants lineup after that Cepeda homer. Thereafter, he faced just 26 batters and retired 24 of them en route to a three-hit complete-game gem. Assisted by "the most lavish (run) support any Dodger pitcher has had in 45 days … Los Angeles flattened second-place San Francisco."[6] Koufax became the first in the majors to reach the coveted 20-win plateau in 1963.

About finally reaching the milestone, Koufax said, "Winning 20 games is not only a statistic to me, but a symbol." He added, "I've been working on it since spring training."[7]

The Dodgers ace told reporters, "It was a bigger thrill than a no-hitter because it was so long in coming. On a no-hitter, you just go out and work a game and you have done it. But it took me nine years to win 20. When it finally arrives, it has to be a top thrill."[8]

The win helped to catapult the Dodgers to the National League pennant and ultimately a sweep of the New York Yankees in the 1963 World Series.

It was a banner year for Koufax. He won five of his next seven starts to finish the season with a 25-5 record, logging the pitcher's triple crown in the process, leading the league in wins (25) tied with Juan Marichal for the lowest ERA (1.88), and leading in strikeouts (306). Koufax also topped the league in shutouts (11). Oh yeah, Koufax threw a no-hitter on May 11 against the Giants.

Koufax won the MVP for the World Series. When the National League MVP votes were tallied, he also won that award. Adding to the trophy case, Koufax won the first of his three Cy Young Awards.

Koufax won 20 games twice more, going 26-8 in 1965 and 27-9 in 1966, his final season before retiring.

SOURCES

The author referred to Baseball Reference and Retrosheet.org for box scores, play-by-play information, and other pertinent data.

https://www.baseball-reference.com/boxes/LAN/LAN196308290.shtml

https://www.retrosheet.org/boxesetc/1963/B08290LAN1963.htm

NOTES

1 "Koufax Shuts Out Colts with 3 Hits," *New York Times*, August 4, 1963: 139. Koufax drew a crowd whenever he pitched in 1963.

2 Frank Finch, "Koufax Misses 20th Victory: Dodgers Win in 16th, 2-1," *Los Angeles Times,* August 22, 1963: B1.

3 Frank Finch, "Braves Nip Punchless Dodgers, 2-1," *Los Angeles Times,* August 25, 1963: K1.

4 Frank Finch, "Record 54,978 See Dodgers Romp, 11-1: Koufax Posts 20th Mound Victory," *Los Angeles Times*, August 30, 1963: B1.

5 Baseball Almanac. "Sandy Koufax 1963 Game By Game Pitching Logs." https://www.baseball-almanac.com/players/pitchinglogs.php?p=koufasa01&y=1963.

6 "Dodgers Rip Giants, 11-1; Lead by 6½; Koufax Wins 20th on a Three-Hit Gem," *Chicago Tribune*, August 30, 1963: C6.

7 Finch, "Record 54,978 See Dodgers Romp, 11-1: Koufax Posts 20th Mound Victory."

8 Al Wolf, "20th Victory Bigger Thrill Than No-Hitter – Koufax," *Los Angeles Times*, August 30, 1963: B1.

Koufax Sets Shutout Record for Southpaws

September 17, 1963: Los Angeles Dodgers 4, St. Louis Cardinals 0, at Busch Stadium, St. Louis

BY GLEN SPARKS

Sandy Koufax made a habit of holding teams scoreless in 1963. He did it for a record-breaking 11th time on September 17 against the St. Louis Cardinals. No left-handed pitcher had ever thrown that many shutouts in one season. Koufax eclipsed the mark set by New York Giants Hall of Famer Carl Hubbell in 1933.

The Los Angeles Dodgers' ace carried a no-hitter into the seventh inning. A baseball great, in the final weeks of his Hall of Fame career, broke up the bid. The Dodgers scored the only run they needed on Jim Gilliam's RBI double in the first inning and won, 4-0, in front of 30,450 fans at Busch Stadium.

"It wasn't my best game, but it was my biggest," Koufax said.[1] Dodgers manager Walter Alston said, "Sandy has great stuff every time he goes out there. This was his usual game."[2]

Koufax raised his won-lost record to 24-5 and lowered his ERA to 1.87. He tossed a four-hitter and did not allow a walk, although he struck out only four batters. The Dodgers (93-59) improved their lead to three games over the surging, second-place Cardinals (91-63).

Reporters asked Alston about the Dodgers' pennant outlook. "It looks better than yesterday," the skipper said. "And I hope I can say the same tomorrow night."[3]

The Dodgers hoped to avoid a repeat of 1962, when they blew a big lead in September and lost a tiebreaker series – as well as the National League pennant – to the San Francisco Giants. Koufax missed several weeks of that campaign after injuring the index finger of his pitching hand and was ineffective when he returned for the stretch run (8⅔ innings in four games, 10 earned runs). He finished with a 14-7 record and a 2.54 ERA.

Koufax got off to a strong start in 1963 and kept going. He hurled his second no-hitter on May 11, against the Giants. His ERA dropped to 1.06 after he blanked the Mets, 1-0, on May 19. It was already his third shutout of the season.

The 27-year-old recorded one more shutout in May and two in June. He began July with three straight scoreless outings, giving him nine in 1963, and tied Hubbell's mark on August 3 at Colt Stadium in Houston, completing a three-hitter in a 2-0 win vs. the Colt .45s. A reporter asked former Dodgers hurler Roger Craig to rate the league's top three pitchers. Craig, now a Met, responded, "Sandy Koufax, Sandy Koufax, and Sandy Koufax. It used to be that one pitcher had the best fastball and one had the best curve. He has both of them."[4]

Curt Simmons started for St. Louis against Koufax. The 34-year-old left-hander was in his 16th season and had been a three-time All-Star with the Philadelphia Phillies. He missed the entire 1959 campaign with shoulder problems and was released by Philadelphia on May 17, 1960. The Cardinals signed him for $30,000.

Simmons led the NL in ERA+ in 1961 (141) and was enjoying another strong season in 1963. He entered this game with a 15-7 record and a 2.50 ERA. Red-hot St. Louis had won 19 of its previous 21 games but lost the opener of this three-game series, 3-1.

LA took an early 1-0 lead against Simmons. Maury Wills singled to lead off the game and stole second base with Gilliam at bat. Wills' theft was the 232nd of his career, tying him with Pee Wee Reese for the Dodgers' modern-day record.[5] Next, Simmons unfurled a wild pitch and Wills sprinted to third. Gilliam hit a double to left field that brought home the run.

Tommy Davis walked but was forced at second base on Frank Howard's groundball. Moose Skowron struck out and Ken McMullen grounded out.

Koufax retired the side in order in the bottom of the first and struck out Stan Musial. The Dodgers went down one-two-three in their half of the second inning, as did the Cardinals. Koufax added his second strikeout. Hard-hitting third baseman Ken Boyer went down swinging.

Simmons recorded another quick inning in the third, while Koufax ran into some trouble after striking out Charlie James to start the bottom half of that frame and plunking Tim McCarver. Simmons slapped a pitch up the middle that Koufax fielded but threw wildly to Skowron at first base. With runners now at second and third, Julian Javier hit a ball that Wills fielded at shortstop and threw home to catcher John Roseboro, who tagged out McCarver. Dick Groat's groundout ended the inning.

"That was our big chance," Cardinals manager Johnny Keane said. "If McCarver had scored it would have been a new ball game. But he didn't." Wills said, "I gambled and won."[6]

The game settled into a pitchers' duel over the next three innings. Simmons gave up just one hit, while Koufax did not allow a baserunner. Simmons was Koufax's fourth and final strikeout victim, closing out the fifth.

LA threatened in the seventh inning. McMullen singled with one out and moved to third on a double by Willie Davis. Simmons, though, got Roseboro to pop out and Koufax to strike out looking.

The Cardinals got their first hit in the bottom of the seventh when Musial singled to center field. Koufax said, "I couldn't afford to set up Musial with a curve. I had to keep the ball in the park. So, I stayed with the fastball, away." Musial, a three-time Most Valuable Player who had announced one month earlier that 1963 would be his final season, told reporters, "I was just trying for a base hit, not slugging with him as I did the first time up. The ball faded and sailed to right field."[7]

One batter later, Boyer launched a ball into deep right field. Howard caught the drive in front of the wall. Boyer said later, "When I hit the ball, I thought it had a chance to go out, and that it would at least hit the fence."[8] Bill White also flied out, and Curt Flood hit a groundball that forced out Gary Kolb, running for Musial.

The Dodgers took a 3-0 lead in the eighth inning. Tommy Davis hit a two-out single and Howard ripped a Simmons pitch over the right-field fence. "I thought it was going to hit the protective screen out there, but it kept going up," Howard said. "I hit a high curveball."[9] It was Howard's first hit of 1963 in 20 at-bats at Busch Stadium.[10] (Afterward, Howard singled out Simmons as a tough lefty opposing pitcher: "Simmons has such good control," Howard said. "He can hit the eyes on a fly."[11])

Koufax gave up two more hits in the bottom of the eighth. McCarver singled with one out, and after pinch-hitter Mike Shannon flied out, Javier singled to put runners on first and second. Groat lined out to end the threat.

Keane asked Barney Schultz to pitch the ninth. McMullen, the first batter he faced, struck out. Willie Davis, next up, singled and stole second base. The speedy outfielder scored on Roseboro's double into right field. Koufax struck out, and Keane brought in Ken MacKenzie to face Wills, who grounded a single to left. Roseboro rounded third base and headed for home, where he was tagged out.

Corky Withrow, pinch-hitting for MacKenzie, grounded out to start the St. Lous ninth, and Boyer did the same. Koufax then got a five-minute breather. Ten teenage boys jumped onto the field, and ushers had to round them up before the game could continue.[12]

After the delay, Bill White singled past the right side of the Dodgers' infield. That brought up Curt Flood, who lined to Tommy Davis in left for the final out.

The last pitcher to throw more shutouts in a season than Koufax was right-hander Grover Cleveland Alexander, who tossed 16 for the 1916 Philadelphia Phillies.[13]

About the records and accolades, Koufax said, "I appreciate [them]. But really all I want to do every time I pitch is just to win or if I don't, to have some other Dodger pitcher win. This is a team thing. I don't care if I win 10 or 30 games, as long as we get into the World Series."[14]

Keane insisted that his team could still overtake the Dodgers. "We never considered this game or any other up to now a 'must' one," he told reporters. Musial sounded less optimistic. He said, "We just have to win every game from now on."[15]

The Cardinals, though, lost the finale against the Dodgers, 6-5, and five of their next seven games to finish 93-69. LA won the pennant with a mark of 99-63.

Koufax started twice more in 1963 after blanking St. Louis but did not throw another shutout. He ended the season with a record of 25-5 and topped the National League in several categories, including strikeouts (306) and ERA (1.88).

The Dodgers swept the Yankees in the fall classic. Koufax won both of his starts and gave up just three runs in 18 innings while striking out 23. Writers voted him the World Series Most Valuable Player. He also earned NL MVP and Cy Young Award honors.

SOURCES

In addition to the sources cited in the Notes, the author consulted Baseball-Reference.com and Retrosheet.org.

https://www.baseball-reference.com/boxes/SLN/SLN196309170.shtml

https://www.retrosheet.org/boxesetc/1963/B09170SLN1963.htm

NOTES

1   Neal Russo, "Koufax's 'Biggest' Win Puts Dodgers in Command," *St. Louis Post-Dispatch*, September 18, 1963: 34.

2   Don Johnson, "Magic No. Seven; Richert on Call," *Pasadena Independent*, September 18, 1963: 18.

3   George Lederer, "Sandy Sets Records During KO Punch," *Long Beach* (California) *Press-Telegram*, September 18, 1963: 43.

4   Jerry Wynn, "Man to Man," *Long Beach Press-Telegram*, August 4, 1963: 27.

5   "Groat Yields Batting Lead to Clemente," *St. Louis Post-Dispatch*, September 18, 1963: 34.

6   "Still Can Win, Claims Keane," *Long Beach Independent*, September 18, 1963: 43.

7   "Groat Yields Batting Lead to Clemente."

8   "Groat Yields Batting Lead to Clemente."

9   Johnson, "Magic No. Seven; Richert on Call."

10 "Things Look Pretty Good Now, Says Alston," *Los Angeles Times*, September 18, 1963: 35.

11 Russo, "Koufax's 'Biggest' Win Puts Dodgers in Command."

12 Frank Finch, "Win Hikes L.A. Lead to Three," *Los Angeles Times*, September 18, 1963: 35.

13 Ed Wilks, "Sandy Orbited When He Learned to Throw Missiles," *St. Louis Post-Dispatch*, September 18, 1963: 34.

14 Johnson, "Magic No. Seven; Richert on Call."

15 "Still Can Win, Claims Keane."

Sandy Koufax Sets World Series Strikeout Record, Fanning 15 Yankees

October 2, 1963: Los Angeles Dodgers 5, New York Yankees 2, at Yankee Stadium

BY ANDY MCCUE

For the first time in seven years, the Yankees and the Dodgers resumed their World Series rivalry in 1963. In the decade from 1947 through 1956, they had met six times. Since the Dodgers had moved to Los Angeles in 1958, they had missed postseason competition with each other.

The New York Yankees entered their fourth consecutive World Series with confidence. "We've got a better all-round ball club than the Dodgers," said manager Ralph Houk, "and we're going to win it."[1] The Yankees had won 104 games, beating the second-place White Sox by 10½ games. They were second in the American League in most runs scored and fewest runs allowed while leading the league in defensive efficiency. After a mediocre start, and with a rash of injuries, the Yankees had taken over the league lead for good on June 18 and clinched on September 13.

The Dodgers were quieter. Unlike the Yankees, they had not been picked to win in many of the preseason polls. Their epic collapse at the end of the 1962 season weighed on the prognosticators, and on the team.[2] They had started the 1963 season slowly, taking over first place for good on July 2, and seemed to be cruising when the St. Louis Cardinals won 19 of 20 between August 30 and Sunday, September 15. That same weekend, the Dodgers were blowing two games to the Phillies in a carnival of misplays. On the 16th, the Dodgers came into Busch Stadium with the revived "choke artists" label in their ears. The lead was down to one game. But they won all three games from the Cardinals and clinched six days later. They had won 99 games, finishing six ahead of the Cardinals. As per their reputation, they led the National League in fewest runs allowed and lowest earned-run average, while finishing sixth in runs scored. Less noticed was that they finished eighth in defensive efficiency, a weakness hidden because their pitchers avoided letting the ball into play by leading the league in strikeouts.

The experts generally agreed with the Yankees. Expectations, after all, had been set. Said Yankees owner Del Webb: "When we won with [manager Casey] Stengel in 1949, I got 292 congratulatory telegrams. This year I got six."[3] While giving due credit to the Dodgers' pitching, the analysts

Yogi Berra was near the end of his playing career when the Yankees met Sandy Koufax and the Dodgers in the 1963 World Series. Courtesy of National Baseball Hall of Fame.

emphasized the Yankees' greater depth, bigger power, and more diversified skills.

The Sporting News was typical, featuring the Yankees' winning boast on the front page and turning the parallel feature on the NL winners into a Fred Lieb rundown of the Bronx Bombers' six-to-one domination of the Dodgers in earlier World Series. The cover showed Willard Mullins's famous Brooklyn Bum, spiffed up with sunglasses and a Hawaiian shirt by cartoonist Lou Darvas. He was marveling at the tall buildings and the Yankee stars. In New York, the betting was 3-2 Yankees and the odds for a Dodger sweep were 25-1.[4]

New York Times columnist Arthur Daley was one of the few to pick the Dodgers, noting that he was risking ridicule by bucking the tide of predictions. For Daley, "the thing that would make it totally embarrassing is the Yankees winning in four straight, which they could do. There's no conceivable way of seeing the Dodgers doing that."[5]

Both managers were thoroughly familiar with Yankee Stadium. Houk, in his third straight World Series, knew to pitch a left-hander in the Stadium with its distant fences in left and short porch in right. Inevitably, his choice was Whitey Ford, making his 20th World Series start with a 10-5 record in the classic. The Dodgers' Walter Alston, in his fourth World Series and second in Yankee Stadium, also had his top left-hander available. Sandy Koufax, who was named that year's National League Most Valuable Player and Cy Young Award winner, had made one previous World Series start, in a seven-inning, one-run loss to the White Sox in 1959.

The Yankees' lineup was pretty much set. For the Dodgers, third baseman Ken McMullen had pulled a hamstring and was questionable. Alston moved Jim Gilliam to third base and inserted Dick Tracewski, who had spent most of the year as a defensive replacement, at second. Alston's big decision was to replace Ron Fairly at first base with former Yankee Moose Skowron. Skowron's regular-season performance had been abysmal, with a .203 batting average and only four home runs in 256 plate appearances. Alston hoped Skowron, an experienced, if streaky, right-handed hitter, would get hot against the Yankee left-handers. "I hope I can do something to help this team," Skowron said, "I've failed them this year."[6]

In 76-degree weather, 69,000 people crammed into Yankee Stadium for the first game. Ford cruised through the top of the first, but Koufax served notice in the bottom half by striking out Tony Kubek, Bobby Richardson, and Tom Tresh in short order.

In the top of the second, the game turned the Dodgers' way. With one out, Frank Howard blasted a double to the base of the wall in center field. Skowron followed with a bouncer up the middle that barely eluded Ford and Richardson, scoring the lumbering Howard. An infield single by Tracewski moved Skowron to second. Ford hung a low curve to Johnny Roseboro, who hooked the ball barely fair into the right-field bleachers and the Dodgers led 4-0. It was the worst inning in Ford's World Series career. It was Roseboro's first homer off a left-hander that season, when he often didn't start against lefties.

Koufax continued his work with slight variation in the second, striking out Mickey Mantle and Roger Maris and getting American League Most Valuable Player Elston Howard to pop up to Roseboro. As he left the plate, Mantle turned to Roseboro and said, "How in the fuck are you supposed to hit that shit?"[7] In the next inning, Skowron singled in Willie Davis for the last Dodger run.

Now the story became Koufax. Clete Boyer got the Yankees' first fair ball in the third, a groundout that Koufax deflected to Tracewski; Elston Howard got the first hit, an opposite-field single in the fifth with two outs. It started a troublesome inning for the Dodger hurler. Joe Pepitone followed with a single and Tracewski's diving, backhand knockdown of Boyer's line drive single kept Howard from scoring. Koufax rallied to strike out Hector Lopez, pinch-hitting for Ford.

"I felt a little weak in the middle of the game. Then I got some of my strength back, but I was a little weak again at the end," said Koufax.[8] The left-hander's elbow had started to tighten, said Dodgers pitching coach Joe Becker. Koufax pressed and reached back for more, which led to the base hits in the fifth and two consecutive walks in the sixth. So Koufax dropped the curve and relied on his fastball the rest of the game.[9] In the Yankees eighth, a Kubek single and Tresh's home run to left gave the Yankees their only runs of the afternoon.

Koufax took the mound in the bottom of the ninth with a three-run lead and the knowledge that he had a chance to break Carl Erskine's record for strikeouts in a World Series game. Exactly 10 years earlier to the day, the Dodgers' Erskine had struck out 14 Yankees. Koufax already had 14. Howard lined out to start the inning, and Pepitone's second single was followed by a fly out from Boyer. Up to the plate came right-handed pinch-hitter Harry Bright. With two strikes, Bright managed a soft roller down the third-base line, which Gilliam allowed to roll foul. With a fastball, Koufax put Bright away for the new record.

The strikeout record dominated the headlines the next morning. Roseboro, who also snared three foul pops, also set a record – for putouts by a catcher in a World Series game (18). Only one out was recorded by a Dodgers outfielder. The Yankees' Richardson, who had 22 strikeouts in 668 plate appearances during the regular season, was kayoed three times. Said Clete Boyer: "Bobby just doesn't strike out. Not three times. That's an act of God."[10]

Other Yankees were impressed. Yogi Berra on Koufax: "I wonder how come he lost five games this year."[11] Said Mickey Mantle: "Koufax just showed me that everything written about him is true."[12]

SOURCES

In addition to the sources mentioned in the Notes, the author consulted Baseball-Reference.com, Retrosheet.org, and the following books, video, and digitized box scores:

Koufax, Sandy, with Ed Linn. *Koufax* (New York: Viking, 1966).

Leavy, Jane. *Koufax: A Lefty's Legacy* (New York: HarperCollins, 2002).

Spink, C.C. Johnson, compiler. *Official Baseball Guide for 1964* (St. Louis: Charles C. Spink & Son, 1964).

"Major League Baseball Presents the World Series of 1963" (retrieved August 17, 2020, at youtube.com/watch?v=HFjFvooJagA)

baseball-reference.com/boxes/NYA/NYA196310020.shtml

retrosheet.org/boxesetc/1963/B10020NYA1963.htm

NOTES

1   Til Ferdenzi, "'We're Going to Win It,' Yanks Chorus," *The Sporting News*, October 5, 1963: 1.

2   The 1962 Dodgers had a four-game lead as late as September 17, then faded into a tie with the San Francisco Giants. The Giants won a three-game tiebreaker series to take the 1962 NL pennant.

3   "They Said It," *Sports Illustrated*, September 30, 1963: 18.

4   "Odds Favor Yanks, 7½-5," *Los Angeles Times*, October 1, 1963: C1.

5   Arthur Daley, "Look Ma, No Hands," *New York Times*, October 1, 1963: 64.

6   William Leggett, "Koo-Foo the Killer," *Sports Illustrated*, October 14, 1963: 18.

7   Jane Leavy, *The Last Boy* (New York: HarperCollins, 2010), 262.

8   "Sandy Felt 'Tired and Weak' While Setting Strikeout Mark," *Los Angeles Times*, October 3, 1963: B1.

9   Leonard Koppett, "Koufax Stopped Throwing Curve When Elbow Began to Tighten in Mid-Game," *New York Times*, October 3, 1963: 55.

10   Will Bradbury, "The Yankees in Defeat: Subdued and Impressed but Hardly Shaken," *New York Times*, October 3, 1963: 56.

11   Shirley Povich, "Yanks Agog at Sandy: 'How'd He Lose Five?' – Yogi," *Los Angeles Times*, October 3, 1963: B5.

12   Bradbury, "The Yankees in Defeat."

Koufax Stifles Yankee Bats Again As Dodgers Sweep World Series

October 6, 1963: Los Angeles Dodgers 2, New York Yankees 1,at Dodger Stadium, Los Angeles

BY ANDY MCCUE

As the New York Yankees arrived at Dodger Stadium for the fourth game of the 1963 World Series, they knew no team had ever come back from a three-game deficit to win. "The knowledge of defeat could not be disguised in the quiet but calm Yankee clubhouse," wrote the *New York Times*'s Leonard Koppett after the third game.[1]

Days before, as the Yankees' team bus left for the airport and Los Angeles, third baseman Clete Boyer joked that what the Yankees needed was more Jewish holidays. "You mean like Yom Koufax," said Mickey Mantle.[2] Now they would have to face Sandy Koufax, the Los Angeles Dodgers'Jewish left-hander who had set a strikeout record beating them in Game One. Before they left their hotel that morning, the Yankees packed their bags, at once a standard practice and a foreshadowing.[3]

A mild fall afternoon with temperatures in the high 70s greeted Koufax and the Yankees' Whitey Ford, meeting in a rematch. With the exception of Héctor López, subbing for the injured Roger Maris in right field for the Yankees, it was the same lineup as that game, a 5-2 Dodgers victory.

Hidden from the Yankees was an open sore between the last two toes of Koufax's left foot, the one he used to push off from the mound. A corn had torn off two days before and had not healed. Dodgers team physician Robert Kerlan had given the area a shot of novocaine and the trainer was primed to give him more if needed. It was not.[4]

As with all the games in this Series, there was a premium on runs. As the Dodgers came up in the bottom of the fifth, they had managed one single. The Yankees had a single and a double. Nobody had any runs. With one out, Frank Howard came to the plate and launched the first home run ever hit into the second deck down the left-field line, a blow estimated at 450 feet.[5]

Koufax set the Yankees down in the sixth and got Tom Tresh to pop out leading off the seventh. But Mickey Mantle, limited to a fluke bunt single so far in the series, launched a Koufax fastball over the 380-foot sign in left-center to tie the score. It was Mantle's 15th World Series home run, tying him with Babe Ruth for the most round-trippers in Series history. The Yankees had never led a game the entire Series and now had barely edged into a tie.

The tie lasted five batters. Koufax shut out the Yankees in the rest of the seventh inning. Jim Gilliam led off the Dodgers' seventh with a high bouncer to Boyer, who leapt high in the air to glove the ball, came down, and launched a belt-high throw across the diamond. The throw hit first baseman Joe Pepitone on inside of his right forearm and bounced down along the right-field stands. Gilliam wound up at third and scored on Willie Davis's sacrifice fly to give the Dodgers a 2-1 lead.

"It was a perfect throw. I didn't see it. It got lost in the shirts behind third base. It hit me on the side of the glove and wrist and went on by," said Pepitone of the game's crucial play.[6]

There was one final bit of drama in the Yankees' ninth. With two outs and Bobby Richardson on first, Elston Howard hit a groundball to Maury Wills, who threw to Dick Tracewski for the force out. Koufax leapt off the mound, hands high in the air, nearly reaching third base before realizing Tracewski had dropped the short hop and Richardson was safe. Koufax returned to the mound and got Héctor López to ground slowly to Wills. This time, Tracewski held on to the throw. This time Koufax kept leaping and was joined by his teammates.

"I don't feel anything – I'm numb," said Koufax afterward.[7] His teammates were focused on a larger picture. "They won't call us choke artists any more," said Gilliam, harking back to the Dodgers' epic collapse at the end of the 1962 season, which had haunted them through 1963.[8] "This makes up for last year," echoed Johnny Podres. Asked to compare this game with his victory over the Yankees in the seventh game of the 1955 World Series, Podres exclaimed: "Damn right it's better than '55. Why, you just can't beat those guys four straight."[9]

Los Angeles Times columnist Jim Murray gloated: "There's been a bunch of guys out here masquerading as the New York Yankees. It's the clumsiest impersonation I've ever seen."[10]

The Sporting News was awed. It was "pitching that bordered on the fantastic," wrote Fred Lieb, "[w]hile Ralph Houk's versatile New York Yankees entered the Series as odds-on favorites, the Dodger victory was hardly an upset. The sweep, though, came as a shocker."[11] The Dodgers weak offense had taught them how to manufacture runs against good pitching. It was a skill the Yankees had never had to learn.

Mickey Mantle joined in the praise. "I never saw pitching like that. In our league, we see good pitching for a game or two, but never for four straight games. These guys are the best I have ever seen."[12]

Those guys were also few in number. Alston used only 13 players in the four games – eight basic position players plus Ron Fairly, three starting pitchers and one inning of relief from Ron Perranoski. With the pinch-hitters and relief pitchers necessary for come-from-behind tactics, Houk used 20. The four games took a total of 8 hours and 17 minutes.

The 55,912 people in the stands that day pushed total series attendance to 247,279 and total gate receipts to $1,995,189.09, There was also $3.5 million from NBC and Gillette for television rights.[13] The players' share came to $1,017,546.43 with the Dodgers passing out full shares worth $12,794 and Yankees disbursing $7,874.32 per share.[14] Both were the largest ever. Because the Series went only four games, the commissioner's office, and the two leagues would not participate in the receipts. The teams would take home smaller amounts. Nevertheless, Dodgers owner Walter O'Malley would describe the sweep as his greatest thrill in baseball.[15]

Summed up Red Smith: "An hour and a quarter after the game, the eleganti still lapping it up in the stadium club overlooking right field saw a gaggle of young men in business suits emerge from the dugout and trudge toward an exit gate. Most of the Yankees, for it was indeed they, wore black. All walked ever so slowly as to – hell, write your own simile."[16]

SOURCES

In addition to the sources mentioned in the Notes, the author consulted Baseball-Reference.com, Retrosheet.org and the following books, video, and digitized box scores:

"Major League Baseball Presents the World Series of 1963" (retrieved August 17, 2020, at youtube.com/watch?v=HFjFvooJagA)

baseball-reference.com/boxes/LAN/LAN19631006o.shtml

retrosheet.org/boxesetc/1963/B10060LAN1963.htm

NOTES

1   Leonard Koppett, "It Isn't Dodgers Pitching, Says Houk, It's a Yankee Batting Letdown," *New York Times*, October 6, 1963: 198.

2   Jane Leavy, *The Lost Boy* (New York: HarperCollins, 2010): 262.

3   "Yanks Packed Their Bags Before Game, Just in Case," *New York Times*, October 7, 1963: 38.

4   "Sandy Won Decider with Ulcerated Toe," *Los Angeles Times*, October 8, 1963: B2. In *The Sporting News* of October 19, 1963, Bob Hunter reported that the drug used was morphine. The information is on page 2 in a story that begins on page 1 with the headline "Couldn't Be Done – But Dodgers Did It."

5   William Leggett, 'Koo-foo the Killer," *Sports Illustrated*, October 14, 1963: 24.

6   John Hall, "It Was a Perfect Throw. … I Didn't See It' – Pepitone," *Los Angeles Times*, October 7, 1963: B4.

7   Bill Becker, "Manager Praises Koufax's Hurling," *New York Times*, October 7, 1963: 38.

8   Bob Hunter, "Couldn't Be Done – but Dodgers Did It," *The Sporting News*, October 19, 1963: 1. In 1962 the Dodgers had a four-game lead as late as September 17, then faded into a tie with the San Francisco Giants. The Giants won a three-game tiebreaker series to take the 1962 NL pennant.

9   Dan Hafner, "We've Made Up for Last Year,'" *Los Angeles Times*, October 7, 1963: B2.

10   Jim Murray, "Bring on the Yanks!" *Los Angeles Times*, October 7, 1963: B1.

11   Frederick G. Lieb, "Review of Series," in *Official Baseball Guide for 1964* (St. Louis: Charles C. Spink & Son, 1964): 177.

12   Dick Young, "Yanks in for Razzing; They Won't Forget It," *Los Angeles Times*, October 7, 1963: B4.

13   Bob Burnes, "Unbelievable! That's Story of Dodger Sweep," *The Sporting News*, October 19, 1963: 5. The NBC and Gillette figures are in Clifford Kachline, "'Broadcasting' Says Sponsors Will Rush to Back Fetzer Plan," *The Sporting News*, October 19, 1963: 14.

14   "Splitting Swag," *The Sporting News*, October 26, 1963: 6.

15   Bob Oates, "O'Malley's Top 10 and 20," *Los Angeles Times*, March 2, 1977: E1.

16   Red Smith, quoted in *The Sporting News*, October 19, 1963: 22.

Koufax Stifles Cardinals in Only Career Opening Day Start

April 14, 1964: Los Angeles Dodgers 4, St. Louis Cardinals 0, at Dodger Stadium, Los Angeles

BY ANDREW HARNER

"A full season of pitching stretches the muscles of the arm. Over the winter, the muscles relax back into place, and whatever little injuries may have occurred in either the stretching or the relaxing develop scar tissue or, as they are more commonly called, adhesions. … When the scar tissue tears away, a certain amount of bleeding and swelling will take place, and the pitcher may be out of action for ten days to two weeks. In 1964, my adhesions did not tear loose during spring training. I got to pitch the opening game, finally."

– Sandy Koufax[1]

While he did not overpower the St. Louis Cardinals in the way he had tortured so many teams during the previous campaign, Sandy Koufax put the Los Angeles Dodgers in the win column on April 14 by throwing the National League's only Opening Day shutout of 1964.[2] Allowing six hits, Koufax struck out a modest five batters, but he did not issue a walk and allowed only one runner to reach second base at Dodger Stadium in a 4-0 victory.

"He belongs in a higher league," said St. Louis pitcher Roger Craig, Koufax's former Dodgers teammate, now in his first season with the Cardinals.[3]

But others from the Cardinals organization suggested that Koufax had lost some of the pizzazz that made him the National League MVP and the first unanimous Cy Young Award winner in 1963. Five of St. Louis's six hits came on Koufax's curveball, a pitch that had wiped out scores of hitters since he debuted as a 19-year-old in 1955.

Cardinals manager Johnny Keane noted that his players hit Koufax "surprisingly hard,"[4] even though he allowed only singles and Bill White reached second base only due to a wild pitch. "I thought Koufax was very ordinary," added St. Louis coach Howie Pollet. "He got by on reputation, as Warren Spahn and others often do. Even when a great pitcher doesn't have his good stuff, the batters keep looking for it."[5]

Regardless, Koufax ended the Cardinals' three-year winning streak in season openers by tossing the Dodgers' first Opening Day shutout since 1940.[6]

"I've been getting worked up for days. It's a thrill," Koufax said. "We're all charged up. I always get excited before every start, but the first game of the season is something extra."[7]

But before the umpires yelled. "Play ball!" on the first-ever Opening Day meeting between the Dodgers and Cardinals, a litany of unusual incidents spoiled the ambiance. Due to a traffic snafu outside the ballpark, officials delayed the game five minutes to allow fans more time to get into their seats. Then, during the National Anthem, Wagnerian opera tenor Lauritz Melchior lost power in his microphone, allowing only the final line of the song to come through the stadium speakers. Finally, future major leaguer Larry Yount,[8] a member of the Woodland Hills Pony League national runner-up squad, delivered the ceremonial first pitch – six months later than scheduled. The Dodgers initially planned Yount's first pitch for Game Five of the 1963 World Series, but LA's sweep prevented it.

After inducing a fly out on the second pitch of the game, Koufax cut down Dick Groat and White on back-to-back strikeouts to energize baseball's largest Opening Day crowd of the season (50,451). But St. Louis starter Ernie Broglio – four years removed from an NL-leading 21-win season – showed some of that old spark, holding back LA's offense in the early going.

Dodgers rookie Johnny Werhas singled in his first career at-bat in the third. Werhas became the seventh straight different Opening Day third baseman for the Dodgers since the franchise relocated to Los Angeles in 1958.[9] He also started LA's only double play of the game with no outs in the ninth and wore a "grin that covered the entire dressing room"[10] after a dazzling debut in front of a hometown crowd.[11]

Offensive action otherwise remained quiet until the Dodgers broke a scoreless tie in the sixth when Willie Davis singled, stole second, moved to third on a groundout, and scored on Ron Fairly's single up the middle.

"I should have caught that ball Fairly hit through the box to score Davis," Broglio said. "That was the turning point. You give Koufax a run, and he gets pretty tough."[12]

LA's offense used the small-ball approach to produce another tally in the seventh as John Roseboro reached on an error, moved to second on Koufax's sacrifice, advanced to third on a Maury Wills single, and scored when Jim Gilliam poked a grounder through the right side. In the eighth, Frank Howard – happy to see Broglio lifted from the game – delivered a crushing blow, launching reliever Ron Taylor's low fastball more than a dozen rows up into the left-field bleachers for a two-run home run, the 100th of his career.

"That Broglio was fooling around with me," Howard said of striking out to end the second and sixth innings. "He was licking his chops. He knew he had a big fish up there. He got me out both times with his curve. His curve is as good as anyone's in the big leagues."[13]

Koufax allowed a hit in each of the final three innings, but the Cardinals never got a chance to start a rally. The victory gave Koufax 10 straight wins, dating to August 17, 1963, and including his two victories as the Dodgers swept the New York Yankees in the World Series.[14] Dating to June 5, 1963, the Opening Day triumph marked his 21st victory over his past 23 decisions and his fifth straight winning decision against the Cardinals, who had not scored off Koufax in 24 innings.[15]

"Koufax pitched a heckuva game," said Dodgers manager Walter Alston. "He held his stuff real good. He made a few more bad pitches than he will a month from now, but any time you shut out the Cardinals, you're doing a whale of a job."[16]

Eight days later, this time at Busch Stadium in St. Louis, Koufax faced the Cardinals again, and Keane, Pollet, and others learned why he did not dominate on Opening Day. After throwing a curveball to White that bounced in front of the plate, Koufax knew his adhesions had ripped away. He felt "something tear in my forearm,"[17] and Alston pulled him after he allowed three runs in the first inning. It marked a tough break for Koufax, who certainly wanted to put on a show for the fans a day after the St. Louis chapter of the Knights of the Cauliflower Ear and the St. Louis Baseball Writers Association presented him with the J. Roy Stockton Award for outstanding achievement during the 1963 season.[18]

"Sandy told me his arm had been hurting on and off since spring training," recalled Cardinals doctor I.C. Middleman. "He hadn't bothered to report it, feeling he could work it out. He is extremely tender and has a swelling on the inside of his left forearm. It is rigid and just like a hot dog."[19]

Koufax returned 12 games later, throwing a 13-strikeout, 10-inning gem to seemingly leave his arm troubles in the past. He won 15 of his 16 decisions between Memorial Day and his final start in August. He fired a no-hitter on June 4 and reeled off shutouts in two of his next three starts in one of the most dominating four-game stretches of his career. But as the season wore on, arthritic pain seeped in and cut Koufax's season short

Sandy Koufax shut out the Cardinals in the only opening-day start of his big-league career. Courtesy of National Baseball Hall of Fame.

in August after his NL-leading seventh shutout gave him 19 victories on August 22. But even though his season ended with some disappointment, he forever had the memory of his only Opening Day start and ultimately finished his career with back-to-back Cy Young Awards and World Series appearances in 1965 and 1966.

SOURCES

In addition to the sources cited in the Notes, the author consulted the Baseball-Reference.com, Stathead.com, and Retrosheet.org websites for pertinent materials and the box scores noted below. He also used information obtained from coverage by *The Sporting News*, the *Los Angeles Times*, and the *St. Louis Post-Dispatch*.

https://www.baseball-reference.com/boxes/LAN/LAN196404140.shtml

https://www.retrosheet.org/boxesetc/1964/B04140LAN1964.htm

NOTES

1   Sandy Koufax with Edward Linn, *Koufax* (New York: Viking Press, 1966), 218-219.

2   Juan Marichal was the only other NL pitcher to fire a complete game on Opening Day, outdueling Warren Spahn in San Francisco's 8-4 win over the Milwaukee Braves.

3   Paul Zimmerman, "He's Better Than 'Big League' – That's What Cards Call Sandy," *Los Angeles Times*, April 15, 1964: 44.

4   Zimmerman.

5   Neal Russo, "Power-Short L.A. Short Circuits Cardinals' Opening Streak, 4-0," *St. Louis Post-Dispatch*, April 15, 1964: 4E.

6   In that game, on April 16, 1940, Brooklyn's Whit Wyatt surrendered five hits during a 5-0 win over the Boston Bees.

7   John Hall, "Just a Human," *Los Angeles Times*, April 15, 1964: 47.

8   Larry Yount suffered an injury while firing warm-up pitches for his major-league debut in 1971, and he never appeared in another big-league game. His brother, Robin, built a Hall of Fame career with the Milwaukee Brewers.

9   The other six, listed chronologically: Dick Gray, Jim Baxes, Jim Gilliam, Tommy Davis, Daryl Spencer, and Ken McMullen. The streak continued with John Kennedy in 1965, before Jim Lefebvre made consecutive starts in 1966 and '67.

10   John Hall, "Werhas Rates Raves in First Game," *Los Angeles Times*, April 15, 1964: 48.

11   Though born in Michigan, Werhas played high-school baseball in Los Angeles at San Pedro Prep and in college at the University of Southern California.

12   Zimmerman.

13   Russo.

14   Koufax had four no-decisions down the stretch of the 1963 season. The Dodgers finished 3-1 in those games.

15   St. Louis last scored against Koufax in the sixth inning on August 21, 1963. He pitched the next six frames of an eventual 16-inning win for the Dodgers. Koufax also fired a shutout against the Cardinals on September 17.

16   United Press International, "Old Pro Dodgers Display Enthusiasm for Opening," *Lompoc* (California) *Record*, April 15, 1964: 4-A.

17   Koufax with Linn, 219.

18   The game served as Opening Day for Busch Stadium, and the 31,410 fans who attended marked a St. Louis record for the first home game of a season.

19   Jane Leavy, *Sandy Koufax: A Lefty's Legacy* (New York: HarperCollins, 2003), 150.

Sandy Koufax's Third No-Hitter

June 4, 1964: Los Angeles Dodgers 3, Philadelphia Phillies 0, at Connie Mack Stadium, Philadelphia

BY MARC Z AARON

The Los Angeles Dodgers (21-25, and in eighth place) came to Philadelphia to play the league-leading Philadelphia Phillies (27-15). It was a great pitching matchup: Sandy Koufax (5-4) and Chris Short (3-2, 0.64 ERA).

Both pitchers set the side down in order in the first inning. In the second inning Tommy Davis singled but was erased on an inning-ending double-play ball. Koufax looked dominant from the beginning of the game, needing only six pitches to set the Phillies down in order in the second and picking up his third strikeout. Johnny Callison, Dick Allen, and Gus Triandos had all gone down swinging.

In the top of the third, Koufax lined a single to center with two out, but Willie Davis fouled out to third baseman Dick Allen. In the bottom half, Tony Taylor went down looking, Ruben Amaro hit a popup to first baseman Ken McMullen, and Chris Short went down swinging.

In the bottom of the fourth with two out, Koufax fell behind in the count 3-and-0 to Dick Allen. Two strikes and one foul ball later, Koufax walked Allen on a fastball that was three inches below the strike zone. Koufax later commented that he shook off the curve to throw the fastball.[1] Allen was erased from the basepaths when he attempted to steal on a 2-and-2 count with Danny Cater at bat. After the game Koufax said, "(Doug) Camilli had called for a curve, but I shook him off … then right in the middle of my windup I realized I had made a mistake, that Allen would be looking for the fast one. But just like you don't stop a golf shot on the backswing, I kept right on going. There was no doubt about the call. It was a ball."[2]

In the fifth inning Cater went down swinging, Triandos flied to center, and Roy Sievers fouled out to first. In the sixth Taylor hit a grounder back to Koufax, and both Amaro and Short went down swinging at the air.

After six innings there had been only three hits, one error allowing a base, and just the one walk to Allen. A real pitching duel. The Dodgers had not scored a run in 19 straight innings.

In the top of the seventh, Jim Gilliam grounded a ball up the middle and went to third on a line-drive single to right by Tommy Davis. On the next pitch from Chris Short, Frank Howard crushed his 14th home run of the season, the ball taking one hop on the arched roof of the left-field pavilion. Ken McMullen then singled to left but was out trying to stretch it into a double. Doug Camilli hit a fly ball to right for the second out. Dick Tracewski doubled to left, chasing Short from the mound. Ed Roebuck came in and got Koufax, his former teammate on the Dodgers, to ground out to short.

The Dodgers made some lineup changes in the bottom of the seventh. Wes Parker was now the right fielder and Ron Fairly came in to play first base. They replaced Frank Howard and Ken McMullen. Koufax faced Cookie Rojas and with two strikes Rojas flied out to left. Johnny Callison grounded back to Koufax and Allen hit a high chopper to Gilliam at third. Gilliam came running hard to grab it on the short hop and throw Allen out by three steps.

Sandy Koufax threw just 97 pitches in his no-hitter against the Phillies. He struck out 12 and walked one. SABR: The Rucker Archive.

In the eighth Ray Culp replaced Roebuck. The Dodgers went down in order. In the bottom half of the inning Cater was out on a hard liner to right on the first pitch, and Triandos and Sievers went down swinging.

In the ninth, Tony Taylor struck out. Amaro, swinging at the first pitch, fouled out to first baseman Fairly, who caught the ball about 20 feet behind first. With two outs, Bobby Wine, batting .205 and 1-for-17 against Koufax, batted for Culp. With the count 1-and-2, Wine went down swinging. But not before he had fouled off the second pitch into the dirt. The ball bounced up and hit home-plate umpire Ed Vargo in the throat. Vargo didn't want to hold up the game and allow Koufax to cool off, even though he was having trouble breathing.[3]

Final score: Dodgers 3, Phillies 0. A crowd of 29,704, the biggest of the season so far, witnessed Koufax's third no-hitter. (The crowd for the game against the San Francisco Giants the next night exceeded the Dodgers' crowd by 2,000.) The game took 1 hour 55 minutes to play as Koufax faced the minimum 27 batters. He threw just 97 pitches and the only three-ball count was the one to Allen that resulted in Koufax's lone walk. Koufax struck out 12 Phillies in what was to be the only time he was to shut out the Phillies during his career. It was the 54th time he had struck out 10 or more batters. He joined Bob Feller as the only pitchers to throw three no-hitters in the twentieth century.[4]

Before the no-hitter the Dodgers had been defeated by the Phillies in eight of their nine previous contests.

Koufax remarked after the game, "This was the first time this season that I have been able to put everything together."[5] He was throwing differently than he had earlier in the season. He wasn't stepping as far to the left and not throwing as much across his body. He seemed to have better leverage on his follow-through. He had his old rhythm back. The fastball was overpowering and the curve cut the corners.[6]

Prior to this start, Koufax came across an issue of *Sport* magazine that featured a photo of him during his 1963 no-hitter against the Giants. From the photo angle, Koufax was able to

detect a flaw in his stride.[7] He could see that he had to open up a little.[8]

On the bus from the stadium, Koufax remarked to pitcher Joe Moeller, "You know, I got away with a pitch. I hung a curve to Wine."[9] He faced the minimum number of batters and all he could think about was the one pitch that got away. Typical Koufax.

Don Drysdale, who lost 1-0 in 11 innings the night before, was not traveling with the team. When he heard the announcer reporting that Koufax had pitched his third no-hitter, Drysdale asked impatiently, "But did he win?"[10]

SOURCES

In addition to the sources cited in the Notes, the author also consulted Baseball-Reference.com and an article by Bob Hunter in the June 20, 1964, issue of *The Sporting News*.

NOTES

1   John Brogan, "Sandy Shook Off Curve, Fast Ball Walked Allen," *Philadelphia Bulletin*, June 5, 1964.

2   Associated Press, "Koufax Pitches His 3rd No-Hitter," June 4, 1964.

3   Allen Lewis, "Ump Vargo Refused to Leave Contest in spite of Painful Injury From Foul," *The Sporting News*, June 20, 1964. (Vargo would again be behind the plate when Koufax pitched his perfect game against the Cubs in 1965.)

4   Larry Corcoran and Cy Young accomplished the feat in the nineteenth century.

5   Associated Press, "Sandy Found a Flaw, Corrected It, and...," *Los Angeles Times*, June 5, 1964: B1.

6   "Koufax Pitches His 3rd No-Hitter."

7   Jane Leavy, *Sandy Koufax, a Lefty's Legacy* (New York: HarperCollins, 2002), 152.

8   Sandy Koufax with Ed Linn, *Koufax* (New York: Viking Press, 1966), 220.

9   Leavy, 154

10 Leavy, 154.

Sandy Koufax Blanks Cardinals But Receives Ominous Medical Diagnosis

August 16, 1964: Los Angeles Dodgers 3, St. Louis Cardinals 0, at Dodger Stadium, Los Angeles

BY CHAD MOODY

"On August 8 I won a tough game in Milwaukee," Sandy Koufax recounted of his second victory over the Braves in 1964. "Tougher than I thought."[1] Indeed, the star Los Angeles Dodgers lefty had to struggle through a complete game after jamming his throwing arm while diving back to second base and avoiding a fifth-inning pickoff attempt. Despite battling the resulting pain and swelling, four days later he went the distance again in an impressive win over the Cincinnati Reds. And on August 16 the reigning Cy Young Award winner loosened up his ailing arm enough to start the first game of a twin bill against the St. Louis Cardinals. Although tossing what he called one of his "better games of the year," it turned out to be his last appearance of the season – and portended the premature end of a Hall of Fame career.[2]

Both Los Angeles and St. Louis entered the contest in the middle of the National League pack after having finished first and second respectively in 1963. Koufax on the other hand – leading the league at the time in the pitching Triple Crown categories – remained in top form. Rookie left-hander Gordie Richardson was given the challenging task of squaring off against Koufax, who was riding a 24⅓-inning scoreless streak at home against the Cardinals. A reported 38,072 spectators were on hand at Dodger Stadium for the afternoon tilt.

Neither club could muster a serious offensive threat until the Dodgers broke through in the bottom of the fifth. Ron Fairly led off with a walk and advanced to third on a wild pitch and stolen base. Third baseman – and the season's eventual MVP – Ken Boyer argued with umpire Chris Pelekoudas that he tagged out the sliding Fairly on the theft, but to no avail. After Nate Oliver walked, Koufax's batterymate, John Roseboro, delivered an RBI single and ended up at second on Gold Glove center fielder Curt Flood's uncharacteristic errant throw to third. After the play Boyer, still stewing from the earlier call on Fairly, was ejected from the game after he "renewed his complaints" with Pelekoudas.[3] Richardson was able to retire the next pair of batters but fell victim to Dick Tracewski's two-out single that scored

Oliver. On the same play, Roseboro was cut down at the plate by burgeoning star left fielder Lou Brock to end the damage.

After Koufax blanked St. Louis in the top of the sixth, the home team added to its lead in the bottom of the inning when two-time batting champion Tommy Davis connected on a solo home run to left field. With neither club able to manufacture any runs the rest of the way, Los Angeles secured a 3-0 triumph.

Richardson, making only his fourth big-league start, performed admirably in his six innings of work against the reigning World Series champs before handing the ball to reliever Ron Taylor, who delivered two scoreless frames. But it was Koufax who was truly magnificent in his complete-game blanking that improved his record to 19-5 and lowered his ERA to 1.74. "He's a great, great pitcher," Cardinals manager Johnny Keane said of Koufax after the game. "He's just ahead of the field."[4] Dodgers pitching coach Joe Becker quipped that he wished his team "had a couple more like him."[5]

Koufax's 13 strikeouts tied a season high for him and produced a major-league-record 61st time that he fanned 10 or more batters in a game. "I held my stuff right through the ninth inning," he said.[6] Although some lauded the experimental forkball recently added to his arsenal after having trouble with the straight change, Koufax downplayed its role in his success in the game. "The forkball had nothing to do with it," he said. "I threw it only four times all afternoon. It's nothing special. Speed and the curve are still my pitches."[7]

In any case, St. Louis's offense managed to collect only one walk and seven scattered hits. "So it's not the real good hitters you've got to get out," Koufax once opined. "It's the others. They're the ones that'll beat you."[8] In line with his philosophy, the southpaw allowed four of the hits to Flood, who also flirted with the record books over the course of the day. The veteran star – en route to back-to-back seasons with 200 or more hits – added another four in the second game of the doubleheader to fall just one short of major-league records for the both most hits and most consecutive hits in the same day. "Flood's always tough," Koufax admitted. "It was one of those days with him. He was hitting good pitches."[9] Flood had an opportunity to tie the marks in the ninth inning of game two but struck out against workhorse Los Angeles reliever Ron Perranoski. "I'm mighty happy to have gotten eight hits even though I couldn't get that last one," Flood said. "I've never been able to hit Perranoski very well and I guess I might have had a negative attitude facing him in that one inning."[10]

Some off-field excitement ensued for both clubs shortly after the day's contests. While leaving the stadium parking lot, coach Leo Durocher got into a verbal and physical altercation over an autograph request that sent a fan to the hospital with an injured jaw.[11] Although no charges were filed, the scuffle resulted in a civil lawsuit against the fiery Dodgers coach.[12] The next day, news broke that longtime St. Louis general manager Bing Devine and Cardinals business manager Art Routzong had resigned. Later it was uncovered that Cardinals owner Gussie Busch had actually fired the two executives for what Devine believed was mainly due to "the Redbirds' inability to win a pennant."[13] Devine was nevertheless named major-league Executive of the Year by *The Sporting News* for the second consecutive season when St. Louis went on to win the 1964 World Series with the team he had constructed. However, nothing could top the postgame drama surrounding The Left Arm of God.

The morning after his league-leading seventh shutout, Koufax was unable to straighten his throwing arm. "The joint squished," wrote author Jane Leavy in *Sandy Koufax: A Lefty's Legacy*. "Pockets of fluid protruded from beneath the skin like hard-boiled eggs. His elbow was as big as his knee. The only difference was his knee bent."[14] Quickly running tests and X-rays, the Dodgers team physician (and famed pioneer of sports medicine), Dr. Robert Kerlan, identified the injury as traumatic arthritis, an incurable ailment degrading Koufax's elbow cartilage. Because the diagnosis was not publicly disclosed until just before the following season, hope still sprang eternal among fans for his quick return despite the missed starts that piled up, but Koufax and his "waterlogged log" of an arm were done for the year.[15]

The jammed elbow Koufax suffered on the basepaths against the Braves eight days earlier was most certainly the flashpoint that eventually led to his premature exit from the campaign. However, in his 2013 book *Baseball Injuries: Case Studies, by Type, in the Major Leagues*, W. Laurence Coker, MD, surmises that it was a pitch tossed back on April 22 that may have hastened the onset of his arthritis symptoms. "As I came over the top to throw a curve ball [to Cardinal Bill White], I could feel something tear in my forearm," Koufax recounted of the incident that caused him to leave the game after only one inning and be shut down for 12 days.[16] Coker contends that this likely signaled a partially torn ulnar collateral ligament, which "makes the elbow more unstable and speeds up the arthritis process."[17] Unfortunately, medical MRIs were not yet available at that time to confirm the cause.

Despite missing the final month and a half of the season, Koufax nonetheless finished in third place in the National League Cy Young Award voting. At season's end, he led the NL in a number of rate statistics, including ERA, ERA+, FIP, won-lost percentage, and WHIP. And he was even among league leaders in several counting statistics, finishing first in shutouts, second in pitching WAR, fourth in wins and strikeouts, and sixth in complete games. Enduring frequent and severe pain, Koufax managed to make it through the 1965 and '66 campaigns – amazingly winning the Cy Young Award in each – before his Hall of Fame career was cut short due to the arthritis that plagued him.

SOURCES

The author accessed Baseball-Reference.com (https://www.baseball-reference.com/boxes/LAN/LAN196408161.shtml) for box scores/play-by-play information and other data, as well as Retrosheet.org (https://www.retrosheet.org/boxesetc/1964/B08161LAN1964.htm). In addition to the sources cited in the Notes, the author accessed GenealogyBank.com, NewspaperArchive.com, Newspapers.com, Paper of Record, and Stathead.com.

NOTES

1 Sandy Koufax and Ed Linn, *Koufax* (New York: Viking Press, 1966), 222.

2 Koufax and Linn, 224.

3 "Flood Tides Cards Over in Split," *St. Louis Post-Dispatch*, August 17, 1964: 4C.

4 "Flood Tides Cards Over in Split."

5 George Lederer, "Koufax, Simmons Swap Shutouts," *Long Beach* (California) *Independent*, August 17, 1964: C-5.

6 Lederer.

7 Bob Hunter, "Sandy Makes Hay With a New Pitch – It's His Forkball," *The Sporting News*, August 22, 1964: 11; John Hall, "Please, Please – Sandy Is NO Fork-Baller," *Los Angeles Times*, August 17, 1964: Part III-2.

8 "Koufax on Koufax," *Sports Illustrated*, December 20, 1965: 38.

9 Hall.

10 Alex Kahn, "Sandy Nabs 19th Victory," *Los Angeles Citizen-News*, August 17, 1964: B-2.

11 "Fan Says Leo Hit Him in Lot," *Pasadena Star-News*, August 17, 1964: 14.

12 Associated Press, "No Charges Filed Against Durocher," *Palo Alto* (California) *Times*, September 1, 1964: 3.

13 Bob Broeg, "Bing Devine, Routzong Resign Card Jobs," *St. Louis Post-Dispatch*, August 17, 1964: 4C.

14 Jane Leavy, *Sandy Koufax: A Lefty's Legacy* (New York: Perennial, 2003), 153.

15 "Koufax Sidelined by Elbow Arthritis," *Los Angeles Times*, April 3, 1965: Part II-1; Leavy, 153-154.

16 Koufax and Linn, 219.

17 W. Laurence Coker, M.D., *Baseball Injuries: Case Studies, by Type, in the Major Leagues* (Jefferson, North Carolina: McFarland & Company, 2013), 81-83.

Koufax Strikes Out 13 Over 10-Plus Innings in an Epic Pitching Duel

May 17, 1965: Los Angeles Dodgers 5, Houston Astros 3, at the Astrodome, Houston

BY QUENTIN SALLAT

It's difficult to find the right words to describe the 10⅓ innings Sandy Koufax pitched against the Houston Astros on May 17, 1965, allowing three runs. But this game, astounding on its own, looks even better when seen through its context: only four days before, Koufax had pitched a shutout against the same Houston Astros. In a way, this was Koufax at his peak, playing in a season where he got both a pitching Triple Crown and a Cy Young Award, in what was his next to last season.

When Koufax stepped onto the mound at the Astrodome that evening, everybody had in mind the previous series against Houston, played in Los Angeles a few days earlier. The Dodgers dominated the series, and won on May 12 thanks to an impressive complete-game performance by pitcher Don Drysdale.

The next day, May 13, Koufax pitched a shutout. Close to 21,000 fans watched the lefty pitch a gem at Dodger Stadium, allowing only three hits and no walks, with 13 strikeouts. The Dodgers won, 3-0.

Facing the man who shut them out a few days before might not have been to the taste of the Astros. They might even have hoped Koufax would be resting. Indeed, in 1965, Koufax had already been suffering pain in his arms because of traumatic arthritis. But the Dodgers pitcher tried a new way of reducing the pain in 1965: He simply skipped his usual sideline throwing between starts. This simple resting technique was enough to create a change. Koufax finished the season with 335⅔ innings pitched, a career high. On top of that, he broke the Modern Era strikeout record, until then owned by Rube Waddell. Rube had 349 in 1904, Koufax finished with 382.

All these achievements are a testimony not only to Koufax's talent but also his sheer determination. Breaking records is one thing. Doing it while suffering terrible pain from a medical condition is another. This would end his career early. But in 1965 the new routine was effective enough that the version of Koufax on the field was stellar.

This is how, on May 17, Koufax was able to pitch again, after a then-common four-day rest. And he was on a roll against the Astros: he had defeated them eight straight times. Maybe even more worrying, Houston was in the middle of a six-game losing streak. This game was going to be the Dodgers' introduction to the brand-new Astrodome. And several of them seemed to be charmed. "This is the greatest thing I've played in since I played at Carnegie Hall," said outfielder Al Ferrara, a former talented piano player.[1]

Koufax was also eager to see this new ballpark. "I've never heard ball players talk about a park as much as they have about this one," he told Frank Finch of the Los Angeles Times a few days earlier.[2]

Koufax's opponent on this day was Bob Bruce, who would throw more than 10 innings in this pitching duel while allowing three runs. It was Bruce who faced Koufax a few days before and took the loss. Probably determined not to suffer the same fate, Bruce started the game by retiring the side in order.

The first hit came from Houston's Bob Lillis, who singled to center field to lead off the Astros' first inning. But the next batter, future Hall of Famer Joe Morgan, grounded into double play. Koufax finished the inning by retiring Jim Wynn on a fly ball to center field.

The Dodgers got their first hit in the top of the second, a single by the five-time All-Star John Roseboro. The threat didn't go further, as the next two batters grounded out.

The first real scoring opportunity for the Astros came in the bottom of the second inning, when Joe Gaines tripled to center field with one out. Once again Koufax rose to the occasion and struck out the next two batters.

The Dodgers' Dick Tracewski led off the top of the third with a single to left field and stole second while Koufax was at the bat. Two outs later, Wes Parker doubled, giving Los Angeles a 1-0 lead. (Parker was out trying to stretch his hit into a triple.)

The Astros countered in the bottom of the fourth. Koufax started it by walking Wynn leading off and Joe Gaines with one out. Eddie Kasko's single to center, drove in Wynn. Koufax shook it off and retired the next two batters on a fly ball and an infield pop.

Fans had to wait until the top of the seventh inning to see any further action on offense. Ron Fairly reached first base on a one-out error by second baseman Morgan. Roseboro singled him to second base. But the 1965 Rookie of the Year Jim Lefebvre grounded into a double play, and the inning was over.

Still tied 1-1, the game went into extra innings with both starters still in the game. In the 10th, despite base hits by Roseboro and Lefebvre, the Dodgers were unable to score. The Astros didn't do better, despite Kasko drawing a leadoff walk.

The Dodgers broke through in the top of the 11th. With one out, Bruce gave up a single to center by Koufax himself, a notoriously weak hitter who retired with a .097 career batting average. Koufax took second when the next batter, Maury Wills, also singled to center.

After Wills' hit, Astros manager Lum Harris replaced Bruce with reliever Hal Woodeshick, who walked Parker, loading the bases for Willie Davis. Woodeshick struck him out. Fairly, however, hit a line drive to center field for a single. Koufax scored on the hit and Wills came home when Joe Morgan mishandled the relay, his second error of the game. It was a nightmare of a game on defense for Morgan, as he also allowed the next batter, Roseboro, to reach first on yet another error. Parker and Fairly scored. Despite the three errors, Houston manager Harris defended his second baseman after the game, telling sportswriters, "I told him that Babe Ruth made errors."[3] (That didn't prevent the *Baytown (Texas) Sun* from headlining its game story "Morgan's Misplays Aid LA's Bum Win."[4]

Woodeshick struck out Lefebvre to end the inning with the Dodgers leading, 5-1.

Koufax, after pitching 10 impressive innings and sparking the Dodgers' offense, was back on the mound in the bottom of the 11th, facing the top of Houston's batting order. He retired Lillis but gave up a single to Morgan (who was greeted at the plate by boos), hit Wynn with a pitch, and allowed a run-scoring single to Bob Aspromonte.

After 10⅓ innings, Koufax was replaced by Bob Miller, who despite allowing a run on a groundball got Kasko on a game-ending pop fly to second. Koufax had his fifth victory on his way to a 26-8 season. Adding to the satisfaction of Dodgers manager Walt Alston was the fact that it was his 1,000th win as the Dodgers' manager. "I hope the next few aren't as tough as the thousandth," he declared after the game.[5]

The rest of the season would prove to be as eventful as this game. Koufax pitched a perfect game on September 9, becoming the first pitcher to throw four no-hitters. (Bob Feller had three; Nolan Ryan finished his career with seven).

The Dodgers made it to the World Series. Koufax refused to pitch in Game One because it was being played on Yom Kippur, the holiest day in the Jewish religion. Los Angeles won the Series in seven games over the Minnesota Twins.

Koufax won the first of his two pitching Triple Crowns that season, along with the second of his three Cy Young Awards, He was the runner-up for the National League MVP and was voted NL Pitcher of the Year.

SOURCES

In addition to the sources cited in the Notes, the author consulted Baseball Reference.com and Retrosheet.org, and the following:

Aaron, Marc Z. "Sandy Koufax," SABR.org., https ://sabr.org/bioproj/person/sandy-koufax/

https://www.baseball-reference.com/boxes/HOU/HOU196505170.shtml

https://www.retrosheet.org/boxesetc/1965/B05170HOU1965.htm

The author would like to thank Rick Bush for providing articles from the *Houston Chronicle*.

NOTES

1   Wells Twombly, "Bubble-Eyed Dodgers Praise Dome," Houston Chronicle, May 18, 1965: 21.

2   Frank Finch, "Dodgers Get 5-3 'Gift' in Dome Debut," Los Angeles Times, May 18, 1965.

3   Associated Press, "Morgan Is Told Ruth Erred, Too," Orange (Texas) Leader, May 19, 1965: 5.

4   Fred Hartman, "Morgan's Misplays Aid LA's Bum Win," Baytown (Texas) Sun, May 19, 1965: 16.

5   "Morgan Is Told Ruth Erred, Too."

Sandy Koufax Wins 5-0 to Remain Undefeated Against the Mets

June 12, 1965: Los Angeles Dodgers 5, New York Mets 0, at Shea Stadium, Flushing, New York

BY THOMAS J. BROWN JR.

The ever-dominant Sandy Koufax owned a 10-0 career record in 11 starts against the New York Mets when he faced them on June 12, 1965. The expansion team — in its fourth season under future Hall of Fame manager Casey Stengel — had scored just 11 earned runs off the Los Angeles left-hander, whose domination included a 2-1 victory in April at Dodger Stadium on John Roseboro's walk-off single against Jack Fisher.[1]

On this sunny Saturday afternoon with temperatures in the mid-70s, a crowd of 38,915 showed up at Shea Stadium to see if the Mets might finally beat their nemesis.[2] The ballpark was filled to capacity as the Mets had advertised free admission to women and children for the game. Al Jackson — at 2-7 — took the mound for New York, which at 20-36 was en route to its fourth consecutive 100-loss season. Koufax was 8-3 after a complete-game victory against Philadelphia five days earlier for the Dodgers, who led the National League at 35-22 and would win their second World Series in three years in October.

Through three innings, the pitchers battled each other. The Dodgers left men in scoring position in all three at-bats but Jackson held firm. Koufax was equal to the challenge as he struck out the final two batters in both the second and third innings with runners on base.

The Dodgers finally scored in the top of a "nightmarish fourth, in which the Mets made three errors (and) saw the Dodgers score three times."[3] Lou Johnson reached on a miscue by Mets shortstop Roy McMillan, then scored on Jim Lefebvre's double. Al Ferrara singled Lefebvre to third to set up Jeff Torborg's RBI bunt base hit. Third baseman Charley Smith then booted Koufax's grounder that loaded the bases ahead of Maury Wills, who bounced to third only to have Mets catcher Hawk Taylor mishandle Smith's throw for another error as Ferrara scored.

"That fourth inning was so bad that the only way that (Jackson) could get an out was to do it himself. He fanned the side while facing nine men," wrote Frank Finch of the *Los Angeles Times*.[4] When Jackson finally struck out Willie Davis for the third out, the Dodgers led 3-0.

"Nobody expects them to hit much but they could field at least," wrote the *New York Daily News*' Joe Trimble. "[T]hey looked a lot like themselves while wearing the holes in their gloves palm upwards. Four errors, three in the fourth inning, made it easy for the Dodgers."[5]

Ron Fairly led off the fifth with a short pop fly to center. Mets fans watched as the ball just cleared the glove of shortstop Roy McMillan. It then popped out of left fielder Danny Napoleon's glove as he raced in to try to make the catch. McMillan grabbed the ball as on one hop and threw it to Jim Hickman at first. Fairly had already rounded first and was headed for second. Hickman threw to second baseman Bobby Klaus who just tagged Fairly "by a whisker. The scoring: E7-6-3-4 – in other words a routine out, as they go at Shea."[6]

The afternoon became painful for Johnson in the fifth when Jackson hit him with a pitch on the right thumb, breaking it and keeping the outfielder out of the starting lineup for almost two weeks.

"The Dodgers scored twice more in the sixth, this time supplying all the momentum themselves."[7] Torborg led off with a double down the left field line. After Koufax fouled out while trying to bunt, Torborg reached third on Wills's single to left. Wills stole second, his second steal of the game and his 38th in 50 attempts. After Jim Gilliam lined out, Davis brought both runners home with a single up the middle, giving the Dodgers a 5-0 lead.

Not that Koufax needed the insurance as he continued to paralyze the Mets, who managed five singles and one walk for the afternoon. The Mets put two runners on base in the second on a pair of singles by Hawk Taylor and Napoleon. "Koufax's answer was to strike out Jim Hickman and Bobby Klaus."[8]

The Mets also put two runners on base in the sixth with consecutive singles. But they came with two outs and Koufax "put an end to the nonsense "by getting Taylor to pop out to third.[9]

Stengel replaced Jackson in the eighth with left-hander Tug McGraw. Jackson fanned seven batters over that stretch but his "support was of little more assistance than a broken crutch."[10]

Koufax led off the eighth with a single, the only hit off McGraw in two innings of relief. It was Koufax's eighth hit of the season, besting his total from 1964.

Koufax retired the last seven batters and finished with eight strikeouts as his career mark against New York improved to 11-0 with a 1.00 ERA. It was a performance that impressed those in attendance despite seeing their Mets "waltzing in a fog…and can't get the act finished."[11] Koufax told reporters afterward that he "didn't have a good curveball, he said. So he just held the cellar club to five singles, three of them scratchy, by overpowering them with his fastball."[12]

The Mets would lose twice more to Koufax that year and lower their record against him to 0-13 over four years before finally winning 5-2 on August 26 before nearly 45,950 at Shea. The Hall of Famer played one more season and retired with a 17-2 record and a 1.44 ERA against the Mets. And no club did worse than New York's .170 batting average, .226 OBP, and .461 OPS in 20 games versus the Brooklyn native.[13]

New York's team fortunes continued with losing seasons the norm until the Amazin' Mets captured the 1969 World Series. Stengel's dugout career would end exactly six weeks after the June 12 game when he busted his hip following Old-Timers' Day.[14] He was less than a week shy of his 75th birthday and had finished last every year with the Mets after 10 American League pennants in 12 seasons with the crosstown Yankees.

But while the Dodgers handled the Mets that year (12-6 vs. the New Yorkers), the Mets cashed in when the Los Angeles club visited Flushing. The Mets were doing well at the gate anyway, with overall ticket sales up more than 60 percent since their first two seasons at the Polo Grounds.[15] In '65, an average of 42,238 fans watched LA play its nine games in eight dates at Shea. That accounted for just over 19 percent of New York's attendance of 1,768,389 in the 10-team NL.[16]

As the Mets struggled on the field, the good times continued for the Dodgers, who won 15 of their final 16 games to erase a 4½-game deficit and capture the NL flag by two games over their archrivals, the San Francisco Giants. Koufax had three shutouts and a save during the late surge and would finish that '65 season with the pitching Triple Crown (26-8, 2.04 ERA, career-high 382 strikeouts, plus a career-low WHIP of 0.855). The effort earned him his second of three Cy Young Awards. After shutting out the Minnesota Twins in Game Five of the Series, Koufax put a bow on the season as Series MVP with another shutout in Game Seven on two days' rest.[17]

Exactly five weeks before that season-ending victory, Koufax had thrown a perfect game against the Chicago Cubs as umpires Bill Jackowski, Chris Pelekoudas, Ed Vargo, and Paul Pryor called the action. Interestingly, those same men in blue were in New York that Saturday in June to watch Koufax dominate the Mets again.

AUTHOR'S NOTE

This was the first major-league game attended by the author. The author's father, a former Brooklyn Dodgers fan, became a Mets fan after the team began play in 1962 and raised the author to be a loyal fan as well.

SOURCES

The author accessed baseball-reference.com, retrosheet.org and baseball-almanac.com for play-by-play, box-score, umpire assignments, attendance, standings, and player and manager career data.

baseball-reference.com/boxes/NYN/NYN196506120.shtml

retrosheet.org/boxesetc/1965/B06120NYN1965.htm

NOTES

1   Koufax eventually was 17-2 with a 1.44 ERA in 20 games against the Mets. He also did well against the Mets' 1962 expansion partner, the Houston Astros, going 14-2 with a 1.90 ERA in 22 appearances. Only the Cincinnati Reds (20-19 in 57 games) had a winning record against Koufax. (baseball-reference.com/players/split.fcgi?id=koufasa01&year=Career&t=p).

2   Weather information from wunderground.com. wunderground. com/history/airport/KJFK/1965/6/12/DailyHistory.html?req_city=&reqstate=&req_statename=&reqdb.zip=&reqdb. magic=&reqdb.wmo

3   Joseph Sheehan, "Dodgers Triumph Over Mets by 5-0," *New York Times*, June 13, 1965: S1.

4   Frank Finch, "Koufax Zeroes in on Mets Again," *Los Angeles Times*, June 13, 1965: C1.

5   Joe Trimble, "LA's Koufax Blanks Mets, 5-0, to String 11-0 Mark," *New York Daily News*, June 13, 1965: 144.

6   Sheehan.

7   Sheehan.

8   Sheehan.

9   Sheehan.

10 Finch.

11 Trimble.

12 Trimble.

13 Johnson did not play for 10 days, and then only as a pinch-runner, before returning to the starting lineup on June 25.(retrosheet.org/boxesetc/1965/B06120NYN1965.htm) and (baseball-reference.com/players/gl.fcgi?id=johnslo01&t=b&year=1965).

14 Accounts differ slightly on details of Stengel's broken hip. His SABR profile (Bill Bishop, sabr.org/bioproj/person/bd6a83d8, SABR BioProject) says he suffered the injury when he slipped at the New York pub Toots Shor's. The *New York Times* obituary from October 1 1975, added that he also fell later that night getting out of a car. (Joseph Durso, "Stengel's Death at 85 Widely Mourned," *New York Times*, October 1, 1975: 93).

15 Joe Trimble of the *New York Daily News* wrote: "About the only place the Mets can do themselves any good is at the box office. The paid attendance was 38,915 – the rest ladies and kids – and brought

the six day total for three with the Giants and two with L.A. to 200,715, which is believed to be the biggest one-week attendance in baseball history." Joe Trimble, "LA's Koufax Blanks Mets, 5-0, to String 11-0 Mark," *New York Daily News*, June 13, 1965: 144.

16　Despite finishing in last place in the National League in 1965, the Mets had the third best attendance behind the Los Angeles Dodgers (2,553,577) and the Houston Astros (2,151,470). https://www.baseball-reference.com/leagues/majors/1965-misc.shtml

17　Koufax was in the midst of a fantastic career-ending four-year run in which he went 97-27 (.782) with a 1.86 ERA, four ERA titles, three strikeout crowns, 31 shutouts, one MVP and two other second-place finishes for NL MVP.

Koufax Bests Spahn, One-Hits Mets

June 20, 1965: Los Angeles Dodgers 2, New York Mets 1, at Dodger Stadium, Los Angeles (first game of doubleheader)

BY KURT BLUMENAU

Sandy Koufax and Warren Spahn, two of the most accomplished left-handed pitchers in baseball history, started against each other six times. Their final faceoff was especially tight and well-pitched – the kind of game fans think about when they imagine two Hall of Famers going head-to-head.

In the first game of a doubleheader[1] at Dodger Stadium on June 20, 1965, 44-year-old Spahn took the mound for the New York Mets, while 29-year-old Koufax started for the Los Angeles Dodgers. Spahn allowed just four hits and two runs in seven innings, with most of the Dodgers' offense limited to the span of three batters in the sixth inning. But Koufax was better. Pitching a complete-game 2-1 victory, he struck out 12 Mets, and only a single mistake denied him his fourth career no-hitter.

The teams entered the game with almost opposite records. Walter Alston's Dodgers were in first place at 41-24, 3½ games ahead of the Milwaukee Braves and four ahead of the Cincinnati Reds. Casey Stengel's Mets were last in the 10-team National League at 21-43 with one tie, 19½ games back. The Dodgers had gone 7-3 in their previous 10 games; the Mets were 1-14 in their previous 15, including a four-game sweep by the Dodgers on June 11 through 13.

The matchup brought together two teams with popgun offenses. For the full 1965 season, the Dodgers and Mets both finished at or near the bottom of the NL in several key offensive categories, including runs per game, doubles, triples, home runs, RBIs, total bases, slugging percentage, and on-base plus slugging percentage (OPS).

Other season statistics, though, painted a fuller picture. The Dodgers were adept small-ballers, skilled at turning steals and sacrifices into run-scoring opportunities, as shown by their league-leading 172 stolen bases and 103 sacrifice bunts.[2] After hustling their way to runs, they relied on formidable pitching to make leads stand up. The Dodgers' staff led the NL in wins, ERA, complete games, and individual and team shutouts, and was second in strikeouts.

Koufax entered the June 20 game with a 10-3 record and a 2.04 ERA, plus a league-leading 135 strikeouts. He already had started twice against the Mets in 1965, spinning complete-game

wins both times. Most recently, on June 12, he threw a five-hit shutout against the New Yorkers at Shea Stadium.

Since the hapless Mets entered the NL in 1962, Koufax had compiled an 11-0 record in 12 games against them, including his first no-hitter. June 20, 1965, happened to be Father's Day,[3] which provided another reminder of the early Mets' futility. On Father's Day the previous year – June 21, 1964 – Jim Bunning of the Philadelphia Phillies had thrown a perfect game against the Mets.

Spahn, who served the Mets concurrently as pitching coach and starting pitcher, had won 360 games in a career that began in 1942 – making him the all-time leader in wins among lefties. The wins dried up, though, after the Braves sold him to New York in November 1964. Spahn entered the game with a 4-8 record and a 3.72 ERA. On April 20 he beat the Dodgers 3-2, pitching a complete game on Opening Night at Dodger Stadium. Spahn pitched another complete game against Los Angeles on June 11, only to lose 2-1 on an eighth-inning homer by opposing pitcher Don Drysdale.

Other than the pitchers, the left fielders for each team were the most notable starters, as both were involved in the game's decisive action.

The Dodgers had lost outfielders Tommy Davis and Willie Davis to injury. Lou Johnson and Wally Moon, inserted to plug the gaps, had also been hurt.[4] So Alston started 36-year-old Jim Gilliam,[5] who began the season as a Dodgers coach but was activated in late May to play third base when John Kennedy and Dick Tracewski hit poorly.[6] Gilliam entered the game hitting .348. Stengel, meanwhile, started 20-year-old rookie Ron Swoboda. Swoboda swung a promising power bat, leading the 1965 Mets with 19 homers, but had a subpar defensive reputation.[7]

With a near-capacity crowd of 52,248 packing Dodger Stadium,[8] the lefty aces set to work. Over the first three innings, Koufax was perfect with four strikeouts. Spahn allowed only a pair of infield singles to Maury Wills, who stalled at first base both times.

Mets second baseman Bobby Klaus entered the game with a .206 average, lowest among qualifying NL batters, but was in the lineup against Koufax because he hit right-handed.[9] With one out in the fourth, Klaus drew a walk on a full count. Mets radio broadcaster Ralph Kiner took pains to note that the New Yorkers wouldn't be perfect-game victims for a second straight Father's Day. Koufax got Charley Smith on a pop and Joe Christopher on a fly to right to end the inning. The Dodgers went down on three grounders in the bottom half.

With one away in the fifth, Mets first baseman Jim Hickman came to the plate. He'd been one of the team's steadier contributors in its first three seasons but was hitting only .143 in 1965 while bouncing between duty at first base, third base, and all three outfield positions. He'd hit three home runs thus far in the season – all off Chicago Cubs pitchers and all at Wrigley Field.[10]

Koufax hung a curve and Hickman jumped on it, drilling the ball over the 390-foot marker in left-center field to give the Mets their first hit and a 1-0 lead. After the game, Koufax told reporters that he "didn't have too good a curve" that day – although he caught the next batter, Roy McMillan, looking on a curve.[11]

Spahn and Koufax swapped one-two-three innings in the bottom of the fifth and the top of the sixth. It looked as though the Dodgers might continue the pattern in the bottom of the sixth: Koufax grounded out, and Hickman made a good play to field Wills' bunt and beat him to the bag.

Gilliam, who hit .267 in 86 career at-bats against Spahn, broke the lefty's streak of nine straight outs by popping a single into "uncatchable territory" in short left-center field.[12] With fans applauding rhythmically,[13] Wes Parker drew a walk, moving a Dodger into scoring position for the first time. Lefty-swinging center fielder and cleanup hitter Ron Fairly was next. He smacked a high slider[14] solidly to the opposite field, where it landed between Swoboda and the left-field line.

On the Mets' radio broadcast, Lindsey Nelson told listeners that the ball took an unexpected hop and Swoboda slipped while changing direction, falling back onto his hand to steady himself. The next day's New York Daily News and New York Times said the rookie overran the ball, while the Los Angeles Times simply said he "let a hit … get away from him."[15] Whether it was bad fielding or bad luck, Swoboda's stumble gave Parker just enough opportunity to steam all the way around from first and follow Gilliam across the plate with the go-ahead run. With Fairly on second base and Galen Cisco warming in the bullpen,[16] Spahn struck out John Roseboro to end the inning, but Los Angeles had moved ahead, 2-1.

Fairly was the game's final baserunner, but more drama was still to come. Spahn worked a perfect seventh with help from right fielder Christopher, who dived in the right-center-field gap to make a rolling, tumbling, inning-ending catch of Tracewski's liner. "There's the play of the ballgame, by far and away … a beautiful play by Joe Christopher," exulted Bob Murphy, the third member of the Mets' radio team.

In the top of the eighth, McMillan struck out for the third time in three at-bats, giving Koufax at least 10 strikeouts in a game for the 68th time in his career.[17] Spahn was scheduled to hit third, but Stengel sent rookie Danny Napoleon – the only right-handed bat on his bench[18] – to hit for the pitcher. Koufax set down Napoleon on three pitches for his 11th strikeout. Righty Larry Bearnarth worked a perfect eighth for New York, and Koufax returned to finish off his masterpiece. Billy Cowan popped foul to Kennedy, and Klaus struck out for Koufax's 12th and final whiff. Smith ended the game with a routine fly to Fairly, wrapping up the game in 1 hour and 52 minutes.[19]

Koufax surrendered only the homer to Hickman and two walks, while Spahn yielded just four hits and one walk. The New York Times described Koufax as "overpowering," adding that the Mets were "completely at the mercy of the hard-throwing Dodger left-hander." Spahn, the Times added, "deserved no worse than a tie."[20]

Koufax ended 1965 as the NL leader in wins, ERA, complete games, innings pitched, and strikeouts (a career-high 382). He picked up his fourth no-hitter on September 9, beating the Cubs 1-0 in a legendary game in which the teams combined for a single hit. Koufax won the NL Cy Young Award and placed second in Most Valuable Player voting behind Willie Mays. To top it off, he won two games – both shutouts – in the World Series as the Dodgers defeated the Minnesota Twins in seven games. One of the few blemishes on Koufax's season for the ages came on August 26: The Mets finally hung a loss on him, 5-2, as Koufax was outdueled by not-quite-21-year-old lefty Tug McGraw.

The Mets finished the season in the basement, but two of their key figures at the start of the year weren't around to see the end. Stengel, the team's manager since its inception, broke his hip after the game of July 24 and was forced into retirement. Spahn beat him out of town: The Mets announced his release as both pitcher and coach on July 14, when his record stood at 4-12.[21] The San Francisco Giants signed him a few days later, and he picked up three more wins in 16 appearances to close his career with 363 victories.

Addendum

Brief summaries of the five other games in which Sandy Koufax and Warren Spahn started against each other:

July 30, 1958: Braves 4, Dodgers 3, in Milwaukee: Spahn scattered six hits in a complete game; Koufax yielded six hits, five walks, and four runs in 7⅓ innings and took the loss.

June 17, 1959: Dodgers 10, Braves 2 (first game), in Los Angeles: Spahn lasted one-third of an inning and was charged with five runs on four hits and a walk. Koufax yielded just five hits – but six walks – in a complete-game win.

September 2, 1961: Braves 4, Dodgers 0, in Milwaukee: Spahn went all the way, giving up seven hits but no walks. Koufax gave up seven hits and four runs – only two earned – in seven innings and took the loss.

September 15, 1961: Dodgers 11, Braves 2, in Los Angeles: Spahn was yanked after facing five batters in the second inning and retiring none; he was charged with five earned runs in an inning-plus of work. Koufax went all the way in a five-hit, 10-strikeout performance.

June 13, 1962: Dodgers 2, Braves 1, in Milwaukee: Koufax pitched a three-hitter, with the only run coming on a homer by Roy McMillan. Spahn was good but not as good, giving up seven hits and two runs in eight innings while striking out seven.

SOURCES

In addition to the sources cited in the Notes, the author used the Baseball-Reference.com and Retrosheet.org websites for general player, team and season data and the box scores for this game:

www.baseball-reference.com/boxes/LAN/LAN196506201.shtml

www.retrosheet.org/boxesetc/1965/B06201LAN1965.htm

The New York Mets radio broadcast of the game was available on the Internet Archive at the time this story was written in January 2023. It served as a general source of background information, in addition to the specific items cited in the endnotes. The author thanks the unidentified person who recorded this game, and numerous other 1960s Mets games, off station WGY in Schenectady, New York, as well as those involved in digitizing the tapes.

NOTES

1 On the Mets' radio broadcast, Lindsey Nelson reported that the four scheduled starting pitchers in the doubleheader – Koufax and Don Drysdale for the Dodgers; Spahn and Frank Lary for the Mets – had combined for 761 career wins.

2 Shortstop Maury Wills accounted for 94 of those steals, leading the NL in that category for the sixth and final season in a row.

3 The Mets' radio broadcast team made several mentions of this.

4 Tommy Davis broke his ankle on the basepaths on May 1 against the San Francisco Giants and appeared in only 17 games that season. Willie Davis suffered a cracked rib in June in a collision with Mets first baseman Hawk Taylor and missed about two weeks. Johnson suffered a thumb injury against the Mets on June 12 when hit on the hand by a pitch from Al Jackson and did not bat again until June 22. Moon, in his last big-league season at age 35, was suffering from a pulled thigh muscle. Paul Hirsch and Mark Stewart, "Tommy Davis," SABR Biography Project, accessed January 19, 2023; Joe Trimble, "Pitching, Speed Could Send LA All the Way," *New York Daily News,* June 23, 1965: C26; Retrosheet box score for Dodgers-

Mets game of June 12, 1965; Bill Miller, "Sandy's One-Hitter Gets Split with Mets," *Pasadena* (California) *Independent,* June 21, 1965: 16.

5 Gilliam is most often thought of as an infielder, but he had played the outfield extensively early in his career with the Dodgers. He made 46 outfield appearances in 1955, 56 in 1956, and 75 in 1958. In the latter season, he made more appearances in left field than at any other position. At the time this story was written in spring 2023, Baseball-Reference and Retrosheet had minor discrepancies regarding Gilliam's game appearances in 1965. According to Baseball-Reference, Gilliam made 80 appearances at third base, 22 in the outfield, and 5 at second base. Retrosheet's breakdown was 82 games at third base, 22 in the outfield, and 3 at second base.

6 Jeff Angus, "Jim Gilliam," SABR Biography Project, accessed January 19, 2023.

7 Swoboda's SABR biography, written by Len Pasculli, makes several references to his struggles in the field, including a quote from manager Stengel: "He will be great, super, even wonderful. Now if he can only learn to catch a fly ball." Several of the news stories cited in these endnotes also mention Swoboda's reputation as a poor fielder.

8 This was the Dodgers' fifth-largest home crowd of the year. They'd had one larger crowd earlier in 1965 (52,357 on June 15 against the San Francisco Giants) and subsequently hosted three more (53,604 on July 28 against Cincinnati; 53,581 on September 6 against San Francisco; and 52,312 on September 29 against Cincinnati.)

9 According to the Mets' radio broadcast, the other second baseman on the team's roster that day was Chuck Hiller, a lefty hitter.

10 Hickman went deep on May 31 off Cal Koonce, then hit two homers on June 1, off Bob Buhl and Lindy McDaniel. Hickman closed 1965 with an average of .236, 15 homers, and 40 RBIs.

11 United Press International, "Koufax 1-Hits Mets as Dodgers Split," *Santa Maria* (California) *Times,* June 21, 1965: 6. The Mets' radio broadcast specified that McMillan struck out on a curve in the fifth.

12 Joe Trimble, "Mets Nip Drysdale, 3-2, After Koo 1-Hits 'Em, 2-1," *New York Daily News,* June 21, 1965: 54.

13 From the Mets radio broadcast.

14 Miller, "Sandy's One-Hitter Gets Split with Mets."

15 Trimble, "Mets Nip Drysdale, 3-2, After Koo 1-Hits 'Em, 2-1"; Joseph M. Sheehan, "Mets Down Dodgers, 3-2, After Koufax's 2-1 One-Hitter," *New York Times,* June 21, 1965: 39; Sid Ziff, "Swoboda Real Met," *Los Angeles Times,* June 21, 1965: Sports: 1. Sheehan and Ziff specified that Parker would have had to stop at third had Swoboda fielded the ball cleanly. At least one reporter also quoted Spahn as saying, "It looks like (Swoboda) overran the ball." Miller, "Sandy's One-Hitter Gets Split with Mets."

16 Mets' radio broadcast.

17 Frank Finch, "It's Bachelor's Day, Too, as Koufax Spins 1-Hitter at Mets," *Los Angeles Times,* June 21, 1965: Sports: 1.

18 Mets radio broadcast.

19 The Mets won the nightcap, 3-2.

20 Sheehan, "Mets Down Dodgers, 3-2, After Koufax's 2-1 One-Hitter."

21 United Press International, "Ask Waivers on Warren Spahn," *Stockton* (California) *Record,* July 14, 1965: 56.

Marichal-Koufax Duel Gets Ugly

August 22, 1965: San Francisco Giants 4, Los Angeles Dodgers 3, at Candlestick Park, San Francisco

BY ALAN COHEN

"For a moment, Watts had spilled over to the National Pastime."[1]

The intensity of a rivalry that began decades earlier on the East Coast heated up once again as the Giants and Dodgers contested yet another National League pennant in 1965. Going into action on August 22, the Dodgers led the league and were being chased by the Braves and Giants. The Braves, in their last year in Milwaukee, were a half-game out of first place, and the Giants trailed by 1½ games, having lost two of the first three games in a four-game series with Los Angeles.

The finale was played during a year of turbulence. In Los Angeles, the Watts riots commenced on August 11 and continued for six days. Although baseball games were played during the disturbances, the impact of the rioting was undeniable, especially on Dodgers players such as John Roseboro, who lived near the unrest. A few thousand miles from California, civil war had broken out in the Dominican Republic, the home country of Giants pitcher Juan Marichal.

The first three games of the series provided a fair amount of excitement. The Thursday game went 15 innings, with the Dodgers prevailing, and in the Friday game tempers flared when Giants catcher Tom Haller was called for interference when his glove made contact with Maury Wills' bat during a bunt attempt. Throughout the game, won by the Giants, the dugouts were alive with antagonism. Extra innings were again needed on Saturday as the Dodgers prevailed.

Sunday's game featured two pitching aces. Marichal (19-9) was going for his third consecutive 20-win season. In his most recent start, he shut out the Mets on three hits at Shea Stadium, lowering his ERA to 1.73. Sandy Koufax (21-4) was having another spectacular season. In his most recent decision, he tossed a 10-inning shutout, his fourth of the season, to defeat Pittsburgh. In each

SANDY KOUFAX
Los Angeles Dodgers—Pitcher

Sandy Koufax took the loss when the Dodgers and Giants brawled on August 22, 1965, at Candlestick Park. SABR: The Rucker Archive.

of his past four decisions, all complete-game wins, he reached double digits in strikeouts. In anticipation of a great mound duel, a season-high crowd of 42,807 fans descended on the ballpark.

The Dodgers gained the early lead when Ron Fairly doubled home Wills, who on the first pitch of the game bunted his way aboard. Koufax proceeded to strike out the side in the bottom of the first. Los Angeles added to its lead in the second. Wes Parker doubled and came home on a single by Roseboro. Wills made the last out of the inning but not before being knocked down by Marichal.

Tempers were getting hot. To start the bottom of the second inning, Koufax threw a pitch high and tight to Willie Mays, the ball sailing over the head of the Giants star. After Mays and Jim Ray Hart were retired on fly balls, light-hitting Giants shortstop Cap Peterson homered to bring the Giants to within a run of the Dodgers.

The Dodgers went down in order in the third inning, but not without incident. Fairly, who had doubled in his first at-bat, received a 90-mph message from Marichal, as a fastball sent him to the ground. Marichal stepped to the plate to lead things off for the Giants in the bottom of the inning. He had been pitching close to the Dodgers batters and the decking of Wills and Fairly had been duly noted by the Dodgers. What was next on the agenda? Umpire Shag Crawford, hoping to defuse the situation, warned both sides that any further head-hunting would result in ejections.

"Why you do that, cono?!" – Juan Marichal to John Roseboro, August 22, 1965[2]

The first pitch to Marichal was strike one. Koufax elected not to seriously retaliate although his second pitch was low and inside. Dodgers catcher Roseboro, in returning the pitch to Koufax, stepped behind Marichal and whizzed the ball past the Giants pitcher's head. A shocked Marichal turned toward Roseboro and asked about the throw back to Koufax.

Marichal then struck Roseboro, still masked, on the forehead with his bat, opening a two-inch gash. Benches cleared and a brawl ensued. Koufax charged the plate to grab the bat from Marichal. Mays left the Giants bench and restrained Roseboro. After 14 minutes, things calmed down and two players had to leave the game. Umpire Crawford (who suffered a spike wound while trying to separate Marichal and Roseboro) ejected Marichal. A wounded Roseboro, who would have his forehead bandaged in the clubhouse, was led off the field by the Dodgers trainer and replaced by Jeff Torborg.

The Giants sent up Bob Schroder to replace Marichal, and he became Koufax's fourth strikeout victim. After getting Tito Fuentes to fly out, Koufax had a loss of control, walking Jim Davenport and Willie McCovey. Mays stepped to the plate. He switched from peacemaker to major weapon and slammed his sixth home run in as many games over the left-field fence, giving the Giants a 4-2 lead. Koufax allowed only one hit over the balance of the game, but the damage had been done.

Ron Herbel came in to pitch for the Giants in the fourth inning and cruised through the Dodgers lineup for the next five innings, scattering three hits. The Dodgers mounted a threat in the ninth inning. With one out, Herbel hit Parker with a pitch, and Torborg singled, advancing Parker to third base. Manager Walter Alston sent up Wally Moon to pinch-hit for Koufax. Moon, though, did not get to bat. Giants manager Herman Franks signaled for a change, and left-hander Masanori Murakami came in from the bullpen. Right-handed hitter Don LeJohn was sent up to pinch-hit for Moon.

Murakami threw a double-play ball to LeJohn. The ball headed to Murakami, but second baseman Hal Lanier dropped the throw. All runners were safe and Parker scored LA's third run. Murakami then retired Wills on a popup and struck out Jim Gilliam to end the game.

Koufax was tagged with the loss, bringing his record to 21-5. Although the usually poor-hitting Koufax had been removed for a pinch-hitter, his bat had been more potent than usual in 1965. He came into the game with a .205 average and had put together a modest five-game hitting streak in July. In seven games that month, he went 8-for-18 (.444). Herbel, on the other hand, was a notoriously bad hitter. His 0-for-2 performance on August 22 brought his average for the season down to .037. His one hit in 1965 came on May 21 at Houston. It was his first big-league hit, and it came in his 56th career at-bat.

Mays's decisive homer was his 38th of the 1965 season and the 491st of his career. He went on to hit 52 home runs that year and received the second MVP award of his career. (Mays was noted as a five-tool player. He had a sixth tool and that was as a peacemaker.[3] This game was not the only time when he calmed things down. Eight years later, during his final season, he played peacemaker when a fight erupted during a playoff series between the New York Mets and the Cincinnati Reds.)

After the game, the teams headed east, the Giants to Pittsburgh and the Dodgers to New York. It was in New York that Roseboro finally made it to the hospital; he received 14 stitches to close the wound. In Pittsburgh, Marichal learned of his fate.

The pitcher received an eight-game suspension (stretched to 10 due to a couple of makeup games) for his role in the brawl and was fined $1,750 by the National League. Most in the area outside of San Francisco thought that the punishment by league President Warren Giles was far too lenient. Marichal did not return to action until September 2. During the balance of the season, he went 3-4. The four losses were ultimately the difference between first and second place for the Giants.

The Giants and Dodgers battled down the stretch. San Francisco won 14 straight games between September 4 and September 16 to take a 4½-game lead over the Dodgers and Cincinnati Reds. Los Angeles won 13 of its last 14 games to win the pennant by two games over the Giants.

Koufax, less than three weeks after the August 22 game, pitched his masterpiece. On September 9 he threw a perfect game against the Chicago Cubs, winning 1-0. Down the stretch he was spectacular. He won his last four decisions (including three shutouts) and finished with a 26-8 record. He brought his ERA down from 2.18 on August 22 to 2.04 and went on to win twice in the World Series against the Twins. He won the Cy Young Award and finished second to Mays in the MVP balloting.

The Dodgers defeated the Twins in the World Series with Koufax winning the clincher.

Roseboro sued Marichal and was awarded $7,500 in February 1970. Years later, the two reconciled and became friends.

SOURCES

In addition to the sources shown in the Notes, the author used Retrosheet.org, Baseball-Reference.com, and the following:

Byrne, Emmons. "Spahn Faces Pittsburgh," *Oakland Tribune*, August 23, 1965: 35, 37.

Finch, Frank. "Mays Breaks up the Fight – and the Ball Game, 4-3," *Los Angeles Times*, August 23, 1965: III-1.

Frizzell, Pat. "Bat Riot Perils Pennant Hopes," *Oakland Tribune*, August 23, 1965: 35, 37.

Kaplan, Jim. *The Greatest Game Ever Pitched* (Chicago: Triumph Books, 2011), 156-167.

Koppett, Leonard. "Marichal Hits Roseboro with Bat and Starts Brawl as Giant Top Dodgers," *New York Times*, August 23, 1965: 24.

Leavy, Jane. *Sandy Koufax: A Lefty's Legacy* (New York: Harper-Collins, 2002), 179-180.

Lederer, George. "Fight Results in Big Duel," *Long Beach* (California) *Independent*, August 23, 1965: C1-C2.

Marichal, Juan (with Lew Friedman). *Juan Marichal* (Minneapolis: MVP Books, 2017), 119-129.

Rathet, Mike (Associated Press). "Marichal Faces Suspension after Bitter Fight," *San Rafael* (California) *Daily Independent Journal,* August 23, 1965: 13.

NOTES

1   James S. Hirsch, *Willie Mays, the Life, the Legend* (New York: Scribner, 2010), 438.

2   John Rosengren, *The Fight of their Lives* (Guilford, Connecticut: Lyons Press, 2014), 113.

3   Hirsch on page 439 mentions how Mays took a seat beside Roseboro in the dugout and did everything in his power to prevent the brawl from expanding.

'A Million Butterflies' and One Perfect Game for Sandy Koufax

September 9, 1965: Los Angeles Dodgers 1, Chicago Cubs 0, at Dodger Stadium

BY MIKE HUBER

On September 9, 1965, Sandy Koufax became the "no-hittingest pitcher of all time,"[1] the first major-league pitcher to throw four no-hitters.[2] His record-setting accomplishment was a 1-0 perfect game against the Chicago Cubs. In front of a relatively small crowd of 29,139 fans at Dodger Stadium, Koufax, who came into the contest with a 21-7 record, locked in a pitchers' duel with a fellow lefty, Bob Hendley. Koufax had been unsuccessful in his previous five starts in winning his 22nd game.

Hendley had just been recalled from the minors. After four seasons with Milwaukee and San Francisco, he had been traded on May 29, 1965, from the Giants (with Harvey Kuenn and Ed Bailey) to the Cubs (in exchange for Dick Bertell and Len Gabrielson). Hendley also pitched a brilliant game, giving up only one hit, and the only run scored off him was unearned. Koufax went him one better.

Cubs center fielder Don Young, in his major-league debut, led off the game. Koufax's first pitch was "a curve ball that bounced in the dirt."[3] After that, his control was nearly perfect, as he retired Young with a popout to second baseman Jim Lefebvre. Koufax then struck out Glenn Beckert and Billy Williams looking. Hendley was equally sharp, getting the first three Los Angeles batters in order. Koufax was in top form, striking out at least one Chicago batter in every inning. Future Hall of Famer Ernie Banks struck out three times, all swinging. According to Dodgers radio announcer Vin Scully, the first Banks strikeout came in the second inning on a forkball. Every Cubs batter except shortstop Don Kessinger struck out at least once. On the other side, Hendley had only three strikeouts, Koufax and Lefebvre (twice).

Hendley was in no danger though the first four innings. The only run of the game came in the fifth. Lou Johnson led off with a walk and advanced to second on a sacrifice by Ron Fairly. Hendley might have had a play at second base when he fielded the bunt, but he dropped the ball and got the sure out at first. With Lefebvre batting, Johnson stole third base and then continued home as Cubs catcher Chris Krug made a throwing error. The run was unearned, and Hendley still had not allowed a hit.

The Cubs had a chance in the sixth inning, when Krug hit a groundball to shortstop Maury Wills. Wills' throw to first was in the dirt, but Wes Parker dug the ball out for the first out of the inning, preserving the string of consecutive outs. This was the only threat to Koufax's perfect game. Kessinger then hit a grounder to third and was just erased, as third baseman Jim Gilliam was playing in for a possible bunt. Koufax then struck out Hendley to end the inning.

Both pitchers had no-hitters intact until the seventh inning, when Koufax retired the side on a strikeout and two fly outs. That's when Koufax "really started to feel as though I had a shot at [the perfect game]."[4] In the home half, the Dodgers had several exciting at-bats. Lead-off batter Gilliam hit a grounder to third baseman Ron Santo, who fielded the high bouncer and just threw out Gilliam at first. Willie Davis followed with a slow grounder to first. Banks fielded the ball and then tagged out Davis, who tried sliding into the bag to avoid the tag. Johnson then hit a ball past first base that barely made it to the outfield grass before rolling into foul territory. By the time Banks retreated to field it, Johnson had motored to second base for a two-out double. However, he was stranded there as Fairly grounded out to short, and the Dodgers did not score, but Hendley's bid for a no-hitter was gone.

In the top of the eighth inning Koufax, facing the middle third of the Cubs' order, struck out Santo looking and Banks and Byron Browne swinging. The Dodgers tried to add a run in their half of the eighth, but Jeff Torborg's long fly to left was caught by Browne in front of the bullpen gate.

Before the ninth inning, Vin Scully told his producers, "Let's make a recording."[5] Fans can still hear Scully call the final three outs. The Cubs had sent up two pinch-hitters. After Krug struck out, Joey Amalfitano pinch-hit for Kessinger and struck out swinging. The broadcast climaxed when Scully exclaimed, "Swung on and missed, a perfect game!" as Harvey Kuenn, who batted for Hendley, struck out to end the game.[6] The game lasted one hour and 43 minutes. The final six Chicago batters (and seven of the final nine) went down on strikes.

The next day, *Los Angeles Times* writer Frank Finch started his story with, "A Michelangelo among pitchers, Sandy Koufax produced his masterpiece when he pitched a perfect no-hit, no-run game against the Chicago Cubs."[7] After the historic game, Koufax had told reporters, "I had a real good fastball, and that sort of helps your curve."[8] He added, "The last three innings I had the best stuff I threw all night, and perhaps all year."[9]

With his accomplishment, Koufax surpassed the record of three career no-hitters held by three different pitchers: Larry Corcoran, Cy Young, and Bob Feller.[10] This was just the eighth perfect game pitched in major-league history.[11]

As of the beginning of the 2023 season, this was the only perfect game thrown by a Dodgers pitcher.[12] Further, this marked the fourth consecutive season in which Koufax had pitched a no-hit game. His record of four career no-hitters stood for 16 years, until Houston Astros fireballer Nolan Ryan pitched his fifth no-hit game on September 26, 1981, against the Los Angeles Dodgers.[13]

Hendley faced only 26 batters in his eight-inning gem. On any other day, his performance would have grabbed the top headlines. Five days after Koufax's perfect game, on September 14, 1965, he and Hendley faced each other again, this time at Chicago's Wrigley Field. The Cubs prevailed, as Hendley beat Koufax 2-1.

The Cubs had only three groundball outs. Koufax's 14 strikeouts were the highest strikeout total in a perfect game (equaled by Matt Cain on June 13, 2012). Koufax finished the season with 382 strikeouts, which bested Rube Waddell's twentieth-century record of 349 set in 1904. But Ryan topped this mark eight years later, striking out 383 in 1973.

Teammates congratulate Sandy Koufax after the left-hander hurled his perfect game against the Chicago Cubs in 1965. Courtesy of National Baseball Hall of Fame.

Koufax finished the 1965 campaign with a record of 26-8. His earned run average was 2.04, and he pitched 27 complete games out of 41 starts. He was the unanimous choice for the 1965 Cy Young Award and finished second in the NL's Most Valuable Player Award voting.[14]

AUTHOR'S NOTE

This game was reminiscent of another pitchers' duel, when Chicago's Hippo Vaughn and Cincinnati's Fred Toney pitched a double no-hitter through regulation on May 2, 1917. Vaughan held the Reds hitless for 9⅔ innings, before two hits produced a run. Meanwhile, Toney pitched 10 hitless innings for the win and part of history.

An abridged version of this article was published in SABR's book *No-Hitters* (2017), edited by Bill Nowlin. As Scully described Krug's ninth-inning at-bat against Koufax, the future Hall of Fame broadcaster uttered the timeless phrase, "There's 29 thousand people in the ballpark and a million butterflies."[15]

SOURCES

In addition to the sources mentioned in the Notes, the author consulted Baseball-Reference.com, MLB.com, Retrosheet.org, SABR.org and the following sources:

"The Cubs haven't been no-hit since Sandy Koufax pitched," https://ftw.usatoday.com/2013/08/the-cubs-havent-been-no-hit-since-sandy-koufax-pitched.

"Sandy Koufax pitches perfect game," http://history.com/this-day-in-history/sandy-koufax-pitches-perfect-game.

To listen to Vin Scully call the final strike of Sandy Koufax's perfect game on September 9, 1965, type https://www.mlb.com/video/koufax-s-perfecto-c13062863 into your internet browser.[16]

https://www.baseball-reference.com/boxes/LAN/LAN196509090.shtml

https://www.retrosheet.org/boxesetc/1965/B09090LAN1965.htm

NOTES

1   "Sandy Now No. 1 on No-Hit Parade," *Los Angeles Times*, September 10, 1965: 46.

2   Koufax's other no-hit games were pitched on June 30, 1962, May 11, 1963, and June 4, 1964.

3   "Koufax Eyed 'Perfection' All the Way," *Chicago Tribune*, September 10, 1965: 53.

4   Charles Maher, "Even Koufax Admits Game 'Nearly Perfect," *Los Angeles Times*, September 10, 1965: 45.

5   "Recorded History: Vin Scully Calls a Koufax Milestone," found online at https://www.npr.org/2007/04/23/9752592/recorded-history-vin-scully-calls-a-koufax-milestone. Accessed January 2023.

6   Harvey Kuenn, who struck out to end the perfect game, also made the last out in Koufax's 1963 no-hit game against the San Francisco Giants. In that game, Kuenn grounded out to the pitcher, Koufax.

7   Frank Finch, "Hendley Loses, 1-0, on 1-Hitter," *Los Angeles Times*, September 10, 1965: 45.

8   Maher.

9   "Koufax Eyed 'Perfection' All the Way."

10 The first to achieve this total was Chicago White Stockings hurler Larry Corcoran, whose no-nos took place on August 19, 1880, against the Boston Red Caps; September 20, 1882, against the Worcester Worcesters; and June 27, 1884, against the Providence Grays. Next was Cy Young, who pitched his first no-hitter as a member of the Cleveland Spiders on September 18, 1897, against the Cincinnati Reds; followed by two as a pitcher for the Boston Americans and Red Sox on May 5, 1904, against the Philadelphia Athletics; and June 30, 1908, against the New York Highlanders. Cleveland Indians star Bob Feller was the third pitcher to tie the mark, on April 16, 1940, against the Chicago White Sox; April 30, 1946, against the New York Yankees; and July 1, 1951, against the Detroit Tigers.

11 For the complete list, see https://www.mlb.com/news/all-time-perfect-games. Accessed January 2023.

12 "Los Angeles Dodgers no-hitters," found online at http://nonohitters.com/los-angeles-dodgers-no-hitters/. Accessed April 2015.

13 "Baseball Sisco Kid Style: Sandy Koufax Becomes the First Pitcher to Throw 4 No-Hitters September 9, 1965," http://baseballsiscokidstyle.blogspot.com/2014/09/sandy-koufax-becomes-first-pitcher-to.html. Accessed April 2015.

14 In 1965, Koufax led the majors in victories (26), earned-run average (2.04), innings pitched (335⅔) and strikeouts (382). He received all 20 first-place votes for the Cy Young Award. Koufax finished second to San Francisco's Willie Mays in the MVP race, receiving six first-place votes (177 vote points) to Mays' nine first-place votes (224 vote points). Before 1967, only one pitcher was awarded the Cy Young Award. Koufax won his third Cy Young Award in 1966, the season before MLB began the practice of awarding a winner from each league.

15 Found online at https://ia800701.us.archive.org/16/items/VinScullyCallsThe9thInningOfSandyKoufaxsPerfectGame/VinScully-1965-KoufaxPerfectGame9thInning_64kb.mp3. Accessed April 2015 and January 2023.

16 Hear Vin Scully call just the final strike at https://www.mlb.com/video/koufax-s-perfecto-c13062863.

On Two Days' Rest, Koufax Sends Dodgers to World Series

October 2, 1965: Los Angeles Dodgers 3, Milwaukee Braves 1, at Dodger Stadium

BY JAKE BELL

By October, exhaustion was a standard part of every game for Sandy Koufax. But one out from clinching a World Series berth, the Los Angeles Dodgers ace reached new depths of fatigue. "I don't remember ever being so tired in my life," Koufax later confessed, but downplayed it for manager Walt Alston. "I'm dog-tired, but I think I have enough left to get this guy."[1] The manager nodded and strolled back to the dugout as Denis Menke stepped into the batter's box.

Koufax had ample reason to be tired. Even before taking the mound for this penultimate game of the 1965 season on just two days' rest, the lefty led the majors in innings pitched, batters faced, and complete games.[2]

Despite Los Angeles leading the National League standings most of the year, this opportunity to clinch the pennant seemed unlikely just two weeks earlier. In September, the San Francisco Giants posted a record of 21-9, including a 14-game winning streak, putting them 4½ games ahead of L.A. and the Cincinnati Reds. But the Dodgers bounced back, finishing the month with 13 straight wins and a two-game lead in the standings.

Koufax, who led all of baseball with 25 wins, won three games during that streak, all of them shutouts. When considered with his perfect game, Koufax hadn't allowed a run in a win since September 5. A 26th Koufax win would not only send the Dodgers to the World Series, it would also tie the NL record for wins by a left-hander.[3]

The only pitcher with a chance to tie Koufax's wins total was on the mound for the opposition. With 24 wins, Tony Cloninger had cemented himself as the Milwaukee Braves' ace in the two years since Warren Spahn had left the team. His hope for a 25th victory wasn't unfounded, as the Braves were the only team that had scored any runs off Koufax in his previous four starts. Eleven days earlier, in their final game in

Sandy Koufax won eight games for the Dodgers in September-October of 1965.
SABR: The Rucker Archive.

Milwaukee, the team's hitters sent Koufax to the showers in the third inning, plating five runs on two home runs, including the only grand slam of Frank Bolling's career.

Before the game, the Dodgers watched some of the Giants-Reds game before taking infield practice, knowing that, for pennant purposes, a San Francisco loss would be as good as an LA win. But Cincinnati stranded three runners in scoring position through the first three innings. "Let's go win it ourselves!" shouted rookie Jim Lefebvre.[4]

Milwaukee leadoff hitter Felipe Alou went down on Koufax's 370th strikeout of his record-shattering season. Two games earlier, he surpassed the major-league record of 349 K's, set by Rube Waddell of the Philadelphia Athletics in 1904.[5] A groundout by Hank Aaron and his 371st strikeout, of Gene Oliver, ended the inning.

Cloninger started the game third in the NL in walks, and with the second batter he faced, Jim Gilliam, he tied teammate Wade Blasingame at 116 apiece. When the 36-year-old Gilliam stole second, catcher Oliver fired the ball into center field, allowing Gilliam to advance to third.

Cloninger also began the game with the major-league lead in wild pitches and threw his 22nd with two outs. His first pitch to Ron Fairly was high and away, just beyond Oliver's mitt, putting Gilliam and the Dodgers up a 1-0 in a hitless inning.

In the second, Koufax struck out the side. Cloninger responded with a three-up-three-down inning of his own.

Woody Woodward slapped a single up the first-base line to lead off the third, but when Alomar attempted to bunt him over, Koufax pounced on the ball and fired to second for the out. Cloninger, attempting to sacrifice Alomar to second, reached on a throwing error by third baseman Gilliam, but Milwaukee failed to capitalize. Alou struck out for a second time and Aaron smashed a line drive directly into Gilliam's glove to end the inning.

After Cloninger retired the Dodgers in order again, Oliver tied the game with a leadoff solo home run, his career-high 21st of the year. Left fielder Lou Johnson tracked the ball and gave Dodger fans some hope that it might be reachable, but he crashed into the wall as it fell into the stands.

Pain radiated through Koufax's arthritic elbow, but he managed to get three more outs, two of them K's. He also issued his first walk of the game, to Mack Jones.

With the score tied, Cloninger set down the Dodger hitters in order again. It was around this time that the PA announcer at Dodger Stadium informed the crowd of 41,574 that San Francisco had beaten Cincinnati, 3-2.

About 350 miles up the California coastline, some Giants players turned on a transistor radio in the locker room at Candlestick Park. They couldn't pick up Vin Scully's play-by-play, but a local station was reading updates between songs. A few players sliced into a watermelon while manager Herman Franks, having discarded his uniform pants, paced the floor and sucked on an ice cream cone.[6]

Koufax struck out Cloninger and Aaron in a scoreless fifth. Cloninger opened the bottom of the fifth by walking Johnson, the first Dodger baserunner since Gilliam walked. "[Cloninger's] a great competitor," Spahn, now a 44-year-old fifth starter for the Giants, assured his teammates around the radio.[7]

Lefebvre, on his way to being named NL Rookie of the Year, hit a pop foul, but first baseman Joe Torre lost the easy out in the sun. Several pitches later, the rookie cracked a grounder toward third baseman Miguel de la Hoz. It appeared to be a double-play ball, but became the Dodgers' first hit, shooting into left field to bring Johnson around to third.[8]

Wes Parker slapped a groundball toward first, and Torre quickly relayed home, sending Johnson scurrying back. Oliver's throw to third appeared to be in time to catch Johnson, but umpire Tony Venzon signaled safe. "Caramba!" shouted de la Hoz as the Milwaukee bench erupted in protest.[9]

Cloninger walked John Roseboro on five pitches, and when his next three to Koufax were all balls as well, manager Bobby Bragan gave him the hook. "He was trying too hard," Bragan lamented. "He wanted to get that 25th victory."[10]

Ken Johnson's first pitch missed the strike zone, walking Koufax and bringing Lefebvre home for a 3-1 Dodgers lead. The walk was charged to Cloninger, his 119th, which tied him with Pittsburgh Pirates All-Star Bob Veale for the NL lead.

"There's nothing we can do about it now," Franks declared while chomping a cigar, "We're still alive. For four innings, anyway."[11]

The next three Dodger hitters went down in order, ending the 29-minute half-inning. Despite the break, Koufax was still exhausted and changed his approach. For the rest of the game, he worked from a stretch, even without runners on base. "I didn't have to raise up my arms so high and I didn't have to kick my leg up either," he later explained. "Kicking that leg took too much effort."[12] He retired the side in order.

The longer the game wore on without a Milwaukee runner advancing beyond first base, the quieter the San Francisco clubhouse grew. Willie Mays was one of the first Giants to leave.[13] "He's got a two-run lead in the seventh inning?" one Giants player grumbled to another. "I'll listen to the rest of it in my car."[14]

"If I wasn't so old, I'd cry," muttered Franks.[15]

When the ninth inning finally came, Koufax was out of steam. He surrendered a leadoff single to de la Hoz, who was replaced by pinch-runner Ty Cline. Alston began to worry about his pitcher tiring, noting, "He was getting the ball high and that generally is a tell-tale sign."[16] But Koufax struck out Jones,[17] and Roseboro snapped the pitch to second base to catch Cline stealing.

Needing one more out, Koufax walked Woodward on five pitches, then threw a ball to Menke, prompting the meeting with Alston at the mound.

"I told him, 'Yes, I'll get 'em out.' After you tell the manager that, you'd better get them out," Koufax later recalled.[18] With the count at 2-and-2, Menke hit a towering fly ball to left field.

"I thought it was never coming down," recounted Lou Johnson, the 31-year-old who'd spent 13 years in the minors, bouncing around various systems, including Milwaukee's. As he settled underneath, fans began to rush the field. "The onliest way I wasn't going to catch it was if the good man up above got in my way."[19]

The Dodgers swarmed Koufax, dancing and hugging in celebration. As they popped bottles of champagne and sprayed each other in the clubhouse, Koufax declined the bubbly and went to sit alone in a tiny kitchenette. "I'm tired. Very tired," the sweaty pitcher whispered through his pain. "I don't believe I could have gone any longer."[20]

"Hey, Sandy," reliever Bob Miller interrupted, pouring champagne over the back of Koufax's head before the Los Angeles ace could turn around to acknowledge his name.[21]

"I feel like I'm 100 years old," Koufax said.[22]

SOURCES

In addition to the sources cited in the Notes, the author accessed Baseball-Reference.com, Stathead.com, and Retrosheet.org.

https://www.baseball-reference.com/boxes/LAN/LAN196510020.shtml

https://www.retrosheet.org/boxesetc/1965/B10020LAN1965.htm

NOTES

1   Associated Press, "Koufax Admits He's Tired: 'Feel Like I'm a Hundred,'" *Santa Cruz* (California) *Sentinel*, October 3, 1965: 19.

2   His 326⅔ innings pitched at the game's start represented two complete games more than the 308⅓ innings of teammate Don Drysdale, the only other pitcher over 300. Both had faced 1,262

hitters, well ahead of Bob Gibson's 1,198 in third place, and Koufax's 26 complete games were two better than Juan Marichal. With his 20th complete game in the next day's season closer, Gibson finished third in the NL with 299 innings pitched and 1,233 batters faced. New York Yankee Mel Stottlemyre led the American League in all three categories with 291 innings pitched, 1,188 batters faced, and 18 complete games.

3   Rube Marquard set the record of 26 wins in 1912, which was matched by Carl Hubbell in 1936. Koufax beat the record the following year when he went 27-9. Twenty-seven wins remain the NL record for lefties, matched by Steve Carlton with a 27-10 record in 1972. Lefty Grove holds the major-league record with 31 wins for the Philadelphia Athletics in 1931.

4   Paul Zimmerman, "Weary Koufax Still Calmest in Midst of Victory Celebration," *Los Angeles Times,* October 3, 1965: D4.

5   He'd also long since passed his own NL record of 306, set in 1963. Koufax's mark represented the modern record, but was the third highest total in baseball history. In 1884, Old Hoss Radbourn and Charlie Buffinton struck out 441 and 417 batters, respectively.

6   Jack McDonald, "Bye Bye World Series," *San Francisco Examiner,* October 3, 1965: III-3.

7   McDonald, "Bye Bye World Series."

8   Lefebvre knocked another single in the sixth, giving him both of the Dodgers' only hits for the game.

9   Frank Finch, "It's All Over!," *Los Angeles Times*, October 3, 1965: D1. Blasingame was ejected for his complaints to the umpire.

10   Joseph St. Amant, "Bedlam in Dodger Clubroom," *San Francisco Examiner*, October 3, 1965: III-3. Bragan was ejected by home-plate umpire Al Forman in the eighth inning for arguing balls and strikes.

11   George Ross, "Champagne in L.A. – Party's Over in S.F.," *Oakland Tribune*, October 3, 1965: 39.

12   Associated Press, "Koufax Admits He's Tired."

13   Charles Maher, "Giants Players Not Interested in L.A. Game," *Los Angeles Times*, October 3, 1965: D4.

14   Ross, "Champagne in L.A."

15   Ross, "Champagne in L.A."

16   Zimmerman, "Weary Koufax Still Calmest."

17   Jones was Koufax's 382nd strikeout victim of the campaign, which remains the record for NL pitchers and the major-league record for left-handed pitchers. In 1973, right-hander Nolan Ryan struck out 383 as a member of the California Angels.

18   Zimmerman, "Weary Koufax Still Calmest."

19   Sid Ziff, "Dodgers Steal It," *Los Angeles Times*, October 3, 1965: D3; Zimmerman, "Weary Koufax Still Calmest in Midst of Victory Celebration."

20   Associated Press, "Koufax Admits He's Tired."

21   St. Amant, "Bedlam in Dodger Clubroom."

22   "Koufax Admits He's Tired."

Koufax's Clutch Hitting (!) Gives Dodgers the Series Lead

October 11, 1965: Los Angeles Dodgers 7, Minnesota Twins 0, at Dodger Stadium, Los Angeles
Game Five of the 1965 World Series

BY NORM KING

This edition of the fall classic had so many bizarre twists and turns that they might as well have had Rod Serling do the pregame show. First there were the Twins beating both of the Dodgers' best pitchers, Don Drysdale and Sandy Koufax. Then the punchless Dodgers turned around and won the next two games by a combined score of 11-2, hitting as many home runs in the victories (two) as the powerful Twins. The strange twists continued in Game Five, which the Dodgers won by a touchdown, 7-0. Cue the music.

Koufax started Game Five. He had lost Game Two, but was so dominant a pitcher in 1965, winning the pitching triple crown with 26 wins, a 2.04 ERA, and a then-record 382 strikeouts, that even Serling's vivid imagination couldn't see him losing two games in a row. He didn't, pitching a four-hitter and striking out 10. The Dodgers offense helped with 14 hits off three Twins pitchers, and by driving Twins catcher Earl Battey ... well, batty, with four stolen bases, three by center fielder Willie Davis and one by shortstop Maury Wills. The Dodgers raised their team batting average for the Series to .302, 60 points higher than their regular-season average.

Jim Kaat once again started for the Twins, but unlike his start in Game Two, when he went all the way in a 5-1 Twins victory, this was not to be his day, as he pitched only 2⅓ innings, giving up four runs (three earned) on six hits. The carnage started with the leadoff hitter, Wills, who led off the bottom of the first with a ground-rule double to right. Third baseman Jim Gilliam followed with a single that scored Wills. Davis followed that with a bunt attempt. Twins third baseman Harmon Killebrew handled it cleanly, but second baseman Frank Quilici, who was covering first, lost sight of Killebrew's throw. The ball ended up in the outfield, allowing Gilliam to score and Davis to reach third. It was Quilici's second error of the Series.

Davis stole his first base of the game in the third after singling to right with one out. Left fielder Lou Johnson singled to center, scoring Davis. Right fielder Ron Fairly then doubled to left-center. Fairly's hit ended Kaat's day much earlier than Jim had anticipated.

By the fourth inning, knowing that it was Koufax who had the 4-0 lead, the Dodgers began messin' with the Twins' heads. Wills beat out an infield hit and with Gilliam up, pitcher Dave Boswell threw to first six straight times in an effort to keep Wills close to the bag. He should have known that wasn't going to work, because Wills, on his way to a four-hit day, stole second anyway, and scored when Gilliam singled to right-center field, making it 5-0.

"I didn't know [Boswell] before the game, so I had no line on him," said Wills. "But it became a challenge. I just wanted to make sure I got a good jump because I was determined to steal the first time he threw home."[1]

Meanwhile, ho-hum, Koufax was perfect through four. Killebrew broke up the perfecto with a single to center in the fifth that, according to newspaper accounts, Davis should have caught but lost in the background of fans' white shirts. Koufax still ended up facing the minimum that inning as the next batter, Battey, grounded into a double play and left fielder Bob Allison struck out.

"In the fifth, Harmon Killebrew looped a hit into center field," wrote Ted Smits. "Willie Davis ... misjudged it. When he finally ran in, it was too late. He managed to catch the ball momentarily in his glove but dropped it in a sliding fall."[2]

The perfect illustration of what kind of day it was for the Twins came in the seventh. Fairly hit a ball to deep short off pitcher Jim Perry that resulted in an infield hit. He advanced to second on first baseman Wes Parker's sacrifice. With first base open and facing the number-eight hitter, catcher John Roseboro, the Twins made the standard move of walking him to face the pitcher. Koufax, with an .097 lifetime batting average, singled to center to drive in Fairly. Wills singled to drive in Roseboro for the final run of the game.

The Twins got two meaningless singles in the ninth, but the game ended when center fielder Joe Nossek hit a liner to Wills, who capped a great day by catching the ball, then throwing to second for a game-ending double play.

Although Koufax put in a magnificent performance, he wasn't entirely happy with the way he pitched that day: "I'm not disappointed with the way I pitched, but I have pitched better," he said. "I was behind the hitters too much and I became awfully tired after the seventh inning."[3]

This modest self-assessment was of little comfort to the Twins, who came into Los Angeles with a 2-0 Series lead but headed back to Minneapolis down 3-2. Twins third-base coach Billy Martin griped before Game Five about the hardness of the Dodger Stadium infield, saying balls traveled faster as a result.

"This infield is hard as a rock and the sun bakes it down," he said. "And they use a 1,200-pound roller on it. That makes the infield exceptionally hard. Balls will go through this infield that wouldn't go through in other ballparks."[4]

The Twins were happy to leave Dodger Stadium, but it's not as if they were unfamiliar with the locale. They played the California Angels there nine times that season (the Angels moved to Anaheim in 1966).

Anyway, the Twins flew back to Minneapolis after the game and were greeted into the warm bosoms of more than 1,000 fans upon their return. At least the bosoms would have been warm if the temperature weren't 37 degrees.

SOURCES

In addition to the sources cited in the Notes, the author consulted *Sports Illustrated* and Baseball-Reference.com.

https://www.baseball-reference.com/boxes/LAN/LAN196510110.shtml

https://www.retrosheet.org/boxesetc/1965/B10110LAN1965.htm

NOTES

1   Mike Rathet (Associated Press), "Koufax Fans Too Many, Wills Says," *Appleton* (Wisconsin) *Post-Crescent,* October 12, 1965.

2   Ted Smits (Associated Press), "Only Second Guessing Was How Twins Got Four Hits." *Appleton* (Wisconsin) *Post-Crescent,* October 12, 1965.

3   Joe Reichler (Associated Press), "Modest Sandy Wasn't Angry," *San Bernardino* (California) *Daily Sun,* October 12, 1965.

4   Associated Press, "Dodger Infield 'Too Hard,' Twins Complain," *San Bernardino* (California) *Daily Sun,* October 12, 1965.

Koufax Has Nothing to Atone for with Classic Game Seven Performance

October 14, 1965: Los Angeles Dodgers 2, Minnesota Twins 0,
at Metropolitan Stadium, Bloomington, Minnesota
Game Seven of the 1965 World Series

BY NORM KING

Unfortunately for the Minnesota Twins, there were no Jewish holidays that would prevent Sandy Koufax from pitching for the Los Angeles Dodgers in Game Seven of the 1965 World Series. As a result, he came. He pitched. He shut the Twins out, 2-0. That's really all you need to know.

Actually, there's a little bit more to Game Seven than that. Dodgers manager Walter Alston elected to start Koufax on two days' rest, rather than Don Drysdale, who hadn't pitched in four days. Alston made it clear during a pregame meeting that Drysdale would take over if Koufax faltered.

Jim Kaat started for the Twins, also on two days' rest, and Twins manager Sam Mele was not afraid to change pitchers at the first sign of trouble. He ended up using five pitchers in the game, all of whom shut the Dodgers out after Kaat gave up two runs in the fourth.

"You hate to lose but we didn't disgrace ourselves," said Mele. "We were beaten by the best pitcher that there is anywhere."[1]

Oddly enough, Koufax didn't breeze through the early innings. Some luck, plus good defense, kept the Twins off the scoreboard until he found his rhythm in the middle frames. He walked right fielder Tony Oliva and third baseman Harmon Killebrew back-to-back in the first inning with two out, prompting Alston to get Drysdale up in the bullpen. But Koufax struck out catcher Earl Battey to escape any damage. In the third, Drysdale began warming again after shortstop Zoilo Versalles singled with one out. Versalles stole second, but had to return to first when center fielder Joe Nossek was called out for batter interference. Koufax then struck out Oliva for the third out.

Lou Johnson opened the fourth with a home run to deep left, giving the Dodgers a 1-0 lead. Ron Fairly followed that with a double and scored on a single by first baseman Wes Parker. That was the end of the season for Kaat, who was replaced on the mound by Al Worthington.

The Twins' most serious threat came in the fifth. With one out, second baseman Frank Quilici doubled to left. Koufax walked the next batter, Rich Rollins, who was pinch-hitting for Worthington. Versalles was up next and he hit a scorcher toward third base that could have scored one, possibly two runs. However, third baseman Jim Gilliam made an outstanding backhanded stab and touched the bag for the force on Quilici. Nossek then grounded into a force play at second and the inning, and the Twins, were done.

"I didn't even have time to think about (the play)," said Gilliam. "It was about a foot from the bag and as I grabbed it, I slipped to one knee. But I saw the runner and knew I had time so I got up and stepped on the bag."[2]

"Gilliam's play could have been the turning point," said Mele. "Rollins has a chance to score from first, depending on what happens in the left-field corner. It was a great play, no doubt about it."[3]

Minnesota went three-up-three-down in the sixth, seventh, and eighth. Killebrew got a base hit with one out in the ninth, but – stop me if you've heard this one – Koufax struck out the next two batters to win the game with a flourish.

The game capped a remarkable World Series for Koufax, who was chosen Series MVP for the second time (he also earned the honor in 1963 when the Dodgers swept the New York Yankees). He went 2-1 and gave up only one earned run in 24 innings pitched (a 0.38 ERA), struck out 29, and threw two shutouts. He even had a hit and an RBI.

While Koufax deserved the award, he wasn't the only suitable candidate. Ron Fairly had 11 hits in the Series, for a .379 batting average, with two home runs, three doubles, and a 1.069 OPS. Wills also had 11 hits, for a .367 average. If they had an unsung-hero award, Lou Johnson would have won easily. Johnson was a 31-year-old career minor leaguer with only 96 games of major-league experience prior to the 1965 season. After playing for six different organizations in such far-flung outposts as St. Jean, Quebec, and Ponca City, Oklahoma, he got his big break in 1965 when regular left fielder Tommy Davis broke his ankle on May 1. Johnson proved to be a sparkplug for the Dodgers, helped carry them to the pennant, and batted .296 with two home runs in the fall classic, one of which was the Series-winning hit.

Associated Press sportswriter Joe Reichler summed up the reasons for the Dodgers' victory quite succinctly: "In the final essence, it was Dodger pitching with the shutouts and the ability of Los Angeles' supposedly weak hitters to all but match the Twins in home run power that swung the balance to the Dodgers."[4]

As for Mele, if he didn't have enough on his plate during the Series, his wife, Connie, was several days overdue with the couple's fifth child. In fact, Sam was told during Game Five that she had gone into labor, but that turned out to be a false alarm. Connie gave birth to their fifth child, Scott, four days after the Series ended.

SOURCES

In addition to the sources cited in the Notes, the author consulted Baseball-Reference.com and Retrosheet.org.

https://www.baseball-reference.com/boxes/MIN/MIN19651014o.shtml

https://www.retrosheet.org/boxesetc/1965/B10140MIN1965.htm

NOTES

1   William Leggett, "The Final Strength Was Sandy," *Sports Illustrated*, October 25, 1965.

2   Jack Hand, "Shutout Sandy Stymies Twins to Give Dodgers World Series," *San Bernardino* (California) *Daily Sun*, October 15, 1965.

3   Hand.

4   Joe Reichler, "Koufax Dominant Figure of World Series Champions," *Janesville* (Wisconsin) *Daily Gazette*, October 15, 1965.

Sandy Koufax and Jim Bunning Face Off, Combine for 28 Strikeouts Over 11 Innings

July 27, 1966: Los Angeles Dodgers 2, Philadelphia Phillies 1 (12 innings), at Dodger Stadium, Los Angeles

BY AARON TALLENT

The 2005 US House Government Reform Committee hearing that put Mark McGwire, Sammy Sosa, José Canseco, Rafael Palmeiro, and Curt Schilling on a witness panel to testify on steroid use is a widely remembered event in baseball history. What is often forgotten is that the sole witness on the first panel was then US Senator and Hall of Fame pitcher Jim Bunning [Republican of Kentucky], who closed his testimony by saying, "I remembered players didn't get any better as they got older. We all got worse. When I played with Henry Aaron and Willie Mays and Ted Williams, they didn't put on 40 pounds and bulk up in their careers and they didn't hit more home runs in their late 30s than they did in their late 20s."[1]

Bunning was not being hyperbolic. His statistics did decline in the later years of his career, but before Father Time started catching up with him, he and Sandy Koufax faced off in a barnburner with both men pitching at the top of their game. The Los Angeles Dodgers won 2-1 over the Philadelphia Phillies at Dodger Stadium on July 27, 1966, in the first-ever meeting between pitchers who had thrown perfect games.[2]

The two had been competing against each other since college and not always on the baseball diamond. As a member of the University of Cincinnati freshman basketball team in the 1953-54 season, Koufax averaged 9.7 points a game[3] and also played crosstown rival Xavier, whose freshman team was coached by Bunning.[4]

"He was pretty good. But I think he made the right career choice, don't you?" Bunning later joked.[5]

They both made their major-league debuts in 1955 and Bunning recorded his first and only 20-win season in 1957 with the Detroit Tigers. Koufax, of course, took a little longer to hit his stride before recording arguably the best six-season run of pitching in major-league history from 1961 to 1966.

Bunning's perfect game was a 6-0 Phillies win over the New York Mets at Shea Stadium on Father's Day, June 21, 1964.

Koufax's came the next season when he blanked the Chicago Cubs 1-0 at Dodger Stadium on September 9, 1965.

When they met in July of 1966, the Dodgers were 57-40 and riding a five-game winning streak. They were 1½ games out of first place behind the San Francisco Giants, while the Phillies were 7½ games back with a record of 52-37 and had lost seven of their last 10 games.[6] A crowd of 44,937 was on hand that night as Koufax took the mound in the first inning.

He struck out Cookie Rojas before giving up a single to John Briggs. However, Harvey Kuenn hit into a double play and Bunning followed with a hitless bottom of the first. Phillies third baseman Dick Allen opened the second inning with a 430-foot home run deep to left field, his first since July 8, and his 22nd of the season, for a 1-0 lead.[7] Koufax then took control of the inning, striking out Jackie Brandt and Bill White. The strikeout of White was the 2,267th of Koufax's career, surpassing Lefty Grove's total and putting him at 10th on the all-time list. Koufax finished his career with 2,396 strikeouts.

In the bottom of the inning, Bunning hit catcher John Roseboro in the shin – the first of three batters he plunked with pitches – forcing Roseboro to leave the game in the fourth inning (x-rays were negative), but a pop fly by John Kennedy got Philadelphia out of the inning with Roseboro and Jim Gilliam on base. (Bunning went on to hit a National League-high 19 batters. Don Drysdale, a pitcher more famous for plunking batters, hit 17. To add another point on Koufax's greatness, he did not hit a single batter that season.)

Koufax struck out Bunning for the first time in the game in the third inning. Bunning would return the favor in the bottom of the inning and neither let the other on base for the entire contest.

After pitching five straight scoreless innings, Bunning started the sixth by giving up a double to left fielder Jim Barbieri and hit shortstop Maury Wills with a pitch. A fly ball by Willie Davis sent Barbieri to third and Bunning walked first baseman Dick Stuart to load the bases. A sacrifice fly by Jeff Torborg, who had replaced Roseboro at catcher, drove in Barbieri to tie the game at 1-1.

Neither pitcher allowed a hit in the seventh inning, but Bunning found himself in trouble in the eighth. First, he gave up a single to Barbieri. Wills sacrificed him to second. Bunning then hit Willie Davis, putting runners on first and second base, before recovering by retiring Stuart on a pop fly and striking out Torborg.

The next two innings saw little offensive action, with Koufax only giving up a single to Dick Allen in the ninth and walking Bob Uecker in the 10th. Bunning opened the 11th by giving up consecutive singles to Davis and Stuart before getting ground-outs by Torborg and Ron Fairly. After intentionally walking Jim Gilliam, he struck out Jim Lefebvre.

By the end of 11th inning, Koufax had thrown 163 pitches and struck out a season-high 16 batters, giving him at least 200 for the sixth straight year, Bunning fanned 12 in a game that was still tied.[8] Neither pitcher would get the win or loss.

"I was reluctant to pitch Koufax even as many as 11 innings. The last time he worked that long was three years ago when he pitched 12 innings against St Louis," said Dodgers manager Walter Alston.[9]

Alston replaced Koufax with Phil Regan to start the 12th inning and he made quick work of the middle of the Phillies' batting order, striking out Johnny Callison and forcing ground-outs from Allen and Bob Uecker. Darold Knowles took over for Bunning and started by walking second baseman Nate Oliver on four pitches. Catcher Clay Dalrymple, whom Phillies manager Gene Mauch had tapped to replaced Uecker, let a pitch to Lou Johnson get past him, putting Oliver in scoring position on second base. Johnson fouled off two bunt attempts before lining drive down the left-field line to send Oliver home for a 2-1 win. Regan got the win for one inning's work, putting his record at 8-1; Knowles took the loss.

Koufax had received a cortisone shot in the arthritic elbow of his left pitching arm three days before the game[10] and said after the contest, "I felt better last night than at any time this year. For one of the few times, I had both a good fastball and curve."[11] Describing the latter, Bunning said, "I guarantee you his ball when he threw a curve did very unphysical things."[12]

But Koufax's left arm was at a point where he could no longer fully straighten it and he retired after the 1966 season, but not before one more showdown with Bunning. The Dodgers led the San Francisco Giants by two games going into the last day of the season and needed to win one game of a doubleheader against the Phillies at Philadelphia's Connie Mack Stadium to clinch the pennant. Los Angeles dropped the first game, 4-3, so it was up to Koufax to seal the deal. This time he pitched a complete game and struck out 10 in a 6-3 win, giving Bunning the loss.

Koufax finished the year with career highs of 27 wins, 27 complete games, and a 1.73 ERA. The three personal bests led both leagues. He also tallied 317 strikeouts and won his third Cy Young Award in four years. Bunning finished with 19 wins, a major-league-leading 41 game starts, and 314 innings pitched. As he portended in his congressional testimony nearly 40 years later, he never reached those milestones again.

While Koufax retired after the 1966 season, Bunning continued to play until 1971, and finished his career with a 224-184 record, a 3.27 ERA, and 2,855 strikeouts.

SOURCES

In addition to the sources cited in the Notes, the author consulted Baseball-Almanac.com, Baseball-Reference.com, and Retrosheet.org.

https://www.baseball-reference.com/boxes/LAN/LAN196607270.shtml

https://www.retrosheet.org/boxesetc/1966/B07270LAN1966.htm

NOTES

1 Bunning's comment is included in "Restoring Faith in America's Pastime: Evaluating Major League Baseball's Efforts to Eradicate Steroid Use," the record of a hearing by the US House Government Reform Committee, March 17, 2005. https://www.govinfo.gov/content/pkg/CHRG-109hhrg23038/html/CHRG-109hhrg23038.htm.

2 Jane Leavy, *Sandy Koufax: A Lefty's Legacy* (New York: HarperCollins, 2002), 229.

3 Gregory Orfalea, "The Incomparable Career of Sandy Koufax," *The Atlantic*, October 6, 2016. Retrieved on February 20, 2024. https://www.theatlantic.com/entertainment/archive/2016/10/sandy-koufax/503036/.

4 Leavy, 51.

5 Steve Wulf, "Sandy Koufax' final victory might have been his best," ESPN.com, September 30, 2016. Retrieved on February 20, 2024. https://www.espn.com/mlb/story/_/id/17671148/los-angeles-dodgers-pitcher-sandy-koufax-relives-finest-game.

6 "Baseball Standings," *Pasadena Independent*, July 27, 1966: 23.

7 Bill Conlin, "Even Great Effort by Bunning Can't Pull Phils Out of Tailspin," *Philadelphia Daily News*, July 28, 1966: 60.

8 Frank Finch, "Johnson's Hit in 12th puts L.A. Half Game Out," *Los Angeles Times*, July 28, 1966: CC1, CC3.

9 Alex Kahn, "Koufax, Bunning Praised." *Hollywood Citizen-News*, July 28, 1966: 14.

10 United Press International, "Shot of Cortisone Helps Koufax Keep Groove Against Phils," *Lebanon* (Pennsylvania) *Daily News*, July 28, 1966: 36.

11 Kahn.

12 Leavy, 8.

Sandy's Last Shutout

September 11, 1966: Los Angeles Dodgers 4, Houston Astros 0 (first game of doubleheader), at Dodger Stadium

BY PAUL SEMENDINGER

He had walked up the small hill 391 previous times in his big-league career. Standing atop that mound, he had accomplished so much: four no-hitters, including the only perfect game in Dodgers history, and 39 total shutouts among the many highlights. What Sandy Koufax did not know that Sunday afternoon was that he was about to throw the 40th and final regular-season shutout of his illustrious career.

On September 11, 1966, Koufax was the starting pitcher for the Los Angeles Dodgers in the first game of a doubleheader against the Houston Astros at Dodger Stadium. The Dodgers came into this game in second place in the National League,[1] a half-game behind the Pittsburgh Pirates. By the time this day was over, the Dodgers were in first place, never to relinquish that top spot in the standings.

The Astros were a second-division club in their fifth season of existence. To date in the season, they had won 63 games against 82 losses, while the Dodgers, the reigning World Series champions, were 81-59.

The Dodgers had won the two preceding games from Houston, both by shutouts. On Friday night September 9, Claude Osteen threw a three-hitter and won, 7-0. On Saturday afternoon Don Drysdale threw 8⅓ innings of four-hit scoreless ball and was relieved by Phil Regan, who got the win in the bottom of the 10th.[2]

On the mound opposing Koufax was 19-year-old right-hander Larry Dierker, who over the course of his career won 139 major-league games. On this day he was in just his second full season but already one of the better Astros pitchers, one of three that year who won 10 or more games. Dierker won in double figures nine times in his career, including winning 20 games in 1969 (one of two seasons when he was an All-Star). When he entered the game to face Koufax that Sunday afternoon, Dierker had an 8-6 record with a 3.47 ERA.

Koufax, already a two-time Cy Young Award winner, boasted a 22-8 record and a 1.87 ERA.

This might have looked like a mismatch, but three months earlier, on June 14, these two pitchers had faced each other at Dodger Stadium and Dierker got the better of the matchup, pitching a five-hit shutout and and handing Koufax only his second loss of the season. In Dierker's last start, on September 5, he shut out the St. Louis Cardinals.

The first batter to face Koufax was right-handed-hitting Ron Davis. Davis reached the big leagues briefly with Houston in 1962, and now in 1966 had finally made it back to the big leagues. He was no match for Koufax and struck out to begin the game.

If Koufax had thoughts about a no-hitter, he didn't have much time to entertain them. Shortstop Sonny Jackson, the next batter, reached on an infield hit to second base. But Joe Gaines lined out to center field and Chuck Harrison was Koufax's second strikeout victim.

Sandy Koufax's final shutout was the 40th of his career and fifth of the 1966 season. SABR: The Rucker Archive.

In their half of the first inning, despite a leadoff single by Maury Wills, the Dodgers went down quietly after Jim Gilliam hit into a double play.

On this day, Koufax did not have it easy. That became evident in the top of the second inning. Future Hall of Famer Joe Morgan began the inning with a single and went to third on a double by the next batter, catcher John Bateman. With runners at second and third, and no outs, Koufax got Bob Aspromonte to ground out to third, struck out Aaron Pointer, and got Dierker on a pop fly to second.

On the mound in the early going, Dierker proved to be Koufax's match. He retired the Dodgers in order in the second inning.

In the third, Koufax retired the Astros in order. Dierker allowed a leadoff hit to Lou Johnson, who was thrown out trying for a double. The next two batters were retired quickly.

In the fourth inning, Koufax again retired the Astros in order. Wills led off the Dodgers half with a bunt single. He was sacrificed to second by Gilliam. One out later, Ron Fairly singled home Wills with the first Dodgers run.

The Astros tried to answer back quickly. Aspromonte led off the fifth with a double. After Pointer flied out and Dierker struck out, Davis walked. The scoring threat ended when Jackson grounded out to second base.

The Dodgers gave Koufax a comfortable cushion in their half of the fifth. With one out, Lou Johnson reached on an error by Astros shortstop Jackson. Wes Parker walked, and the runners moved up when Astros catcher John Bateman threw wild to first on a pickoff attempt. The notoriously weak-hitting Koufax walked to load the bases. Wills' infield single brought home the Dodgers' second run. One out later, Willie Davis doubled home the Dodgers' third and fourth runs. That fourth run was the second-to-last time Koufax ever scored in a game.

In the Astros' sixth, Koufax walked a batter and in the seventh he allowed two more singles. Pointer, who hit the second single in the seventh inning, was the last Astro to reach base. A double-play grounder ended the inning, and Koufax retired the Astros in order in the eighth and ninth.

Though Koufax had to pitch out of trouble occasionally, the *Fort Worth Star Telegram* noted that he "breez[ed] to his 23rd victory."[3] By this point in his career, Koufax pitching well – especially against a second-division club – wasn't big news. The *Los Angeles Times* commented that Koufax was "in trouble only occasionally."[4]

Koufax was a great strikeout pitcher, but in this game he got by, especially in the final innings, without striking out many batters. He struck out six Astros in all and walked two. The last player to strike out against Koufax in this game was Gaines to start the sixth inning. That was the 2,357th punchout of Koufax's career and tied him for seventh place on the all-time strikeout list with Robin Roberts.[5] In his next start, against the Pittsburgh Pirates, Koufax struck out Gene Alley to take sole possession of seventh place.[6]

After the game, noting his lack of strikeouts in the final innings, Koufax remarked, "I had a good curve early, but in the last four innings I stuck mostly with my fastball."[7]

This 40th shutout was the last of Koufax's career. Plagued by pain in his pitching elbow, he retired in November at the age of 30. But his shutout, combined with a 1-0 whitewashing of the Astros in the second game gave the Dodgers sole possession of first place. The win in the second game closed out a four-game series with the Astros, a series in which Houston failed to score a single run.[8]

SOURCES

In addition to the sources cited in the Notes, the author consulted Baseball-Reference.com and Retrosheet.org.

https://www.baseball-reference.com/boxes/LAN/LAN196609111.shtml

https://www.retrosheet.org/boxesetc/1966/B09111LAN1966.htm

NOTES

1　The major leagues did not go to division play until 1969, when both leagues expanded to 12 teams.

2　The win improved Regan's won/lost record to 13-1. Mike Cuellar went the distance for the Astros, but gave up a leadoff single to Maury Wills, who was sacrificed to second, took third on an infield grounder, and scored on a single by Al Ferrara.

3　"LA Wins Two, Takes Top Spot," *Fort Worth Star Telegram*, September 12, 1966: 15.

4　Frank Finch, "Blank, Blank - Dodgers Lead Loop," *Los Angeles Times*, September 12, 1966: 47.

5　"Astros Lay Goose Egg, and Dodgers on Top," *Los Angeles Evening Citizen News*, September 12, 1966: 16.

6　Christy Mathewson was sixth on the all-time list, with 2,507.

7　"Wills Beef Cleared Air," *San Francisco Examiner*, September 12, 1966: 64.

8　The win in the second game closed out a four-game series with the Astros, a series in which Houston failed to score a single run. The game scores were 7-0, 1-0, 4-0, and 1-0.

Sandy Koufax's Last Regular Season Hurrah

October 2, 1966: Los Angeles Dodgers 6, Philadelphia Phillies 3 (second game of doubleheader), at Connie Mack Stadium, Philadelphia

BY MARK KANTER

Sandy Koufax, the Los Angeles Dodgers' superstar left-hander, won his final major-league game on Sunday October 2, 1966.

The Phillies had taken the first game of a doubleheader, 4-3, in Philadelphia, when Chris Short came on in relief and won his 20th game.[1]

When the Dodgers lost the opener of the doubleheader, they had to keep tabs on the San Francisco Giants' game against the Pittsburgh Pirates. The Dodgers wanted to avoid a three-game playoff by winning the second game. Koufax, who had 26 wins in the season far, was pitching on two days of rest. While waiting to learn about the outcome of the second Giants-Pirates game, he reportedly said something akin to "The hell with it. Let's win the goddamn game."[2] The Giants and Pirates went into extra innings before the Giants finally won, 7-3, in 11 innings, while the Dodgers and Phillies were playing their second game of the day.

Jim Bunning, who was 19-13, started strong in the top of the first inning when both shortstop Maury Wills and third baseman Dick Schofield went down on strikeouts. Center fielder Willie Davis grounded out, Bunning to first baseman Bill White. Koufax had a slightly more difficult start. Center fielder Jackie Brandt led off the bottom of the first with a single to Wills. Right fielder Cookie Rojas sacrificed Brandt to second base when the bunt was hit to Koufax, who threw the ball to Jim Lefebvre covering first base. Dick Groat singled to third baseman Schofield, leaving men on first and third with one out. Koufax struck out third baseman Dick Allen. Left fielder Harvey Kuenn grounded out to third.

Bunning made it through the top of the second inning when Dodgers right fielder Ron Fairly singled to right. Lefebvre flied out to Kuenn. Left fielder Lou Johnson popped out to second baseman Tony Taylor and catcher John Roseboro popped out to third baseman Allen.

Taylor and White went down on strikes against Koufax to start the Phillies' half of the inning. Catcher Bob Uecker grounded out to Wills, who threw the ball to first baseman Wes Parker to finish out the inning.

The Dodgers scored three times in the third inning. Parker worked a walk against Bunning. He stole second base while Koufax was batting. After Koufax struck out, Wills hit a fly ball to Kuenn. Schofield drove a single to center field to score Parker. Davis hit a long two-run home run to right field that increased the score to 3-0. Fairly then flied out to Taylor.

Koufax, for his part in the bottom of the third, got Bunning to hit a comebacker. Brandt flied out to Fairly and Rojas lined out to Wills.

Lefebvre led off the top of the fourth with a double to right field. Johnson got a bunt single that put runners on first and third. Roseboro hit a sacrifice fly to Brandt, making the score 4-0. Johnson stole second base and moved to third on catcher Uecker's throwing error. Bunning intentionally walked Parker to get to Koufax, who struck out. Wills grounded out to Groat to end the inning.

Groat led off the bottom of the fourth and reached base on Wills' error. Allen, who was emerging as a big star with 40 home runs and 110 RBIs, went down on strikes. Kuenn flied out to right field for the second out. Taylor reached on an infield single to third, putting runners on first and second. Koufax got out of trouble by striking out White.

Bunning got the Dodgers out in order in the top of the fifth inning: Schofield grounded to shortstop, Davis flied to center, and Fairly grounded to shortstop.

After Koufax struck out Uecker leading off the bottom of the fifth, he started to feel some discomfort in his back, especially after working to pinch-hitter Gary Sutherland, batting for Bunning. For the rest of the game, between innings, the Dodgers trainers and retired pitching legend Don Newcombe popped Koufax's back into place.[3] Sutherland flied out to Johnson in left field for the second out. Brandt grounded out to second baseman Lefebvre to end the inning.

The Phillies brought in 21-year-old Rick Wise to pitch in the top of the sixth inning.[4] Lefebvre flied out to center fielder Brandt. Johnson beat out an infield hit to third. Roseboro flied to Brandt for the second out of the inning. Johnson stole second base. Wise intentionally walked Parker to face Koufax. Shortstop

Groat fielded Koufax's grounder and got an unassisted force out at second base.

Koufax was still feeling the effects of the knot in his back but had an easy sixth, getting Rojas to pop out to third and striking out Groat and Allen, ending the inning with the Dodgers still leading 4-0.

Wise had an easy seventh, striking out Wills and getting Schofield and Davis on groundballs. Koufax, in the bottom of the inning, got Kuenn on a fly ball to right field and Taylor on a groundball to shortstop. With two outs, White doubled to right field, but Uecker grounded out to third base.

The Dodgers' Fairly doubled to left to begin the eighth. Lefebvre bunted and third baseman Allen's error put runners on first and third with nobody out. But Phillies shortstop Groat snagged Johnson's liner and doubled Lefebvre off first. But Phillies second baseman Taylor booted Roseboro's grounder and Fairly scored, giving the Dodgers a 5-0 lead. Wise struck out Parker to end the inning.

Johnny Briggs, pinch-hitting for Wise, coaxed a walk out of Koufax to begin the bottom of the eighth. Center fielder Davis caught Brandt's fly ball, Rojas popped out to Schofield at third, and Groat grounded to shortstop Wills, who stepped on second base to force out Briggs.

Darold Knowles relieved Wise in the top of the ninth inning. He struck out Koufax, then walked Wills and surrendered a single to Schofield, with Wills stopping at second base. Willie Davis's groundout to second moved the runners up, Taylor to White, advancing both baserunners. Fairly's single to right scored Davis; Schofield also attempted to score, but right fielder Rojas's throw home snuffed him out at home plate. Koufax and the Dodgers had a comfortable 6-0 lead heading into the bottom of the ninth. Dodgers manager Walter Alston decided to let Koufax finish the game.

Sandy Koufax struck out 10 and beat the Phillies in his last regular-season start. SABR: The Rucker Archive.

It was a near thing. Leadoff batter Dick Allen reached base on an error by third baseman Lefebvre and Kuenn singled to left. With runners at first and second base, Tony Taylor's single to center gave the Phillies their first score of the game, and there were still runners at first and second for Bill White, whose double to right field scored both and made it a 6-3 game with no outs. But Koufax made quick work of the Phillies, fanning Uecker for the first out, getting pinch-hitter Bobby Wine on a grounder to shortstop, and striking out Brandt – his 10th strikeout of the game – to seal his 27th win of the season and his last career win.

Koufax said, after the game, "Thank God it's over." Some sportswriters suggested that "it" was culmination of winning the National League pennant on the final day of the season as compared to the Baltimore Orioles, who had won the American League pennant by nine games. Many, including ESPN's Steve Wulf, have suggested that this may have been Koufax's most consequential win.[7] Pitching on short rest, he navigated through a tense ninth inning with a bad back. He knew the ramifications that emanated from this game. He got the last three batters with a flourish and finished his regular-season major-league career.[8]

Koufax finished his final season with a record of 27-9. He led the majors in wins, ERA (1.73), strikeouts (317), and complete games (27), Not surprisingly, Koufax won his third Cy Young Award.

A final note

The author had a virtual front-row seat watching this event. Sandy Koufax's last major-league win was the first full game that the author, as a 10-year-old boy, ever watched on television. The game was telecast in the Philadelphia region on Philadelphia's Channel 6, WFIL. Byrum Saam, Bill Campbell, and former Phillies legend Richie Ashburn were the announcers.

SOURCES

In addition to the sources cited in the Notes, the author consulted Baseball-Reference.com and Retrosheet.org.

https://www.baseball-reference.com/boxes/PHI/PHI196610022.shtml

https://www.retrosheet.org/boxesetc/1966/B10022PHI1966.htm

NOTES

1   David Skelton, "A Season-Ending Doubleheader and Its Impact on the 1966 World Series," *Baseball Research Journal,* Fall 2014. https://sabr.org/journal/article/a-season-ending-doubleheader-and-its-impact-on-the-1966-world-series/, accessed March 12, 2023.

2   Steve Wulf, "Sandy Koufax' Final Victory Might Have Been His Best," ESPN.com, September 30, 2016. https://www.espn.com/mlb/story/_/id/17671148/los-angeles-dodgers-pitcher-sandy-koufax-relives-finest-game, accessed May 8, 2023.

3   George Lederer, "Sandy's Dramatic Win Clinches Pennant Dodgers' Magic Number 32," (32 is Koufax's uniform number. Lederer is suggesting that the number 32 is magic for Koufax and the Dodgers.) *Long Beach* (California) *Press Telegram,* October 3, 1966: 25.

4   Wise was later traded for Steve Carlton. Joseph Durso, "Cardinals Trade Carlton to Phillies and Get Wise," *New York Times,* February 26, 1972: 21.

5   Glenn Stout and Richard Johnson, *The Dodgers: 120 years of Dodgers Baseball* (New York: Houghton Mifflin Company. 2004), 296.

6   Associated Press, "Victory Bath: Champagne and Shaving Cream," *Los Angeles Times,* October 3, 1966: III, 1.

7   Wulf.

8   Koufax did pitch in Game Two of the 1966 World Series, giving up just one earned run in six innings, but was bested by Baltimore's Jim Palmer, who threw a four-hit shutout.

Contributors

MARC Z AARON is a lifelong Yankees fan, having grown up in the Bronx. Despite this fact, he idolized Sandy Koufax and had the thrill of speaking with Sandy in connection with the SABR biography of Koufax he authored. Marc has been to games in Dodger Stadium and has contributed numerous bios to the SABR BioProject. He now resides in Pinehurst, North Carolina, where he does not play golf but continues to play competitive tournament tennis.

JAKE BELL is a writer who lives in the shadow of Camden Yards in Baltimore's Pigtown neighborhood. Despite living in Phoenix for more than 30 years and his parents being Diamondbacks season-ticket holders, he'd never seen a Dodgers game in person until they visited the Nationals in 2024.

CHARLIE BEVIS is the author of *Baseball Biography: A Comprehensive History*, a web-book freely accessible on his website, Bevis Baseball Research. During his 40 years as a researcher and writer of baseball history, he has written eight hard-copy books, two dozen journal articles, and more than 65 biographical profiles for the SABR BioProject. He writes baseball from his home in Chelmsford, Massachusetts.

LUIS BLANDÓN, a Washington, DC, native, is a producer, writer, and researcher in video and documentary film production and in archival, manuscript, historical, film, and image research. His creative storytelling has garnered numerous awards, including three regional Emmys®, regional and national Edward R. Murrow Awards, two TELLY awards, and a New York Festival World Medal. His writing has been published in several platforms. He was senior researcher and manager of the story development team for two national television programs. He served as the principal researcher for several authors including for *The League of Wives* by Heath Hardage Lee and her current biography project, *The Mysterious Mrs. Nixon: The Life and Times of Washington's Most Private First Lady*. Luis has a master's degree in international affairs from the George Washington University.

KURT BLUMENAU is a former journalist who now works in corporate communications in the Boston area. He is a regular contributor to SABR's Games Project and BioProject.

THOMAS J. BROWN JR. is a lifelong New York Mets fan. He also became a Durham Bulls fan after moving to North Carolina in the early 1980s. Tom was a national-board-certified high-school science teacher for 34 years before retiring in 2016. He taught science to ELL students during the last 10 years of his career and continues to provide support and guidance for his former ELL students. Tom joined SABR in 1995 after a visit to Cooperstown on his honeymoon. He became active in SABR after his retirement and has written numerous biographies and game stories, mostly about the Mets. Tom also travels as much as possible with his wife. He has traveled to five continents and all 50 states. Tom and his wife also visit major-league and minor-league ballparks across the country whenever they travel. He also loves to cook, keeping track of what he cooks on his blog, Cooking and My Family.

PAUL BROWNE is the author of *The Coal Barons Played Cuban Giants: A History of Early Professional Baseball in Pennsylvania, 1886-1896*, published by McFarland & Company, Inc. His article on the Cuban Giants' first victory over a major-league team appears in *Inventing Baseball: The 100 Greatest Games of the Nineteenth Century*. His *Mundell's Solar Tips* appears in the 2013 *National Pastime*. Browne has been a member of SABR since the mid-1990s and has had several player biographies posted at the SABR BioProject site. He has also contributed articles to McFarland's journal *Black Ball*, SABR's Nineteenth Century and Minor Leagues committees, as well as local newspapers. Browne is executive director of the Carbondale Technology Transfer Center.

A lifelong White Sox fan now living in Cedarburg, Wisconsin, **KEN CARRANO** works as the business operations manager for SABR. He has been a SABR member since 1992 and has contributed to several SABR publications and the SABR Games Project. Ken and his Brewers fan wife Ann share two children, two golden retrievers, and a mutual disdain for the blue side of Chicago.

ALAN COHEN has been a SABR member since 2011. He chairs the BioProject fact-checking committee, serves as vice president-treasurer of the Connecticut Smoky Joe Wood Chapter, and is a datacaster (MiLB stringer) with the Eastern League Hartford Yard Goats, the Double-A affiliate of the Colorado Rockies. He also works with the Retrosheet Negro Leagues project and serves on SABR's Negro League Committee. His biographies, game stories, and essays have appeared in more than 70 baseball-related publications. He cheered the Giants on in his youth and was a fan of Sandy Koufax. In 1964 he had the opportunity to visit both Candlestick Park and Dodger Stadium after graduating from high school. He has four children, nine grandchildren, and one great-grandchild, and resides in Connecticut with his wife, Frances, their cats, Zoe and Ava, and their dog, Buddy.

CARTER CROMWELL spent 11 years as a sportswriter for daily newspapers – covering athletics at the high school, collegiate, and professional levels – and followed that with a career in corporate public relations. Currently he works with an independent pro baseball team in the U.S., writes for baseball-related websites, and has contributed to multiple projects of SABR. His other passions include family, world travel, and rescue dogs.

RICHARD CUICCHI joined SABR in 1983 and is an active member of the Schott-Pelican Chapter. Since his retirement as an information technology executive, Richard authored *Family Ties: A Comprehensive Collection of Facts and Trivia about Baseball's Relatives*. He has contributed to numerous SABR BioProject and Games publications. He does freelance writing and blogging about a variety of baseball topics on his website, TheTenthInning. com. Richard is a regular contributor to CrescentCitySports.com, where he writes about New Orleans baseball history. Richard lives in New Orleans with his wife, Mary.

LARRY DEFILLIPO is a retired aerospace engineer who lives in Kennewick, Washington, with his wife, Kelly. A left-handed Jewish pitcher born in Brooklyn, he briefly played in college and so for obvious reasons he's been an avid Koufax fan as long as he can remember. His work has been published in SABR's *Baseball Research Journal, The National Pastime* and *Yankee Stadium 1923-2008: America's First Modern Ballpark;* and he has presented at the Fred Ivor-Campbell Nineteenth Century Baseball Conference. He's authored an array of ballplayer and ballpark biographies for SABR's BioProject and dozens of game stories for SABR's Games Project, with an emphasis on uncovering firsts and otherwise undocumented records.

JOHN FREDLAND is an attorney and retired Air Force officer. As an undergraduate at Rice University, he covered Rice's nationally ranked baseball teams for the school newspaper, the *Rice Thresher*. John received his law degree at Vanderbilt University, then served as an active-duty attorney in the Air Force's Judge Advocate General's Corps for 20 years. He lives in San Antonio, Texas, and chairs SABR's Baseball Games Project Research Committee.

CRAIG GARRETSON was born and raised in New Jersey, but his father-in-law is a Brooklyn native who as a boy in the 1950s would have much rather been at the ballpark than in Hebrew school. Craig, a member of SABR since 2019, makes his third appearance in a SABR publication following his contributions to *Yankee Stadium 1923-2008 - America's First Modern Ballpark* and *Willie Mays: Five Tools.*

ED GRUVER has been a sportswriter for four decades, covering the Philadelphia Philles and Baltimore Orioles, the World Series, playoffs, and All-Star Games. He is the author of 12 sports books, including two on baseball – *Koufax* and *Hairs vs. Squares: The Mustache Gang, the Big Red Machine, and the Tumultuous Summer of '72*. He is a contributor to SABR's BioProject and Games Project as well as more than 30 sports books.

VINCE GUERRIERI is a journalist and author in the Cleveland area. He's the secretary/treasurer of the Jack Graney SABR Chapter, and has contributed to the SABR BioProject, the SABR Games Project, and several SABR anthologies. Additionally, he's written about baseball history for a variety of publications, including *Ohio Magazine, Cleveland Magazine, Smithsonian,* and *Defector.* He can be reached at vaguerrieri@gmail.com, or found on Twitter @vinceguerrieri.

A love of baseball was instilled in **ANDREW HARNER** from childhood, but since he had next to no athletic skills, he instead dove into the game's history and pored over box scores as often as he could. And because baseball history wasn't offered as a college major, he settled for the next best thing – a bachelor's degree in sports journalism with a minor in history. He graduated from Bowling Green State University in 2010 and spent nearly seven years as a sports editor before leaving the newspaper industry to pursue a career in hospitality management. Andrew has since published baseball research for *HowTheyPlay* and spent a little over a year producing online NFL content for *Sports Illustrated*. He has been married to his wife, Elizabeth, since 2011, and they have two daughters.

BRUCE HARRIS has been a SABR member since 2006. A New Yorker, he became a Cubs fan after seeing the Cubbie patch on the uniform sleeve of Lou Brock's 1964 Topps card. He still thinks about his beloved 1969 Cubs and wishes things had turned out differently. He has contributed to SABR's Biography Project; Games Project; *Metropolitan Stadium: Memorable Games at Minnesota's Diamond on the Prairie, Yankee Stadium, America's First Modern Ballpark;* and the *Baseball Research Journal.*

JEFF HOWARD is a lifelong resident of the Northwest Side of Chicago and is a frequent contributor to the SABR Games Project. Jeff attended Luther College, played DIII football, had a weekly sports column, and read news for the campus radio station. On graduation, he worked in the insurance industry and recently retired from a research analyst position handling claim appeals. He has mentored youth and organized multiple community baseball, softball, and basketball teams as a volunteer, teaching kids to appreciate and love the games they play.

MIKE HUBER is a professor of mathematics at Muhlenberg College. He studies various rare events in baseball, such as pitching a no-hitter or perfect game, using statistical approaches to predict the next one. He joined SABR in 1996 and enjoys writing for SABR's Games Project.

MARK KANTER grew up in Bristol, Pennsylvania, where he became a lifelong Philadelphia Phillies fan. He got the itch watching the last few outs of Jim Bunning's perfect game against the Mets on Father's Day in 1964. As a member of SABR since 1985, he has made numerous presentations at SABR meetings and conventions, as well as writing several articles for the *Baseball Research Journal, The Northern Game and Beyond,* and the *National Pastime 43: From Swampoodle to South Philly,* and several SABR BioProject biographies. He was the editor of the *Northern Game and Beyond,* the 2002 Boston SABR Convention publication. He has won 12 SABR team trivia contests since 1997. He and his wife, Lynne, who is a great baseball fan in her own right, have discussed and watched baseball in Cuba, Puerto Rico, Great Britain, Australia, Japan, South Korea, Canada, and the United States. Since retirement after 31 years as an engineer for the US Navy, he has been preparing taxes for AARP Tax Aide and playing Stratomatic365 baseball online. He and Lynne live in the idyllic seaside community of Portsmouth, Rhode Island, where he is on the town's canvassing board.

NORM KING (1957-2018) of Ottawa, Ontario, joined SABR in 2010 and became a prolific contributor to the SABR BioProject and Games Project until his untimely death from a rare form of bile duct cancer in 2018. He was the lead editor and author of *Au jeu/Play Ball: The 50 Greatest Games in the History of the Montreal Expos,* published in 2016, and wrote chapters for a number of other SABR books, including *Thar's Joy in Braveland: The 1957 Milwaukee Braves; Winning on the North Side: The 1929 Chicago Cubs;* and *A Pennant for the Twin Cities: The 1965 Minnesota Twins.* He was an active member of SABR's Quebec Chapter and a friendly face at the SABR national convention each year.

KEVIN LARKIN was a police officer for over 20 years and has been going to baseball games since he was five years old. After retiring, he continued his love for the sport by writing about the game. He joined SABR in 2015 and began to fact-check articles and write stories for the Games and Biography Projects. He also has his own monthly local radio show. He has a keen interest in the Civil War and has written about that period of United States history as well. According to Mr Larkin, "Baseball is a great way to learn and I am honored to be able to do this."

LEN LEVIN is a longtime newspaper editor in New England, now retired. He lives in Providence with his wife, Linda, and an overachieving orange cat. He now (Len, not the cat) is the grammarian for the Rhode Island Supreme Court and copy-edits its decisions. He also copy-edits many SABR books, including this one. He is just down the interstate from Fenway Park, where he has spent many happy – and not-so-happy – hours.

SCOTT MARTIRE was born and raised in the Philadelphia suburbs and has been a member of SABR since 2022. He holds the Level One SABR Analytics Certification. This is Scott's first article for SABR and he looks forward to writing many more. He has particular interest in the business side of baseball and the catcher position. With a background in education, finance, and real estate, Scott currently works in lumber and building materials sales. He enjoys skiing, music, reading about history, and being outdoors.

LES MASTERSON is an editor at Forbes Advisor, a consumer website, where he covers insurance. During his career he's covered news, health care, insurance, business, financial services, credit cards, content marketing, mortgages, and history, to name a few. He's received awards for his writing and editing from the New England Press Association, Massachusetts Press Association, and the American Society of Business Publication Editors. Masterson has contributed to six SABR books.

ANDY MCCUE, a former president of SABR, won the Seymour Medal for *Mover and Shaker: Walter O'Malley, the Dodgers, and Baseball's Westward Expansion.* He is also the author of *Baseball by the Books: A History and Complete Bibliography of Baseball Fiction,* and *Stumbling Around the Bases: The American League's Mismanagement in the Expansion Eras* (University of Nebraska Press, 2022). He is a retired newspaper reporter, editor, and columnist, and a winner of the Bob Davids Award.

CHAD MOODY is a nearly lifelong resident of the Detroit area, where he has been a fan of the Detroit Tigers from birth. An alumnus of the University of Michigan and Michigan State University, he has spent 30-plus years working in the automotive industry. Chad has contributed to numerous SABR and Professional Football Researchers Association projects. He and his wife, Lisa, live in Plymouth, Michigan, with their dog, Daisy.

BILL NOWLIN is in the Hall of Fame. As one of the founders of Rounder Records, he left being a professor of political science to follow the music. Rounder released more than 3,000 record albums in its first 50 years and landed its founders in the International Bluegrass Music Hall of Fame. Pursuing a passion that began as a Ted Williams and Red Sox fan in the late 1950s, he has been to somewhere around 1,000 games at Fenway Park – and has written more than 1,000 articles for SABR, while also helping edit many SABR books. Sadly, he never saw Sandy Koufax pitch.

TIM ODZER has a law degree from the University of Chicago and litigates cases in Miami, Florida. In his free time, he enjoys writing articles for SABR and watching baseball. In 2022 he contributed an article on Rube Foster to Jay Caldwell's book *Black Baseball In Living Color.* Although Tim never saw Sandy Koufax pitch, he proudly owns a Sandy Koufax bobblehead and enjoyed writing about one of his old dominant games.

TIM OTTO grew up in northeast Ohio, 35 miles from Cleveland's Municipal Stadium. His first memories of major-league baseball date to the spring of 1960 when, as a second-grader, he was fascinated by the controversy surrounding the trade of Rocky Colavito to the Tigers for Harvey Kuenn. Shortly thereafter he started monopolizing the sports section of the *Cleveland Plain Dealer* each morning at breakfast, and that June attended his first major-league game. He became an instant Koufax fan after skipping school to watch the opening game of the 1963 World Series.

BYRON PETRAROJA is a retired Syracuse city public-school teacher and a current SABR member. During the early stages of his teaching career, he was introduced to the field of storytelling and has since told stories in the classroom and at various community settings including the National Baseball Hall of Fame in Cooperstown, New York. This is his initial experience as a contributor to a SABR book project and he has thoroughly enjoyed the process.

BILL PRUDEN has been a teacher of American history and government for over 40 years. A SABR member for over two decades, he has contributed to SABR's BioProject and Games Project as well as a number of book projects. He has also written on a range of American history subjects, an interest undoubtedly fueled by the fact that as a seven-year-old he was at Yankee Stadium to witness Roger Maris's historic 61st home run.

CARL RIECHERS retired from United Parcel Service in 2012 after 35 years of service. With more free time, he became a SABR member that same year. Born and raised in the suburbs of St. Louis, he became a big fan of the Cardinals. He and his wife, Janet, have three children and he is the proud grandpa of two.

HOWARD ROSENBERG has been a baseball fan since the Dodgers played in Brooklyn. His baseball interests include writing SABR game stories, editing BioProject articles, tweeting about the Mets (@Metbaseball), and doing statistical analyses using R. He received his Ph.D. from Syracuse University, where he investigated complex systems using system dynamics. A college teacher, he teaches a course on sports communication, culture, and identity, enjoys writing poems about baseball, including one that was the Baseball Poem of the Month in *Spitball Magazine* in July 2010, and drawing baseball-related pictures.

QUENTIN SALLAT is a software engineer, video game developer and creator of Astonishing Sports Games. He joined SABR in 2016 and has written for the Games Project as well as the Games and Simulations Research Committee. He was born in France and now lives in Montreal.

PAUL SEMENDINGER, Ed.D., retired as a school principal in 2022 and now serves as an educational consultant and adjunct college professor. He is the author of numerous baseball-themed books including *The Least Among Them* and *From Compton to the Bronx* (written with Roy White). Paul has also contributed to a number of SABR publications.

PAUL SINCLAIR retired after a 38-year career as an investment professional for a leading Canadian life insurance company. A graduate of the University of Toronto, he is a lifelong Toronto resident, baseball player, and fan. As a player he tried out for both the Montreal Expos and Toronto Blue Jays. Highlights of his lifelong fandom include watching spring training with the Detroit Tigers in the mid-'70s, enduring the snow and cold of the first Blue Jays game ever and throwing out the first pitch at a Blue Jays game in August 2015.

GLEN SPARKS is a lifelong Dodgers fan and enjoyed learning more about Sandy Koufax through working on this book. He wrote the first full-length biography of Hall of Fame shortstop Pee Wee Reese, published by McFarland in 2022. Glen majored in journalism at the University of Missouri and worked for many years in the newspaper industry. He and his wife, Pam, share a house with two cats, Kasper and Buster (not named for the former Giants catcher), and an aquarium filled with tropical fish.

RUSS SPEILLER lives in Cincinnati with his wife and two children. Russ has a chemical engineering degree from the University of Pennsylvania. He is an avid New York Yankees fan and has been a SABR member since 2023, having contributed stories to SABR books and the SABR BioProject, as well as journals. Though not his first article published by SABR, the Koufax piece represents the first article he penned for submission as a SABR member.

The son of a fan of the Brooklyn Dodgers but born about two years after Koufax retired, **MARK S. STERNMAN** would likely have rooted for his coreligionist except in the 1963 World Series against the Yankees.

AARON TALLENT is a writer whose work has appeared in the *Washington Post*, the *Washington Times*, the *Advocate & Democrat*, *Athlon Sports*, The Sweet Science, *Oncology Business Review*, and FOX Sports' Outkick the Coverage. He writes extensively about sports history and lives in the Washington, DC, area with his wife and two cats.

WILLIAM M. "MATT" VINES is a trial lawyer who has practiced in Jackson, Mississippi, since 1994. He is a lifelong baseball fan and collector of baseball cards. His collection includes a 1955 Topps Roberto Clemente (rookie card), a 1933 Goudey Babe Ruth (#144), and a 1909-11 T206 Walter Johnson (hands at chest).

STEVEN C. WEINER, a SABR member since 2015, is a retired chemical engineer and a lifelong baseball fan starting with the Brooklyn Dodgers of the 1950s. During his undergraduate years at Rutgers University, Steven worked in the sports information office and broadcast baseball and basketball play-by-play on WRSU radio. Steven obtained his doctoral degree in engineering and applied science from Yale University and has been a contributor to the technical literature on hydrogen and fuel cell safety. Steven served as assignments editor for the SABR Games Project with essay contributions in SABR books, the *Baseball Research Journal*, and Jackie Robinson 75: Baseball's Re-Integration. He is currently a volunteer teacher in local middle school English classes and mentors students at the University of Maryland's College of Information Studies.

SARAH WEXLER is a reporter/producer for MLB.com. She has been on SABR's editorial board since 2020. Previously she contributed to *Dodgers Digest*, *The Hardball Times*, and *FanGraphs*. She resides in her hometown of Los Angeles with her husband, Jack, and dogs, Nellie and Boomhauer.

PAUL WHITE, a SABR member since 2001, is a native of Boston and lifelong fan of the Red Sox. He writes a daily newsletter on baseball history at www.lostinleftfield.com, and has contributed several entries to the SABR Games Project and the SABR BioProject, including a contribution to the recent SABR publication *One-Win Wonders*. His book *Cooperstown's Back Door: A History of Negro Leaguers in the Baseball Hall of Fame*, will be published by McFarland Books in February 2025. Paul and his wife live near Kansas City.

BRIAN WILLIAMS began writing as a high-school sports stringer before launching a broadcast, writing, and voiceover career at age 15. He has performed radio play-by-play for PIAA state championship baseball and football as well as some minor-league baseball. After he built a new FM radio station with three partners, added an AM, and sold both in 2001, Brian switched gears to a career in medical equipment software, where he authored several articles for national trade magazines. Brian continues to write and voice projects (brianwilliamscreative.com), and currently works with a middle-school emotional support team and coaches high-school baseball in Harrisburg, Pennsylvania.

GREGORY H. WOLF was born in Pittsburgh, but now resides in the Chicagoland area with his wife, Margaret, and daughter, Gabriela. A professor of German studies and holder of the Dennis and Jean Bauman Endowed Chair in the Humanities at North Central College in Naperville, Illinois, he has edited more than 15 books for SABR. Since January 2017 he has been co-director of SABR's BioProject, which you can follow on Facebook and X.

The SABR Digital Library

•••

Print & Ebooks

SABR.ORG
OR
WHEREVER
BOOKS ARE
SOLD

The Stars Shone on Philadelphia: The 1934 Phila. Stars

ISBN 978-1-960819-04-8 $9.99 ebook

ISBN 978-1-960819-05-5 $29.95 paperback

Biographies of Ed Bolden's 1934 Negro National League champions, including Biz Mackie and Jud Wilson.

Yankee Stadium: America's First Modern Ballpark

ISBN 978-1-960819-16-8 $9.99 ebook

ISBN 978-1-960819-21-5 $39.95 paperback

Essays about the history of Yankee Stadium and recaps of over 50 historic games and other events there, including papal visits, football, and more.

Ebbets Field: Great, Historic, and Memorable Games at Brooklyn's Lost Ballpark

ISBN 978-1-960819-16-1 $9.99 ebook

ISBN 978-1-960819-17-8 $39.95 paperback

Relive Jackie Robinson's and Sandy Koufax's debuts, and over 90 other heartbreaks and triumphs in Brooklyn, plus essays on the ballpark.

Nichibei Yakyu: Volume II: 1960-2019

ISBN 978-1-960819-14-7 $9.99 ebook

ISBN 978-1-960819-15-4 $34.95 paperback

Fascinating recaps of the exhibition tours and MLB games by US baseball teams in Japan.

Sox Bid Curse Farewell: The 2004 Boston Red Sox

ISBN 978-1-960819-18-5 $9.99 ebook

ISBN 978-1-960819-19-2 $34.95 paperback

Biographies of every player and coach on the 2004 World Championship team, as well as essays about the season, effects of the win on fans, and more.

Dodger Stadium: Blue Heaven on Earth

ISBN 978-1-960819-20-8 $9.99 ebook

ISBN 978-1-960819-21-5 $29.95 paperback

Essays about the history of Dodger Stadium and recaps of over 50 historic games there, from Fernandomania to Vin Scully's bow.

One-Win Wonders

ISBN 978-1-960819-13-0 $39.95 paperback

ISBN 978-1-960819-12-3 $9.99 ebook

Biographies of 78 players whose entire major league pitching record consisted of just one win, from the tragic, like Nick Adenhart, to the improbable, like catcher Brent Mayne.

Willie Mays: Five Tools

ISBN 978-1-960819-02-4 $9.99 ebook

ISBN 978-1-960819-03-1 $29.95 paperback

Twenty essays on Mays' life and career, plus recaps of 30 historic games.

www.ingramcontent.com/pod-product-compliance
Lightning Source LLC
Chambersburg PA
CBHW080957120626
46546CB00010B/2927